In Defence of Cosmopsychism

Also available from Bloomsbury:

Cross-Cultural Approaches to Consciousness edited by Itay Shani and Susanne Kathrin Beiweis

Consciousness Mattering by Peter D. Hershock

In Defence of Cosmopsychism

A Fundamental Approach to the Problem of Consciousness

Khai Wager

BLOOMSBURY ACADEMIC
LONDON • NEW YORK • OXFORD • NEW DELHI • SYDNEY

BLOOMSBURY ACADEMIC
Bloomsbury Publishing Plc, 50 Bedford Square, London, WC1B 3DP, UK
Bloomsbury Publishing Inc, 1359 Broadway, New York, NY 10018, USA
Bloomsbury Publishing Ireland, 29 Earlsfort Terrace, Dublin 2, D02 AY28, Ireland

BLOOMSBURY, BLOOMSBURY ACADEMIC and the Diana logo are
trademarks of Bloomsbury Publishing Plc

First published in Great Britain 2026

For legal purposes the Acknowledgements on p. x constitute an
extension of this copyright page.

Cover image: BIOSPHOTO / Alamy Stock Photo

A catalogue record for this book is available from the British Library.

A catalog for this book is available from the Library of Congress

ISBN: HB: 978-1-3505-0861-3
ePDF: 978-1-3505-0862-0
eBook: 978-1-3505-0863-7

Typeset by Integra Software Services Pvt. Ltd.

For product safety related questions contact productsafety@bloomsbury.com.

To find out more about our authors and books visit www.bloomsbury.com
and sign up for our newsletters.

Dedicated to Watson

Thank you for being a friend rather than a doctor or a priest.

Contents

Figures

Acknowledgements

It is difficult to say when work on this book began and even harder to say when it will be finished. Regardless, the process has spanned my time at the University of Oxford and the University of Birmingham and has benefitted from both rich intellectual contexts. The book is largely grounded in research made possible by generous funding from the UK Arts and Humanities Research Council, first via a one-year research preparation studentship and then via a three-year PhD studentship award. I am incredibly grateful to have been one of the lucky ones.

I owe a particularly enormous debt of gratitude to my former MA and PhD supervisor and current friend, Yujin Nagasawa. The research presented here is underpinned, in one way or another, by many years of his support, encouragement, inspiration and collaboration. Yujin supervised my Master's thesis on cosmopsychism in 2010–11, before the term 'cosmopsychism' was in use in the philosophical literature. Indeed, it was a co-authored paper by Yujin and me, *Panpsychism and Priority Cosmopsychism,* that introduced the term 'cosmopsychism' sometime back in 2012, when it circulated widely before formal publication. It would take an age to list individually the many things for which I owe Yujin my gratitude, but suffice it to say that this book would not exist without him.

I am also grateful to Mark Wynn, who kindly welcomed me to Oxford and offered his support and timely encouragement to pursue this publication. In addition, I have shared many illuminating conversations on this book's themes at Oxford, Birmingham, and other places at home and abroad over the years. I sadly cannot mention them all, but conversations with Itay Shani, Godehard Brüntrup, Philip Goff, David Chalmers and Hedda Hassel Mørch are particularly noteworthy.

I thank my wonderful mum, Nadia Wager, for her near-miraculous support and my (also wonderful) partner, Simona Olexova, for putting up with my absentmindedness and still encouraging me to 'finish' what I 'started'. And I thank the rest of my family, Kama, Angel, Tia, Charlie, Dave, Jon, Ian, Landy, Poppy and Phoebe, for their essential non-technical assistance along the way. It would, of course, be a crime to omit thanks to my amazing non-human animal family, who make life so colourful: Watson, Dexter, Mowmow, Monster and Polly.

Finally, I thank Colleen Coalter, Aimee Brown, Suzie Nash and the wider Bloomsbury team for their fantastic editorial support, and several anonymous reviewers for exceptionally thoughtful and constructive feedback over two rounds of peer review.

1

Uncovering a landscape of fundamental consciousness

1.1 Introduction

Let me begin with an outlandish claim: the cosmos itself is a conscious entity, and you are conscious right now because you are a part of its vast conscious expanse. In the pages that follow, I aim to demonstrate to you that as outlandish as it sounds on first hearing, this is a philosophical idea that deserves to be taken seriously. In this book, I explore hitherto unexplored, or at least underexplored, regions of what I call *the landscape of fundamental consciousness*. By way of this exploration, I provide a defence of cosmopsychism, a fundamental approach to the problem of phenomenal consciousness, which says that the cosmos as a whole is conscious and that it is in virtue of this cosmic consciousness that ordinary individuals like us are conscious.

Before we proceed, it will be helpful to situate the upcoming exploration within the broader context of the mind-body problem and, within that, the problem of phenomenal consciousness. After this, we can position it more narrowly within the landscape of fundamental consciousness, which will serve as the local setting for our upcoming study. These introductory remarks will track a well-worn path for readers familiar with the mind-body problem, its main approaches and the challenges they encounter. However, for those less familiar, it will provide the necessary context for what lies ahead.

The mind-body problem is the overarching challenge of explaining the nature of the mind and its relationship to the body (and, more specifically, the brain). There are two broad approaches to the problem: substance dualism and substance monism. Substance dualism asserts that the body and mind are ultimately composed of two distinct substances: the body is made of a material substance, while the mind is made of a mental substance. Meanwhile, substance monism contends that the body and mind are ultimately composed of the same substance. From herein, when I refer to 'dualism' and 'monism' without further qualification, it can be assumed that I refer to substance dualism and substance monism. There are two main types of monism: materialism and idealism. Materialism posits that the mind and body are ultimately material, whereas idealism claims that the mind and body are ultimately mental. Each of these main types of monism can be further categorized into sub-types. Regarding materialism, one variant asserts that only material entities exist and that anything that appears mental is illusory in some sense. Another variant says that non-material things exist but that these ultimately depend on material entities. A parallel can be seen in the sub-types of idealism: one variant posits that anything non-mental exists only in an illusory sense, while another asserts the existence of non-mental entities, which nonetheless ultimately depend on mental entities.

At this point, it is important to note that through conventional implicature, 'materialism' implies 'physicalism' – the view that the mind and body are both ultimately *physical* – despite physicalism including entities not historically covered by materialism (e.g. forces, fields, laws of nature, etc.). In line with contemporary literature, I will focus on physicalism in what follows. The mind-body problem can be subdivided into numerous sub-problems, including the problems of mental causation, intentionality, personal identity and the existence of other minds. The relevance, seriousness and form of these sub-problems vary depending on which of the above approaches is adopted. Arguably, the most challenging aspect of the overarching problem in contemporary debates is the problem of phenomenal consciousness. This problem will be the focus of our present inquiry. The prevailing approach to the mind-body problem today is physicalism, and it is to physicalism that the problem of phenomenal consciousness presents a significant challenge. The issue arises when we recognize that when we are in conscious states, it *feels like something* for us to experience them. That is, consciousness comes with a qualitative feel. Consider the conscious states we experience when we smell fresh coffee, listen to music, look at a painting, or run our fingers through a dog's coat. These experiences feel like something. The problem arises when we try to explain this phenomenal aspect of consciousness in terms of the structure and dynamics of the brain. The brain, at least according to physicalism, is fundamentally a wholly physical affair. When we examine its microphysical components, we do not find these qualitative feelings, so how do they arise?

As we can see from this formulation, neither dualism nor idealism faces the problem of consciousness because neither holds that consciousness is ultimately physical. However, each faces its own considerable difficulties in reconciling the physical and the mental, and, in large part, these difficulties account for the predominance of physicalism. Before we expand on the problem of consciousness, it will be helpful to outline the core problems for dualism and idealism as these motivate both physicalism and the alternative approaches that will be our core concern in this volume.

1.1.1 Idealism

Numerous distinct versions of idealism exist, and each invariably has its challenges. However, two challenges that all versions share are the difficulty of motivating the fundamental base (i.e. why should we take the proposed mental foundation of reality seriously) and the problem of the external world (i.e. how is the 'physical' world explained in virtue of the mental foundation of reality). Regarding the first problem, in each case, a principal motivation will be its success in accounting for the mind-body problem and reality more broadly, but the key thing is that this is done without introducing further problems. Regarding the second problem, either the physical world is an illusion, or it is real but dependent on the mental, but either way, it must explain the apparent reality of the physical world (i.e. external objects and their persistent existence). If it is an illusion, how does it explain the fact that the illusion seems so convincing, appears and behaves so consistently to distinct individual minds, and indeed in the absence of minds?

Idealism unfolds in various, more precise ways. One example that posits the external world as illusory is George Berkeley's (1710) subjective idealism. According to Berkeley's idealism, external objects are ideas in individual minds. This raises the challenge of why the external world appears so persistent and consistent across time and between individual minds. Berkeley tackles this problem by appealing to God; the external world persists and remains consistent due to being an idea in *God's* mind. Another example of this kind is John McTaggart's (1921, 1927) personal idealism. According to McTaggart, reality consists solely of minds and their perceptions. However, McTaggart does not invoke God to explain the persistence and consistency of external objects. Instead, he contends that this arises from a close binding of all individual minds (through relations of love). It may be unfair to describe the external world as 'illusory' on McTaggart's view; rather, it is a construction of the interrelated collection of minds upon which it always depends.

Meanwhile, the absolute idealisms of Hegel (1977) and F. H. Bradley (1930) represent views according to which the external world exists independently of any individual mind but is ultimately reliant on the mental, as it forms part of an underlying mind or mental process. For Hegel, this is the Absolute Spirit, and for Bradley, it is the Absolute Reality. At first glance, these views encounter fewer difficulties than the previous ones in accounting for the persistence and consistency of external objects, as they exist independently of individual minds. However, they face a rather formidable challenge in justifying their overall metaphysical accounts of the Absolute.

1.1.2 Dualism

Let us now turn to dualism. Like idealism, it does not face the problem of phenomenal consciousness because it does not claim that consciousness is ultimately physical. Instead, it posits that mental properties are formed from a fundamentally distinct mental substance. However, unlike idealism, dualism does maintain that the physical world is ultimately real (i.e. it does not depend on some deeper reality). Dualism's most persistent challenge revolves around accounting for the interaction between the mental and physical domains. This is known as *the interaction problem*. One especially pressing aspect is *the problem of mental causation*, which is the problem of explaining how mental properties have causal efficacy. These issues are grounded in the desirability of maintaining two widely accepted notions: first, that the physical domain is a closed causal system, and second, that mental properties have causal efficacy. Maintaining the former is desirable because all physical effects appear to have sufficient physical causes, and the latter because it certainly seems like our own minds have causal power: our mental *thinking* of making a cup of tea causes us to then go and make it. Various responses to the interaction problem have been proposed. Dualism can endorse interactionism, epiphenomenalism, parallelism or occasionalism. Let us briefly survey these.

Interactionism says that the mental and physical domains, although fundamentally distinct, causally interact, with mental properties being causally efficacious in accordance with our common intuitions. This response requires pinpointing a location and mechanism of interaction. Descartes (1649/1989), the most well-known proponent of this view, proposed the pineal gland in the brain as the location of mental-physical interaction. However, this proposal violates the principle of the causal closure of the physical because some physical effects do not have sufficient physical causes (i.e. those effects caused by mental properties interacting with the pineal gland).

Alternatively, *epiphenomenalism* allows dualism to avoid the difficulty of explaining mental causation by dropping the claim that mental properties are causally efficacious. Nevertheless, it maintains one-way physical-to-mental causation because mental properties are causally influenced by physical properties but not *vice versa*. However, this epiphenomenalist approach violates the intuitive notion that mental properties, like our *thinking* about making a cup of tea, cause physical effects, like our *making* a cup of tea. It must also explain the mechanism of interaction between the two domains – in particular, how physical causes can have mental effects.

Another option is *parallelism*, which says that the mental and physical domains run alongside one another without any causal interaction. Parallelism acknowledges a strong correlation between specific physical properties (e.g. brain states) and mental properties (e.g. conscious states). Yet, it claims that any apparent causal interaction is merely an illusion resulting from the perfectly parallel nature of the two domains, each governed by distinct laws. Leibniz (1989) proposed a version of parallelism underwritten by 'a pre-established harmony', a perfect synchronization of the two domains established by God at the point of creation. While this view avoids the interaction problem, it fails to account for the intuitive sense that our mental states really do play a causal role in the physical world. More importantly, it is a metaphysically uneconomical view, relying on a complex theistic deterministic framework and two fundamentally distinct domains of reality.

Finally, *occasionalism* (Malebranche, 1674/1997), like Leibniz's parallelism, affords God a key role, but rather than pre-establishing harmony between the domains at the point of creation, this view holds that God manually implements each case of apparent interaction between the physical and mental domains, which, in actual fact, have no direct causal interaction. While occasionalism does offer an explanation of physical-mental interaction and allows for the appearance of mental efficacy (and, in so doing, satisfies the intuitive sense that our minds have causal efficacy), it comes at the cost, as does parallelism, of relying on a complex theistic framework and two fundamentally distinct domains of reality.

1.1.3 Physicalism

Having very briefly surveyed idealism and dualism and the problems entailed by their various formulations, we can now return to physicalism – the position within the mind-body debate most directly burdened by the problem of phenomenal consciousness. Before we motivate that problem and note physicalist responses, let us first outline physicalism itself, which is, simply put, the view that everything is physical.

Two contentious issues that arise when articulating physicalism are the questions of what counts as 'physical' and how the scope of the physical encompasses *everything*. Typically, in addressing these issues, physicalists will draw on two mutually supporting notions: first, the view that what counts as physical is tied to the subject matter of physical science and second, that the physical domain is causally closed (we have just seen how dualism struggles to maintain both mental causation and causal closure).

Regarding the issue of how to demarcate the physical in accordance with physics, Daniel Stoljar (2001, 2010) outlines two options: an object-based conception of the physical and a theory-based conception of the physical. As the name suggests, the object-based approach says that what counts as physical are those objects currently studied in physics: the fundamental physics of particles, fields, forces and spacetime. Meanwhile, the theory-based conception focuses on whatever current or future physics describes. This highlights a dilemma in formulating physicalism, known as Hempel's Dilemma (Hempel, 1965): either the formulation of physicalism is defined in terms of current physics, which is too restricted, or future physics, which is too indeterminate. The former seems to be an overly restricted view of the physical since it is widely accepted that current physics is incomplete. The latter seems overly vague since we do not know what future physics will involve. It is interesting to note that the latter view risks self-defeat, as it is conceivable that dualism or idealism could turn out to be versions of physicalism under this proposal, should 'mental' entities fall within the purview of future physics. Thus, on this construal, physicalism is at risk of lacking distinctiveness. The object-based conception of the physical seems to face the first horn of the dilemma and the theory-based conception the second.

Regarding the issue of the operative account of the physical being complete (i.e. including everything), physicalists typically invoke the causal closure of the physical. This means that all physical effects have sufficient physical causes. The important thing here is that the physical domain is taken to be causally sealed; nothing outside the physical domain has causal efficacy.

Thus, we can see how responses to the questions of *what is physical* and how *everything* is physical complement each other. The physical entities are those posited by current or future physics, depending on whether an object-based or theory-based approach is adopted, and these entities form a causally closed system, meaning that all physical effects have sufficient physical causes.

Let us now return to the physicalist approach to the mind-body problem, which concerns how mental properties are explainable in physical terms. This includes explaining consciousness and its varied aspects (e.g. phenomenality, intentionality, agency, cognition). We will very briefly survey how common forms of physicalism respond to this general problem before returning to the problem of *phenomenal* consciousness, specifically.

Eliminative materialism (Churchland, 1981; Stitch, 1983; Churchland, 1986) asserts that there is no *problem* of consciousness because there is no consciousness. One version of eliminative materialism is *illusionism* (Dennett, 1991, 2016), which posits that consciousness is merely an illusion. The *mind-brain identity theory* (Smart, 1959; Lewis, 1999) claims that conscious states are identical to brain states, meaning that conscious states are purely physical brain states and nothing more. *Functionalism*

(Putnam, 1967) elucidates mental states in terms of the functional roles realized by physical systems. *Non-reductive physicalism* (Kim, 1993) asserts that consciousness depends on, but is not reducible to, the physical. *First-order representationalism* (Dretske, 1995; Tye, 1995) maintains that consciousness results from physical systems (namely, brains) generating representations of the world. Lastly, *higher-order thought theory* (Carruthers, 2000; Rosenthal, 2005) contends that a mental state is conscious when it is the object of a higher-order thought.

Arguably, all the aforementioned physicalist approaches hit a roadblock when they try to account for the phenomenal aspect of consciousness. Hence, we arrive at the problem of *phenomenal* consciousness. Recall that this is the challenge of accounting for the phenomenal feel of experience in terms of entirely non-phenomenal physical matter (and interactions among physical matter).

Various prominent arguments against physicalism underpin the problem. Let us briefly summarize. *The knowledge argument* against physicalism (Jackson, 1982, 1986) purports to show that physical explanations cannot account for phenomenal consciousness. The argument proceeds via a thought experiment asking us to consider Mary, a scientist who knows all the physical facts about colour vision but has never actually seen colour because she gained her complete physical knowledge of colour in monochromatic surroundings. We are then asked to consider Mary as she leaves her monochromatic surroundings and gazes at a red rose, seeing colour for the first time. The idea is that Mary learns something new when she sees the red rose for the first time because she learns *what it is like* to see red. Therefore, the argument concludes that physical facts do not capture phenomenal properties (i.e. the what-it-is-like-ness of consciousness), so physicalism is false. Similarly, *the explanatory gap argument* (Levine, 1983) posits that physicalism is false (or at least its truth cannot be established) because physical explanations of phenomenal consciousness leave an explanatory gap regarding phenomenal consciousness.

The conceivability argument is another influential argument against physicalism (Chalmers, 1996). It starts from the claim that if phenomenal properties are identical to, or depend on, physical properties, must necessitate phenomenal properties. With this claim in place, the argument moves from the conceivability of phenomenal zombies (which are exact physical duplicates of humans but who lack phenomenal consciousness – i.e. they are entirely lacking phenomenal feels) to their possibility, and from there to the falsity of physicalism: Given that we can conceive of phenomenal zombies, and that conceivability is a guide to possibility, it follows that phenomenal zombies are possible. If they are possible, then physicalism is false because, in the case of zombies, at least, phenomenal properties are not necessitated by physical properties.

Chalmers (2002) categorizes broadly reductive physicalist responses to these arguments into three categories: type-A, type-B and type-C materialism.[1] Type-A materialism says that there is no ontological or epistemological gap between physical

[1] He also includes type-D and type-E dualism, and type-F monism. Type-F monism includes views that populate the landscape of fundamental consciousness.

and phenomenal properties. This category includes eliminative materialists who say the phenomenal knowledge that Mary supposedly gains is illusory, and that zombies are inconceivable because what we call consciousness is merely brain processes.

Type-B materialism says that there is an epistemic gap but not an ontological gap. Included in this category are typical identity theorists, functionalists and those following the phenomenal concepts strategy (PCS). Identity theorists say Mary gains a new concept, but not a new fact, when she sees the red rose for the first time (i.e. she gains a new way of thinking about existing knowledge), and that zombies are conceivable but not possible (i.e. they reject that conceivability equals possibility). Functionalists assert that Mary does not gain new facts but new abilities (i.e. she gains an ability to recognize physical facts in new ways), and that zombies are conceivable but not possible (because their being possible would involve them lacking functional organization). Proponents of the PCS (e.g. Loar, 1990; Papineau, 2002) claim that Mary learns not new facts about the world but new ways of conceptualizing it (i.e. she learns phenomenal concepts). Meanwhile, they maintain that zombies are conceivable (although not possible) because we confuse a conceptual distinctness between the physical and phenomenal with a metaphysical distinctness.

Type-C materialism holds that there is no ontological gap, but there is currently an epistemic gap, albeit one that will be closed by future physics. Physicalists of this kind assert that Mary's new knowledge highlights a gap in our current scientific knowledge that will eventually be closed as neuroscience progresses, and that zombies are conceivable to us now but will not be once this epistemic gap has been closed (with the advent of complete neuroscience, for example).

There are two types of non-reductive versions of physicalism worth noting. *Non-reductive physicalism*, in general form, holds that phenomenal properties depend on, but are not reducible to, physical properties. Some (Kim, 1993) appeal to supervenience relations, holding that phenomenal properties supervene on physical properties, while others (Putnam, 1967; Davidson, 1970; Fodor, 1974) appeal to different senses in which phenomenal properties resist physical reduction. According to non-reductive physicalism, Mary's new knowledge marks a conceptual rather than ontological shift because she learns a new way of conceptualizing physical processes – via direct experience of phenomenal properties – but does not gain knowledge of any ontologically new facts. Meanwhile, zombies are conceivable but not metaphysically possible. We can conceive of them because consciousness is not reducible to physical processes, but they are metaphysically impossible due to lawful dependency between physical processes and consciousness.

Another non-reductive view, and borderline case of physicalism, is *strong emergentism* (Broad, 1925; O'Connor, 1994). This says that phenomenal properties constitute a fundamentally new ontological category that emerges from physical processes in a way that is neither reducible to nor predictable from its physical base. Strong emergentism agrees that Mary does indeed gain genuinely new knowledge; she learns about new fundamental properties that are ontologically, not merely conceptually, distinct from physical properties. Regarding the conceivability argument, strong emergentists respond that zombies are not even conceivable because consciousness necessarily emerges from its physical base owing to fundamental laws that govern emergence. This resembles the non-reductive physicalism response, but the strong emergentist position is more extreme because phenomenal properties represent an ontologically new category of reality, making it arguably not a form of physicalism.

A common objection to reductive forms of physicalism and their responses to the above arguments is that they still do not explain phenomenal consciousness; that is, they do not explain why physical processes are accompanied by conscious experience rather than simply being devoid of it. The aforementioned responses leave an explanatory gap untouched. Meanwhile, non-reductive forms of physicalism seem to face problems similar to dualism in accounting for mental causation without violating the causal closure of the physical; either consciousness involves novel causal powers and therefore violates causal closure, or it lacks novel causal powers and therefore cannot account for mental causation.

1.1.4 An alternative: Fundamental consciousness

While physicalist views collectively constitute a majority in the contemporary literature, there is a growing minority that is, on one hand, unconvinced that reductive physicalism does due justice to the reality of phenomenal consciousness and, on the other, see non-reductive physicalism, substance dualism and idealism as too problematic to be viable. This minority has a different suggestion: Consciousness is present at the fundamental level of reality, and it is from consciousness at this fundamental level that we derive our human forms of consciousness. In the logical space of approaches to phenomenal consciousness, this is the area I call the landscape of fundamental consciousness, and it will serve as the local setting for our present exploration.

This view that consciousness is fundamental is underwritten in large part by the non-emergence argument, which is an argument *for* fundamental consciousness and *against* physicalism. Despite the focus on 'emergence' here, it is important to note that this argument targets all physicalists and not just the emergentists about whom we have just learned. Thomas Nagel (1979) and Galen Strawson (2006) have both offered similar versions of the argument, and we will have occasion to visit them at various points in the book. For now, a rough outline will suffice: The argument begins with the acknowledgement that conscious states are real features of organisms like us. It then follows with the claim that everything, including us, is ultimately made of the same matter (e.g. my brain is made of the same fundamental components as the contents of my compost bin). Then comes the crucial non-emergence clause, the assertion that for any given complex system, it will be possible to derive whatever properties it has from the properties of its fundamental parts (i.e. the fundamental matter that it is made out of). Finally, we have the claim that we cannot derive our conscious states from the physical properties of matter. It concludes that matter – the stuff everything is made out of – must also have non-physical properties. These non-physical properties must be conscious or else be protoconscious in some sense that renders conscious states intelligible. In either case, the conclusion is that consciousness or protoconsciousness is present at the fundamental level of reality.

Another argument, which can be deployed either in conjunction with the non-emergence argument or independently, is the intrinsic nature argument. This argument exemplifies a line of reasoning inspired by Bertrand Russell (1927, 1959), and the resultant position is aptly referred to as Russellian monism (although similar lines of thinking go back further than Russell). Russellian monism will be a central feature of our current study, so we will return to it in more detail later. Here, let us just outline the argument: it starts from the claim that physics describes the world externally, in terms of its structure and dynamics, but remains silent on the internal nature (i.e. the categorical grounds) of the structure and dynamics. Another way to say this is that something intrinsic is needed to ground the structure and dynamics that physics reveals, but about this, physics is silent. It then asserts that the required intrinsic nature is phenomenal consciousness (either wholly or in part). Put simply, consciousness is posited as the categorical ground of physics because it provides the only example we have of matter's intrinsic nature. Our conscious states are the intrinsic nature of our brain states.

We will have many opportunities to explore these arguments in more detail as the book progresses. Now that we have located the broad contours of this landscape of fundamental consciousness within the broader terrain of approaches to the mind-body problem and the problem of phenomenal consciousness, we are in a position to delve deeper. Before pushing on, let us pause to outline some core tenets of the upcoming study. We can then explore, in finer detail, the positions that occupy the landscape of fundamental consciousness before we commence, in earnest, our exploration of cosmopsychism.

1.2 Core tenets of the present study

To restate, when I say 'fundamental consciousness', I refer to approaches to the problem of phenomenal consciousness that claim consciousness is a fundamental feature of reality and that fundamental reality is (in some sense) consonant with the physical universe. From this, we can derive five core tenets that form the foundation of the upcoming exploration and warrant clear articulation from the outset:

1. **Realism about the physical universe**: The view that the physical universe exists.
2. **Realism about phenomenal consciousness**: The view that phenomenal consciousness exists.
3. **Fundamentality of the physical universe**: The view that fundamental reality is consonant with the physical universe (i.e. the physical universe is not derivative of some distinct, more fundamental reality).
4. **Fundamentality of consciousness**: The view that phenomenality is a fundamental feature of the universe.
5. **Substance monism**: The physical universe and consciousness are not formed of fundamentally distinct substances.

These core tenets indicate that this study will not take idealist approaches to the problem of consciousness as its focus. Idealist approaches might reject (1) or (3). As we have just seen, some forms of idealism maintain that the physical universe does not exist, while others claim that while the physical universe exists, it does so only as a derivative of some more fundamental reality. I will have cause to mention idealist views along the way, but my core focus is on views that affirm (1) and (3). Neither will the focus be on those views which deny (5) and take a substance dualist stance. We surveyed some of the deep and persistent problems facing such views a moment ago. Furthermore, the present study will not be primarily concerned with convincing those who reject (2) or (4). These are our physicalists. Some reject that phenomenal consciousness exists entirely, while others accept that it exists but deny that it is fundamental. I will refer to such views, of course, but they will not be the primary focus. Instead, I will concentrate on those views which affirm the complete set of tenets. With our remit now outlined, we can begin our exploration. Let us start with a map of the landscape of fundamental consciousness; this landscape will be our local setting.

1.3 A map of the landscape of fundamental consciousness

Here, I will provide a map of the landscape of fundamental consciousness and situate the present book's chapters within it. However, I intend the map to have some value over and above embedding the book's chapters in a broader context. The argument contained in this opening chapter, insofar as there is one, is that the landscape of fundamental consciousness is much richer and more expansive than is typically acknowledged, and expeditions therein are still in their infancy. In particular, I will highlight that a whole tranche of the map remains little explored. I call this unexplored region *the cosmopsychism pathway*. The map I provide charts views that exist in the logical space of fundamental consciousness; some defended, some merely possible. Indeed, some may be ultimately indefensible, but I offer all as potential avenues for further research.

It is important to note that I refer to Figure 1 as *a* map rather than *the* map. The reasoning is that this is far from a complete map of the logical space, and there are various possible ways to carve up the landscape. There are undoubtedly many additional fundamental approaches to the problem of consciousness – actual and possible – that I do not include here. Thus, it is not my intention to provide a complete taxonomy of fundamental approaches or an authoritative map of *the* landscape. Instead, I offer one possible way to view it.

With that caveat in place, my suggestion is that until very recently, fundamental approaches to consciousness have been limited to uncovering and exploring micropsychism (the left tranche of the map), leaving cosmopsychism (the right tranche of the map) uncharted. However, mapping the right tranche reveals a rich and fruitful extension to the landscape that may yet hold the key to solving the problem of phenomenal consciousness. It will be useful, at this point, to define what I mean by 'fundamental approaches to consciousness', 'micropsychism' and 'cosmopsychism' more formally:

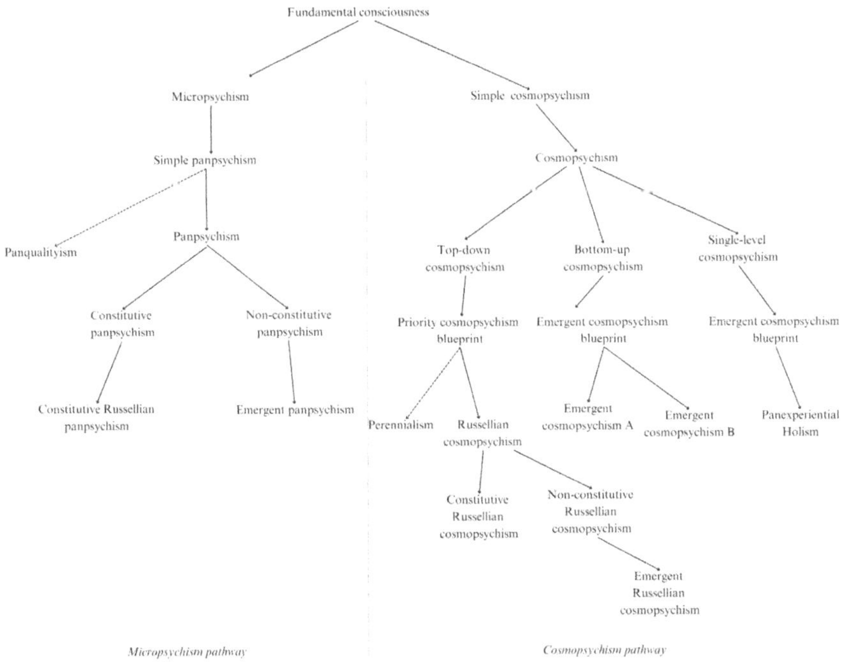

Figure 1 A map of the landscape of fundamental consciousness.

Fundamental consciousness: A fundamental approach to consciousness is one that affirms consciousness as a fundamental feature of reality.

Micropsychism: The view that at least some microphysical ultimates instantiate phenomenal properties.

Cosmopsychism: The view that the ultimate cosmos instantiates phenomenal properties.

From the above definitions, it is clear why the map diverges from the starting point of fundamental consciousness into two distinct pathways: micropsychism and cosmopsychism. Proceeding from the acceptance of fundamental consciousness, there are two options available because there are two potentially fundamental levels to reality; either there is a plurality of microphysical ultimates at the bottom level of reality, or the cosmos is the single ultimate at the top level of reality. This translates into our two options for the proponent of fundamental consciousness: either consciousness is fundamental because it is instantiated by microphysical ultimates, or it is fundamental because it is instantiated by the cosmos.[2]

[2] To be clear, I do not rule out the possibility that the fundamental level is some intermediary level between the top and bottom (e.g. Thompson (2016) argues for metaphysical interdependence, a view of fundamentality that rejects that the top and bottom levels of reality are fundamental), but I

Before going any further, it will be helpful to cover two more preliminaries. First, it will be useful to introduce a conception of a stratified reality that I will rely on throughout the book. I will typically treat reality as being stratified into three levels: micro, macro and cosmic. The micro-level is the smallest level of reality (or the level that is typically taken to be the smallest, at least). The micro-level is the level of the microphysical ultimates of matter (i.e. sub-atomic particles). The cosmic level is the biggest level of reality. The cosmic level is, unsurprisingly, the level of the cosmos as a whole. The macro-level is anything in between the micro and cosmic levels. I will sometimes refer to 'sub-cosmic entities' or 'entities on sub-cosmic levels'; when I do this, I refer to entities on all levels below the cosmic level. Second, it will be helpful to clarify my use of a few important terms relating to consciousness. Unless stated otherwise, by 'consciousness', I mean *phenomenal* consciousness. I also use the term 'phenomenality' to refer to phenomenal consciousness. By 'phenomenal properties', I mean the properties that characterize phenomenal consciousness. As a result, these terms will sometimes be used interchangeably. As the book progresses, there will be cause for further clarification on these terms and others, but we need not overcomplicate things at this early stage.

As mentioned, the principal aim of this chapter is to orient readers in the landscape of fundamental consciousness, which the present inquiry takes as its stage. With this in mind, the remainder of the chapter is structured as follows: In the next section, I suggest that consideration of fundamental consciousness, until very recently, has been almost exclusively centred on the micropsychism region of the landscape, which I call *the micropsychism pathway*. The first task will be to canvas views inhabiting this pathway, and we will note nearly all views along this pathway are vulnerable to a serious challenge in the form of the combination problem. In the subsequent section, we focus on the alternative branch of the map: *the cosmopsychism pathway*. Typically, the views there do not face the combination problem. As we will see, this distinction will be an important point of focus for the inquiry that follows. Our present emphasis, however, will be to explore the kinds of views populating this logical space rather than critically engage with them. Following this, I demonstrate how the upcoming chapters of the book fit into the landscape of fundamental consciousness. Finally, I discuss the relationship between cosmopsychism, as I conceptualize it here, and some historical views.

1.4 Fundamental consciousness and micropsychism: A synonymy

Until recently, the landscape of fundamental consciousness has been narrowly conceived within the contemporary philosophy of mind literature despite the significance of fundamental approaches to the problem of phenomenal consciousness. The view that consciousness is, or might be, fundamental is not exactly new. For instance, versions of panpsychism and idealism are well documented throughout history, with both typically

do not know if such a position, with regard to fundamental consciousness, is tenable. For my present purposes, I omit this option from the map.

affirming fundamental consciousness. For our present exploration, I am interested in fundamental approaches in the context of contemporary analytic philosophy that seek a place for consciousness in the physical world. It is in this context that taking consciousness as fundamental is a relatively recent endeavour. However, this recent endeavour has equated fundamental consciousness with micropsychism and, as such, has left the whole cosmopsychism tranche of the map uncharted. Recall that when I say 'micropsychism', I mean the view that at least some microphysical ultimates instantiate phenomenal properties.

As indicated earlier, the revival within the analytic philosophy of mind of the view that consciousness is fundamental was stimulated by Frank Jackson's *knowledge argument* (1982, 1986) against physicalism and then again, more explicitly, by David Chalmers's *conceivability argument* (1995, 1996, 1997, 2002). To recap: the knowledge argument allegedly shows that a complete physical description of the world leaves phenomenality out of the picture. Mary, the scientist who has complete physical knowledge of the world but has only ever experienced it monochromatically, is said to learn a new fact when she finally sees red for the first time. She learns *what it is like* to experience colour. Thus, the knowledge argument concludes that a complete physical picture of the world leaves out phenomenal properties (i.e. the properties that characterize the *feel* of conscious experience). The conclusion of the knowledge argument does not imply micropsychism exclusively; it also motivates dualism, for example. However, it certainly paved the way for micropsychism.

Similarly, the conceivability argument says that if we can conceive of exact physical duplicates of humans who lack consciousness, then such non-conscious physical duplicates are metaphysically possible. If they are metaphysically possible, then our physical descriptions of the world are incomplete (because the physical facts should necessitate the conscious facts). Chalmers's work from the mid-1990s onwards has been instrumental in arguing against physicalism and advocating for a fundamental theory of consciousness. Arguably, the fact we are in a position where it makes sense to present a map of fundamental consciousness in relation to contemporary literature is largely thanks to Chalmers's efforts. However, explorations by Chalmers and others have thus far been limited to the micropsychism pathway.

Let us explore this a little. Following the micropsychism pathway on the map, the next position we arrive at is 'panpsychism':

> **Panpsychism**: The view that all physical ultimates instantiate phenomenal properties.

Galen Strawson (2006) provides the most well-known defence of panpsychism. It is based on a version of the non-emergence argument that we mentioned earlier. In his version, he argues that physicalism entails panpsychism. The first part of his argument can be summarized in just two premises: (1) everything is entirely physical, and (2) consciousness is a real thing. From these two premises, he concludes that consciousness is physical. This does not get him all the way to panpsychism, however. He further reasons that if consciousness is physical, then it must either already be present in the microphysical ultimates (e.g. sub-atomic particles) or else emerge from them (and interactions among them). However, the kind of emergence required if they are to emerge would be strong emergence,[3] which, Strawson says, is impossible. Thus, the microphysical ultimates of matter must themselves be conscious. You may have noticed that this still does not bring us to panpsychism, just micropsychism. Strawson has not yet established that *all* microphysical ultimates are conscious as opposed to just *some* of them. He justifies the move from micropsychism to panpsychism on the grounds that the former would represent a radical heterogeneity at the fundamental level that seems out of sync with other fundamental entities: 'I think that the idea that some but not all physical ultimates are experiential would look like the idea that some but not all physical ultimates are spatio-temporal (on the assumption that spacetime is indeed a fundamental feature of reality). I would bet a lot against there being such radical heterogeneity at the very bottom of things' (Strawson, 2006, p. 25). As mentioned already, the non-emergence argument for panpsychism is widely accepted as the strongest argument for micropsychism (including panpsychism) and it will be covered in much more detail as the book progresses.

At this point, I should distinguish between panpsychism and what I call *simple panpsychism*. Panpsychism, understood in the most literal terms, is the view that everything is conscious. Such a broad understanding of the position is useful, because it captures, under a single term, the great variety of related views throughout history that posit consciousness ubiquitously.[4] However, in recent philosophical discussions, it is more readily understood as the view that consciousness is ubiquitous and fundamental, and it is from this that I take my definition of 'simple panpsychism':

> **Simple panpsychism**: The view that consciousness is fundamental and ubiquitous.

Panpsychism, as I define it above (as 'panpsychism'), is the most typical development on simple panpsychism, so much so that until recently, 'simple panpsychism', practically speaking, has implied 'panpsychism'. What is interesting is that simple panpsychism does not dictate that any given level of reality be considered fundamental. It says simply that consciousness is ubiquitous and fundamental. It is owing to this that I will later claim that many versions of cosmopsychism are also versions of panpsychism (because they are versions of *simple panpsychism* in virtue of maintaining that consciousness is both ubiquitous and fundamental).

Continuing along the path from panpsychism, we observe another branching. This time, one branch leads to 'constitutive panpsychism', while the other leads to 'non-constitutive panpsychism'. We can define these views as follows:

> **Constitutive panpsychism**: The version of panpsychism that says that macro-consciousness, like our own, is constituted by a combination of micro-consciousness at the microphysical level.

3 This kind of emergence is sometimes referred to as 'brute emergence' or 'radical emergence'. In this book, I will tend to refer to it as 'strong emergence', but in doing so I do not mean to distinguish between strong emergence, brute emergence and radical emergence.

4 For a good overview of historical accounts of panpsychism, see Skrbina (2005). Also see Clarke (2004).

Non-constitutive panpsychism: The version of panpsychism that says that macro-consciousness, like our own, is not constituted by a combination of micro-consciousness at the microphysical level.

Constitutive panpsychism is by far the most common version of panpsychism, and is usually taken to be the most promising (Chalmers, 2017a, 2017b). Much of what I have to say in this book focuses on constitutive panpsychism, given that it is considered the most auspicious. However, non-constitutive forms of panpsychism have received increasing attention, with some novel proposals (Rosenberg, 2004; Seager, 2010, 2017; Mørch, 2014; Brüntrup, 2017). One particularly promising version of constitutive panpsychism is 'constitutive Russellian panpsychism', which adds that phenomenal properties are fundamental and ubiquitous because they ground the spatiotemporal structure that is revealed by physics:

Constitutive Russellian panpsychism: A version of constitutive panpsychism that says that consciousness is fundamental and ubiquitous because phenomenal properties ground the spatiotemporal structure that physics describes.

Meanwhile, a promising version of non-constitutive panpsychism is emergent panpsychism, which says that macro-consciousness emerges from micro-consciousness. It may seem strange to endorse a version that postulates the *emergence* of macro-consciousness, but it must be stressed that consciousness per se does not emerge. It is only that macro-consciousness emerges from micro-consciousness:

Emergent panpsychism: A version of non-constitutive panpsychism that says that macro-consciousness emerges from micro-consciousness.

However, such views still rely on some concept of emergence, which raises an emergence problem of sorts. Nevertheless, it is arguably less severe because consciousness does not need to emerge from the entirely non-conscious, as is the case for many physicalist approaches to the problem of phenomenal consciousness. A few interesting versions of emergent panpsychism have been proposed in recent years. All state that macro-consciousness emerges from micro-consciousness but differs in other respects. Some (Rosenberg, 2004; Brüntrup, 2017) propose that the emergent macro-consciousness and the submergent micro-consciousnesses co-exist post-emergence, while others (Seager, 2010, 2017) state that the submergent micro-consciousnesses cease to exist post-emergence. Another view (Mørch, 2014) argues that micro-consciousness and macro-consciousness co-exist post-emergence, but that the emergent macro-consciousness is ontologically prior (i.e. is fundamental) to the submergent micro-consciousness base. Non-constitutive views are not a central concern for the present work, but we will consider them in some detail in Chapter 7.

In the above discussion of micropsychism, panpsychism and simple panpsychism, I have referred to how 'phenomenal properties' or 'consciousness' factor into their definitions. It is important to note that there is space on the micropsychism pathway for views that are identical to these except that they do not maintain that *consciousness* or *phenomenal properties* are fundamental, but instead maintain the fundamentality of *proto*consciousness or *proto*phenomenal properties. Fundamental protophenomenal properties are not full-blown phenomenal properties but are instrumental in giving rise to them in certain conditions. Let us set these alternatives out clearly:

> **Simple panprotopsychism**: The view that protoconsciousness is fundamental and ubiquitous.
>
> **Microprotopsychism**: At least some microphysical ultimates are protoconscious.
>
> **Panprotopsychism**: All microphysical ultimates are protoconscious.

One example of such a view is panqualityism (Lockwood, 1989; Coleman, 2017), which could be formulated as a version of either Microprotopsychism or panprotopsychism. It occupies an especially interesting position on the map because it overcomes arguably the most pressing aspect of the combination problem for panpsychism: the subject combination problem. It does so by denying that there are subjects of experience at the micro-level of reality, which is to say that it denies that microphysical ultimates are subjects of experience. Thus, it is not a version of micropsychism or panpsychism (because panpsychism involves micro-level subjects of experience) but is instead a version of microprotopsychism or panprotopsychism:

> **Panqualityism:** The view that microphysical ultimates instantiate phenomenal qualities.

However, in its most typical form, it is closely related to panpsychism because, like panpsychism, it posits phenomenality (broadly construed) as fundamental and says that all microphysical ultimates instantiate phenomenality. In this case, the phenomenality referred to is phenomenal *quality*. These are the qualities that characterize conscious experience, such as visual qualities, auditory qualities and olfactory qualities. The critical problems for panqualityism are as follows: (1) it is widely considered a conceptual truth that conscious experience implies a subject of experience instantiating phenomenal properties, so the panqualityist must motivate a departure from such a perceived conceptual truth. Furthermore, (2) it must explain how subjects like us arise from a fundamental level devoid of subjecthood. We will explore panqualityism and the subject combination problem in more detail in later chapters.

I hope to have illustrated in this section that there has been a significant groundswell of interest in fundamental consciousness over the last two to three decades. Although this interest is welcome because micropsychism offers a way around the knowledge and conceivability arguments and avoids the problem of strong emergence, each version of micropsychism comes with its challenges. Chief among these challenges are variations of the combination problem; the problem of accounting for the combination of micro into macro-level consciousness. My main contention is that until recently, there has been an implied synonymy between fundamental consciousness and micropsychism. Meanwhile, an entire parallel pathway has remained uncharted, branching out from fundamental consciousness in a different direction. Let us now contour this alternative pathway.

1.5 Mapping the uncharted landscape: The cosmopsychism pathway

The uncharted pathway I refer to is the cosmopsychism pathway on the right-hand side of the map. As mentioned, this region of the map, unlike the micropsychism region, has remained unexplored in analytic philosophy until very recently. Cosmopsychism, in its most simple formulation, can be understood as the view that there is a cosmic consciousness. There are many ways that this could be cashed out. However, I am primarily interested in how it is most often defined, as this version also holds the most potential for addressing the problem of phenomenal consciousness. Consider the following definitions of 'simple cosmopsychism' and 'cosmopsychism':

> **Simple cosmopsychism:** The view that there is a cosmic consciousness.
>
> **Cosmopsychism:** The view that there is a cosmic consciousness, which is also the fundamental form of consciousness.

As we can see, cosmopsychism is to simple cosmopsychism what panpsychism is to simple panpsychism. 'Simple cosmopsychism' is the most literal definition of the view, while 'cosmopsychism' is the definition that is considered standard. From this point, as I see it, three potential paths are branching off: a top-down route, a bottom-up route and a single-level route. The top-down, bottom-up and single-level ascriptions denote something about how the cosmic consciousness relates to sub-cosmic consciousness:

> **Top-down cosmopsychism:** Sub-cosmic consciousness derives from the fundamental cosmic consciousness
>
> **Bottom-up cosmopsychism:** The fundamental cosmic consciousness derives from sub-cosmic consciousness.
>
> **Single-level cosmopsychism:** The fundamental cosmic consciousness is the only form of consciousness.

The limited attention that cosmopsychism has received has been focused on top-down cosmopsychism. This is with good reason, as we will see. However, it is right to draw attention to the other two routes as they are potential avenues of further research (but I do not claim they are ultimately tenable). For each of the routes just outlined, we can formulate a blueprint on which to build more well-developed views. Such blueprints provide a schema on which to base more detailed and systematically articulated views of that kind. Consider the following blueprints:

> **Priority cosmopsychism blueprint:** The cosmos, as a whole, exhibits the fundamental form of consciousness, and all sub-cosmic forms of consciousness derive from the cosmic consciousness.
>
> **Emergent cosmopsychism blueprint:** The cosmos, as a whole, exhibits the fundamental form of consciousness, and the cosmic consciousness emerges from sub-cosmic consciousness.

Existence cosmopsychism blueprint: The cosmos, as a whole, exhibits the fundamental form of consciousness, and the cosmic consciousness is the only form of consciousness.

Each blueprint can be taken as a guide to how cosmic consciousness relates to sub-cosmic consciousness in a broad sense. Each will bring a particular set of advantages to any future development based on it and will likely permit various such developments. For example, there have been numerous developments stemming from, or consistent with, the priority cosmopsychism blueprint, as proposed by Nagasawa and me (2017), which I cover in more detail in Chapter 2. In fact, cosmopsychism has become synonymous with versions of priority cosmopsychism. Let us consider one development on the priority cosmopsychism blueprint, called 'Russellian cosmopsychism', and then two further developments stemming from it:

Russellian cosmopsychism: The cosmos has both revealed and concealed forms. The revealed form is the world as revealed by physics, while the concealed form is its consciousness, and furthermore, its concealed form is the categorical ground of its revealed form. The cosmic consciousness is the fundamental form of consciousness, from which all sub-cosmic consciousness derives. The cosmos as a whole, in its revealed concrete form, is the fundamental concrete entity from which all sub-cosmic concrete entities derive.

I have outlined and argued for Russellian cosmopsychism in various places (Wager, 2011, 2020; Nagasawa & Wager, 2017),[5] and further examples can be found in Shani (2015), Goff (2017, 2020) and, albeit in quite different terms, Mathews (2011). In addition to following the priority cosmopsychism blueprint, Russellian cosmopsychism implies commitments to priority monism (as exemplified in its view of the structure of concrete reality) and Russellian monism (as exemplified in its view of the cosmos as having both a revealed and concealed form). From Russellian cosmopsychism, we have two further branches:

Constitutive Russellian cosmopsychism: The version of Russellian cosmopsychism that says that sub-cosmic consciousnesses are *constituted* by the cosmic consciousness.

Non-constitutive Russellian cosmopsychism: The version of Russellian cosmopsychism that says that sub-cosmic consciousnesses exist but are *not constituted* by the cosmic consciousness.

[5] As a footnote to history, Yujin Nagasawa and I introduced the term 'cosmopsychism' in our paper, 'Panpsychism and Priority Cosmopsychism', which was widely circulated from 2012, and generated significant academic interest prior to its much-delayed formal publication in 2016. Before 2012, I had referred to the version of cosmopsychism I defended in my 2011 Master's thesis – combining panpsychism, priority monism, and Russellian monism – as 'dual-aspect priority monism' and, for a brief period, 'priority panpsychism'.

These branches are characterized by their view of how fundamental consciousness relates to derivative consciousness. They are versions of cosmopsychism, so we know that the cosmic consciousness is considered fundamental in both cases. The difference between them is how they account for the derivation of derivative consciousnesses from the fundamental cosmic consciousness. In the case of *constitutive* Russellian cosmopsychism, derivative consciousnesses are grounded in the cosmic consciousness as its partial aspects. This is an approach I have suggested (Wager, 2020), as have Goff (2017, 2020) and Shani (2015). Meanwhile, *non-constitutive* Russellian cosmopsychism says that derivative consciousnesses are not grounded in the cosmic consciousness. There are several more specific ways the non-constitutive approach could be developed. However, the only version in the literature (to my knowledge) that could be construed as a case in point is Mathews (2011). Perhaps the best way to formulate non-constitutive Russellian cosmopsychism is as a kind of emergentist view, such as:

> **Emergent Russellian cosmopsychism:** The version of Russellian cosmopsychism that says that macro-consciousnesses emerge from the cosmic consciousness but are not constituted by it.

Let us now turn to emergent cosmopsychism (note that this is distinct from the top-down emergent Russellian Cosmopsychism just covered). As far as I am aware, there are no versions of emergent cosmopsychism extant in the literature, but I will outline two possible developments on the emergent cosmopsychism blueprint. One is a cosmopsychist equivalent of the emergent panpsychism proposed by Seager (2010) and Mørch (2014) (call this 'emergent cosmopsychism A'), and the other is a cosmopsychist equivalent of the emergent panpsychism offered by Rosenberg (2004) and Brüntrup (2017) (call this 'emergent cosmopsychism B'):

> **Emergent cosmopsychism A:** A version of emergent cosmopsychism that says that the fundamental cosmic consciousness emerges from fundamental sub-cosmic consciousness, and that the emergence of the former supersedes the latter.

> **Emergent cosmopsychism B:** A version of emergent cosmopsychism that says that the fundamental cosmic consciousness emerges from fundamental sub-cosmic consciousness, and that the emergent and submergent coexist post-emergence.

Interestingly, one version of emergent cosmopsychism B might be similar to Mørch's (2014) emergent panpsychism, whereby the submergent base (consisting of sub-cosmic consciousnesses) coexists with the emergent cosmic consciousness, such that submergent sub-cosmic consciousnesses become dependent on the cosmic consciousness post-emergence.

I do not aim to provide details on how the above approaches could be fruitfully developed further. My goal of outlining possible positions is more modest. However, we can say that emergent views like those listed above will face a version of the problem of emergence: how can we make sense of the cosmic consciousness's emergence from a submergent base of sub-cosmic consciousnesses? They will also have to answer questions about the cosmic consciousness's co-existence with, or elimination of, the base of sub-cosmic consciousness. Furthermore, an additional question would be whether emergent cosmopsychism could offer advantages over and above emergent panpsychism. It may even turn out that specific versions of emergent panpsychism entail cosmopsychism. However, these questions are beyond the remit of our current exploration.

Finally, let us turn to the existence cosmopsychism blueprint. To my knowledge, there is only one view in the literature that might be considered a development on it: Jaskolla and Buck's (2012) 'panexperiential holism':

> **Panexperiential holism:** The view that there is precisely one entity, the cosmos, and that that entity is conscious.

This view faces challenges because it presupposes existence monism (i.e. the view that only one entity – the cosmos – exists), which introduces various problems, several of which are inherited by panexperiential holism due to its commitment to existence monism. For example, it must account for the existence or non-existence of the universe of multiplicity and our commonly held intuitions about it (by 'universe of multiplicity', I just mean our commonsense view of the world as populated by distinct objects). It also faces the problem of explaining the apparent existence of a multitude of sub-cosmic subjects of experience.

Before concluding this brief exploration of the landscape, it is worth drawing attention to two further views: cosmoqualityism and perennialism. Earlier, I mentioned that there is a thread running through the panpsychism pathway, which replaces consciousness at the fundamental level with *proto*consciousness. As noted, the resultant views are referred to as pan*proto*psychism rather than panpsychism and micro*proto*psychism rather than micropsychism. The same thread runs through the cosmopsychism pathway, too. We can call views picking up on this thread versions of cosmoprotopsychism. Let us define 'simple cosmoprotopsychism', the proto equivalent to simple cosmopsychism and 'cosmoprotopsychism', the proto equivalent to cosmopsychism:

> **Simple cosmoprotopsychism:** The view that there is a cosmic protoconsciousness.
>
> **Cosmoprotopsychism:** The view that the cosmos as a whole exemplifies fundamental protoconsciousness.

Two developments following this thread, along the route of the priority cosmopsychism blueprint, are 'cosmoqualityism' and 'perennialism' (the latter proposed by Albahari, 2020):

> **Cosmoqualityism:** The view that the cosmos as a whole exemplifies fundamental phenomenal quality, but the cosmos itself is not a subject of experience.
>
> **Perennialism:** The view that the universe of multiplicity is grounded in a universal non-dual consciousness (non-dual in the sense of being beyond the subject-object distinction).

Both of the above views reject the premise that the cosmos is itself a subject of experience, which arguably allows them to avoid the subject derivation problem for cosmopsychism (we will cover this problem in detail in the upcoming chapters). However, there are obvious questions about both. Albahari's perennialism posits an ultimate ground of unconditioned, non-dual, universal consciousness. Therefore, it must explain how the universe of multiplicity (again, that is, the commonsense world of objects with which our everyday experience acquaints us) can be grounded in such an unconditioned, non-dual universal consciousness. Moreover, a related problem concerns how subjects of experience might be derived from a fundamental level beyond the subject-object distinction. Albahari's perennialism is not strictly speaking a fundamental approach to the problem of consciousness, as I have conceived it, because it does not take the physical universe to factor into fundamental reality. Moreover, it is not strictly speaking a version of cosmopsychism or cosmoprotopsychism either because its fundamental non-dual consciousness is not a property of the cosmos, but the cosmos is a property of non-dual consciousness. It would thus be more accurate to describe the view as 'supracosmopsychism' or 'supracosmoprotopsychism' (we will cover this view in Section 1.7). Nevertheless, perennialism will be a central focus of Chapter 3, owing to its purported promise as an alternative to cosmopsychism.

Meanwhile, cosmoqualityism is the cosmopsychist version of panqualityism. Recall that panqualityism says that the microphysical ultimates are phenomenally qualitied but not subjects of experience. In fact, it does away with macro-subjects, too. What we call macro-level subjects, it says, are really just instances of the awareness of phenomenal qualities. For Colemans's panqualityism, for instance, such awareness arises as a result of there being a higher-order thought about phenomenal qualities. Cosmoqualityism is similar in that it says that macro-subjects are really just awareness of phenomenal qualities. However, in this case, all phenomenal qualities are derivative of the cosmic quality. A core challenge for cosmoqualityism is whether or not the position has any advantages over panqualityism. While I suspect it does, direct exploration of the view is beyond the scope of this book.

1.6 Exploring the landscape: The upcoming chapters

Now that we have revealed more of the landscape of fundamental consciousness, I can situate the chapters of this book within it. Our principal focus will be on a comparison between constitutive panpsychism and constitutive cosmopsychism, as they are arguably the most promising and also the most comparable versions of views along each of our two main pathways. This is not to say other areas of the map charted above will not ultimately turn out to be more fruitful; rather, space requires us to narrow the scope of our present inquiry.

Chapter 2, *The Priority Cosmopsychism Blueprint*, provides a blueprint for an approach to the problem of phenomenal consciousness, which turns panpsychism on its head. On the map, this is the blueprint for priority cosmopsychism. Rather than positing micro-consciousness that must sum to form macro-consciousness, it posits a cosmic consciousness from which macro-consciousness derives. The chapter shows that panpsychism faces both the combination problem and the problem of infinite decomposition. It motivates the priority cosmopsychism blueprint on the grounds that it can avoid both of these problems. However, it states that the blueprint paves the way for a new problem for cosmopsychism, called *the derivation problem*. Rather than providing a detailed solution to the problem of phenomenal consciousness, the blueprint outlines a general approach that offers certain advantages and remains open to more detailed development in various ways. The blueprint can be seen as setting the scene for much of the cosmopsychist tranche of the map.

Chapter 3, *Beyond Panpsychism and Cosmopsychism*, focuses on the two views – panqualityism and perennialism – on the map (one from the panpsychism tranche and one from the cosmopsychism tranche[6]) that reject full-blown consciousness at the fundamental level in favour of fundamental proto-consciousness. These views occupy especially interesting positions on the map because they reject the typical stipulation that the fundamental form(s) of consciousness are themselves subjects of experience. It is this move that purportedly allows them to sidestep the combination problem and the derivation problem. Albahari's perennialism is touted as the natural successor to cosmopsychism; avoiding its subject derivation problem while maintaining a cosmic consciousness. Meanwhile, Coleman's panqualityism is touted as a natural successor to panpsychism; avoiding its combination problem while maintaining that phenomenality is present at the level of the microphysical ultimates. However, I show that both of these views appear considerably less appealing upon closer examination and, as such, they do not seem well-suited to serve as successors to panpsychism or cosmopsychism. Perennialism, for example, faces the problem of motivating the very idea of non-dual consciousness, let alone the further stipulation that non-dual consciousness grounds the universe of multiplicity. Additionally, it faces tough questions relating to the existence and emergence of conscious perspectives. Panqualityism also faces problems relating to its subjectless phenomenally qualitied ground, as well as issues relating to how to think about perspectives.

Chapter 4, *The Subject Problem for Panpsychism and Cosmopsychism*, targets, arguably, the hardest problems for constitutive panpsychism and constitutive cosmopsychism: the subject combination problem and the subject derivation problem, respectively. Cosmopsychism is touted as a promising alternative to panpsychism because it can avoid the combination problem while maintaining some other of its advantages. However, it faces the derivation problem, which is cosmopsychism's equivalent to the combination problem. If it is to be considered a genuine alternative to panpsychism, then it must (at least) avoid its derivation problem being any more of a challenge to solve than the combination problem. In this chapter, I take the most difficult aspects of the two problems, which pertain to the combination (for panpsychism) and derivation (for cosmopsychism) of subjects of experience. I show that the two problems are almost identical, both hinging on the entailment of what I call synchronous perspectives scenarios. There are existing arguments from

6 In Figure 1, these two views are indicated with dotted lines to indicate that they are non-standard cases. Both reject subjects at the fundamental level, and perennialism does not equate fundamental reality with the cosmos so is not strictly speaking a 'fundamental approach'.

metaphysical impossibility against such scenarios, but I also provide alternative epistemic implausibility arguments that turn on an apparent inconsistency between what we should expect our everyday experience to be like (given panpsychism and cosmopsychism's stance on subjects) and what our everyday experience is actually like (through introspection). However, I provide a possible model of how to envisage synchronous perspective scenarios unproblematically. I also provide several alternative responses. I conclude that if there is a way to determine which of the two views to support, it is not to be found by comparing their respective subject problems. However, far from leaving panpsychism and cosmopsychism where I found them, the responses I provide to the various arguments leave both views in a significantly stronger position.

Chapter 5, *Problems of Phenomenal Quality and Structure*, takes as its target the two remaining aspects of the combination and derivation problems: those which relate to the combination or derivation of phenomenal qualities and structure. Taking, first, the quality combination problem for panpsychism, it explores two pressing aspects: the palette problem (which poses the challenge: how is it that a very small number of micro-level phenomenal qualities combine to form the rich array of qualities we are acquainted with in our macro-level experience?) and the quality grain problem (which poses the challenge: given that the macro-level phenomenal qualities we are acquainted with in our experience are composites of numerous distinct micro-qualities, how is that they appear smooth and continuous rather than as composites?). It then explores the equivalent derivation problems for cosmopsychism (or, indeed, whether or not there are such problems). It then explores two especially pressing aspects of the structure problem for panpsychism: the (structure) grain problem and the structural mismatch problem. The (structure) grain problem is a challenge to panpsychism because it asks: how is it that the phenomenal structure of our macro-level human experience does not appear to be formed of fragments of micro-level structure when that is precisely what constitutes it? The structural mismatch problem, which is a little more complicated to grasp, presents the challenge: how can we explain the mismatch between the physical structure of the brain and the phenomenal structure of our experience, given a purported isomorphism between the microphysical structure and micro-phenomenal structure at the fundamental (micro) level? It then considers the derivation equivalents of the structure problems for cosmopsychism. The chapter concludes that the ability to avert the problems of phenomenal quality and structure marks a key distinction between panpsychism and cosmopsychism, with cosmopsychism significantly better placed to respond. This is especially pertinent given the rather surprising conclusion of Chapter 4, which placed the two views on an equal footing with regard to the subject problems.

Chapter 6, *An Account of Cosmopsychism*, provides an account of – and motivation for – a version of cosmopsychism that I call CRP cosmopsychism. This version of cosmopsychism is created on the priority cosmopsychism blueprint and has three further key commitments: simple panpsychism, priority monism and Russellian monism. The chapter motivates these commitments both individually and in combination. Furthermore, I argue that cosmopsychism should be preferred over panpsychism owing to considerations concerning internal relations. I end the chapter by responding to some possible objections to the account on offer.

Chapter 7, *Non-Constitutive Alternatives and the Broader Significance of Cosmopsychism*, concludes the present enquiry by returning to a central division in the landscape of fundamental consciousness between constitutive and non-constitutive views. While the book primarily focuses on comparing constitutive versions of panpsychism and cosmopsychism, this final chapter offers a valuable opportunity to reflect on the non-constitutive alternatives that contrast with the proposals that have been our primary concern. I explore SED cosmopsychism, which is an influential non-constitutive version of cosmopsychism, as well as three versions of emergent panpsychism. Finally, I close with some brief reflections on the potential significance of cosmopsychism (or broadly cosmopsychist thinking) beyond its relevance to the problem of phenomenal consciousness. As a brief illustrative case study, I discuss how a cosmopsychism-based pantheist view might contribute to ongoing discussions in the philosophy of religion.

1.7 Cosmopsychism and enduring currents of human thought

Despite cosmopsychism representing a novel approach to the problem of phenomenal consciousness in contemporary philosophy of mind, it can be seen as partaking in enduring currents of human thought stretching back thousands of years. The broad thinking that there is some form of indwelling supra-human mind or consciousness has been expressed many times throughout history, including the more specific idea that the indwelling supra-human mind is the mind of the cosmos. Before proceeding with our exploration of the landscape, I will highlight a small number of views rooted in these enduring currents of thought and briefly note how they relate to cosmopsychism (as I conceptualize it). The aim is not to give full accounts of the views highlighted, nor is it to highlight all the views partaking in these enduring currents of thought. Instead, the aim is to demonstrate that broadly cosmopsychism-related thinking is not without precedent, as it bears varying degrees of resemblance to historical positions.

Let us begin with views that, on the surface, might seem like versions of cosmopsychism but which, on reflection, might be more accurately described as versions of *supracosmopsychism*. We can define supracosmopsychism as the view according to which there is a kind of indwelling consciousness that in some sense outstretches the physical cosmos (and we might also include under this term views wherein the cosmos is conscious but where the conscious cosmos does not equate to ultimate reality).

1.7.1 Historical supracosmopsychism

Let us take first an early example. The pre-Socratic philosopher Anaxagoras presents a picture of the cosmos in which Nous (mind) plays a central but mysterious role. At the risk of oversimplifying, according to Anaxagoras, the cosmos was originally a homogenous, static mixture of fundamental ingredients. In this mixture, every ingredient was present at each location: '[I]n everything there is a share of everything' (B11, cited in Curd, 2007, p. 23). At some point, Nous caused this static cosmic mixture to begin rotating. This movement resulted in increasing heterogeneity, with compound entities forming as varying localized concentrations of ingredients: 'When Nous began to move [things], there was separation off from the multitude that was being moved, and whatever Nous moved, all this was dissociated' (B13, cited in Curd, 2007, p. 25). In other words, the movement of the cosmic mixture, which Nous occasions, generates the universe of discrete objects. Unlike ingredients, Nous is not present in the cosmic mixture, and is clearly distinct from the ingredients. However, Nous is present *to* some compound entities (e.g. living things), and in such cases, it controls their movement: '[I]n everything there is a share of everything except Nous, but there are some things in which Nous, too, is present' (B11, cited in Curd, 2007, p. 23). The precise relation of Nous to the cosmos is hard to pin down. Anaxagoras's view is better described as a form of supracosmopsychism rather than cosmopsychism because, on his view, it is not strictly the case that the cosmos is conscious; rather, there is a kind of supra-cosmic consciousness (Nous) on which the cosmos (at least in its differentiated form) depends.

In Anaxagoras, there are echoes of the Advaita Vedānta tradition in Hinduism. In Advaita Vedānta, we also find a kind of supracosmopsychism, albeit of a different form. Advaita Vedānta refers to non-dual interpretations of the latter Vedas. Common to such interpretations is that the physical cosmos is grounded in a non-dual consciousness. However, interpretations differ with respect to the precise metaphysical status afforded to the physical cosmos in relation to the non-dual ground. Śaṅkara[7] is arguably the most well-known proponent of Advaita Vedānta. On the most common interpretation of his work, there is no reality beyond Brahman (i.e. non-dual consciousness), and the physical cosmos is a dream-like illusion. Radhakrishnan (1923) presents an alternative interpretation of Advaita Vedānta, according to which the physical cosmos is not an illusion but rather possesses a lower degree of reality than Brahman. Again, in Advaita Vedānta, we find related strands of human thought: that there is a supra-human consciousness in virtue of which human consciousness exists. However, again, these views are distinct from cosmopsychism because, on the Advaita view, the physical cosmos is not conscious; rather, a supra-cosmic consciousness underpins the physical cosmos in one sense or another.[8] It is worth noting that Albahari's (2020) perennialism, which will be explored in Chapter 3, is very closely related to Advaita Vedānta. In Chapter 3, I will present some problems for Albahari's view and at least some of these will also apply more broadly to the Advaita Vedānta tradition.

Additionally, we can detect cosmopsychism-adjacent ideas in Plato. In the *Timaeus* (see Cornford, 1935), Plato's Timaeus provides an account of the origin of

7 See Gambhirananda (1989) for Śaṅkara's commentaries on the Upaniṣads.

8 I recommend interested readers wishing to investigate the links between cosmopsychism and Indian philosophy further see a recent special issue of *Mind* on the topic (volume 105, issue 1, January 2022), titled 'Cosmopsychism and Indian Philosophy', edited by Shani and Ganeri. Also see Shani's (2022) edited book *Cross-Cultural Approaches to Consciousness: Mind Nature and Ultimate Reality*, and especially his contribution to the volume titled 'Cosmopsychism and Non-Sankaran Traditions of Hindu Non-dualism: In Search of a Fertile Connection'.

the cosmos. He posits the cosmos as a living being with a soul and intelligence. The cosmos's soul and intelligence ensure its rational order (or its unfolding according to a divine plan). On his account, the cosmos was created out of chaos (i.e. not out of nothing) by a demiurge. The demiurge mixed the elements of fire, water, earth and air to form the physical cosmos (these elements are, in turn, constituted by various triangular atoms, he says). The demiurge then created a soul from a mixture of Being, the Same, and the Different, which was diffused into the physical cosmos, imparting it with life and intelligence. In the same manner, the demiurge created more souls, less pure than the world soul, which were imparted into celestial objects to make heavenly gods. These gods were then instructed to make human beings by implanting even lesser souls into human physical bodies. These human souls were also made by the demiurge – from leftovers from the purer souls of the world and the celestial bodies – and given to the gods to implant into human bodies. To add further metaphysical complexity, on Timaeus's picture, reality has two realms: the physical (in which things come into being and are characterized by change) and the eternal (in which things are eternal and unchanging). The demiurge modelled the physical cosmos according to a perfect version existing in the eternal world. Plato's account in Timaeus raises many complex metaphysical questions, such as those regarding the metaphysical status of the demiurge and souls in relation to the cosmos and the eternal world. We can bracket most of these questions since our present interest regards how Timaeus's account relates to cosmopsychism. Timaeus's view is similar to cosmopsychism in some respects because we can interpret his world-soul as a kind of cosmic consciousness. However, in other respects, it is distinct from to cosmopsychism (as I conceptualize it in this book) because, on Timaeus's view, neither the cosmos nor its soul is fundamental; both are the creation of a demiurge. Moreover, unlike cosmopsychism's cosmic consciousness, Timaeus's world-soul does not ground human souls; instead, human souls are formed by the demiurge (by way of a mixture similar to the one that formed the world-soul).

Perhaps the most *prima facie* obvious example of a historical analogue of a cosmopsychist is Spinoza. In Spinoza (2000), we find another expression of these enduring currents of human thought that posit a supra-human mind associated with the cosmos. On an overly simplistic interpretation of his work, one might contend that Spinoza is a cosmopsychist because he claims that the world is God and that God is conscious. However, a closer consideration of his position seems to reveal him as less of a cosmopsychist and, like others mentioned above, more of a supracosmopsychist. On his view, fundamental reality is envisioned as a single substance, which he calls 'God or Nature'. This God has an infinite number of expressions (which can be understood, roughly speaking, as ways that God can be registered). Extension (which, for our purposes, we can think of as physical matter) and thought (which we can think of as consciousness) are two of the infinite number of God's expressions, and, moreover, these are the only two extensions that we can register. For example, my body is a mode of God under its expression of extension, and my consciousness is a mode of God under its expression of thought. It is not clear that it is correct to say, on Spinoza's view, that the cosmos is conscious, since the cosmos is merely a mode of God under its expression of extension. It is more accurate, I think, to say that *God* is conscious, and that God is not merely the cosmos (i.e. both the cosmos and consciousness are modes of God, but God outstrips both the cosmos and consciousness because God has an infinite number of expressions unknown to us but distinct from thought and extension). Spinoza's view can also be seen as a form of supracosmopsychism because, if thought is an expression of God, and God outstrips the cosmos, then it seems incorrect to say the cosmos is conscious; it is more accurate to say that God is conscious and God is the cosmos (It is worth noting that the reasoning I am expressing here is related to a debate about whether Spinoza should be properly considered a pantheist or panentheist. If he is a pantheist, then he might more correctly be considered a cosmopsychist. If he is a panentheist, then he might better be described as a supracosmopsychist).

Further examples of broadly cosmopsychism-related thinking can be found among the absolute idealists: first, the German idealists of the nineteenth century – perhaps most notably Schelling (1988) and Hegel (1977), and then the British idealists that followed – F. H. Bradley (1930) is a prime example. Although the views of absolute idealists vary considerably, they share the view that reality is a single interconnected whole (the Absolute) and that that whole is mental or mind-like in nature. Moreover, they typically hold that features of our everyday reality (objects, relations, concepts, etc.) are structured by mind. Importantly, absolute idealists (and here Hegel is the prime example) often posit ultimate reality as in the process of development towards its complete self-consciousness. The ideas of absolute idealists are difficult to fully grasp, and I cannot do justice to them here, but it is clear there are some points of similarity with the cosmopsychism we are interested in. For them, reality is a unified whole, which is associated with a form of consciousness. However, the views of the absolute idealists also differ considerably from cosmopsychism (again, as I conceptualize it). For example, for the absolute idealist, it is not so much that the physical cosmos is itself a conscious entity, but rather that the physical cosmos is *really* consciousness. Furthermore, on some absolute idealist views (again, I am thinking of Hegel especially), reality is developing towards a specific end of the Absolute's complete self-consciousness. This is a metaphysically complex and expensive claim unlikely to be mirrored by cosmopsychists.

Although each of the aforementioned cases can be seen as sharing in the same broad currents of thought as cosmopsychism, we can see that none of them are versions of cosmopsychism, and none are fundamental approaches to the problem of consciousness, as I am conceptualizing them. Therefore, the cosmopsychism I explore in this book is a rather different proposition.

1.7.2 Fechner's (simple) cosmopsychism

Perhaps the closest historical analogue of cosmopsychism was presented by Fechner in his *Zend-Avesta*.[9] Fechner argued for a cosmic consciousness, and his argument was analogical in form. It starts by acknowledging what human beings are like; we

[9] It is difficult to find Fechner's work in English. Perhaps the most detailed account of his view is offered by William James in Lecture IV of his *A Pluralistic Universe* (1909).

are organic bodies with souls. He then argues that the Earth can be seen as analogous to the human body, noting various things that the Earth has in common with the human body, including that it is a unified whole consisting of numerous parts working together in an organized way. Next, he says that since we know human organisms have souls, we can infer that the planetary organism likewise has a soul. He then extends the analogy from the Earth to the whole cosmos. Here, we can take souls to equate to consciousnesses.

Let us investigate the analogy a little deeper. Fechner starts with the observation that in our own cases, the sense data from each sense are unknown to every other sense. For example, right now, I am sensing the *smell* of coffee and the *sound* of a busy coffee shop, but these are not present to each other. However, these two discrete sense data come together in my consciousness. He then suggests that, likewise, our consciousnesses, which seem entirely unrelated to each other, come together in some even larger consciousness. This analogical thinking is then repeated until we reach the *cosmic* consciousness in which all sub-cosmic consciousnesses come together. Crucially, it is not only entities human and above that are conscious. He also argues that plants are conscious. And, in fact, the cells that constitute them and, in turn, the particles out of which those cells are constituted. For Fechner, the larger consciousnesses are, in part, constituted by smaller consciousnesses. The reason larger consciousnesses are not *fully* constituted by smaller ones is that larger instances are not mere aggregates of smaller instances in the same way that our conscious experience is not simply a mere aggregation of data from each of our senses, because by including the overall purview of data from all of our senses (as well as thoughts and memories, etc.) it involves something over and above the collection of sense data. Smaller consciousnesses contribute to larger consciousnesses analogously to how data from each of our human senses contribute to our overall conscious experience. On Fechner's view, our human consciousnesses contribute to a larger consciousness in just the same way – the larger consciousness unifies the smaller consciousnesses into a larger overall conscious field. Human consciousnesses, then, are seen as analogous to sense-organs of larger consciousnesses.

Interestingly, Fechner's views on consciousness are overtly spiritual in nature, with his views on human consciousness and its relation to the cosmic consciousness forming the basis of his account of immortality. Intriguingly, larger consciousnesses have thought and memory in some way analogous to how humans do. Just as human thoughts and memories persist in the absence of immediate sense data, so too do the thoughts and memories of human consciousnesses persist in the larger consciousness after the human forms cease to exist. Another spiritual dimension of Fechner's view of consciousness is that entities and their consciousnesses, which are intermediate between the human level and the cosmic level, act as sort of intermediaries through which human beings can understand their parthood of the cosmic order. In particular, for Fechner, the Earth is a kind of angel, through which we can understand our connection to and dependence on the cosmos as a whole (by understanding our connection to and dependence on the Earth).

So how does Fechner's view compare to cosmopsychism as I conceptualize it? Recall *simple cosmopsychism* from the map, which is the broad view that the cosmos is conscious. Fechner's view is certainly a form of simple cosmopsychism. However, it is a little less clear to me that it is a version of cosmopsychism, as I conceptualize it: the view that the cosmos is conscious and that the cosmic consciousness is the fundamental form of consciousness. I say this because, at least according to James's (1909) account of his view, Fechner maintains that sub-cosmic consciousnesses constitute (at least in part) the cosmic consciousness. Here is how James describes the generation of the cosmic consciousness on Fechner's view:

> [W]e must suppose that my consciousness of myself and yours of yourself, altho in their immediacy they keep separate and know nothing of each other, are yet known and used together in a higher consciousness, that of the human race, say, into which they enter as constituent parts. Similarly, the whole human and animal kingdoms come together as conditions of a consciousness of still wider scope. This combines in the soul of the earth with the consciousness of the vegetable kingdom, which in turn contributes its share of experience to that of the whole solar system, and so on from synthesis to synthesis and height to height, till an absolutely universal consciousness is reached.
>
> (1909, pp. 155–6)

The cosmic consciousness is not a mere sum of sub-cosmic consciousnesses, as James explains below, but, nonetheless, sub-cosmic consciousnesses do partly constitute the cosmic consciousness:

> The special thought of Fechner's with which in these lectures I have most practical concern, is his belief that the more inclusive forms of consciousness are in part *constituted* by the more limited forms. Not that they are the mere sum of the more limited forms. As our mind is not the bare sum of our sights plus our sounds plus our pains, but in adding these terms together also finds relations among them and weaves them into schemes and forms and objects of which no one sense in its separate estate knows anything.
>
> (1909, pp. 168–9)

This calls into question whether the cosmic consciousness is the fundamental form of consciousness because if it is, even in part, constituted by sub-cosmic consciousnesses, then it depends on them. So, the chain of dependence on Fechner's view appears to be bottom-up rather than top-down. If this is right, it distinguishes his view from cosmopsychism, as I conceptualize it here. Nevertheless, the resultant simple cosmopsychism would be a close relative of the views I will focus on in this book. For now, we do not need to concern ourselves with the precise metaphysical mechanics of Fechner's view. It is enough for our present purposes to draw attention to the close relation of his view to the conceptualization of cosmopsychism we will most concern ourselves with here.

1.8 Conclusion

The hope is that by spotlighting the landscape and conducting the explorations noted two sections back, the book will serve a dual purpose: to make a modest contribution to contemporary debates on the problem of consciousness (principally, but not exclusively, by providing a defence of cosmopsychism) and to catalyse further explorations. It is my view that fundamental approaches to the problem of consciousness, in general, but especially those following the cosmopsychism pathway, are teeming with potential yet untapped. There are many positions still un(der)explored, which future expeditions into the landscape will no doubt chart. Some will undoubtedly turn out to be dead-ends, but any genuine explorers searching for the solution to the problem of phenomenal consciousness would do well not to ignore vast regions of the map. With that said, we are now in a position to proceed to the next phase of our present inquiry: to outline the priority cosmopsychism blueprint.

References

Albahari, M. (2020). 'Beyond cosmopsychism and the great I am: How the world might be grounded in universal Advaitic consciousness'. In W. Seager (Ed.), *The Routledge handbook of panpsychism* (pp. 229–48). New York: Routledge.

Berkeley, G. (1710). *A treatise concerning the principles of human knowledge*. Edited by J. Dancy. Oxford: Oxford University Press, 1998.

Bradley, F. H. (1930). *Appearance and reality: A metaphysical essay*. Oxford: Clarendon Press.

Broad, C. D. (1925). *The mind and its place in nature*. London: Routledge & Kegan Paul.

Brüntrup, G. (2017). 'Emergent panpsychism'. In G. Brüntrup & L. Jaskolla (Eds.), *Panpsychism: Contemporary perspectives* (pp. 48–72). New York: Oxford University Press.

Carruthers, P. (2000). *Phenomenal consciousness: A naturalistic theory*. New York: Cambridge University Press.

Chalmers, D. J. (1995). 'Facing up to the problem of consciousness'. *Journal of Consciousness Studies*, 2(3), 200–19.

Chalmers, D. J. (1996). *The conscious mind: In search of a fundamental theory*. New York: Oxford University Press.

Chalmers, D. J. (1997). 'Moving forward on the problem of consciousness'. *Journal of Consciousness Studies*, 4(1), 3–46.

Chalmers, D. J. (2002). 'Consciousness and its place in nature'. In D. J. Chalmers (Ed.), *Philosophy of mind: Classical and contemporary readings* (pp. 247–72). New York: Oxford University Press.

Chalmers, D. J. (2017a). 'The combination problem for panpsychism'. In G. Brüntrup & L. Jaskolla (Eds.), *Panpsychism: Contemporary perspectives* (pp. 179–214). New York: Oxford University Press.

Chalmers, D. J. (2017b). 'Panpsychism and panprotopsychism'. In G. Brüntrup & L. Jaskolla (Eds.), *Panpsychism: Contemporary perspectives* (pp. 19–47). New York: Oxford University Press.

Churchland, P. M. (1981). 'Eliminative materialism and the propositional attitudes'. *Journal of Philosophy*, 78(2), 67–90.
Churchland, P. S. (1986). *Neurophilosophy: Toward a unified science of the mind-brain.* Cambridge, MA: MIT Press.
Clarke, D. S. (Ed.) (2004). *Panpsychism: Past and recent selected readings.* Albany, NY: State University of New York Press.
Coleman, S. (2017). 'Panpsychism and neutral monism: How to make up one's mind'. In G. Brüntrup & L. Jaskolla (Eds.), *Panpsychism: Contemporary perspectives* (pp. 249–82). New York: Oxford University Press USA.
Cornford, F. M. (1935). *Plato's cosmology: The Timaeus of Plato.* Indianapolis, IN: Hackett Publishing.
Curd, P. (2007). *Anaxagoras of Clazomenae: Fragments and testimonia.* Toronto: University of Toronto Press.
Davidson, D. (1970). 'Mental events'. In L. Foster & J. W. Swanson (Eds.), *Experience and theory* (pp. 79–101). London: Humanities Press.
Dennett, D. C. (1991). *Consciousness explained.* Boston: Little, Brown.
Dennett, D. C. (2016). 'Illusionism as the obvious default theory of consciousness'. *Journal of Consciousness Studies*, 23(11–12), 65–72.
Descartes, R. (1649). *The passions of the soul.* Translated by S. H. Voss. Indianapolis, IN: Hackett Publishing, 1989.
Dretske, F. (1995). *Naturalizing the mind.* Cambridge, MA: MIT Press.
Fechner, G. T. (1851). *Zend-Avesta oder über die Dinge des Himmels und des Jenseits. Vom Standpunkt der Naturbetrachtung.* Leipzig: Leopold Voß.
Fodor, J. A. (1974). 'Special sciences (or: The disunity of science as a working hypothesis)'. *Synthese*, 28(2), 97–115.
Gambhirananda, S. (1989). *Eight Upaniṣads: With the commentary of Śaṅkaracarya* (2nd ed.). 2 Volumes. Calcutta: Advaita Ashram.
Ganeri, J., & Shani, I. (Eds.) (2022). *Cosmopsychism and Indian philosophy* [Special issue]. *The Monist,* 105(1).
Goff, P. (2017). *Consciousness and fundamental reality.* New York: Oxford University Press.
Goff, P. (2020). 'Cosmopsychism, micropsychism and the grounding relation'. In W. Seager (Ed.), *The Routledge handbook of panpsychism* (pp. 144–56). New York: Routledge.
Hegel, G. W. F. (1977). *Phenomenology of spirit.* Oxford: Oxford University Press.
Hempel, C. G. (1965). *Aspects of scientific explanation and other essays in the philosophy of science.* New York: Free Press.
Jackson, F. (1982). 'Epiphenomenal qualia'. *Philosophical Quarterly*, 32(127), 127–36.
Jackson, F. (1986). 'What Mary didn't know'. *Journal of Philosophy*, 83(5), 291–5.
James, W. (1909). *A pluralistic universe.* Cambridge, MA: Harvard University Press.
Jaskolla, L., & Buck, A. (2012). 'Does panexperiential holism solve the combination problem?' *Journal of Consciousness Studies*, 19(9–10), 190–9.
Kim, J. (1993). *Supervenience and mind: Selected philosophical essays.* New York: Cambridge University Press.
Leibniz, G. W. (1989). 'Monadology'. In R. Ariew & D. Garber (Eds.), *G. W. Leibniz philosophical essays* (pp. 213–24). Indianapolis, IN: Hackett.
Levine, J. (1983). 'Materialism and qualia: The explanatory gap'. *Pacific Philosophical Quarterly*, 64(October), 354–61.
Lewis, D. (1999). 'Reduction of mind'. In *Papers in metaphysics and epistemology* (pp. 291–324). Cambridge: Cambridge University Press.

Loar, B. (1990). 'Phenomenal states'. *Philosophical Perspectives*, 4, 81–108. https://doi.org/10.2307/2214188.
Lockwood, M. (1989). *Mind, brain and the quantum: The compound 'I'*. Oxford: Blackwell.
Malebranche, N. (1997). *The search after truth*. Translated by T. M. Lennon & P. J. Olscamp. Cambridge: Cambridge University Press.
Mathews, F. (2011). 'Panpsychism as paradigm'. In M. Blamauer (Ed.), *The mental as fundamental* (pp. 167–84). Frankfurt Heusenstamm: Ontos Verlag.
McTaggart, J. M. E. (1921). *The nature of existence* (Vol. I). Cambridge: Cambridge University Press.
McTaggart, J. M. E. (1927). *The nature of existence* (Vol. II). Cambridge: Cambridge University Press.
Mørch, H. H. (2014). *Panpsychism and causation: A new argument and a solution to the combination problem* (PhD thesis, University of Oslo).
Nagasawa, Y., & Wager, K. (2017). 'Panpsychism and priority cosmopsychism'. In G. Brüntrup & L. Jaskolla (Eds.), *Panpsychism: Contemporary perspectives* (pp. 113–29). New York: Oxford University Press.
Nagel, T. (1979). 'Panpsychism'. In Nagel's *Mortal Questions* (pp. 181–95). Cambridge: Cambridge University Press.
O'Connor, T. (1994). 'Emergent properties'. *American Philosophical Quarterly*, 31(2), 91–104.
Papineau, D. (2002). *Thinking about consciousness*. Oxford: Oxford University Press.
Putnam, H. (1967). 'Psychological predicates'. In W. H. Capitan & D. D. Merrill (Eds.), *Art, mind, and religion* (pp. 37–48). Pittsburgh, PA: University of Pittsburgh Press.
Radhakrishnan, S. (1923). *Indian philosophy*. 2 Volumes. Delhi: Oxford University Press.
Rosenberg, G. (2004). *A place for consciousness: A place for consciousness*. New York: Oxford University Press.
Rosenthal, D. M. (2005). *Consciousness and mind*. New York: Oxford University Press.
Russell, B. (1927). *The analysis of matter*. London: Keagan Paul.
Russell, B. (1959). *My philosophical development*. London: Routledge.
Schelling, F. W. J. Von (1988). *Ideas for a philosophy of nature*. Cambridge: Cambridge University Press.
Seager, W. (2010). 'Panpsychism, aggregation and combinatorial infusion'. *Mind and Matter*, 8(2), 167–84.
Seager, W. (2017). 'Panpsychist infusion'. In G. Brüntrup & L. Jaskolla (Eds.), *Panpsychism: Contemporary perspectives* (pp. 229–48). New York: Oxford University Press.
Shani, I. (2015). 'Cosmopsychism: A holistic approach to the metaphysics of experience'. *Philosophical Papers*, 44(3), 389–437.
Shani, I. (2022). 'Cosmopsychism and non-Sankaran traditions of Hindu non-dualism: In search of a fertile connection'. In I. Shani & S. K. Beiweis (Eds.), *Cross-cultural approaches to consciousness: Mind, nature and ultimate reality* (pp. 45–70). New York: Bloomsbury Academic.
Shani, I., & Beiweis, S. K. (Eds.) (2022). *Cross-cultural approaches to consciousness: Mind, nature and ultimate reality*. New York: Bloomsbury Academic.
Shani, I., & Keppler, J. (2018). 'Beyond combination: How cosmic consciousness grounds ordinary experience'. *Journal of the American Philosophical Association*, 4(3), 390–410.
Skrbina, D. (2005). *Panpsychism in the West*. Cambridge, MA: MIT Press.
Smart, J. J. C. (1959). 'Sensations and brain processes'. *Philosophical Review*, 68(2), 141–56.
Spinoza, B. (2000). *Ethics*. Oxford: Oxford University Press.

Stitch, S. P. (1983). *From folk psychology to cognitive science: The case against belief.* Cambridge, MA: MIT Press.
Stoljar, D. (2001). 'Two concepts of the physical'. *Philosophy and Phenomenological Research*, 62(2), 253–81.
Stoljar, D. (2010). *Ignorance and imagination: The epistemic origin of the problem of consciousness*. New York: Oxford University Press.
Strawson, G. (2006). 'Realistic monism: Why physicalism entails panpsychism'. *Journal of Consciousness Studies*, 1(10–11), 3–31.
Thompson, N. (2016). 'Metaphysical interdependence'. In M. Jago (Ed.), *Reality making* (pp. 38–56). Oxford: Oxford University Press.
Tye, M. (1995). *Ten problems of consciousness: A representational theory of the phenomenal mind*. Cambridge, MA: MIT Press.
Wager, K. (2011). *Dual-aspect priority monism and the combination problem for panpsychism* (MA thesis, University of Birmingham).
Wager, K. (2020). *Panpsychism and cosmopsychism* (PhD thesis, University of Birmingham).

2

The priority cosmopsychism blueprint

2.1 Introduction

Now that we have an overview of the landscape of fundamental consciousness in place and having removed some of the thicket concealing the underexplored cosmopsychism pathway, I can begin to sharpen the focus on the more specific target of this book: priority cosmopsychism. The purpose of this short chapter is to present a blueprint for priority cosmopsychism.[1] The idea here is to outline and motivate a general approach to the problem of consciousness, on which more specific approaches can be based, to promising effect. In a nutshell, where panpsychism says that phenomenality is prevalent because the ultimate constituents of matter on the microphysical level instantiate phenomenal properties, priority cosmopsychism, which, again, is a blueprint rather than a fully-fledged theory, says that phenomenality is prevalent because the cosmos as a whole instantiates fundamental phenomenality. The purpose of this chapter is to pitch priority cosmopsychism as a potentially promising alternative to panpsychism because it can inherit its advantages while overcoming its most prominent problems.

The chapter will unfold as follows: To begin, I will discuss two metaphysical positions that are relevant to the framing of priority cosmopsychism: panpsychism and priority monism. Then, I will introduce the priority cosmopsychism blueprint before outlining how following the blueprint overcomes two of the main challenges for panpsychism: the combination problem and the problem of infinite decomposition. Finally, I will provide brief responses to some possible objections to the blueprint.

2.2 Panpsychism and priority monism

Priority cosmopsychism is parallel in structure to both panpsychism and priority monism, so I will outline each of these before formulating the priority cosmopsychism blueprint in the following section.

[1] This chapter is based on the ideas contained in my 2017 paper titled 'Panpsychism and Priority Cosmopsychism' (co-authored with Yujin Nagasawa), which is published in Brüntrup & Jaskolla (2017).

2.2.1 Panpsychism

Much of this book will be focused on panpsychism, so I will not give a comprehensive account of it here but will instead summarize its aspects that relate most directly to the blueprint I am to propose. The most literal version of panpsychism can be formulated in terms of ordinary minds or mental states. According to this literal version, everything has a mind or mental states in the same sense that humans do. Although there is still a tendency for panpsychism to be understood in this way, this formulation is highly implausible and contemporary proponents of panpsychism rarely, if ever, formulate the position along these lines. In their ascriptions of consciousness to all things, proponents do not mean to ascribe human-like minds or mental states to things like slippers and dog toys. As noted in Chapter 1, a more accurate general formulation of panpsychism is what I call simple panpsychism: the view that consciousness (or protoconsciousness) is fundamental and ubiquitous. This formulation indicates that consciousness (or protoconsciousness), whatever it is, is both a fundamental feature of reality and spread throughout it. This is still a very general formulation as it does not yet indicate where we are to find consciousness. This brings us to the operative definition of panpsychism for our present purposes. As outlined in the opening chapter, in its most typical contemporary construal, panpsychism is the extreme form of micropsychism. Micropsychism is the view that at least some microphysical ultimates instantiate phenomenal (or protophenomenal) properties. Panpsychism is the extreme form of micropsychism because it maintains that *all* microphysical ultimates instantiate phenomenal (or protophenomenal) properties.

The parenthetical alternatives above indicate the proto versions of the standard views, as identified in Chapter 1. Recall that panpsychism and micropsychism are sometimes articulated in terms of protoconsciousness (formally defined as 'panprotopsychism' and 'microprotopsychism'). In such cases, the claim is that rather than instantiating full-blown consciousness (i.e. phenomenal properties), microphysical ultimates only instantiate protoconsciousness or protophenomenal properties. Chalmers distinguishes panpsychism from panprotopsychism as follows[2]:

> There are two ways this might go. Perhaps we might take experience itself as a fundamental feature of the world, alongside space-time, spin, charge, and the like. That is, certain phenomenal properties will have to be taken as *basic* properties. Alternatively, perhaps there is some other class of novel fundamental properties from which phenomenal properties are derived ... these cannot be physical properties, but perhaps they are nonphysical properties of a new variety, on which phenomenal properties are logically supervenient. Such properties would be related to experience in the same way that basic physical properties are related to nonbasic properties such as temperature. We could call these properties

[2] Here Chalmers is distinguishing between phenomenal and protophenomenal versions of 'Type-F monism', which includes versions of panpsychism. My focus here is narrower than his broader Type-F monism category but this distinction is equally applicable.

> *protophenomenal* properties, as they are not themselves phenomenal but together they can yield the phenomenal.
>
> (Chalmers, 1996, pp. 126–7)

Since the blueprint herein is compatible with protoconsciousness, for simplicity, in this chapter, 'panpsychism' and 'cosmopsychism' include their proto forms.

Panpsychism is a promising alternative to physicalism. The main reason for holding panpsychism over physicalism is its avoidance of the problem of strong emergence. For physicalism, this problem arises due to the unexpectedness of phenomenal properties given the physicalist picture. On both panpsychism and physicalism, phenomenal properties are instantiated by physical entities – for example, aggregates of neurons in human brains. On physicalism, phenomenal properties arising from such aggregates are unexpected and surprising because neurons themselves are fundamentally non-phenomenal. This raises the question: how can phenomenality arise out of aggregates of neurons themselves devoid of phenomenality? Strawson (2008) argues that such an emergence of the phenomenal from an utterly non-phenomenal base is as extraordinary as the emergence of a spatially extended entity from a non-spatial base. He claims that the emergence of phenomenality on the physicalist picture is a 'miracle every time it occurs' (2008, pp. 64–5) because it violates the following principle of emergence: 'For any feature *Y* of anything that is correctly considered to be emergent from *X*, there must be something about *X* and *X* alone in virtue of which *Y* emerges, and which is sufficient for *Y*' (2008, p. 65).

Panpsychism does not face the problem of strong emergence because it stipulates that the physical ultimates that compose neurons are themselves phenomenal. On the panpsychist picture, it is, therefore, unsurprising that aggregates of neurons (in human brains, for instance) instantiate phenomenal properties. The problem of strong emergence will be covered in more detail in the following chapters since it forms an important backbone of the panpsychist approach (and also the cosmopsychist approach that I will soon present). However, for now, it is enough that we just outline this crucial advantage of panpsychism over physicalism.

2.2.2 Priority monism

Before I present the blueprint for priority cosmopsychism, it is also important to outline priority monism, which is in some sense structurally parallel to the blueprint I will propose. Priority monism is a position in metaphysics that states that the cosmos is the one and only *basic* concrete object. It is important to distinguish priority monism from existence monism.[3] Existence monism says that exactly one concrete object exists and that the one concrete object is the cosmos. Unlike existence monism, priority monism is compatible with the existence of multiple concrete objects since it stipulates only that there is exactly one *basic* concrete object, which leaves room for other objects provided they are non-basic. Therefore, on the priority monistic view, the cosmos

[3] See Horgan and Potrč (2000, 2008) for detailed discussions of existence monism.

is the one and only basic concrete entity, but this does not preclude the existence of other concrete objects – parts of the cosmos, for example – it only stipulates that the cosmos is ontologically prior to them. That is, all concrete objects, except the cosmos, are derivative of the cosmos, which is fundamental.[4]

Priority monism might seem *prima facie* counterintuitive. We tend to think of parts of things as ontologically prior to the things they compose. It might initially feel like something of a stretch to maintain that a whole could be prior to its parts. For example, it seems like the pieces of a puzzle are ontologically prior to the picture that they jointly compose, or that the grains of sand in a heap are prior to the heap. However, there are other examples where it does seem that the whole is more fundamental than its parts. For instance, the body seems to be prior to its organs, and the circle seems to be prior to the semicircles of the circle (Schaffer, 2008, 2010). To explain this commonsense distinction, Schaffer distinguishes between 'mere heaps' and 'genuine unities'. The pieces composing a puzzle and the grains of sand forming a heap are mere heaps, while the circle, the body and the cosmos are genuine unities.

It is important to note that priority monism, as formulated by Schaffer, is concerned only with concrete objects (and, more precisely, the relationship between the cosmos as a concrete whole and the concrete objects which are its parts). All else is excluded from its purview, as we can see in the following passage from Schaffer:

> I assume that there is a maximal actual concrete object – the cosmos – of which all actual concrete objects are parts. I should emphasize that I am only concerned with actual concrete objects. *Possibilia*, *abstracta*, and actual concreta in categories other than *object* are not my concern (deities and spirits, if such there be, are not my concern either). When I speak of the world – and defend the monistic thesis that the whole is prior to its parts – I am speaking of the material cosmos and its planets, pebbles, particles, and other proper parts.
>
> (2010, p. 33)

As we can see, phenomenal properties sit outside the scope of priority monism as they are not concrete objects.

2.3 The priority cosmopsychism blueprint

We are now able to formulate the priority cosmopsychism blueprint. Recall that it is intended to be a *blueprint* for an approach to the problem of phenomenal consciousness rather than a full account of an approach. The intention is to provide a basic framework around which more full-bodied approaches can be formed. The idea is it will permit developments in various directions.

As mentioned previously, priority cosmopsychism is, in a sense, structurally parallel to both panpsychism and priority monism. Let us outline these structural parities one

[4] Here I treat the terms 'basic' and 'fundamental' as synonymous.

at a time, starting with priority monism. Recall that priority monism says that exactly one basic concrete object – the cosmos – exists. Priority cosmopsychism has a structure parallel to this because it says that exactly one basic consciousness – the cosmic consciousness – exists. As we just saw, priority monism is only concerned with concrete objects. In parallel to this, priority cosmopsychism is only concerned with phenomenal (or protophenomenal) properties. Recall also the distinction between priority monism and existence monism, where the principal difference is that priority monism admits the existence of concrete objects in addition to the basic concrete cosmos, providing they are derivative of it, while existence monism does not. In parallel to this, priority cosmopsychism is compatible with the existence of multiple consciousnesses because it says only that there is exactly one *basic* consciousness: the cosmic consciousness. Consider the distinction with existence cosmopsychism here, according to which there is exactly one consciousness. Clearly, existence monism is not compatible with additional consciousnesses. Priority cosmopsychism admits other consciousnesses in addition to the fundamental cosmic consciousness, providing that they are derivative of it. On priority cosmopsychism, all consciousnesses except the cosmic consciousness itself are derivative of it, much as concrete objects are derivative of the concrete cosmos on priority monism.

To be clear, priority cosmopsychism does not adopt priority monism. It merely applies a structurally analogous approach to the domain of consciousness. As will become apparent in the following chapters, I do think it makes sense to adopt priority monism but the priority cosmopsychism blueprint does not dictate that one must.

Let us now consider the parallel structure between panpsychism and priority cosmopsychism. Recall that panpsychism says that all microphysical ultimates instantiate phenomenal properties. That is, all physical entities on the fundamental level of reality – which on panpsychism is taken to be the microphysical level – instantiate phenomenal properties, and those phenomenal properties at the microphysical level are the most fundamental instances of phenomenality. On panpsychism, the phenomenal properties of ordinary individuals like us are derivative of those fundamental instances. In parallel to this, priority cosmopsychism maintains that the phenomenal properties instantiated at the cosmic level are the fundamental instances of phenomenal properties and that those of ordinary individuals like us are derivative of phenomenality in its fundamental form.

It is worth highlighting at this point that the conjunction of priority monism and priority cosmopsychism entails a unique form of panpsychism. Recall that panpsychism is formulated in terms of physical ultimates, that is, in terms of the fundamental physical entities. Note that earlier I define panpsychism in terms of *micro*physical ultimates, because panpsychists typically take it that the ultimate physical entities occupy the micro-level of physical reality. But they need not. On priority monism, there is exactly one physical ultimate, which is the cosmos itself. Here, the physical ultimate is not at the micro-level of physical reality but at the cosmic level. If we define panpsychism as the view according to which all physical ultimates instantiate phenomenal properties, the conjunction of priority monism and priority cosmopsychism entails a unique form of panpsychism because it says that the concrete cosmos – the one and only physical ultimate – instantiates phenomenal properties.

Moreover, it says, like panpsychism, that the phenomenal properties instantiated at the ultimate physical level are the fundamental forms of phenomenality. While the following chapters will explore in detail the conjunction of priority monism and the priority cosmopsychism blueprint, it is important to stress that the blueprint does not dictate the adoption of priority monism. The two are independent of each other at the blueprint stage. It might be that time will show the two to be ultimately incompatible. Nevertheless, such an eventuality would not thereby rule out priority cosmopsychism because it is not dependent on priority monism. The priority cosmopsychism blueprint remains neutral with regard to its compatibility with priority monism.

Importantly, the blueprint also remains neutral about the nature of the cosmic consciousness. There are many possible ways to conceive of the cosmic consciousness that are compatible with the blueprint. For example, some formulations might position the cosmic consciousness as some kind of higher being or God, perhaps which shares in the experiences of ordinary individuals. Other formulations could maintain that the cosmic consciousness is only protophenomenal, with instances of, say, human phenomenal consciousness being somehow derived from that ultimate protophenomenal base. These issues are not crucial to our discussion of a blueprint. Again, what I am presenting here is not a full-bodied approach to the problem of phenomenal consciousness, but a framework of an approach that can be adopted and filled in various ways. It is, however, a framework that brings with its adoption some significant advantages over typical versions of panpsychism. Let us now turn to these advantages.

2.4 Priority cosmopsychism versus panpsychism

One might wonder why priority cosmopsychism should be taken seriously as an alternative to panpsychism. The contention I will make is that following the blueprint allows one to maintain the main advantage of panpsychism while also overcoming two of its most persistent problems. Before turning our attention to the problems that the blueprint overcomes, let us first consider how priority cosmopsychism maintains the main advantage of panpsychism. Recall that the central motivating force behind panpsychism is its avoidance of the problem of strong emergence. Unlike physicalist positions, it does not face this problem because it does not purport that phenomenality is instantiated by something itself entirely devoid of phenomenality. On many physicalist views, consciousness inexplicably emerges from a submergent base of neurons (and the matter which compose them) that are entirely non-conscious. Panpsychism is not committed to this inexplicable emergence because it says that consciousness is, in some form, there in the neurons and the matter which composes them; therefore, consciousness does not miraculously break into existence. Like panpsychism, priority cosmopsychism is not vulnerable to the problem of strong emergence because it, too, rejects the claim that phenomenality is instantiated by something itself entirely devoid of phenomenality. Rather, like panpsychism, it says that ordinary consciousness is derived from some more fundamental form of consciousness.

Perhaps more importantly, in virtue of its structural parity with priority monism, priority cosmopsychism avoids two of the most persistent problems for panpsychism. These are *the problem of infinite decomposition* and *the combination problem*. Let us take these one at a time.

2.4.1 The problem of infinite decomposition

Panpsychism holds that all microphysical ultimates instantiate phenomenal properties, which means that it presupposes fundamentalism. Fundamentalism equates fundamental reality with the entities on the bottom (i.e. the microphysical) level of reality.[5] For example, consider a common version of physicalism, which says that the ultimate level of reality is physical because everything in the actual world supervenes on fundamental subatomic particles, the properties and behaviour of which are described by microphysical theory. This entails that entities at the fundamental level of reality are entirely physical and, therefore, that everything in the actual world is ultimately physical. Panpsychism, in the formulation we are most interested in here, in effect, takes this form of physicalism and supplements its fundamental subatomic particles with phenomenal natures (insofar as those fundamental particles are said to instantiate phenomenal properties). In this sense, panpsychism is closely related to physicalism, and it is due to this close relation that panpsychism faces a pressing problem.

Schaffer (2003) and Montero (2006) have considered the argument that physicalism is false as a consequence of fundamentalism being false. We can call this *the argument from infinite decomposition*. Physicalism, in the form just outlined, entails fundamentalism because it equates the fundamental level of reality with the microphysical level. Therefore, if fundamentalism is false, then physicalism (as so construed) is false. The argument says that if the cosmos is stratified infinitely into levels – that is, the entities on any given level of reality will always be composed of entities on a lower level – then fundamentalism cannot be true because it states that the fundamental level of reality is the microphysical level. We then have the falsity of physicalism following from the falsity of fundamentalism, owing to the former's commitment to the latter. However, the falsity of fundamentalism also entails the falsity of panpsychism because it, too, presupposes fundamentalism.

Schaffer argues that it is at least metaphysically possible that the cosmos is infinitely decomposable – that is, that it is infinitely stratified into levels – by appealing to the conceivability and logical consistency of infinite decomposition (Schaffer, 2003, p. 501). He begins by arguing that it is metaphysically possible because it is conceivable that everything has parts. It is perfectly conceivable that everything is extended and that every extended thing can be decomposed into further things, *ad infinitum*.

[5] Fundamentalism can be formulated in various ways, as Montero notes (2006, p. 181). One way to formulate it is in terms of decomposition, whereby fundamental entities are undecomposable proper parts out of which all else is constituted. It might also be formulated in terms of supervenience, whereby fundamental entities are those on which all others supervene, but which do not supervene on any others themselves. Other possible formulations might be in terms of explanation, realization, reduction, determination, etc. I focus here on decomposition as it seems to me the most intuitive, but the claims made will apply equally to other formulations.

If we take conceivability to entail possibility, then infinite decomposition is possible. Next, Schaffer suggests it is metaphysically possible because it is logically consistent. Meaning that there are no logical contradictions in a picture of reality according to which matter is infinitely decomposable. He argues that since there are consistent models of mereology that permit infinite decomposition, there is no *a priori* ground for rejecting it as a metaphysical possibility. I say more about the troubles that the mere metaphysical possibility of infinite decomposition might pose for panpsychism and other approaches to the problem of consciousness in Chapter 6. Perhaps more strikingly, Schaffer asserts that infinite decomposition might not only be possible but also actual. His reason for suggesting that it might be actual is because the idea that it is a feature of the universe is taken seriously by scientists and posited as a feature of serious scientific theories about the actual world. For example, he points out that David Bohm (1957) says that his formulation of physics is 'consistent with an infinity of levels'. While Hans Dehmelt (1989) proposes an infinite regression of subelectron structure. The takeaway from this is not that we have compelling reasons to conclude that the world lacks the microphysical ultimates that both physicalism and panpsychism (in their popular contemporary construals) rely on, but rather that we should take seriously the possibility that they do not exist.

To recap, if fundamentalism is false because there are no microphysical ultimates, then panpsychism is also false because there are no microphysical ultimates to instantiate phenomenal properties. It is tempting to think that the panpsychist has a simple way around this problem by holding that it is not microphysical *ultimates* that instantiate phenomenal properties but rather some nonbasic microphysical entities. The problem with this move is that it seems to be arbitrary; why is it that entities on that microphysical level instantiate phenomenal properties and not those entities on the level below? Also, it would seem that the problem of strong emergence resurfaces. If the phenomenal-property-instantiating microphysical entities depend for their existence on entities at lower levels, but the lower-level entities do not instantiate phenomenal properties, then from where do they emerge?

In contrast, because it does not rely on fundamentalism, priority cosmopsychism is not vulnerable to the problem of infinite decomposition because it attributes the fundamental form of consciousness to the cosmos. The cosmos is on the top level of reality, whereas the microphysical ultimates (if they exist) are on the bottom level of reality. Therefore, the question of whether or not there is indeed a bottom level of reality, at which the microphysical ultimates preside, is inconsequential for the cogency of priority cosmopsychism. All priority cosmopsychism requires is that the cosmos exists, and indeed, the cosmos does exist. These considerations around the infinite decomposability of concrete objects give us good reason to prefer the priority cosmopsychism approach over panpsychism.

What I have said so far relates only to concrete objects, but the same thinking can also be extended to phenomenal properties. For example, Chalmers (1996, p. 126) indicates that phenomenal properties might be proper arrangements of protophenomenal properties, when he says that phenomenal properties logically supervene on appropriately arranged sums of protophenomenal properties. If that were the case, it would leave open the possibility that phenomenal properties or protophenomenal properties are infinitely decomposable, with instances of protophenomenal properties on one level always divisible into more primitive ones on lower levels. This possibility would undermine panpsychism because the whole point of panpsychism is to avoid the problem of strong emergence by introducing (proto)phenomenal properties on the ultimate micro-level of reality as the fundamental building blocks of macro-level phenomenality. If phenomenal properties are infinitely decomposable, then they cannot be the fundamental building blocks of phenomenal reality.

Priority cosmopsychism is not undermined by such an eventuality because it regards cosmic-level phenomenality as ontologically prior to phenomenality at sub-cosmic levels. That is, on priority cosmopsychism, the cosmic consciousness is the one and only fundamental form of consciousness, from which all sub-cosmic consciousnesses derive. The question, therefore, of whether or not there exists such a thing as the smallest phenomenal level does not concern priority cosmopsychism.[6]

2.4.2 The combination problem

Panpsychism's most severe and persistent challenge is *the combination problem*.[7] The combination problem arises as a result of the panpsychist claim that microphysical ultimates instantiate the fundamental forms of phenomenal properties and that macro-level consciousness (like human consciousness) is constituted by combinations of these micro-level phenomenal properties. The combination problem is the challenge of accounting for such a combination.

It is generally accepted that the combination problem comprises several sub-problems or has multiple aspects. Principal among these are the more specific problems relating to the combination of phenomenal qualities, structure and *subjects* of experience. The extent to which these aspects of the combination problem apply will depend on the precise formulation of panpsychism under consideration. For example, the subject aspect of the combination problem will only arise for accounts of panpsychism affirming the subjecthood of microphysical ultimates. Each of these sub-problems or aspects will be dealt with in detail in the course of this book, but at this stage, we can limit our focus to the combination problem in a general form.

The view that the combination problem represents the most severe and persistent problem for panpsychism is a widely accepted view; as Goff (2022) points out in his *Stanford Encyclopedia of Philosophy* entry on panpsychism, 'It is generally agreed, both by its proponents and by its opponents, that the hardest problem facing panpsychism is what has become known as the "combination problem"'. For example, Chalmers has described it as 'certainly the hardest problem for any sort of Russellian view [which includes panpsychism, as formulated here]' (Chalmers, 1996, p. 307). Similarly,

6 Talk of size here is metaphorical since phenomenal properties are not spatially extended.

7 The combination problem was first highlighted by James (1890). Although it is typically referred to as 'the combination problem' (Chalmers, 2002; Coleman, 2006; Goff, 2006, 2009), it has also been called the 'generation problem' (Seager, 1999), 'the structural mismatch' (Stoljar, 2001, 2006) and the 'constitution problem' (Strawson, 2008).

Seager states that it is 'the most difficult problem facing any panpsychist theory of consciousness' (1995, p. 280).

Priority cosmopsychism does not face the combination problem because it denies that macro-level phenomenal experiences are constituted by phenomenal properties instantiated by microphysical ultimates. Recall that priority cosmopsychism attributes fundamental consciousness to the cosmos and maintains that macro consciousnesses (like us) are derivative of it. Therefore, according to priority cosmopsychism, instances of macro consciousness are derivatives of a larger consciousness (i.e. the cosmic consciousness) rather than aggregates of smaller instances of consciousness (i.e. the phenomenal properties of the microphysical ultimates), as is the case for panpsychism. In effect, panpsychism faces the combination problem because it is a bottom-up view, according to which 'small' instances of consciousness – the phenomenal properties instantiated by the microphysical ultimates – combine to form 'larger' instances, such as the phenomenal properties characterizing macro-level conscious experience, like ours. The combination problem resides in how to make sense of such a combination. Priority cosmopsychism does not face the combination problem because it does not maintain that smaller instances of consciousness combine to form larger ones. Rather, it is a top-down view, according to which macro-level consciousness is derived from an even larger consciousness. Thus, there is no need, on this approach, to make sense of the combination of smaller into larger instances of phenomenality. Nagasawa and I use the following analogy to illustrate how its top-down approach allows priority cosmopsychism to avoid the combination problem:

> Suppose, *per impossibile*, there is an absolutely perfectly smooth painting, which is analogous to a smooth, homogenous phenomenal experience. Such a painting cannot be an aggregate of small dots, which are analogous to phenomenal or protophenomenal properties of physical ultimates, but it can be a segment of a larger painting that is equally smooth and homogenous, which is analogous to the cosmic consciousness.
>
> (Nagasawa & Wager, 2017, pp. 121–2)

One might contend that priority cosmopsychism still faces a version of the combination problem because instances of macro-level consciousness still combine to form the cosmic consciousness, even if macro-level consciousness is not constituted by micro-level consciousness. However, this is a misunderstanding of priority cosmopsychism, which says that the cosmic consciousness is ontologically prior to sub-cosmic forms of consciousness, meaning that sub-cosmic forms of consciousness are derived from cosmic consciousness. On panpsychism, the fundamental building blocks of consciousness are at the micro-level; for cosmopsychism, there is only one fundamental building block of consciousness, and that is at the cosmic level.

2.4.3 The derivation problem for priority cosmopsychism

However, priority cosmopsychism does face the following crucial question: How could macro-level consciousnesses be derived from the cosmic consciousness? Let us call this *the derivation problem*. While the derivation problem will arguably be the most pressing challenge for accounts that take as their basis the priority cosmopsychism blueprint, the precise form the derivation problem will take will depend on the specifics of the cosmopsychist account. Just as the combination problem will have different aspects, partially dependent on the specific details of a particular account, so will cosmopsychist accounts built on the priority cosmopsychism blueprint. For example, the derivation problem for priority cosmopsychism may, like the combination problem for panpsychism, have aspects relating to the derivation of phenomenal qualities, structure and subjects of experience. As such, the task at this stage will not be to provide a detailed response to the derivation problem. Recall that we are presenting here only a *blueprint* of an approach to the problem of phenomenal consciousness on which to develop fuller-bodied accounts. Those fuller accounts will invariably postulate more about the nature of consciousness attributed to the cosmos and will face the derivation problem accordingly. The blueprint remains neutral as to the precise nature of the cosmic consciousness.

Nevertheless, at this stage, we can provide some very general support to the plausibility of derivation by comparing the cosmic consciousness to human consciousness. On any development on the blueprint, the cosmic consciousness will be somewhat comparable to the consciousness we are acquainted with in our ordinary experience because the cosmic consciousness will be, after all, a form of consciousness. We might then provide some initial support to the idea that consciousness on the macro-level (e.g. human consciousness) derives from a more extensive form of consciousness by considering if our ordinary consciousness can be divided into smaller, less fundamental segments. We would then have reason to think that the cosmic consciousness could be divided into less fundamental segments. Indeed, it seems plausible that the consciousness of an ordinary individual can be divided into smaller segments. Consider, for example, an ordinary visual experience – perhaps the visual experience a person might have when looking out across a rocky beach to the ocean beyond it as the sun is setting. We can consider such a visual experience to be a unity which can be segmented into distinguishable colour or spatial experiences. For example, it will include distinguishable colour experiences corresponding to the green-blue ocean and orange-red sky hues. It will also include distinguishable spatial properties corresponding to the left and right-hand sides of the visual field. However, the visual experience seems to be a unity that is more fundamental than any such segmentation. We might then consider the cosmic consciousness to unify the sub-cosmic consciousnesses similarly, with instances of sub-cosmic consciousness derived from the cosmic consciousness as partial aspects.

Let us recap. Panpsychism faces the infinite decomposition problem because it relies on fundamentalism. Priority cosmopsychism avoids this problem because it does not rely on fundamentalism. Additionally, panpsychism faces the combination problem (widely regarded as its most serious challenge) because it maintains that macro-level consciousnesses are constituted by combinations of micro-level consciousness. Priority cosmopsychism avoids this problem because it denies that macro-level consciousness is so constituted. Views built on the priority cosmopsychism blueprint will face the derivation problem, but there is *prima facie* reason to think that derivation is plausible.

2.5 Possible objections

Following the priority cosmopsychism blueprint overcomes two of the most persistent challenges for panpsychism, but one may argue that priority cosmopsychism seems more implausible than panpsychism. Let us review some of the most likely initial objections that one might have, related to its relative implausibility. Of course, this book will explore such objections in more detail, but addressing some initial concerns at this early stage will be helpful in clearly establishing the *prima facie* plausibility of the priority cosmopsychism blueprint.

2.5.1 The inexplicability of the cosmic consciousness

One initial objection to the blueprint might be that it remains silent about the precise nature of cosmic consciousness. Given that the blueprint's defining feature is its attribution of phenomenality to the cosmos, one might claim that it is incomplete without further explaining its nature.

In response, it is worth stressing, once again, that what is proposed here is a *blueprint* of an approach to the problem of phenomenal consciousness. The blueprint provides a framework for an approach to the problem of consciousness that can be elaborated on in various ways. If the blueprint is followed, the resultant views will inherit the advantages laid out in the previous section. However, by design, the blueprint dictates only a little about how the cosmic consciousness must be conceived. Nevertheless, the blueprint is not *entirely* silent about what the cosmic consciousness must be like. First, as mentioned previously, it must be a form of consciousness; its form of phenomenality must be similar in some respect to that of ordinary individuals because it is called upon to solve the problem of phenomenal consciousness after all. If positing a cosmic consciousness is to help solve the problem of phenomenal consciousness, then it must be in some way equivalent to human consciousness. Second, the cosmic consciousness must be the fundamental form of phenomenality on which all sub-cosmic forms depend.

Additionally, recall that the purpose of this chapter is to present a blueprint for addressing the problem of phenomenal consciousness, which represents a promising alternative to panpsychism. Therefore, the aim is to compare priority cosmopsychism with panpsychism and to show that the former is more advantageous than the latter insofar as it avoids its most persistent problems while retaining its most significant motivation. Consequently, the present interest is more directly in how priority cosmopsychism fairs, regarding its relative silence about the precise nature of the cosmic consciousness, compared to panpsychism. When considered as a general approach to the problem of consciousness, we find that panpsychism also does not commit one to any precise account of the nature of consciousness at the fundamental (i.e. micro) level. It is arguably as tricky for panpsychists to imagine precisely what micro-level consciousness might be like as it is for cosmopsychists to imagine the precise nature of the cosmic consciousness. However, this issue does not cut against the possibility of their existence. Indeeed, Chalmers (1996) makes exactly this point (about the kind of micro-level protophenomenal properties that panpsychists might posit): 'Of course it is very hard to imagine what a protophenomenal property could be like but we cannot rule out the possiblity that they exist' (p. 127). So, in terms of comparing the two, priority cosmopsychism does not come off any worse for not stipulating details of the cosmic consciousness (at least when we are comparing the two as general approaches to the problem of consciousness). However, significant distinctions will likely be borne out in the details of more specific versions of these approaches.

2.5.2 Counterintuitiveness

Alternatively, one might object to priority cosmopsychism because it is simply too counterintuitive to be taken seriously. Again, the intended comparison at this stage is between panpsychism and priority cosmopsychism. Therefore, the aim of responding to this possible objection is to show that the latter is not more counterintuitive than the former. As we mentioned, the two are structurally equivalent. Panpsychism says that there is a fundamental bottom level of reality and adds that the microphysical ultimates forming the bottom level instantiate phenomenal properties. Similarly, priority cosmopsychism says that the cosmos is on the top level of reality and that it instantiates fundamental phenomenal properties. In both cases, macro-level phenomenal properties depend on those fundamental forms of phenomenality on different levels of reality. Thus, they are structurally similar, and there is no immediate reason to think of either as distinctively more counterintuitive than the other.

However, one might still claim that attributing phenomenality to the cosmos is especially absurd. One might contend, for instance, that animal brains instantiate phenomenal properties due to their bearing an appropriate level of structural complexity, but that this does not appear to be mirrored in the cosmos taken as a whole. While this might be a challenge that ultimately arises for those following the priority cosmopsychism blueprint (depending on the precise details of their filled-out cosmopsychist account), it *prima facie* cuts equally against panpsychism because panpsychism faces an objection of the same form. According to panpsychism, macro-level consciousness (that we typically associate with animal brains) is constituted by the consciousness of microphysical ultimates; however – much like the cosmos – microphysical ultimates do not have the structural complexity exhibited in brains. Therefore, panpsychism and priority cosmopsychism must both account for the counterintuitiveness of the claim that macro-level consciousness associated with brains arises from consciousness instantiated by apparently less structurally complex entities.

Furthermore, it is worth noting that panpsychism often faces objections on the grounds of its counterintuitiveness. For example, John Searle (1997) calls it an 'absurd view' and describes Chalmers's defence of it the following way: 'when faced with a *reductio ad absurdum* argument he just accepts the absurdity' (p. 156). Panpsychists emphasize that panpsychism should not be dismissed based on its counterintuitiveness, and priority cosmopsychists can echo this response. Thus, again, counterintuitiveness *per se* does not cut against priority cosmopsychism any more than it does against panpsychism. Indeed, the same can be said for many other possible objections to priority cosmopsychism. For example, one might object on the basis that there is no sign that the cosmos is conscious (we can call this the *no sign problem for priority cosmopsychism*), or because there is no empirical test to prove a cosmic consciousness (we can call this *the no test problem for priority cosmopsychism*). The priority cosmopsychist could respond to these objections. For instance, they might respond to the no signs problem by claiming that there is no sign that the cosmos is conscious because it is not structured such that it behaves in accordance with its phenomenal nature (unlike the way human bodies behave in accordance with *their* phenomenal natures). Alternatively, the priority cosmopsychist might respond to the no test problem by conceding that there is no empirical test to affirm the cosmic consciousness while pointing out that this is also true of the consciousness of higher animals – the problem of animal minds (and other minds) is intractable for this reason. However, potential responses to these objections are not relevant here since we are interested in a comparison between panpsychism and priority cosmopsychism, and we can see that panpsychism faces its own versions of the no sign problem and no test problem. For example, it faces a no sign problem in so far as we see no sign that microphysical ultimates are conscious, and a no test problem because there is no definitive empirical test to confirm that they are conscious entities.

2.5.3 Estrangement from current science

Finally, one might contend that priority cosmopsychism is less favourable on account that it is more estranged from current science than panpsychism. For instance, one might be particularly concerned that priority cosmopsychism is especially estranged from current science because it is not concerned with the same physical ultimates that are the focus of current physics. In contrast, they might argue that panpsychism is preferable because it is concerned with precisely the same physical ultimates described by current physics (since it holds that fundamental phenomenal or protophenomenal properties are instantiated by such ultimates).

A more specific objection following this line of reasoning might be that priority cosmopsychism is unable to adhere to the principle of the causal closure of the microphysical (given that, presumably, the priority cosmopsychist would like the cosmic consciousness to be causally efficacious). This principle says that the world's causal efficacy is fully accounted for in terms of the causal efficacy of its microphysical ultimates. One might claim that panpsychism is able to adhere to this principle while cosmopsychism is not. Panpsychism, they might say, can adhere to the principle by claiming that since all microphysical ultimates instantiate phenomenal properties, any causal efficacy they may have is already accounted for in current physics. On the other hand, they might say that priority cosmopsychism cannot account for the principle in the same way because it does not say that microphysical ultimates instantiate phenomenal properties.

Again, it should be emphasized that the priority cosmopsychism blueprint is not a detailed approach to the problem of phenomenal consciousness but a blueprint on which more detailed views can be developed. The blueprint remains silent about the precise relation between phenomenal properties and physical properties; since it is in the details of such a relation that it will become apparent if priority cosmopsychism can adhere to the causal closure of the microphysical, this objection can only be addressed in the context of a more fully developed stance on the priority cosmopsychism blueprint. However, it should be noted that the priority cosmopsychism blueprint is consistent with more detailed versions of cosmopsychism that take a broadly dual-aspect view, according to which the phenomenal and physical are co-extensive in some sense, and where the level of the cosmos is taken to be fundamental with respect to both aspects. On such views, it is arguably plausible that cosmopsychism can adhere to the causal closure of the physical owing to the phenomenal already being accounted for in our current physics. I will not detail such a response here, but we will investigate this line of thinking in forthcoming chapters (most notably in Chapter 6).

2.6 Conclusion

The purpose of this short chapter has been to present a blueprint of an approach to the problem of consciousness that is an alternative to panpsychism. Importantly, it preserves the key motivation behind panpsychism (i.e. bypassing the problem of strong emergence) while also avoiding its most intractable problems (i.e. the problem of infinite decomposition and the combination problem). The blueprint, as we have seen, achieves this by prescribing an approach according to which a cosmic consciousness, rather than micro-level consciousness, is the fundamental form of consciousness and, macro-level consciousnesses (like human consciousnesses) are derived in a top-down manner from the cosmic consciousness rather than built up in a bottom-up manner from combinations of micro-level consciousness. As indicated, this blueprint gives rise to the derivation problem. Although we have *prima facie* reason to believe it is easier to solve than panpsychism's combination problem, those following the blueprint will ultimately have to answer to it. The remainder of this book marks an inquiry into the promise of the priority cosmopsychism blueprint. It is important to note that there are numerous avenues of potential development on the blueprint that I will not delve into in this book. Part of the reason for including a brief chapter on this minimal blueprint is to provide others with an outline of a promising approach they can develop according to their own ideas. With that said, and with the blueprint now in place, we can proceed to the next phase of our present inquiry. In the next chapter, we will investigate recent developments on the blueprint in more detail. This investigation will reveal what appears to be a serious problem for such developments: the subject derivation problem, along with its counterpart in panpsychism, the subject combination problem. As a result, much of the following chapter will explore closely related alternatives to panpsychism and cosmopsychism that purport to avoid these problems.

References

Bohm, D. (1957). *Causality and chance in modern physics*. London: Routledge & Kegan Paul.

Chalmers, D. J. (1996). *The conscious mind*. New York: Oxford University Press.

Chalmers, D. J. (2002). 'Consciousness and its place in nature'. In D. J. Chalmers (Ed.), *Philosophy of mind: Classical and contemporary readings* (pp. 247–72). New York: Oxford University Press.

Coleman, S. (2006). 'Being realistic – why physicalism may entail panexperientialism'. *Journal of Consciousness Studies*, 13(10–11), 40–52.

Dehmelt, H. (1989). 'Triton, … electron, … cosmon … : An infinite regression?' *Proceedings of the National Academy of Sciences*, 86(22), 8618–19.

Goff, P. (2006). 'Experiences don't sum'. *Journal of Consciousness Studies*, 13(10–11), 53–61.

Goff, P. (2009). 'Why panpsychism doesn't help us explain consciousness'. *Dialectica*, 63(3), 289–311.

Goff, P., Seager, W., & Allen-Hermanson, S. (2022). 'Panpsychism'. In E. N. Zalta (Ed.), *The Stanford encyclopedia of philosophy* (Summer 2022 ed.). Retrieved from https://plato.stanford.edu/archives/sum2022/entries/panpsychism/.

Horgan, T., & Potrč, M. (2000). 'Blobjectivism and indirect correspondence'. *Facta Philosophica*, 2(2), 249–70.

Horgan, T., & Potrč, M. (2008). *Austere realism: Contextual semantics meets minimal ontology*. Cambridge, MA: MIT Press.

James, W. (1890). *The principles of psychology*. London, England: Dover Publications.

Montero, B. (2006). 'Physicalism in an infinitely decomposable world'. *Erkenntnis*, 64(2), 177–91.

Nagasawa, Y., & Wager, K. (2017). 'Panpsychism and priority cosmopsychism'. In G. Brüntrup & L. Jaskolla (Eds.), *Panpsychism: Contemporary perspectives* (pp. 113–29). New York: Oxford University Press.

Schaffer, J. (2003). 'Is there a fundamental level?' *Noûs*, 37(3), 498–517.

Schaffer, J. (2008). 'Monism'. In E. N. Zalta (Ed.), *The Stanford encyclopedia of philosophy* (Fall 2008 ed.). Retrieved from http://plato.stanford.edu/archives/fall2008/entries/monism/.

Schaffer, J. (2010). 'Monism: The priority of the whole'. *Philosophical Review*, 119(1), 31–76.

Seager, W. (1995). 'Consciousness, information and panpsychism'. *Journal of Consciousness Studies*, 2(3), 272–88.

Seager, W. (1999). *Theories of consciousness: An introduction*. New York: Routledge.

Searle, J. (1997). *The mystery of consciousness*. New York: New York Review of Books.

Stoljar, D. (2001). 'Two conceptions of the physical'. *Philosophy and Phenomenological Research*, 62(2), 253–81.

Stoljar, D. (2006). *Ignorance and imagination: The epistemic origin of the problem of consciousness*. New York: Oxford University Press USA.

Strawson, G. (2008). 'Realistic monism: Why physicalism entails panpsychism'. In *Real materialism and other essays* (pp. 53–74). Oxford: Oxford University Press.

Wager, K. (2011). *Dual-aspect priority monism and the combination problem for panpsychism* (MA thesis, University of Birmingham).

3

Beyond panpsychism and cosmopsychism? *Panqualityism and perennialism*

3.1 Introduction

Panpsychism occupies an interesting space when considering the hard problem of consciousness. It sits between the extremes of physicalism and dualism, explaining conscious experience neither as something captured by our current physics nor as something substantially distinct from physical matter. Instead, panpsychism states that consciousness is already present at the start. It is literally *in* everything. An upshot of this is that everything is also said to be a *subject* of experience. This gives rise to *the subject combination problem*, which is severe enough that it has led some who are drawn to the panpsychist project to explore alternative views inspired by, but distinct from, panpsychism.

Cosmopsychism is a view that has built a reasonable following in recent years. Its proponents typically claim that, rather than panpsychism being true because all microphysical ultimates are conscious, it is true because the cosmos as a whole, as the one physical ultimate, is conscious (Wager, 2011, 2020; Shani, 2015; Goff, 2017, 2020; Nagasawa & Wager, 2017). The positive implication of this is that the subject combination problem can be averted because subjects, according to cosmopsychism, do not *combine*. However, it faces an equivalent, perhaps equal in difficulty, in *the subject derivation problem*: how are macro-subjects, like you and me, derived from the cosmic subject?

One promising way forward is to reject the stipulation that physical ultimates – whether microphysical ultimates, as in the case of panpsychism, or the cosmos itself, as in cosmopsychism – are subjects of experience. Doing so straightforwardly sidesteps the subject combination problem and the subject derivation problem since, on such a proposal, there are no subjects at the purported fundamental level to combine into, or from which to derive, macro-subjects. In this chapter, I focus on two such alternatives: one maintaining a focus on the microphysical, like panpsychism, and one keeping the focus on the cosmos, like cosmopsychism. The former is the view known as *panqualityism*, while the latter is *perennialism*. Both of these views were very briefly introduced in Chapter 1. In this chapter, I consider them in more detail to ascertain whether they can rescue the fruitful middle ground between physicalism and dualism that panpsychism and cosmopsychism occupy, a middle ground which appears to be threatened by their respective subject combination and derivation problems. However, I conclude that in both cases, we see a resurgence of the same problems faced by existing approaches, as well as some new ones unique to these alternatives. This conclusion will ultimately motivate us to revisit the subject combination and derivation problems and evaluate them more deeply, a task we will take up in Chapter 4.

Returning to the present chapter, it proceeds as follows: The first two sections recap and build on key views and problems briefly outlined in preceding chapters. First, Section 3.2 introduces, in more detail than previously, panpsychism and its combination problem. Then, Section 3.3 introduces cosmopsychism and its derivation problem. After briefly restating the priority cosmopsychism blueprint presented in the previous chapter, it summarizes some developments on it. Importantly, this section highlights Albahari's (2020) objection to cosmopsychism on the grounds of the subject derivation problem. The next two sections critically assess the two proposed successors to cosmopsychism and panpsychism that drop the stipulation that subjects are present at the fundamental level of reality. Section 3.4 focuses on Albahari's (2019, 2020) perennialism, a potential successor to cosmopsychism, while Section 3.5 focuses on Coleman's (2012, 2014, 2017) panqualityism, a potential successor to panpsychism.

3.2 Panpsychism

Let us begin by recapping panpsychism once again. Panpsychism is the view that consciousness is a fundamental and ubiquitous feature of the cosmos.[1] Meaning consciousness is not explained in terms of anything else and is spread throughout the whole of the cosmos. It holds an interesting position in the philosophy of mind, especially as an approach to the problem of phenomenal consciousness, since it does away with the problematic implications of substance dualism while avoiding the need for consciousness to suddenly break into the world in rare and seemingly miraculous circumstances. A rare and miraculous breaking into the world is an implication of physicalism, and physicalism is arguably the most popular approach to the problem of phenomenal consciousness. Consequently, it is easy to see why panpsychism marks an exciting departure from orthodoxy.

3.2.1 The problem of strong emergence

The main reason for holding panpsychism is that it avoids the problem of strong emergence. This problem was sketched out in the first two chapters, but it will now be helpful to gain a deeper understanding. The problem arises from the unexpectedness of consciousness. On a somewhat standard view, consciousness is instantiated by entirely physical entities such as aggregates of neurons. However, this is unexpected and a surprise each time it happens because neurons are ordinarily taken to be

[1] Note here that this is what I referred to as 'simple panpsychism' in Chapter 1.

fundamentally non-conscious. Any view stating that consciousness arises from matter entirely devoid of consciousness faces the problem of strong emergence.

Emergence, per se, is not the problem here. There are numerous examples of emergent phenomena that are unproblematic. For example, the emergence of a solid from a liquid when the temperature of water drops 0°C. Such cases are not concerning. The difficulty is specifically with *strong* emergence. To get a handle on what makes strong emergence *strong* and other kinds of emergence *weak*, it is helpful to refer to Chalmers's (2006) distinction between strong and weak emergence. Regarding strong emergence, he says: 'We can say that a high-level phenomenon is *strongly emergent* with respect to a low-level domain when the high-level phenomenon arises (in some sense) from the low-level domain, but truths concerning that phenomenon are not *deducible* even in principle from truths in the low-level domain' (2006, p. 244). While about weak emergence, he says: 'We can say that a high-level phenomenon is weakly emergent with respect to a low-level domain when the high-level phenomenon arises from the low-level domain, but truths concerning that phenomenon are *unexpected* given the principles governing the low-level domain' (2006, p. 244).

Chalmers highlights that the two conceptions of emergence are not mutually exclusive since cases of strong emergence will likely imply weak emergence (as defined). However, cases of weak emergence will not imply strong emergence. He says that while the existence of weakly emergent phenomena does not challenge our conception of nature, the existence of strongly emergent phenomena does. Strong emergence is especially concerning because, as he says: '[I]f there are phenomena whose existence is not deducible from the facts about the exact distribution of particles and fields throughout space and time (along with the laws of physics), then this suggests that new fundamental laws of nature are needed to explain these phenomena' (2006, p. 245).

It is not hard to get a feel for why strong emergence is such a problematic concept if its existence means we need new fundamental laws to account for its instances. Proponents of theories that rely on, or imply, strong emergence do not, typically speaking, want to invoke new fundamental laws of nature to explain consciousness. A core issue with panpsychism from physicalists' perspectives will likely be precisely its expansion of fundamental reality by way of adding consciousness to the set of fundamental things. Since it is only by invoking new fundamental laws that there could be said to be a connection between the low- and high-level domains, strong emergence represents a significant problem without those laws because the strongly emergent phenomena float free of their submergent bases. Interestingly, in the face of apparent strongly emergent phenomena, if we do what Chalmers suggests we must do and introduce new fundamental laws to account for that phenomena, then we no longer have a case of strong emergence and hence do not face the problem.

Nagel (1979) offered an early and influential argument in favour of panpsychism (or panprotopsychism), which hinges on the notion of emergence. His account of emergence is especially helpful in illustrating the above. He says:

> There are no truly emergent properties of complex systems. All properties of a complex system that are not relations between it and something else derive

> from the properties of its constituents and their effects on each other when so combined. Emergence is an epistemological condition: it means that an observed feature of the system cannot be derived from the properties currently attributed to its constituents. But this is a reason to conclude that either the system has further constituents of which we are not yet aware, or the constituents of which we are aware have further properties that we have not yet discovered.
>
> (p. 182)

Nagel picks up on a critical distinction that is relevant to the problem of emergence. He notes that emergence is an epistemological condition, meaning it signifies nothing more than a gap in our knowledge. Either we are ignorant about the existence of some constituents of a system altogether or about some properties of constituents we already know about. In either case, the suspected emergent properties are only emergent in the weak sense. In contrast, strongly emergent phenomena imply ontological emergence, where the emergent phenomena are not just *seemingly* strongly emergent because of epistemic limitations. Instead, they emerge in the absence of epistemic limitations. The contention is that this ontological emergence is impossible.

As briefly stated in the previous chapter, the most notable defence of panpsychism on the grounds of the problem of emergence is offered by Strawson (2006, 2008). According to him, the instantiation of experiential phenomena by wholly non-experiential phenomena is as extraordinary as the instantiation of spatially extended phenomena by entirely spatially unextended phenomena.[2, 3] Strawson states that such strong emergence (or radical emergence, as he calls it) of the spatially extended from the spatially unextended, and its analogue of the experiential from non-experiential, is impossible due to the truth of the following apparent law: 'For any feature Y of anything that is currently considered to be emergent from X, there must be something about X and X alone in virtue of which Y emerges, and which is sufficient for Y' (2008,

2 To be precise, he says of such an analogy:

'We need an analogy on a wholly different scale if we are to get any imaginative grip on the supposed move from the non-experiential to the experiential.

What might be an analogy of the right size? Suppose someone – I will call him pseudo-Boscovich, at the risk of offending historians of science – proposes that all ultimates, all real, concrete ultimates, are, in truth, wholly unextended entities: that this is the truth about their being; that there is no sense in which they themselves are extended; that they are real concrete entities, but are nonetheless true-mathematical-point entities. And suppose pseudo-Boscovich goes on to say that when collections of these entities stand in certain (real, concrete, natural) relations, they give rise to or constitute truly, genuinely extended concrete entities; real, concrete extension being in this sense an emergent property of phenomena that are, although by hypothesis real and concrete, wholly unextended.

Well, I think this suggestion should be rejected as absurd. But the suggestion that when non-experiential phenomena stand in certain (real, natural, concrete non-experiential) relations they ipso facto instantiate or constitute experiential phenomena, experience being an emergent property of wholly and utterly non-experiential phenomena, seems exactly on a par. That's why I offer unextended-to-extended emergence as an analogy, a destructive analogy that proposes something impossible and thereby challenges the possibility of the thing it is offered as an analogy for' (2008, p. 63).

3 For present purposes we can think of experiential phenomena and conscious phenomena as interchangeable.

p. 65). Strongly emergent phenomena violate such a law, and therefore, Strawson states that it is 'by definition a miracle every time it occurs' (2008, pp. 45–6). He concludes: 'It is built into the heart of the notion of emergence that emergence cannot be brute in the sense of there being absolutely no reason in the nature of things why the emerging thing is as it is' (2008, p. 65). Panpsychism, at least in the guise that I am most interested in here, avoids the problem of strong emergence by stipulating that the microphysical ultimates are themselves conscious. For panpsychism, it is in-principle deducible that aggregates of neurons are conscious because, according to its view, the microphysical constituents of neurons – the microphysical ultimates – are themselves conscious.

3.2.2 Constitutive panpsychism and constitutive Russellian panpsychism

While a simple formulation of panpsychism amounts to the stipulation that phenomenal consciousness is a fundamental and ubiquitous feature of the cosmos, there are numerous ways to develop this simple view into more full-bodied approaches to the problem of consciousness. As indicated in Chapter 1, the most promising form of panpsychism is constitutive panpsychism, according to which micro-level consciousness constitutes macro-level consciousness. On this view, macro-consciousness is grounded, either fully or partially, in micro-consciousness. For macro-consciousness to be fully grounded in micro-consciousness, the former must obtain in virtue of the latter alone. For it to be partially grounded, the former must obtain in virtue of the latter plus some further fact (typically, this will be some fact about structure or dynamics, or a combination thereof).

As we saw in Chapter 1, constitutive Panpsychism is contrasted with non-constitutive panpsychism, the thesis that macro-consciousness is not constituted by micro-consciousness. Again, there are competing versions, but one particularly important one is emergent panpsychism (Rosenberg, 2004; Seager, 2010, 2017; Mørch, 2014, 2019; Brüntrup, 2017). We covered this view in the book's opening chapter, but to recap, emergent panpsychism maintains that instances of micro-consciousness are an important part of the story of how macro-consciousness comes about, but not because certain combinations of them constitute macro-consciousness. Rather, macro-consciousness *emerges* from micro-consciousness. Some versions claim a synchronous existence of micro- and macro-level consciousness, for example, the synchronous existence of the micro-level consciousness of physical ultimates and macro-level human consciousness, where the micro-level gives rise to, and sustains the existence of, the macro-level (Rosenberg, 2004; Brüntrup, 2017). Others maintain that micro-consciousness loses its identity upon the emergence of macro-consciousness from it (Seager, 2017). An especially interesting emergentist account alleges that micro- and macro-level consciousnesses exist synchronically but that, due to the emergence of the macro from the micro-level, micro-level consciousnesses become dependent on macro-consciousness for their existence (Mørch, 2014, 2019). While non-constitutive panpsychism (emergent panpsychism, in particular) marks a potentially fruitful avenue of investigation, it does explicitly endorse the emergence of macro-consciousness from micro-consciousness and thus faces a kind of emergence problem. However, as noted previously, the problem for emergent panpsychism may be less serious since it says only that 'larger' consciousnesses emerge from 'smaller' consciousnesses rather than consciousness emerging from non-consciousness. Still, it represents a significant issue for its proponents. This chapter, and indeed this book, is focused on constitutive panpsychism, so emergentist versions will be largely kept to one side for now.

We can get even more fine-grained and give an account of panpsychism which says more about the relation between the physical and phenomenal at the fundamental level of reality. Constitutive *Russellian* panpsychism supplements what I have said so far about constitutive panpsychism with a view known as Russellian monism. Russellian monism is a version of monism (as regards the mind-body problem) inspired by a claim made by Bertrand Russell in *The Analysis of Matter* (1927). Russell claims that physics describes the world's fundamental constituents – its microphysical ultimates – only in relational or structural terms and remains silent about their categorical nature. Physics may describe what mass, spin, charge, etc., do, but it does not describe what they are. Russellian monism fills this gap by appealing to 'inscrutables' (Montero, 2010; Alter & Nagasawa, 2012, 2015) or 'quiddities' (Chalmers, 2017a, 2017b). Quiddities are properties that are not fully captured in relational or structural descriptions of the world (such as current physics) but that ground the relational or structural nature of physics. Russellian monists claim that at least some quiddities are conscious (or protoconscious).

Constitutive Russellian panpsychism, then, is the view according to which micro-conscious properties are quiddities, and quiddities combine to constitute macro-consciousness. This version of panpsychism is often considered the most promising of all. For instance, Chalmers (2017b) writes, 'I think that constitutive Russellian panpsychism is perhaps the most important form of panpsychism' (p. 27). It is attractive for several reasons, but one significant reason is its ability to alleviate tension between mental causation and adhering to the principle of causal closure of the physical, which, under other views, seems irreconcilable. On the constitutive Russellian panpsychist view, consciousness (human consciousness, for example) has causal efficacy in virtue of it being grounded in quiddities, themselves conscious. Meanwhile, it can also adhere to causal closure of the physical by virtue of the quiddities grounding the microphysical. We will have occasion to explore motivations for Russellian monism in greater detail in Chapter 6. This brief outline will suffice for our purposes in the present chapter.

3.2.3 The combination problem(s) for panpsychism

Let us now recap the central problem of panpsychism. Typically, panpsychists claim that micro-consciousness is instantiated at the level of the fundamental microphysical constituents of matter. Although this avoids the need to explain how consciousness inexplicably emerges from an entirely non-conscious base, it makes way for a significant problem: the combination problem. Some claim this problem is equally as challenging for panpsychism as the problem of strong emergence is for non-panpsychist views. Again, the combination problem is the problem that arises out of the following panpsychist thinking. If micro-consciousness is instantiated at the fundamental microphysical level, then consciousness instantiated at the derivative macro-level (among which are human consciousnesses) must be formed of combinations of these 'smaller' instances of consciousness. The problem concerns explaining how it might be that this combination can happen or at least showing that such combinations are possible.

Although stating the problem this way captures the issue in a broad sense, it is now accepted that the combination problem is not a single issue, but a family of related problems. I will follow Chalmers (2017a) in splitting the combination problem into three sub-problems: a quality problem, a structure problem and a subject problem. The quality combination problem is the challenge of explaining how micro-level phenomenal qualities combine to yield macro-level phenomenal qualities. The structure combination problem is the challenge of explaining how micro-level experiential structure combines to yield macro-level experiential structure. Finally, the subject combination problem is the challenge of explaining how micro-level *subjects* of experience combine to yield macro-level subjects. While a solution to the combination problem will need to rise to each of these challenges, it is the challenge relating to subjects of experience that is generally held to be the most difficult. I will defer a detailed treatment of the subject combination problem until the next chapter. For now, it is enough to bear in mind that the subject aspect of the combination problem for panpsychism is considered the most taxing.

Now let us consider cosmopsychism and its equivalent of the subject combination problem before turning to the central theme of this chapter: a consideration of views that, faced with the seemingly persistent subject-related problems for panpsychism and cosmopsychism, seek to avoid these issues by dropping the stipulation that subjects of experience are present at the fundamental level of reality.

3.3 Cosmopsychism

As we saw in Chapter 1, cosmopsychism, in its most simple formulation, says that the cosmos is conscious. A simple formulation like this does not really help us in our pursuit of a solution to the problem of phenomenal consciousness. However, elaborations on this simple formulation, offered recently, have shown some promise. Of particular promise are developments on the priority cosmopsychism blueprint, as outlined in the previous chapter.

3.3.1 The priority cosmopsychism blueprint

It will not do us any harm to very briefly recap the blueprint. Recall that the priority cosmopsychism blueprint is intended to be a framework around which to develop approaches to the problem of phenomenal consciousness, which allow one to maintain the key advantages of a panpsychist approach whilst overcoming or circumventing its most persistent challenges (e.g. including the combination problem). The blueprint takes inspiration from both the panpsychist approach to the problem of phenomenal consciousness and the priority monist approach to metaphysics. Panpsychism, as I have already noted, is an advantageous approach to the problem of consciousness because it avoids the problem of strong emergence, which it does by positing consciousness at the fundamental microphysical level of reality. The principal downside of panpsychism, as highlighted above, is that it faces the combination problem, which can be defined as the problem of accounting for consciousness at the macro-level in virtue of combinations of consciousness at the micro-level. The priority cosmopsychism blueprint draws inspiration from this approach by positing consciousness at the fundamental level of reality, but for cosmopsychism, the fundamental level is the cosmic, rather than the microphysical. Admitting consciousness to the fundamental level of reality overcomes the problem of strong emergence for cosmopsychism, just as it does for panpsychism. In addition to this, cosmopsychism takes inspiration from priority monism, a view in metaphysics which says that the cosmos as a whole is the one and only fundamental entity, while all its parts are merely derivative of the whole cosmos. The priority cosmopsychism blueprint prescribes a parallel structure to priority monism (albeit in relation to phenomenal reality rather than concrete reality, which is the sole target of priority monism[4]) as it maintains that the cosmic-level consciousness is ontologically prior to all forms of sub-cosmic consciousness, which are merely derivative. Adopting this parallel structure allows cosmopsychists to avoid the combination problem, the reason being that macro-level consciousness is not said to be formed of combinations of micro-consciousness. Hence, there is no *combination* problem to overcome.

We can summarize the blueprint as a commitment to the following three stipulations: (1) The cosmos, as a whole, is conscious. (2) The cosmic consciousness grounds all sub-cosmic consciousness. And, (3) the cosmos is a subject of experience. The first two stipulations demonstrate the similarities with panpsychism and the parallel structure between cosmopsychism and priority monism. While priority monism is only concerned with concrete entities, cosmopsychism (at the blueprint stage) is only concerned with phenomenality. However, the blueprint of cosmopsychism prescribes a structural parity between the two because just as priority monism says that the cosmos is the one and only fundamental *concrete* entity, the cosmopsychist blueprint says that the cosmic consciousness is the one and only *phenomenal* entity. Cosmopsychism and panpsychism are equivalent insofar as they both say that macro-level consciousness (e.g. our human consciousnesses) is dependent on a more fundamental form of consciousness at a non-macro-level. For panpsychism, macro-consciousness is dependent on consciousness at the fundamental micro-level of reality. While, for cosmopsychism, macro-consciousness is dependent on the consciousness at the fundamental cosmic level.

Figure 2 shows the direction of derivation (i.e. the inverse of dependence). We can see that on neither panpsychism nor cosmopsychism is macro-level consciousness fundamental. We can also see how cosmopsychism mirrors the structure of priority monism with the direction of derivation moving from the cosmos downward. It is important to note that although the above diagram does not depict consciousness at the micro-level for cosmopsychism, it does permit micro-level consciousness. It is not

[4] It should be noted that the priority cosmopsychism blueprint is consistent with priority monism, as we shall see. Here I intended only to stress that it is not committed to priority monism, but only to a parallel structure in the phenomenal domain.

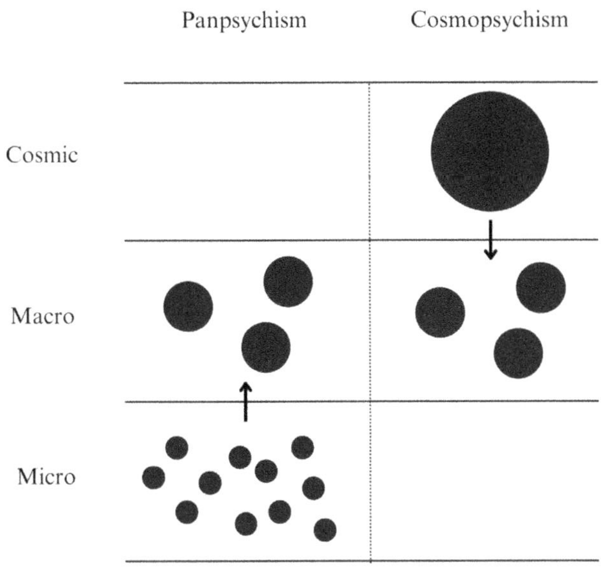

Figure 2 Direction of derivation in panpsychism and cosmopsychism.

depicted because the blueprint of cosmopsychism is silent on the matter of micro-level consciousness. Whether it is posited will be for any given development on the blueprint to stipulate. Similarly, although highly unusual, panpsychists are not logically precluded from positing consciousness at the cosmic level.

Eagle-eyed readers may have found the third stipulation surprising, given that I previously stressed that the blueprint does not commit the cosmopsychist to the presence of subjects of experience at the cosmic level. That is technically true. However, here it can be considered part of a minimal formulation of cosmopsychism because it has been (and is likely to continue to be) a near-unanimous feature of developments on the blueprint that the cosmos is a subject. The reason for this is that it is widely held as a conceptual truth that phenomenal consciousness involves phenomenal properties being instantiated by a subject of experience, so if one holds that the cosmos is conscious then it is very likely that they also hold that it is a subject. We should, of course, bear in mind that the blueprint is technically open to developments rejecting the view that the cosmos is a subject of experience.[5]

3.3.2 The derivation problem(s) for cosmopsychism

As we discovered in the previous chapter, following the blueprint allows the cosmopsychist to avoid the combination problem while still reaping the benefit of

[5] However, in such cases, strictly speaking, the resultant view is likely to be a form of cosmo*proto*psychism rather than cosmopsychism. On such views the cosmos is not conscious but protoconscious.

avoiding the problem of strong emergence. However, it also opens up a new distinct problem called the derivation problem.[6] The derivation problem is the problem of how to account for macro-consciousness (e.g. human consciousness) in virtue of the cosmic consciousness. In other words, it challenges the cosmopsychist to illustrate the plausibility of the derivation of macro-consciousness from the cosmic consciousness, showing, at least, that there are no contradictions in the suggestion. Ideally, they would also provide an account of how the derivation happens. For several reasons, the challenge of showing exactly how the derivation happens is not such a pressing issue, as strange as that may sound. First, all theories of phenomenal consciousness face the challenge of explaining the origins of macro-consciousness. Therefore, even if cosmopsychists cannot provide precise details of the derivation, they may still be on better theoretical footing than other theories. For example, even if we grant for the sake of argument that panpsychism's combination of micro into macro-level consciousness is possible, it is an additional challenge to explain exactly how such a combination happens. In general, panpsychist proposals have not focused on responding to this challenge so much as on simply defending the coherence of the proposed combination.

Second, there may be good reasons for suggesting that the exact details cannot be known, either currently or in principle. For example, Nagasawa and I (2017) have suggested that answering the second challenge may be difficult if we do not (or perhaps cannot) know the precise nature of the cosmic consciousness. The cosmopsychist could argue that there is potential to overcome an epistemic limitation on our detailed understanding of the derivation. For instance, they might claim that the epistemic distance will be countenanced along with future developments in our scientific understanding. Alternatively, they could claim some in-principle limitation on our understanding of the derivation, meaning its precise details will never be known to us. These ideas are closely related to mysterianism, a position in the philosophy of mind which says that it is impossible for human beings to solve the problem of phenomenal consciousness. Mysterianism can be further split into those who claim the problem is in-principle unsolvable – we can call this *strong mysterianism* – and those who claim that it is merely unsolvable at present – we can call this *weak mysterianism*. While mysterianism, in both its weak and strong varieties, invokes mysterianism when addressing the overall problem of phenomenal consciousness, it is clear that cosmopsychists need not do so (nor do panpsychists, for that matter) because they claim that a solution to the overall problem may have been found, but that mysterianism is needed concerning some particular sub-problem. In this case, the sub-problem in question is the part of the derivation problem which demands exact details on how the derivation occurs. Thus, we might say that cosmopsychists can invoke a weak version of either weak or strong mysterianism. Invoking weak-weak mysterianism

[6] Others refer to this broad problem using different names; Wager (2011), Shani (2015) and Chalmers (2020) call it the 'decomposition problem', Matthews (2011) refers to it as 'the combination problem in reverse', while Albahari (2020) names it the 'decombination problem'. I prefer to refer to it as the derivation problem since it strikes me as the least assumptive way of describing what is purportedly going on.

would involve the cosmopsychist claiming there is potential to overcome the epistemic barrier blocking our detailed understanding of the derivation, while invoking weak-strong mysterianism would involve the claim that the epistemic barrier is in-principle insurmountable. With this caveat – that the principal burden on the cosmopsychist is for them to show that the derivation of macro from cosmic-level consciousness is plausible – we can return to the present task of outlining cosmopsychism's equivalents of panpsychism's more fine-grained combination problems.

Recall that it is now widely accepted that the general combination problem for panpsychism is composed of three relatively distinct (though overlapping) problems. As noted above, Chalmers (2017a) distinguishes the three combination problems as the quality combination problem, the structure combination problem and the subject combination problem. To recap, the quality problem refers to the challenge of explaining how micro-qualities can combine to form macro-qualities. The structure problem refers to the need to explain how phenomenal structures at the micro-level can combine to form the phenomenal structure at the macro-level. Finally, the subject combination problem is the problem of accounting for macro-subjects in terms of a combination of micro-level subjects. The problems do not affect all versions of panpsychism equally. For example, it is not a necessary condition of panpsychism that it must include subjects of experience at the micro-level. It stands to reason that the subject combination problem will not be a problem for views that reject micro-subjects (just as subject derivation will not be a problem for a cosmopsychism that does not posit a cosmic subject). It is also important to note that the sub-problems will likely have numerous aspects. For example, Chalmers (2017a) highlights that the structure combination problem has a particularly troubling aspect, which he calls 'the structural mismatch problem', and a challenging aspect of the quality combination problem is 'the palette problem'. We can take the derivation problem for cosmopsychism to be similarly multifaceted, composed of quality, structure and subject-related problems. However, for the cosmopsychist, the challenge is to explain how macro-level phenomenal qualities, phenomenal structure and subjects derive from the phenomenal quality, phenomenal structure and subjecthood of the cosmos rather than microphysical ultimates.

Although the blueprint I have presented does not strictly dictate it, most versions of cosmopsychism affirm that the cosmos is a subject of experience. Consequently, they face the subject derivation problem. As already noted, broadly conceived, the subject derivation problem is the problem of accounting for the derivation of macro-subjects from the cosmic subject. Chalmers suggests that the especially problematic aspect of panpsychism's subject combination problem is the subject-summing problem, which arises because it seems that no group of micro-subjects necessitates the existence of a further macro-subject. Cosmopsychism does not face the subject-summing problem because, on its account, micro-subjects do not combine (or 'sum') to form macro-subjects; instead, macro-subjects derive from the cosmic subject. However, cosmopsychism does face a particularly challenging aspect to its subject derivation problem. I call this *the synchronous subjects problem*.

The basis of the synchronous subjects problem is the stipulation that subjects of experience are inherently perspectival. When I say that subjects are perspectival,

I mean that they are a first-person locus of experience. To put it in a metaphorical key, to have a perspective is to have a unique experiential window, or vantage point, onto the world. I will not defend the stipulation here, but it is commonly regarded as a conceptual truth that a subject of experience is marked by being a conscious perspective. This stipulation lies at the heart of the problem of synchronous subjects because it reveals that the challenge is ultimately that of accounting for synchronous *perspectives*. The problem is that we come up against apparent incompatibilities if we posit synchronous conscious perspectives on different levels of reality, such that those on one level contain, or are contained by, those on another level. For example, problems arise if we posit a cosmic-level perspective that includes macro-level perspectives as partial aspects. To illustrate, we can repurpose an example by Coleman (2014): Imagine two macro-subjects, Red and Blue. The experience of redness to the exclusion of all else characterizes Red's perspective. In contrast, Blue's perspective is characterized by the experience of blueness to the exclusion of all else. Now consider the cosmic perspective, which contains Red and Blue's perspectives as partial aspects. In this case, it seems that what cosmopsychism dictates is that if we are to preserve the defining character of the macro-perspectives, Red and Blue, then the cosmic perspective must be a perspective characterized by the experience of redness-to-the-exclusion-of-all-else *and* blueness-to-the-exclusion-of-all-else, simultaneously. However, the two perspectives are mutually exclusive. When considered as elements of a single perspective, they represent an incoherent set. One perspective – the cosmic perspective – cannot simultaneously be exhausted by the experience of redness (i.e. the experience of experiencing only redness) and exhausted by the experience of blueness (i.e. the experience of experiencing only blueness). Any serious development on the blueprint of cosmopsychism (insofar as the cosmos is taken to be a subject of experience) must address this apparent incoherence.

The full range of combination and derivation problems, including the subject problems, will be given close attention in later chapters. In this chapter, I grant the apparent seriousness of the subject problem and explore the viability of alternatives to cosmopsychism and panpsychism that purport to avoid it.

3.3.3 Developments on the priority cosmopsychism blueprint

Before exploring the potential alternative to cosmopsychism, which purports to avoid the subject derivation problem, we should first consider a couple of developments on the priority cosmopsychism blueprint so that we see the subject problems as they arise for some more full-bodied views.

Although I have presented my own account of cosmopsychism (Wager, 2011, 2020; Nagasawa & Wager, 2017), I will not focus on it here since it will be elucidated further as the book progresses. Instead, I will focus on developments by Philip Goff (2017, 2020) and Itay Shani (2015). I will note that developments on the blueprint, so far, have in common a kind of dual-aspect view according to which the cosmos has both a physical and a phenomenal aspect, with the physical aspect of the cosmos being the fundamental physical entity and the phenomenal aspect being the fundamental form of phenomenality. I noted this in the previous chapter, but here's how Nagasawa and I

(2017) put it in our paper on the blueprint: 'one possible development on the blueprint we offer here is a *dual-aspect* version of priority cosmopsychism, according to which the phenomenal and the physical are co-extensive, with the respective properties at the level of the cosmos being basic' (p. 127). When we mentioned that, on such a view, the phenomenal and physical can be taken as co-extensive, we were anticipating versions of cosmopsychism which incorporate both Russellian monism and priority monism.[7] Indeed, this approach seems to be the preferred way to develop on the blueprint. I outline the most prominent accounts and their subject problems below.

3.3.3.1 Goff

Philip Goff endorses a version of cosmopsychism formed of a combination of priority monism and panpsychism, where the result is a fundamental cosmos which is a subject of experience. According to this view, all sub-cosmic subjects are partial aspects of the cosmic subject. In other words, sub-cosmic subjects are fully grounded in the cosmic subject in virtue of their existing fully formed as a part thereof. Goff acknowledges that the most pressing problem for his version of cosmopsychism, and any other versions of cosmopsychism positing a cosmic subject, for that matter, is the subject derivation problem (he calls it 'the subject decombination problem'). Furthermore, he remarks that its most urgent aspect is the problem of synchronous subjects (which he refers to as the problem of subject-subsuming subjects):

> Cosmopsychism entails the possibility of *subject-subsuming subjects*, i.e. conscious subjects that are aspects of other conscious subjects. Such a thing can seem hard to make sense of. Certainly we cannot imagine such a thing by using our perceptual and/or introspective faculties. But nor can we imagine in this way a four-dimensional object, and we nonetheless take four-dimensional objects to be coherent … The cosmopsychist can plausibly attribute our difficulty positively conceiving of a subject-subsuming subject to the fact that we don't fully grasp the nature of conscious subjects.
>
> (2020, p. 151)

He says, moreover, that his cosmopsychism can be conceived of as a form of constitutive Russellian monism, making it a version of constitutive Russellian cosmopsychism. He proposes that we do not fully grasp the nature of consciousness,[8] and suggests that what we fail to understand is (or might be) a more expansive property termed consciousness+. This 'enfolds experiential and non-experiential aspects in a single unified property' (Goff, 2017, p. 230). He describes his view as follows: 'For the constitutive cosmopsychist, the cosmos is a material entity … While physical science describes the causal structure of the cosmos, its deep nature is constituted by

7 Indeed, I explicitly took this view myself in my Master's thesis *Dual-Aspect Priority Monism and the Combination Problem for Panpsychism* (2011).

8 Recall that this is a move noted earlier in this chapter and in the last, and which Nagasawa and I (2017) anticipated in our paper on the blueprint.

consciousness+. Neuroscience describes the causal structure of the brain, but in its deep nature it is a bearer of consciousness+, and that bearer of consciousness+ is an irreducible aspect of the consciousness+-bearing universe' (Goff, 2017, p. 235). The problem of synchronous subjects is addressed by appealing to a degree of epistemic ignorance. Goff's reasoning can be understood as suggesting that strangeness does not entail impossibility. As already stated, the most crucial issue when responding to the subject derivation problem is to avoid any evident metaphysical incoherence. Goff's suggestion is that not being able to conceive of synchronous subjects scenarios does not entail that they cannot obtain. If there is no apparent metaphysical incoherence, then we do not necessarily have a problem on our hands, so the reasoning goes. Furthermore, Goff provides a positive reason for our inability to conceive of synchronous subjects: we do not fully grasp the nature of consciousness.

3.3.3.2 Shani

Another important development in line with the blueprint is Shani's cosmopsychism (2015). Shani offers a rich and well-developed – arguably the richest and most well-developed – version of cosmopsychism. It bears some resemblance to proposals by others (Matthews, 2011; Wager, 2011, 2020; Nagasawa & Wager, 2016; Goff, 2017, 2020) but is significantly more nuanced. On his view, the cosmos, referred to as 'the absolute', is a vast, internally dynamic entity that operates on what he calls a 'lateral duality principle', according to which it has a co-extensive revealed and concealed nature. Its revealed nature is the world as revealed in our current physics, while its concealed nature is what he calls an 'endo-phenomenological expanse' – a sentient ocean of consciousness. On his view, all sub-cosmic entities are referred to as 'relatives', with 'simple relatives' being sub-cosmic entities existing on the microphysical level. All simple relatives are subjects of experience, but only some complex relatives form subjects. Complex relatives that are also subjects of experience are called 'created subjects', while complex relatives that are not subjects are referred to as 'pure objects'. Both pure objects and created subjects are associated with the revealed nature of the cosmos and subjectivity, but only created subjects exemplify a unified subjectivity of their own. The sense in which pure objects are associated with subjectivity is that they are formed of complexes of simple relatives, each themselves a subject of experience.

A key question for Shani's position is, therefore, why is it that some complexes of simple relatives form a unified subjectivity and become created subjects while others remain only pure objects? In response to this question, he offers an interesting proposal, distinguishing between two kinds of binding that occur in complexes of simple relatives: 'exonectic binding' and 'esonectic binding'. About esonectic systems, he states:

> An esonectic system is a compound whole whose micro-constituents are interrelated in such a manner that the system is not only cohesive in respect of its outward revealed form but is also unified in respect of its concealed experiential domain … esonectic systems are internally interwoven: the endo-phenomenological

reservoirs of their micro-components join together in a coherent fashion, giving rise to a unified experiential domain.

(2015, p. 419)

Whereas, about exonectic systems, he says:

> [A]n exonectic system is a compound whole whose micro-constituents are interrelated in such a manner that the system is woven together only on the outside: it has a cohesive exterior, but it lacks a macro-level inner dimension to match with its macro-level revealed form – the endophenomenological reservoirs of its micro-components remain secluded from each other and do not bind together.
>
> (2015, pp. 419–20)

Pure objects, he says, are exonectic systems, while created subjects are esonectic systems. The reason some complexes of simple relatives are subjects of experience while others are not has to do with how the constituent simple relatives are interrelated.

Understandably, Shani is not able to explain the exact conditions under which esonectic binding occurs; however, he has some insights regarding where to start looking for answers. He agrees with most people that if ever there were clear locales of esonectic binding, it would be in brains. Meanwhile, if there were sure-fire locales of exonectic binding, it would be in minerals. With that in mind, Shani's strategy is to show that there are good reasons to think that the interrelations between constituents of brains and minerals are different in significant ways, which would support his hypothesis. He points out that there are indeed significant differences in the material organization between brains and minerals. In the case of minerals, structural bonds are very strong with next to no communication between spatially distant constituent parts, whereas brains exhibit weak structural bonds and permit massive amounts of communication between all constituent parts. Thus, says Shani, if we take it that all simple relatives are subjects of experience, then we have reasons to expect them to scale up in brains but not in minerals.[9]

Like Goff, Shani acknowledges that the most challenging problem for cosmopsychism is the subject derivation problem and, more specifically, the problem of synchronous subjects. Goff addresses this problem by suggesting that the existence of synchronous subjects scenarios merely *seems* like a serious problem because the idea is strange,

[9] More precisely, Shani says, 'These fundamental differences suggest that there are principled reasons why we should expect consciousness to scale up in humans and animals but to fail to do so in minerals. For suppose, as we have just done, that both types of systems are composed of tiny conscious components. Given the material organization of minerals there is reason to expect that such components will remain largely isolated from each other: each confined to a local, rigidly configured "cell," unable to communicate, or to resonate, with topographically remote locations. In contrast, the dynamical regime of brain-bound organisms gives reasons to expect the contrary: the permeability of organic boundaries, and the intense interconnectedness, synchronous resonance, mutual sensitivity through information transfer, and reciprocal modulation of sub-systems, states, and processes suggest a plethora of possible channels for binding the experiential reservoirs of individual micro-components into an integral whole' (2015, p. 421).

while emphasizing that strangeness does not entail metaphysical impossibility. Shani goes further, illustrating an apparent metaphysical incoherence in such scenarios, before demonstrating why his view does not entail them and thus does not face the problem of synchronous subjects scenarios.

Shani illustrates the apparent metaphysical impossibility of synchronous subjects scenarios by referring to the inherently perspectival nature of subjects of experience. Earlier in the chapter, I illustrated a worry about scenarios involving synchronous subjects, or subject-subsuming subjects, whereby two perspectives, Red and Blue, were both partial aspects of a further perspective. Simply stated, the worry is that it seems incoherent to suggest that an overarching perspective includes two mutually exclusive macro-subjects. The question is: how can one single cosmic perspective be characterized by two mutually exclusive macro-perspectives (e.g. the experience of redness to the exclusion of all else *and* the experience of blueness to the exclusion of all else)?

Goff faces the problem of synchronous subjects because his view asserts that macro-subjects are fully grounded in the cosmic subject, namely, that the cosmic subject includes, as partial aspects, discrete and distinct macro-subjects. His response is that although such scenarios are strange, strangeness alone does not entail impossibility. However, Shani demonstrates that synchronous subjects scenarios appear to be metaphysically precluded on account of them entailing a logical contradiction. He asks us to consider Figure 3 (2015, p. 425), in which P and Q are perspectives.

Considering Figure 3, we can formulate Shani's argument in the following way:

1. Q is a partial (perspectival) aspect of P.
2. In viewing things from viewpoint P one also views things from viewpoint Q.
3. P includes the complement P-Q.
4. Q excludes the compliment P-Q.
5. Therefore, P both affirms and denies P-Q.
6. Therefore, the scenario contains a contradiction.

Clearly, formally speaking, Shani has shown a logical incoherence in scenarios involving synchronous subjects (or, subject-subsuming subjects, as Goff calls them). It

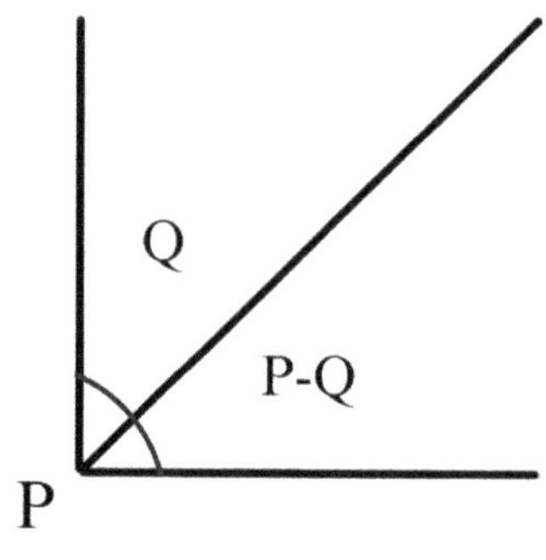

Figure 3 Shani's illustration of incoherent perspectives.

is significant since Goff's approach of dismissing the problem in virtue of such scenarios being merely strange, rather than incoherent, will not stand if Shani's contradiction holds. What I have to say from here, at least in this chapter, will be premised on Shani's contradiction holding.

With our assumption that the contradiction holds in place, we can turn to how Shani proposes to overcome the problem of synchronous subjects. He explains that the problem comes about due to a reliance on fully grounding macro-subjects within the cosmic subject, because the only way for full grounding to work is for macro-subjects to be present, discretely and distinctly, in the cosmic perspective, as its partial aspects. Shani suggests that a different version of cosmopsychism evades the problem by replacing full grounding with partial grounding. Following Rosen (2010) and Fine (2012), Shani contrasts full grounding with partial grounding:

> Partial grounding (partial strict grounding, strictly speaking) is contrasted with full grounding. If B holds in virtue of A, such that A, considered in isolation, is sufficient for B, then A is said to be a full ground for B. In many cases, however, A, although relevant for the grounding of B, is not itself sufficient for a full grounding of B. If A is but one among various facts which, individually, do not suffice to ground B but which do so collectively then it is said to be a partial ground for B.
>
> (2015, p. 404)

Applying the concept of partial grounding to the problem of synchronous subjects (where 'AP' refers to the absolute perspective – or cosmic perspective – and 'RP' refers to a relative perspective – or a macro-perspective), he writes:

> To say that [AP] is a partial ground for [RP] implies that while [RP] depends on [AP] it also amounts to something more and is not exhausted by this particular dependency relationship. Such a state of affairs is expected if there is a certain aspect under which the perspectives of relative subjects are anchored in the perspective of the absolute, and another aspect under which they assert their independence.
>
> (2015, pp. 422–3)

Shani's proposal cleverly avoids the problem of synchronous subjects by claiming that macro-subjects and their macro-perspectives are only *partially* dependent on the cosmic subject and its cosmic perspective. This allows him to reject the claim that macro-perspectives are present, discretely and distinctly, in the cosmic perspective as its partial aspects. To fulfil the requirements of partial grounding, Shani must offer a sense in which the relative perspectives of created subjects (macro-perspectives) are grounded in the absolute perspective (cosmic perspective) as well as a sense in which they are independent of it.

His response is that perspectives have both a 'generic character' and a 'specific character'. Created subjects (and their relative perspectives) are dependent on the absolute for their generic character but independent of it with respect to their specific character. At the risk of oversimplifying, the generic character of a perspective is its being a conscious point of view.[10] In contrast, the specific character is the unique character of the experience from that point of view.[11] It is still an open question as to whether the distinction between the generic and specific character of perspectives, in the way presented, is ultimately defensible. Regardless, it certainly goes a long way towards overcoming the most difficult challenge cosmopsychism faces.

3.3.4 Albahari's objections to cosmopsychism

Miri Albahari (2020) is critical of the approaches of Goff and Shani, and provides objections to each. Let us briefly consider her objections before moving on to investigating perennialism, which is the successor to cosmopsychism that she proposes.

3.3.4.1 Albahari's objections to Goff: The incoherent contents objection

Albahari objects to Goff's cosmopsychism on account of two problems anticipated by William James (1909): *the epistemic problem* and *the perspective problem*, which can be collectively termed *the incoherent contents objection to cosmopsychism*. The epistemic problem arises from the incompatibility between an epistemically all-encompassing cosmic perspective and the content of the relatively ignorant macro-perspectives that share their content with it. The incompatibility arises, Albahari contends, when we consider that macro-perspectives are characterized by content that is not applicable to the cosmic perspective because, for example, it is not finite in the same way, but which, owing to it being an all-encompassing perspective, it nonetheless shares. The example Albahari gives is the fear of mortality; she says that such mental content can only be coherently ascribed to finite subjects. She offers the following thought experiment to demonstrate this:

> Consider Fiona's intense and pervasive fear that she will be annihilated upon death, a fear whose first-personal character is partly owed to its mind-dominating nature. Goff's cosmic subject must directly experience not only Fiona's intense fear of dying but also Fred's overwhelming excitement at his impending reincarnation. Yet qualifying just a fraction of the cosmic mind, it's hard to envisage how each emotion could, from the personal cosmic perspective, retain their defining first-

[10] For Shani, the generic character of sub-cosmic subject is inherited from the cosmic subject, where the generic character is said to be the combination of what he calls 'core-subjectivity' and sentience.

[11] Shani summarizes as follows: 'Each concrete perspective of each relative subject has what I call a specific character, namely, a unique individual profile which cannot be derived from any other perspective (or combination thereof); but, at the same time, all of these perspectives share a generic character, or a basic template, which is, in turn, derived from the subjective, perspectival nature of the absolute. Thus, in respect of its generic character, each conscious perspective of each relative subject is grounded in the fact that the absolute is itself a subject and, as such, the owner of a first-person point of view, but in respect of its specific character it is an independent entity which neither grounds any other perspective, nor being grounded by any' (2015, p. 423).

> personal characters *as* intense and dominating, and hence as those particular emotions. It is also difficult to conceive of how the cosmic subject could first-personally harbour what would, to its singular conscious perspective, be the mass of everyone's contradicting beliefs and identities, e.g. 'there is only one life', 'there is more than one life', 'I am Fiona', 'I am Fred'.
>
> (Albahari, 2020, p. 122)

The perspective problem is essentially what we have been calling the problem of synchronous subjects. The epistemic problem focuses on the incompatibility between the contents of macro-perspectives that imply a degree of epistemic ignorance and the fact they are purportedly shared with an epistemically unlimited cosmic perspective. The perspective problem, on the other hand, focuses on the raw incompatibility of a perspective (the cosmic perspective) subsuming further perspectives (sub-cosmic perspectives). Albahari states that the problem stems from the fact that, on the cosmopsychist view, 'our seemingly unique perspectives also exist as mental objects for the conscious cosmos' (2020, p. 122). A simplistic way to understand Albahari's worry is to imagine three levels of reality: the micro, macro and cosmic. Now consider that we are committed to the view that there are subjects, and so perspectives, on each level of reality, such that the perspectives from any level are partial aspects of (present in) perspectives at all higher levels. For example, a micro-perspective is a partial aspect of a macro-perspective, which itself is a partial aspect of the cosmic perspective. Albahari says that such a picture is incoherent because the very existence of a perspective at one level precludes it from being a partial aspect of any perspectives at higher levels. Her reasoning is informed by Coleman's Argument (2012) – which I adapted earlier to illustrate the subject problem for cosmopsychism – against the possibility of subject-combination for panpsychism. She quotes Shani's summary of Coleman's argument:

> He asks us to imagine two micro-subjects, Red and Blue, such that Red only sees red and Blue only sees blue. Red and Blue combine in turn to form a macro subject, Mac, which integrates the phenomenal worlds into a single perspective. The problem, says Coleman, is that Red's and Blue's perspectives do not survive as points-of-view within Mac's unified perspective. For example, Red's take on the world is that of seeing red, to the exclusion of all else, but Mac's perspective defies this condition: it may contain seeing blue, in addition to seeing red, or it may simply consist of seeing purple … the original perspectives have disappeared from sight.
>
> (Shani, 2015, p. 401)

Albahari could instead call upon Shani's presentation of a metaphysical incoherence in the idea of synchronous subjects to make her case for the perspective problem, since it refers specifically to the challenge for cosmopsychism.

3.3.4.2 Albahari's objection to Shani

Furthermore, Albahari also contends that Shani's cosmopsychism is problematic because it faces a dilemma centred on his stipulation that 'part of what it means to *be* a conscious subject is for any contents within its field of consciousness to be disclosed to its first-personal perspective' (Albahari, 2020, p. 123). Albahari points out that Shani wants to maintain the above while also maintaining that 'the contents of our conscious fields, while embedded within the absolute's field of consciousness, are hidden to the absolute's perspective' (Albahari, 2020, p. 123). Albahari says that these two stipulations are mutually exclusive. She contends that if what it means to be a subject is to have any contents within its field of consciousness disclosed to its perspective, and the cosmos is a perspective-bearing subject of experience (the absolute) that embeds sub-cosmic perspectives (relative perspectives and created subjects, in Shani's system), then, by definition, the contents of sub-cosmic perspectives must be disclosed to the cosmic perspective. The problem is that such disclosure would go against the claim that sub-cosmic perspectives are hidden from the cosmic perspective. The result, according to Albahari, is that Shani must either drop the claim that the contents of sub-cosmic perspectives are hidden from the cosmic perspective or drop the claim that the cosmos is a subject of experience.

I am not convinced that Albahari's dilemma stands up to scrutiny. It appears to be built on a misunderstanding of Shani's nuanced position. I believe this can be understood best with reference to the following passage: 'If our conscious perspectives and their contents are to be embedded within – and illuminated by the sentience of – the absolute's conscious field, then, given that the absolute is a subject, our contents (and perhaps perspectives) must also, by definition, be first-personally revealed to the absolute's perspective' (Albahari, 2020, p. 123).

This excerpt seems to imply that for sub-cosmic perspectives to be embedded in the cosmic perspective, they must thereby be disclosed to it. Such an implication is clearly the case for Goff's cosmopsychism, but Shani seems to have a straightforward answer as to why this is not the case on his view. According to Shani, sub-cosmic perspectives are, by definition, not disclosed to the cosmic perspective because they are only embedded within the cosmic perspective insofar as they inherit its *generic* character. They do not inherit its *specific* character, and as such, the specific characters (i.e. contents) of sub-cosmic perspectives are not embedded in the cosmic perspective and thus are not disclosed to it.

In this chapter, I am interested in the viability of alternatives to panpsychism and cosmopsychism that maintain the advantages of those respective views but overcome their most persistent problems. In the previous chapter, we saw how the priority cosmopsychism blueprint offers a framework for inheriting some key advantages of panpsychism while avoiding its combination problem. However, we also saw that views built on the blueprint also inherit the derivation problem. So far in this chapter, I have given a little more detail on panpsychism and cosmopsychism – including outlining some key developments on the priority cosmopsychism blueprint – and have indicated that the respective subject problems are potentially fatal. I have much more to say about the subject problems and the severity of the challenges they present for panpsychists and cosmopsychists, but I will save that for the next chapter. For the remainder of this chapter, I want to grant that the subject problems are serious, even fatal, and scope two important alternatives, one an alternative to panpsychism and one an alternative to cosmopsychism. We will begin with the purported alternative to cosmopsychism.

Returning to Albahari, she claims that cosmopsychism, as presented by both Goff and Shani, is doomed to failure and that, with this in mind, we should consider her proposal, perennialism, which she sees as the natural successor to cosmopsychism.

3.4 Perennialism

Albahari (2020) aims to situate perennialism as the successor to contemporary cosmopsychism.[12] Perennialism is ostensibly a view maintaining the key advantages that cosmopsychism enjoys over other approaches to the problem of phenomenal consciousness while steering clear of its greatest challenge: the subject derivation problem. Perennialism is the view that there is a universal non-dual consciousness. Unlike cosmopsychism, according to perennialism, the universal consciousness is not a subject of experience since it lacks a conscious perspective. Nonetheless, it is the ground of sub-universal subjects and their perspectives. Moreover, the universal consciousness also grounds all non-perspectival objects; that is, it is the ground of all being. Consider the apparent similarities with cosmopsychism; it agrees with cosmopsychism's claims that:

[12] While it will not be a point of focus for me here, another alternative to cosmopsychism, which, like perennialism, is perhaps best considered an idealistic form of supracosmopsychism, has been proposed by Kastrup (2018). It says that cosmic consciousness is the sole fundamental entity from which all else arises (and, in fact, everything that 'arises' is just its thoughts). Hence, it is a version of idealism. This fundamental entity has self-excitation as an inherent disposition and sub-cosmic forms of consciousness arise from its self-excitations. These excitations (or those that instantiate sub-cosmic consciousnesses) are dissociated segments of the cosmic consciousness analogous to alters in Dissociative Identity Disorder. The problematic synchronous subjects scenarios we will consider in this and the next chapter never arise because the cosmic consciousness is blind to sub-cosmic perspectives. Thus, the derivation problem is purportedly averted. It faces idealism's core challenge of accounting for the external world and responds in the following way: the external world is just the way the cosmic consciousness's thoughts (i.e. the thoughts of alters) are revealed to alters. Kastrup makes the bold claim that the above proposal is preferable to physicalism, panpsychism and cosmopsychism on grounds of parsimony, empirical rigour and explanatory power (because it avoids the hard problem of consciousness facing physicalism and the combination and derivation problems facing panpsychism and cosmopsychism respectively). It is certainly an interesting proposal, but the claim that it is clearly superior to the other views is rather premature, it seems to me. It is unclear how the proposed view has more explanatory power than the others. Moreover, the view is highly speculative, so it is certainly not empirically rigorous in any typical sense. But most importantly, it may be more parsimonious than the other views in so far as it posits only one basic entity, but the important thing is to balance parsimony with theoretical elegance, and in this respect, the proposal falls short; its parsimony comes at a huge cost to its theoretical elegance. Interested readers might like to find further details of Kastrup's intriguing proposal in 'The Universe in Consciousness' (2018) and draw their own conclusions.

- There is a universal (or cosmic) consciousness.[13]
- The universal (or cosmic) consciousness grounds all sub-universal (or sub-cosmic) consciousness.

But it differs insofar as it holds that:

- The cosmos is not a *subject* of experience.

Dropping the universe-as-a-subject premise is supposed to be instrumental in avoiding the subject derivation problem. It is *prima facie* obvious that if the universal non-dual consciousness is not a subject of experience, then the subject derivation problem simply does not arise. However, I will suggest that it is not as simple as it first appears. To get perennialism off of the ground, and to pitch it as a viable alternative to cosmopsychism, Albahari needs to motivate the notion of non-dual consciousness and explain how *universal* non-dual consciousness can ground all being (i.e. how it can ground subjects of experience as well as mind-independent objects) while still maintaining that it is not a subject of experience. I will suggest that perennialism faces a set of serious problems, including an equivalent to the problem of strong emergence, an equivalent to the subject combination problem, and a subject derivation problem. Consequently, I will conclude that perennialism is not a promising successor to cosmopsychism.

Let us summarize Albahari's motivations. She agrees with cosmopsychism that the problem of strong emergence should motivate a panpsychist approach to the problem of consciousness, but also recognizes that panpsychism faces the intractable combination problem. Cosmopsychism, she admits, benefits from avoiding the issue of strong emergence (because it inherits from panpsychism the claim that consciousness is fundamental) as well as the combination problem (because it does not need micro-level instances of consciousness to combine to constitute macro-level consciousness). However, she follows others (Matthews, 2011; Wager, 2011, 2020; Shani, 2015; Goff, 2017; Nagasawa & Wager, 2017) in suggesting that it faces the derivation problem, a challenge equivalent in magnitude to the combination problem.

Albahari suggests that perennialism is a fruitful alternative to cosmopsychism since, like cosmopsychism, it avoids denying fundamental physical reality of consciousness and, as a result, does not face the problem of strong emergence. As she points out, physicalism and dualism, while opposing views, share the view that the fundamental level of physical reality is devoid of consciousness, and this means that they must either admit strong emergence or explain consciousness by means of a distinct fundamental substance. Moreover, like cosmopsychism, perennialism avoids the combination problem for panpsychism because it posits fundamental consciousness at the cosmic rather than micro-level of reality. Most importantly, Albahari claims that perennialism overcomes the subject derivation problem (recall that this is typically considered

[13] As we will see, there is an important difference between Albahari's universal consciousness and cosmopsychism's cosmic consciousness. Unlike the cosmopsychist view, Albahari's universal consciousness is not the consciousness of the cosmos. Therefore, it is not strictly a version of cosmopsychism.

the biggest challenge facing cosmopsychism) because it does not place subjects at the fundamental level of reality. Certainly, it is clear why perennialism is pitched as cosmopsychism's natural successor.

However, on closer examination, the perennialist position faces an especially worrying conjunction of problems. There is a sense in which the problems it faces cover the gamut of central problems for physicalism, panpsychism and cosmopsychism. Consider the approaches from which it wants to distance itself: physicalism, panpsychism and cosmopsychism. Physicalism faces the problem of strong emergence but does not face the combination problem or the derivation problem. Panpsychism faces the combination problem but does not face the problem of strong emergence or the derivation problem. Cosmopsychism faces the derivation problem but does not face the problem of strong emergence or the combination problem. Again, what I demonstrate in the course of this section is that perennialism faces an equivalent of all three problems: a problem of strong emergence, a subject combination problem and a subject derivation problem. Additionally, it faces two further problems, though it shares these with several other approaches: the general plausibility of the ground and the aggregates problem.

This section unfolds as follows: first, I cover the basics of a perennialist reality. Then, I explore the general plausibility of non-dual consciousness before highlighting perennialism's versions of the emergence, combination and derivation problems. I conclude that the view should not be considered a successor to cosmopsychism on the grounds that it faces a uniquely challenging set of problems.

3.4.1 The basics of perennialist reality

Let us first outline the basics of perennialist reality. According to perennialism, the ultimate ground of all reality is a universal non-dual consciousness. The universe of multiplicity[14] is a dream-like emanation from this ultimate backdrop. The contents of the emanation are manifest as subject-object poles, called 'finite centres'. There are both micro- and macro-level finite centres. For argument's sake, we can take it that atoms equate to micro-level finite centres and human brains equate to macro-level ones. Macro finite centres are aggregations of micro finite centres, but not all aggregations of micro finite centres give rise to a macro finite centre. Some form only 'mere aggregates'. While the ultimate ground – universal non-dual consciousness – is *not* a subject of experience, the finite centres it grounds *are* subjects of experience.

The concept of non-dual consciousness refers to an unconditioned consciousness that is beyond subject-object structuring and spatiotemporally unbound. This means it is atemporal, non-spatial, and neither a subject nor an object. On the perennialist picture, there is a *universal* non-dual consciousness which grounds micro- and macro-level subjects of experience, as well as all other objects. I suggest this outline raises several urgent questions for perennialism:

[14] By 'universe of multiplicity' I mean, roughly speaking, the world we experience in our everyday lives and which physics describes.

- **The plausibility of the ground problem:** What motivates the plausibility of non-dual consciousness?
- **The fundamental problem**: How is the emanation grounded in the ground of universal non-dual consciousness?
- **The perspective problem(s) for perennialism**:
  - **The incoherent perspectives problem**: How does perennialism account for synchronous subjects scenarios (or, more accurately, synchronous perspectives scenarios)?
  - **The strong emergence of perspectives problem**: How are perspectives derived from an aperspectival ground?
- **The aggregates problem**: Why do some combinations of micro finite centres give rise to macro finite centres, while other combinations give rise to mere aggregates?

Other approaches also face questions about the plausibility of the proposed ultimate ground, so the first problem is not unique to perennialism. However, I will argue that it is particularly difficult to motivate the notion of non-dual consciousness. I will suggest that the fundamental problem represents a strong emergence problem for perennialism, and the perspective problems represent both a subject combination problem and a form of subject derivation problem.

3.4.2 The plausibility of the ground problem

The first concern is the general plausibility of non-dual consciousness. Both panpsychism and cosmopsychism also face questions about the plausibility of the ground. They both claim the fundamental level of reality (the micro-level for panpsychism, and the cosmic level for cosmopsychism) is both physical and phenomenal in some sense. Arguably, the most popular versions of both approaches justify this claim by alluding to some version of Russellian monism. Perennialism, however, cannot similarly rely on a commitment to Russellian monism to underwrite the plausibility of non-dual consciousness. Due to its counterintuitiveness, the concept of non-dual consciousness needs to be motivated before we even consider whether a *universal* non-dual consciousness could be the ground of all things. It is a task Albahari spends a significant amount of time addressing.

As stated, non-dual consciousness is beyond the subject-object distinction. It can be described as pure subjectless awareness or pure awareness. The idea of subjectless awareness seems contradictory because it is commonly accepted that awareness must necessarily involve a subject of experience, which is the entity being aware. Yet, Albahari suggests we can reasonably easily grasp the idea of subjectless consciousness. Albahari's strategy is to conceptually separate two putative components of consciousness in order to illustrate that we can make sense of the concept of non-dual consciousness. She suggests that phenomenological structure has two components: *witness-consciousness* and a *focal perspective*[15]:

[15] Albahari identifies the proposed components of consciousness as follows: 'The conscious subject, I suggest, has two discernible components: (a) "witness-consciousness" (b) from a focal

Witness-consciousness: The aspect of consciousness that exemplifies a sense of present-moment being, and is luminous, knowing, intransitive and reflexive.

Focal perspective: Witness-consciousness being aware of an object.

Witness-consciousness is the aspect of subjective experience which exemplifies a sense of present moment being and is luminous, knowing, intransitive and reflexive; this equates to pure awareness. The focal perspective is witness-consciousness being aware of an object. As I have indicated previously, it is typically taken as a conceptual truth that to be conscious is to be a subject of experience, and to be a subject of experience is to be a conscious perspective that is aware of phenomenal qualities. However, if Albahari can motivate the separation of the two components – witness-consciousness and a focal perspective – she will thereby motivate the concept of non-dual consciousness and thus underpin the basis of her approach. Albahari seeks to achieve this in two ways: first, through a thought experiment; and second, by demonstrating that separating these two components is uniquely positioned to resolve a tension between two commonly held intuitions.

3.4.2.1 The cognisensory deprivation tank

Albahari presents a thought experiment to highlight the conceivability of witness-consciousness as separable from a focal perspective. If we can conceive of the two components separately, with witness-consciousness existing independently of a perspective, then Albahari can claim that its independent existence is metaphysically possible (given that conceivability equals possibility). She calls the thought experiment the 'cognisensory deprivation tank'. The experiment goes like this: 'Now imagine entering what I will call the "Cognisensory Deprivation Tank". Each conscious perceptual input – sight, sound, proprioception etc. – snuffs out one by one. Next, all conscious cognitive input, attentive or inattentive, goes too, eventually leaving no perceptions, thoughts, memories, imaginings, or emotions' (2020, p. 125). Albahari contends that it is conceivable that with every departing input, witness-consciousness (i.e. pure non-dual consciousness) remains, and remains persistently sharp. It does not 'fade' with each departing input. She suggests that even when the last input has vanished, it is conceivable that we are left not in a 'coma-like vacuum' but rather with pure and unstructured awareness. She continues: 'In the absence of any cues to create inner (self) or outer (world) boundaries, or to mark the passage of time, such

perspective. Witness-consciousness denotes that aspect of consciousness which exemplifies a sense of present-moment being, and is sentiently luminous, knowing, intransitive and reflexive. When directed at objects, witness-consciousness does not take a view from nowhere but appears from a focal, localized perspective whose circumscribed field, whether waking or dreaming, presents for humans as structured by psycho-physical and spatio-temporal parameters. Objects are witnessed attentively or inattentively, as they come and go from the field. An "object," for these purposes, is broadly anything discrete that such a subject could pointedly attend to: physical objects, people, perceptions, thoughts, etc. While a subject's witness-consciousness can be intransitively aware of its own presence, it can never pointedly attend to itself as something discrete; it is not an object' (2020, pp. 124–5).

objectless awareness, if actively present, could well be experienced as boundless, non-dual, unbound by spatial or psychological parameters, and temporally unbounded, not coming or going' (2020, p. 125). The aim of the cognisensory deprivation tank thought experiment is to illustrate the conceivability of pure awareness existing independent of conscious perceptual or cognitive inputs. In the tank, individual inputs dropping out has no effect on the existence of the backdrop of witness-consciousness and, more importantly, the backdrop continues to exist when the last input vanishes.

While I would not want to deny the conceivability of pure awareness outright, I find it hard to pinpoint the difference between imagining being in a coma-like vacuum and experiencing non-dual consciousness. I think the crucial part of the experiment is the move from the final remaining perceptual or cognitive input, to when there are no perceptual inputs at all. This is because it marks a move, according to Albahari, from the existence of a perspective (with one perceptual input) to the absence of a perspective entirely. What Albahari would like us to take away from the experiment is that, without perceptual or cognitive input, rather than a coma-like vacuum, what we have is the persisting backdrop of aperspectival witness-consciousness. However, there is another option available. At the point of zero inputs, one could hold that there is still a perspective, only one that is not *illuminated* by the presence of perceptions or cognitive activity. It is a subtle difference but an important one. We can accept the conceivability of the idea that with every parting input, some sense of consciousness remains while rejecting that what remains is aperspectival pure awareness. Instead, we can maintain that what we are left with after the last input vanishes is an empty perspective, a locus of experience presently free of perceptive or cognitive inputs. I suspect this is what we are conceiving of in the cognisensory deprivation tank thought experiment.

On the alternative view that I suggest, perspectives do not come in and out of existence, as on Albahari's view. In her view, the presence of objects to witness-consciousness gives rise to perspectives. She explicitly rejects the empty perspective idea, claiming that '[t]he subject is not an empty perspective, but must always co-arise with objects that lend to it a structured spatio-temporal viewpoint' (2020, pp. 127–8). It is clear why she cannot accept that what we are left with is an empty perspective because, in her view, perspectives arise out of the co-presence of objects to witness-consciousness, and in this thought experiment, we are asked to conceive of the absence of objects of thought and perception.

3.4.2.2 Accounting for inconsistent intuitions

Albahari provides further motivation for the separation of witness-consciousness from focal perspectives by presenting what she believes are two commonly held intuitions, the holding of which can only make sense if such a separation obtains. Both intuitions centre around our intuitive understanding of the 'now':

> **Intuition 1**: First is the intuition that it is, in some sense, always 'now'; that the present moment has a timeless aspect. Our experience of the 'now' is unmoving in a sense not owing to the objects coming and going within it. Intuitively, Albahari says, this timeless aspect belongs to the perspectival component of our subjective experience.

However, we also hold a second intuition, seemingly inconsistent with the first.

> **Intuition 2**: Second, we have the intuition that the 'now' is not confined to our individual perspectives. We intuitively understand that were we to vanish in an instant the present would continue to be. Albahari maintains it is straightforward to conceive of a flow of objects – the features of the 'now' as continuing to exist without individual perspectives.

How do we account for the timeless aspect of 'now' that appears intimately tied to perspectivality if the 'now' is not confined to individual perspectives? Albahari contends that the only way to account for this is if witness-consciousness is not intrinsically confined to perspectives. In this picture, witness-consciousness, conceived of as non-dual consciousness, is what holds the two intuitions in place. By decoupling these conceptual components, one can maintain that witness-consciousness is the timeless aspect of our sense of 'now' – an aspect not owing to objects within it – without being problematically perspectival in a way that contravenes the first intuition.

However, I do not think there is anything additional to account for. The intuition that 'now' is not confined to our individual perspectives is simply the intuition that there is more to the 'now' than our perspectives (this 'more' is what we ordinarily conceive of as mind-independent objects). It is not the intuition that there is nothing more to the 'now' than them, as Albahari seems to suggest. Thus, again, there is an alternative account on offer; Intuition 1 is maintained by claiming that the timeless sense of 'now' is perspectival, while intuition 2 is maintained due to the continued existence of mind-independent objects beyond any token perspective. This alternative does not require the separation of witness-consciousness from perspectives, and, understood in this way, there is no tension between the two intuitions either.

Are the cognisensory deprivation tank and the motivation from the two intuitions enough to overturn the apparent conceptual truth that consciousness necessarily involves a subject of experience (i.e. a conscious perspective) being aware of phenomenal qualities, and to motivate us to affirm that consciousness comprises two separable components: witness-consciousness and a focal perspective? I do not think so. First, it seems likely that what the reader is conceiving of in the case of the cognisensory deprivation tank is simply an empty perspective (i.e. a perspective that is not aware of anything except its own perspectival nature). Second, regarding the inconsistent intuitions, I believe that once one considers the likelihood that the first intuition is about the existence of mind-independent objects, there is no longer an inconsistent set of intuitions.

Consequently, non-dual consciousness is under motivated, in my view. Since the plausibility of non-dual consciousness underpins Albahari's more extreme claim that *universal* non-dual consciousness is the ultimate ground of everything, her perennialism strikes me as somewhat underpowered from the outset.

3.4.3 The fundamental problem: From the ground to the emanation

Setting aside the plausibility of non-dual consciousness, and indeed the existence of *universal* non-dual consciousness, we turn to the next problem. For argument's sake, suppose we have good reasons to support the existence of universal non-dual consciousness. The perennialist still faces the challenge of how to move from the ultimate ground to the emanation. Recall that the multiplicity of the universe is the manifest content of a dream-like emanation from the ground of universal non-dual consciousness.

Even given the above concessions, if perennialism is to be taken seriously, it needs to provide an account of how the emanation is anchored in pure awareness. Without such an account, the connection between the two is, at best, deeply mysterious and, at worst, unintelligible. So, why should we believe the emanation is grounded in non-dual consciousness? We must have a reason for insisting that there is an asymmetric relation of dependence holding between the ground and the grounded, since that is what a minimal account of any grounding relation must include. However, as far as I can see, Albahari does not provide a reason. Without a compelling rationale for supposing that the two realms are related, we are left with an emergence problem, where there seems to be an inexplicable emergence of the emanation from the backdrop of non-dual consciousness. Thus, the perennialist picture seems to entail a form of strong emergence because, as far as we have been informed, there is nothing about pure awareness, and pure awareness alone, in virtue of which the emanation intelligibly emerges. Conversely, we are given no reason to think that the emanation exclusively implies the existence of a ground of non-dual consciousness.

3.4.3.1 The emergence of emanation from ground

As mentioned earlier in the chapter, there are two conceptions of emergence, which Chalmers (2006) calls 'weak' and 'strong' emergence. First, recall weak emergence. This is the kind of emergence most often alluded to by non-reductive physicalists. The important thing with weak emergence is that the unexpectedness of the emergent seems to be the result of an epistemic limit. The emergent properties are in principle deducible from the basal properties. In cases of weak emergence, the reason that the properties are said to be emergent is that they are unexpected given what we know about the principles governing the low-level domain. However, if we had perfect knowledge of the principles governing the low-level domain, then the emergent properties would be expected. Examples of weak emergence include life or living organisms (Chalmers, 2006), evolution (Chalmers, 2006), liquidity (Strawson, 2006) and the gas-liquid-solid transformation (Popper in Eccles & Popper, 1977).

Albahari could claim that the emanation is weakly emergent from non-dual consciousness, but doing so would imply that the issue around deducing how the emergence happens is merely epistemic, and that if we knew all the relevant facts about universal non-dual consciousness, then we would be able to deduce the emanation's emergence. However, given that the non-dual ground is supposed to be unconditioned, non-spatial and atemporal, it is hard to see how a complete epistemic picture would help with the deducibility.

On the assumption of weak emergence, the emergent fact – the emanation – is only epistemically emergent, so it should still be ontologically reducible to its ground in much the same way as other epistemically emergent facts. We know that other epistemically emergent facts turn out to be deducible from the grounding facts once the epistemic veil has been lifted; they are revealed to be the result of arrangement and interactions at the level of the ground.

Take David Lewis's (1986, p. 14) example of a dot matrix image of a house to illustrate a paradigmatic case of weak emergence. Imagine a picture of a house made up entirely of dots and the space surrounding the dots. There is nothing about the dots and space between the dots that is house-like itself, yet when arranged in a certain way, a house image emerges. The house image is dependent on the dots and spaces because any change in the dots and spaces will correspond to a change in the image of the house. We can see in this example that a dependency relation holds, and we can also see why we might say the house image emerges from the arrangement of dots and spaces. However, in this case, it is also clear that the image of the house does not emerge in any ontological sense since once we know all of the relevant facts about the dots and the spaces, as well as how they combine and interact with one another, the image of the house, although it may still be unexpected, is deducible from the facts about the dots and spaces that ground it. Ontologically speaking, we can reductively explain the house image in terms of the dots and spaces. Thus, although a grounding relation holds in the case of weakly emergent properties, it does so only epistemically.

Weak emergence will not do for perennialism, however. The emanation is not merely the result of the rearrangement of facts at the ground. As mentioned, the ground is unconditioned, beyond the subject-object distinction, atemporal and non-spatial. The emergence of the universe of multiplicity represents the emergence of a substantially different kind of existence. This is a case of strong emergence, the kind of emergence usually alluded to by the British emergentists (or strong emergentists), for example, C. D. Broad, Lloyd Morgan, Samuel Alexander and Karl Popper. The distinguishing feature of strong emergence is that the emergent facts are not necessitated by the grounding facts or configurations of, or relations among, them. The British emergentists (and strong emergentists) claim that emergent facts are brute, meaning that they cannot be explained with reference to facts at the ground and those grounding facts alone. Moreover, they maintain that emergent facts have no explanation. Crucially, this is not owing to an epistemic limitation. Given knowledge of all the relevant facts regarding the principles governing the low-level domain – i.e. the ground – we would still not be able to deduce the emergent facts. The reason is that there is said to be no fact of the matter as to how the emergent facts emerge from the grounding facts. Regarding examples of strong emergence, it is tough to think of any at all; the emergentists who allude to this kind of emergence usually cite examples that turn out to be cases of weak emergence. For instance liquidity and the gas-liquid-solid transformation have both been offered by British emergentists as illustrations of strong emergence.

Given that the universe of multiplicity is accepted as real, it is clear that the emergence of perennialism's emanation from the ground of universal non-dual consciousness is a case of strong emergence. As we have seen already, Strawson (2006) describes the emergence of something with spatial extension from something that is spatially unextended as a paradigmatic case of strong emergence. This is reflected in the emergence of the emanation, with its spatially extended manifestations from the non-spatial ground of pure awareness. The emanation is supposed to be something genuinely novel and must, therefore, be strongly emergent.

There is a particularly serious problem with strong emergentism, and this will be a problem for perennialism, too. The problem concerns the fact that emergent facts are taken to be brute. They are such that it is not possible to explain them or predict them; they are in principle not deducible from the grounding facts – the British emergentists claim that there is no fact of the matter as to how the emergent facts emerge from the base. Hence, theories involving strong emergence posit an ontological emergence as opposed to the epistemic kind associated with weak emergence. The problem, in cases of strong emergence, is that the grounding relation fails. A grounding relation is necessary to keep the relation between the basal facts and the emergent facts meaningful. By meaningful, I mean that it is the grounding relation that predictably links the emergent and basal facts. In the case of strong emergence, the grounding relation fails because the emergent facts are said to be brute with no fact of the matter as to which basal facts they emerge from. Since it is not an epistemic limitation which prevents us from understanding the relation between the basal and emergent facts, there is no basis on which to say that a grounding relation holds.

Let us very briefly unpack the claim that a grounding relation cannot hold between the ground of pure awareness and the emanation. According to a minimal conception of grounding, grounding holds if A-facts ground B-facts and there can be no change in the B-facts without some change in the A-facts. What this means is that without first establishing the B-facts and the A-facts and then establishing an asymmetrical dependency relation among them, it makes no sense to say a grounding relation holds between A-facts and B-facts. In the case of perennialism, there is no way to establish a dependency relation because there seems to be nothing identifiable about universal non-dual consciousness (and universal non-dual consciousness alone) in virtue of which the emanation obtains.

Perennialism tells us that two radically different realms exist: the backdrop of pure awareness – which is unconditioned and outside of space and time – and the emanation – the content of which is the universe of multiplicity. Furthermore, it tells us that pure awareness grounds the emanation. However, we are not given an account of how this grounding is supposed to work or even why we should suppose it does. I have suggested that perennialism is committed to the emanation being a strongly emergent fact and that it, therefore, faces its own problem of strong emergence. Remember that avoiding strong emergence is the main motivation for panpsychism and cosmopsychism over physicalism. Thus, facing a problem of strong emergence puts perennialism, at least in this regard, in the same position as physicalism.

However, there is a way for perennialism to avoid this emergence problem. The perennialist could maintain that while the ultimate ground of universal non-dual consciousness is real, the emanation is not. They could hold that the emanation is merely an illusion, and claim that while the universe of multiplicity may appear spatially extended, it is spatially extended only in the sense that an object in a dream is spatially extended. Such a claim would allow the perennialist to maintain that there is no ontological emergence. However, this would be a difficult position to defend. It seems counterintuitive, but more importantly, perennialism is supposed to be the successor to cosmopsychism. This option would commit them to a radical version of non-realism about the world of multiplicity, thereby undermining any close alignment with current science – a core appeal of panpsychism and cosmopsychism.

Owing to its problem with accounting for the grounding of the universe of multiplicity in the universal pure awareness, perennialism is likely to be too metaphysically expensive (whether it affirms strong emergence or holds that the everyday world is illusory) to attract the panpsychist or cosmopsychist who is looking to overcome their respective subject-related problem. Bear in mind that the central proposal is that perennialism should be favoured over cosmopsychism because it can avoid the subject derivation problem. Would such a metaphysical expense be proportionate to the advantage of avoiding the subject derivation problem? I suspect not. Especially given the additional challenges for perennialism to which we now turn.

3.4.4 The perspective problems for perennialism

Recall the perennialist picture. The universe of multiplicity is a dream-like emanation from a ground of universal unconditioned pure consciousness (or pure awareness). The emanation manifests as an array of finite centres. Each finite centre is a subject-object pole, disposed to appear as an object to other subjects while also being disposed to be a subject when confronted by an object. To say all finite centres are subjectival is to say that all finite centres are perspectival, or, in other words, to say that they all have a conscious perspective: 'The content of the projective emanation will manifest as numerous, inter-connecting subject-object poles: each a finite and unified conscious perspective that is furnished with structured intentional imagistic content, however simple or complex (e.g. atom or human). Following F.H. Bradley, I refer to these subjects as "finite centres"' (2020, p. 127). This definition is explicit that every finite centre is a conscious perspective. However, Albahari also says the following:

> On the proposed Advaitic variant, the substratum, if we can call it that, is not space-time, but non-dual awareness, and each 'arising' is not a property, but a finite centre. Each centre, no matter how simple or complex, has a dispositional and subjective – as opposed to just qualitative – nature, the subjective nature being the appearance of objects to the perspective of a subject. The subject is not an empty perspective, but must always co-arise with objects that lend to it a structured spatio-temporal viewpoint.
>
> (2020, pp. 127–8)

The point here is that finite centres are *disposed* to be perspectival in the presence of objects. Additionally, subjects, being disposed to be objects for other subjects, become objects in the presence of subjects. Therefore, finite centres are not necessarily perspectival because a finite centre unstructured by the co-presence of an object will not be perspectival.

It is not clear if all finite centres are perspectival, as the first quote suggests, or merely disposed to be perspectival, as the second quote suggests. Perhaps all finite centres manifest their disposition *to be perspectival under conditions where an object is present to witness-consciousness* because an object is always present. However, there must be something that *has* the disposition to be perspectival under certain conditions, though it is not clear what that could be. The obvious option is to say that witness-consciousness has the disposition in question, but it is hard to figure out how one could explain its having the disposition without implying that it is already perspective-involving. The empty perspective option appears to make more sense. This option would involve maintaining something like the following: each finite centre is a perspective, the existence of which is illuminated when objects are present to it.

A closer examination of how conscious perspectives fit into the perennialist picture reveals two further problems for the view. The first, the problem of incoherent perspectives, represents a version of the subject combination problem for panpsychism. The second, the problem of the strong emergence of perspectives, is a form of subject derivation problem.

3.4.4.1 The problem of incoherent perspectives

Perennialism faces the same subject combination problem as panpsychism, in the form of the incoherent contents of perspectives problem. A primary motivation behind moving away from panpsychism is that it affirms the existence of incoherent perspectives. In positing perspectives at both the fundamental and macro-levels of reality, both panpsychism and cosmopsychism are vulnerable to incoherent sets of perspectives instantiated in synchronous subjects scenarios, where a perspective on one level is part of a perspective at another level. For panpsychism, macro-perspectives are formed of micro-perspectives, while in the case of cosmopsychism, macro-perspectives are part of the cosmic perspective.

For perennialism, the problem is equivalent to the way it arises for panpsychism. On perennialism's picture, there are both micro finite centres (e.g. atoms or sub-atomic particles) and macro finite centres (e.g. humans), with centres at the macro-level being aggregates (though not *mere* aggregates) of those at the micro-level. Given that all finite centres are perspectival, there will be an incoherence of perspectives at the micro and macro-levels in just the same way there is for panpsychism. This is a grave problem for perennialism since its overall motivation is to avoid the problem of synchronous subjects (for cosmopsychism), which can also be characterized as an argument from incoherent perspectives.

To explain, let us consider Sam Coleman's presentation of the subject combination problem for panpsychism (this is the same argument already referred to at earlier points in the chapter). Coleman offers a scenario purportedly highlighting an incoherence in the notion of subjects of experience combining, based on the notion that *perspectives* do not combine. My suggestion is that the scenario he offers applies equally to perennialism. His scenario is as follows:

> Consider the original duo's points of view. One – Blue's – is pervaded by a unitary blueness, the other – Red's – by redness, and that is all they experience, respectively. To say these points of view were present as components in the experiential perspective of the uber-subject ('Ub') would therefore be to say

> that Ub experienced a unitary phenomenal blueness and a unitary phenomenal redness, i.e. had synchronous experiences as of each of these qualities alone, to the exclusion of all others. For it is these qualities each on their own that characterise, respectively, the perspectives of the original duo. Experience excludes, as well as includes. Yet nowhere does Ub have any such experiences: he precisely combines his predecessors' qualitative experiential contents. Ub doesn't experience red-to-the exclusion-of-(blue-and)-all-else, nor blue-to-the-exclusion-of-(red-and)-all-else, let alone – impossibly – both together. Thus the original points of view are not ingredients in Ub's subjectivity. Only their contents – the redness and blueness – are.
>
> (2014, p. 33)

We see the purported impossibility of two micro-subjects, Red and Blue, combining to form a singular macro-subject, Ub, in virtue of their incoherent perspectival natures. It is not possible, says Coleman, for Ub's perspective to contain the perspective of either Red or Blue (or indeed both) as a partial aspect because, for example, Ub's perspective extends beyond its partial aspect that is characterized by Red's perspective, while Red's perspective excludes anything beyond its own. Ub, as a singular perspective, cannot both include and exclude that which is part of its perspective minus Red. This is the same argument that Shani (2015) makes, as referred to earlier, but Shani's explication is perhaps more clearly illustrated.

The problem arises for perennialism due to two of its stipulations: first, that all finite centres are perspectival, and second, that micro finite centres combine to form macro finite centres. Putting these two together, we arrive at Coleman's scenario: micro-level perspectives (of micro finite centres) combine to form macro-level perspectives (of macro finite centres). Therefore, the same purported incoherence surfaces for perennialism and panpsychism. A token macro-perspective of a macro finite centre cannot be both a unitary, overarching perspective *and* contain within its point-of-view the point-of-views of micro finite centres.

3.4.4.2 The problem of the strong emergence of perspectives

I have shown how perennialism appears to face a version of the subject combination problem for panpsychism, but it also faces a kind of subject derivation problem. Remember that it is the fact that cosmopsychism faces a purportedly intractable subject derivation problem that acts as the core motivation behind a proposed shift to perennialism in the first place. To recap, the subject derivation problem for cosmopsychism is the challenge of accounting for the existence of sub-cosmic subjects in virtue of the cosmic subject (i.e. how are sub-cosmic subjects derived from the cosmic subject?). Clearly, perennialism does not face the same subject derivation problem because it does not posit a cosmic subject. However, it still faces the problem of how to derive sub-cosmic subjects from the universal non-dual consciousness. This problem is very closely related to the one I highlighted earlier. I suggested that the only way for the universe of multiplicity to be derived from the non-dual ground was via strong emergence, hence giving rise to a problem of strong emergence for perennialism. While that argument focused very generally on how to derive the whole universe from the non-dual ground, the subject derivation problem I want to highlight here is one specific aspect of that more general problem.

We can frame the problem like this: how are we to derive sub-cosmic subjects – and thus sub-cosmic perspectives – from a ground entirely devoid of subjecthood, and thus devoid of perspectivality? Stated in this way, it is clear to see that a problem of emergence surfaces again. We can call this *the problem of the strong emergence of perspectives*.

The problem, as just noted, is one aspect of the general problem of the strong emergence of the emanation. However, there is an additional worry aside from the general problem. Let us accept, for the sake of argument, that we have a good explanation for the emergence of the emanation in general. Such an explanation does not necessarily explain the perspective problem. Perspectives, we are informed, are not present in the ground of universal non-dual consciousness, but arise in the emanation in cases of a co-presence of objects and witness-consciousness. Before such co-presences, there are no perspectives (and presumably, this includes the perspectives of micro finite centres, which also come to be perspectival as a result of such a co-presence). So, the question would remain: how can we intelligibly derive conscious perspectives in virtue of the co-presence of witness-consciousness and objects, the nature of both being entirely aperspectival? It seems Albahari's account will rely on the disposition of witness-consciousness to be perspectival under conditions of a co-presence with objects, but, as mentioned, I suspect it will be challenging to give an account of what that amounts to without implying that witness-consciousness is already the bearer of a conscious perspective.

3.4.5 The aggregates problem

It is one thing to show that subjects *can* combine, but another to explain on what grounds such a combination occurs. The aggregates problem relates to the latter (whereas the perspectives problem relates to the former). The aggregates problem is one that Albahari herself recognizes. She says: 'I have been supposing that atoms and animals are finite centres, while tables and toasters are not, and it will be a challenge to arbitrate the principles that sort finite centres from mere aggregates' (2020, p. 128). The problem resides in explaining the principles that govern why some aggregates of micro finite centres give rise to macro finite centres while others do not. As Albahari notes, she takes atoms and animals to be macro centres but not many other ordinary objects. Macro finite centres form from combinations of micro finite centres that give rise to subjective unities, whereas combinations that do not yield such unities remain mere aggregates. But what is it that is special about subjective unities such that their constituents' subjective characters combine to become a single macro-level finite centre? The question remains unanswered.

To be clear, this is not a problem unique to perennialism because panpsychism, cosmopsychism and even physicalism face exactly the same problem; why do only some combinations (or derivations) of the (psycho)physical ultimates give rise to macro-consciousness? I think that, as with panpsychism, it is perfectly respectable for the perennialist to reply that while a complete perennialist theory would need to arbitrate the mechanisms distinguishing subjective unities from mere aggregates, currently, there is an epistemic distance between us and the uncovering of such mechanisms.[16] For now, it will suffice that we have principled reasons to think combination occurs. The pertinent issue is whether or not there are principled reasons to reject the combination of micro-consciousness into macro-consciousness *tout court*. The point of including this here is not to suggest that an answer to the question is required if perennialism is to be taken seriously. Instead, the point is that, in addition to its own problems, perennialism also faces the same old problems as other views.

3.4.6 Perennialism vs cosmopsychism and panpsychism

Let us refresh what has been said about perennialism, comparing it to cosmopsychism (the view that it aims to succeed) and panpsychism (the view that cosmopsychism is purported to succeed). For perennialism to stand as the successor to cosmopsychism, it must overcome at least some of its problems without introducing more of its own. Moreover, it must maintain cosmopsychism's advantages over panpsychism. Let us highlight the main advantages and disadvantages of the respective views, once again. Panpsychism's most powerful motivation is that it avoids the problem of strong emergence (a persistent problem for physicalism). Panpsychism, however, faces the combination problem, with a particularly difficult aspect being the subject combination problem. Cosmopsychism maintains panpsychism's advantage of avoiding the problem of strong emergence by also positing consciousness at the fundamental level, but, moreover, overcomes the combination problem (and its subject combination aspect) by claiming that fundamental consciousness is on the cosmic rather than micro-level of reality. Thus, macro-consciousness is not formed of a *combination* of micro-consciousnesses. However, it does face an equivalent problem in the derivation problem (including a troubling subject derivation aspect) because macro-consciousness (and macro-subjects) must somehow derive from the cosmic consciousness (and cosmic subject). At this point, perennialism enters the picture.

Perennialism is touted as the natural successor to cosmopsychism as it purports to overcome the subject derivation problem. Albahari correctly identifies that the subject derivation problem is dependent on the existence of a cosmic subject that grounds

[16] Chalmers makes this point in reference to type-f monism in general; 'It is not easy to see how a distribution of a large number of individual microphysical systems, each with their own protophenomenal properties, could somehow add up to this rich and specific structure. Should one not expect something more like a disunified, jagged collection of phenomenal spikes? … This is a version of what James called the combination problem for panpsychism, or what Stoljar (2001) calls the structural mismatch problem for the Russellian view (see also Foster, 1991, pp. 119–30). To answer it, it seems that we need a much better understanding of the compositional principles of phenomenology: that is, the principles by which phenomenal properties can be composed or constituted from underlying phenomenal properties, or protophenomenal properties. We have a good understanding of the principles of physical composition, but no real understanding of the principles of phenomenal composition. This is an area that deserves much close attention: I think it is easily the most serious problem for the type-F monist view. At this point, it is an open question whether or not the problem can be solved' (2010, p. 136). Alternatively, see Chalmers (2003).

sub-cosmic subjects. The perennialist approach is to circumvent the subject derivation problem by removing the problematic commitment to a cosmic subject. In doing so, perennialism indeed avoids the subject derivation problem for cosmopsychism. However, as I have shown, it faces a version of its own. More worryingly, as I have demonstrated, perennialism succumbs to the foremost problems for each of the main approaches to the problem of phenomenal consciousness. Like physicalism, it faces a version of the problem of strong emergence (the problem of the emanation from the non-dual ground). Like panpsychism, it faces a subject combination problem (the problem of incoherent contents of perspectives), and, finally, like cosmopsychism, it faces a subject derivation problem (the problem of the strong emergence of perspectives).

Additionally, perennialism arguably has more difficulty defending the plausibility of the ultimate ground than panpsychism and cosmopsychism. Although counterintuitive, both panpsychism and cosmopsychism posit consciousness relatively comparable to our human consciousness at the fundamental level. I do not mean that the consciousness of an electron or the cosmos is the same as human consciousness, but they are at least theorized to be, like us, subjects instantiating phenomenal properties. On the other hand, fundamental consciousness, according to perennialism, diverges significantly from strongly held intuitions, or apparent conceptual truths, about consciousness. For example, the view that consciousness necessarily involves a subject instantiating phenomenal properties. It does this, I have argued, without compelling reasons. All considered, perennialism appears far from a natural successor to cosmopsychism, and what is more, it looks to be behind panpsychism and physicalism in terms of how many serious problems it must overcome.

The final section of this chapter takes us back to where perennialism entered the picture. To overcome the subject derivation problem, perennialism drops the stipulation that the cosmos is a subject of experience. That avenue, as demonstrated, leads us to somewhat of a dead-end. However, there is another option at that juncture. Like perennialism, panqualityism drops the stipulation that the fundamental level of reality is subject-involving, only for panqualityism, like panpsychism, the fundamental level of reality is the micro rather than the cosmic. Let us now explore this possibility.

3.5 Panqualityism

While panqualityism shares similarities with both physicalism and panpsychism, its close relationship to panpsychism is arguably the more significant because, like panpsychism, it takes the striking step of adding consciousness to the set of reality's fundamental building blocks. The focus of this book is, of course, fundamental approaches to the problem of phenomenal consciousness, so the treatment of panqualityism here is focused primarily on a debate between panqualityism and panpsychism. Any focus on physicalism will be tertiary.

The compelling thing about panqualityism is that it is a natural alternative to panpsychism; we might even say its potential successor. As noted, panpsychism faces a seemingly intractable problem of combining small subjects of experience into larger ones like ourselves; panqualityism purportedly avoids this problem while remaining a fundamental approach. It states that phenomenal ultimates are only phenomenally qualitied rather than instantiating phenomenal properties (the important distinction being that the notion of a phenomenal property implies that a subject of experience instantiates it), as panpsychism maintains. The properties we are aware of in experience, according to panqualityism, are perceived phenomenal qualities. For any given phenomenal quality, there is a phenomenal property consisting of awareness of that quality. Crucially, according to panqualityism, phenomenal qualities exist unexperienced too; they can float free from subjects. To put it another way, according to panqualityism, feelings can and do exist unfelt.

It might not yet be clear why such a view can help us with the subject combination problem, but consider that if one explains how macro-experience can be constituted by the awareness of phenomenal qualities rather than the combination of phenomenal properties, then there is no subject combination problem to address, because, while phenomenal properties presuppose a subject of experience (i.e. a subject instantiating the phenomenal property in question), phenomenal qualities do not. On panqualityism, in combining phenomenal qualities, we are not combining subjects of experience.

Although we can now see an outline of how panqualityism can evade a subject combination problem, an account will only be satisfactory if it provides some support for the independent existence of phenomenal qualities. In other words, the panqualityist needs to motivate the idea that phenomenal qualities (such as the feeling of colour experiences, for instance, the feeling of a red-experience or a blue-experience, or the felt olfactory qualities we experience when smelling coffee or a log fire) can exist unfelt, i.e. independent of subjects of experience being aware of them. Does it seem plausible that the qualitative feel of smelling a log fire exists even when it is unfelt, or that the feeling of a red-experience exists even if it is not experienced? For the vast majority, this comes across as very counterintuitive because it seems that feelings are necessarily felt (i.e. *x* is a feeling iff *x* is felt). Some, however, do not toe this line. Sam Coleman, for example, is the stand-out contemporary proponent of panqualityism (2012, 2014, 2017). He maintains that qualities like those just mentioned do indeed exist unfelt.[17]

There is, of course, enough real estate in logical space to accommodate numerous versions of panqualityism. However, in the contemporary literature, proponents are rare, and Coleman is outstanding in his defence of the view. Consequently, it is prudent to focus on his treatment of panqualityism (though much of what I say will be relevant to panqualityism more broadly construed). Coleman offers a panqualityist account of phenomenal consciousness that involves micro-qualities in conjunction with a reductionist account of awareness. On his view, phenomenal consciousness equates to phenomenal qualities plus awareness, where the mechanism for generating awareness is a higher-order thought (HOT). He explains the view like this:

[17] Coleman's panqualityism owes much to Lockwood's (1989) development of a strikingly similar view, albeit not under the name 'panqualityism'. For a good examination of the similarities between Lockwood and Coleman's views, see Shani's (2022) paper 'Eden Benumbed: A Critique of Panqualityism and the Disclosure View of Consciousness'.

> On panqualityism the universe is fundamentally constituted by qualities akin to those we experience, e.g. sensory qualities such as blue and red, but in their natural state these exist non-consciously. Panqualityism is, if you will, panpsychism minus awareness. Though the panqualityist's universe, like the panpsychist's, is bedecked with qualities, awareness of those qualities is restricted, for all we know, to living brains. The qualities constituting all else are 'unfelt qualia' ... what they lack is the light of awareness.
>
> (2017, p. 92)

He elaborates:

> I adopt Feigl's suggestion that in awareness one cerebral area 'scans' qualities in another area, elaborating it via a higher-order theory of consciousness ... on panqualityism a brain is a system of qualities, some portion of which is conscious at a time thanks to the posited special relational property. A group of brain-qualities is within the spotlight of awareness, we may say. The rest are unconscious.
>
> (2017, p. 93)

The 'spotlight of awareness' is a higher-order thought. Since this view utilizes higher-order thought theory's approach to generating awareness, it will help to summarize the view and briefly highlight the notable ways standard HOT theory and HOT panqualityism differ.

3.5.1 Higher-order thought theory of consciousness

For the higher-order thought theory, the problem of consciousness is a general problem relating to why and how some mental states are conscious. Therefore, its focus is on explaining state-consciousness. The *raison d'etre* of the HOT theory is to make sense of the apparent truth that there are both conscious and unconscious mental states. It makes sense of this by providing an account of the difference between those conscious and unconscious states.[18]

The basic idea is that a mental state is conscious if it is the object of a higher-order thought. Unconscious states are those not represented in any HOT. A thought about a mental state is always a higher-order thought, while a thought about something that is not a mental state is always a first-order thought. Therefore, HOTs are consciousness-makers, so it is natural to wonder what it means to be the object of a HOT. The simplest way to understand HOTs is to consider them awareness-generators. Take a first-order mental state such as <a dog is barking>. As a first-order mental state alone, it is unconscious, but now suppose that first-order state becomes the object of a higher-order thought (i.e. there is a thought *about* the first-order state); the resulting mental state represents the first-order thought as the object of the higher-order thought <I am thinking about a dog barking>. The HOT generates awareness of the first-order mental

[18] The most notable proponent of HOT theory is Rosenthal (1993, 2005).

state that the dog is barking, making the resulting state a conscious state. Thus, on the HOT view, consciousness and awareness are closely related.

Whether or not a given state is conscious depends on a HOT generating awareness of that state. *Awareness of* seems to bring about state-consciousness. This gets to an important point: for HOT theorists, state consciousness is explained in terms of transitive consciousness. Transitive consciousness is the consciousness *of* something. Therefore, a mental state is conscious if and only if there is consciousness of that mental state. This sounds circular, but it is saying that state consciousness is explained in virtue of transitive consciousness, which is not circular. For HOT theorists, then, HOTs are consciousness-makers in the sense that they make mental states conscious, and they do so because they are awareness-generators (remembering that transitive consciousness amounts to *awareness of*).

A possible objection to this HOT approach states that we still do not have an intelligible account of *how* consciousness breaks into the world in instances where two non-conscious thoughts are suitably related, i.e. how it is that consciousness emerges when two non-conscious thoughts are arranged with one directed at the other. One might object that it is still seemingly miraculous that we have subjective experience emerging from an entirely non-conscious thought. This is a version of the strong emergence problem for physicalism. I will not focus here on HOT theory responses to such an objection as my interest in the view, for present purposes, is merely tangential. My focus for present purposes is the viability of panqualityism as an alternative to panpsychism and its adoption – in Coleman's contemporary formulation – of aspects of HOT theory. However, recall that panpsychists take the avoidance of the problem of strong emergence as a key motivation for their view. Similarly, Coleman is motivated by the difficulty of strong emergence for physicalism, but while panpsychism avoids the problem by building in consciousness from the start, so to speak, panqualityism posits only phenomenal quality from the start. Presumably, Coleman is concerned that typical HOT theories cannot fully address the problem of phenomenal consciousness. This concern must, at least in part, have to do with the problem of strong emergence. Let us now see how Coleman's panqualityism adopts the HOT theory.

3.5.2 Higher-order thought theory and panqualityism

Like HOT theory, panqualityism, in the form we are interested in, takes higher-order thoughts to be instrumental in generating consciousness. However, HOT theory typically maintains that consciousness is explained without remainder in terms of higher-order thoughts. Meanwhile, panqualityists are concerned enough about the problem of strong emergence (and presumably not satisfied with standard HOT theory responses) that they posit some aspect of consciousness – phenomenal qualities – at the ultimate microphysical level. Thus, the two are only alike in their invocation of HOTs to generate awareness. Again, panqualityism aims to give an account of phenomenal consciousness that does not posit subjects of experience at the microphysical level, in order to avoid the subject combination problem.

Coleman's panqualityism takes HOT theory's method of generating awareness of mental states via HOTs, but applies it to brains as a whole. We can perhaps see

Coleman's view as entailing a massively complex HOT generating awareness of the phenomenal qualities of many states synchronously. It is supposed to work something like this: there is an input to the visual sense, for example, which is attached to a visual phenomenal screen. The visual phenomenal screen is the collection of phenomenal qualities linked to the visual sense. Consequently, the contents of the visual screen change depending on what is presented to the visual sense. This, however, does not yet give us awareness, only a collection, possibly a unity, of qualities. To get awareness of the visual phenomenal screen, a process of phenomenal representation is undergone by means of a second phenomenal screen, a central experiential screen, which all suburban screens (auditory, olfactory, emotional, etc.) feed into. This central experiential screen equates to a higher-order thought which integrates the signals from each suburban screen into a unified phenomenal representation of the whole organism. Awareness is explained, without remainder, Coleman states, by this representation of qualities in the central experiential screen. And this also explains, without remainder, the existence of macro-subjects like you and me. Recall that for the panqualityist, there are no subjects at the fundamental level, so the subject combination problem never arises. Macro-subjects are reduced to awareness, and awareness is generated by the HOT process just described. Awareness does the work of the subject, we might say.

Panqualityism is undoubtedly an important position, elegantly carving a path in the terrain between panpsychism and physicalism. However, to carve this path, it must tamper with a widely accepted conception of phenomenal consciousness; it must jettison subjects of experience from fundamental reality while keeping phenomenal qualities in the absence of subjects. The problem is that it is widely regarded as a conceptual truth that phenomenal consciousness involves a subject of experience instantiating phenomenal properties. This relates to the intuitive idea that phenomenal consciousness necessarily involves a subject being aware of phenomenal qualities, i.e. the idea that phenomenal qualities cannot exist independent of subjects being aware of them. Let us call this *the intuitive notion*. At heart, Coleman's project is to motivate a move away from the intuitive notion to what we can call *the counterintuitive notion:* that phenomenal qualities (again, these are the felt qualities that characterize our conscious experience) can and do exist unfelt; that is, they exist in the absence of subjects to feel them.

In the remainder of this chapter, I show that the support for the counterintuitive notion is weak. The bulk of what I say is focused on a dilemma Coleman poses to those who want to maintain the intuitive notion. The dilemma says that to uphold the intuitive notion, the panpsychist must isolate a phenomenological contribution made by awareness (I call this the awareness-feel), which is not possible. I suggest that the dilemma is ineffective because panpsychists have opportunities to pass through its horns unhindered. I then give one plausible account of the awareness-feel by suggesting that the awareness-feel might be understood as owing to subjects being perspectival. Additionally, I briefly outline a quandary for panqualityism, conditional on my proposal regarding conscious perspectives. Finally, I present what I call the unhappy compromise objection to panqualityism.

3.5.3 Rejecting the intuitive notion: Separating subjects and qualities

To recap, the panqualityist project hinges on being able to metaphysically break apart the conceptual components of subjective experience, leaving a subject, or at least awareness, distinct from phenomenal qualities. Chalmers's (2017b) panqualityist zombie argument is intended as an argument against separating phenomenal qualities from subjects. The thinking is that if we accept that phenomenal qualities can exist apart from subjects, then we can conceive of panqualityist zombies; that is, entities that are exact microphysical and micro-quality replicas of us but who lack awareness of those qualities (remember that for Coleman what we think of as a *subject* is just *awareness* – it is likely that a slightly modified version of this argument could run against other versions of panqualityism too, by replacing 'awareness' with whatever is supposed to do the work of a subject). If this is the case, panqualityism would appear to leave something out of the picture and must, therefore, be false. We can formulate the following argument against panqualityism:

1. It is conceivable that all micro-quality facts (and microphysical facts) obtain without any awareness of qualities.
2. If it is conceivable that all micro-quality facts (and microphysical facts) obtain without any awareness of qualities, then it is metaphysically possible.
3. If it is metaphysically possible that all micro-quality facts (and microphysical facts) obtain without any awareness of qualities, then panqualityism is false.
4. Therefore, panqualityism is false.

Coleman's response to this charge is to maintain that there is nothing lacking in the zombies; thinking otherwise is to imply that there is a phenomenology to awareness itself: 'It's true that if awareness had phenomenology, then this, like sensory quality in general, would be hard to functionalize. But I deny that mere awareness has phenomenology' (Coleman, 2017, p. 270). This rejection of an awareness phenomenology (i.e. an awareness-feel) is central to the panqualityist project. Given that Coleman is the principal contemporary component of panqualityism, we might say that the contemporary panqualityist project turns on the notion of an awareness-feel being unviable.

Coleman maintains that while it is true that *if* there were a phenomenology to awareness (or, to put it another way, if there were such a thing as an awareness-feel), *then* it would be hard to give a functional account of awareness. However, his contention is that there is no such awareness-feel, so the problem of panqualityist zombies never arises. We can see the difference between typical HOT theories, panpsychism and panqualityism play out here; panqualityists (in Coleman's mould) are, like panpsychists, convinced that functional accounts of phenomenal consciousness like HOT theories (as well as other typical physicalist accounts) cannot be complete because they do not adequately account for phenomenality (i.e. the what-it-is-like-ness of conscious experience). Thus, they propose that phenomenality is a fundamental feature of the universe. As we have seen, panpsychists and panqualityists disagree about what physicalist theories like HOT theories leave out of the picture, with the former saying subjects and phenomenal qualities are missing, and the latter that only phenomenal qualities are missing. Recall that Coleman wants to do away with subjects instantiating phenomenal properties and replace them with the awareness of phenomenal qualities (where awareness is achieved via a HOT). The problem is that when subjects of experience are replaced by HOTs, which are a distinctly functional affair, there is no room for awareness to have a phenomenology because any such phenomenology would be hard to functionalize. Coleman's strategy, as I understand it, is multifaceted. He aims to offer intuitive reasons for the positive claim that phenomenal qualities exist independent of subjects, together with presenting a dilemma for proponents of the notion that awareness has a phenomenology (these I call awareness-feel proponents).

Consider this binary decision: we must hold either that phenomenal qualities can exist unexperienced or that they cannot. The widely accepted view is that phenomenal qualities are necessarily experienced because they are the properties that characterize a subject's experience. With this in mind, it seems that, when considering the viability of panpsychism over panqualityism (or vice versa), panpsychism has a *prima facie* advantage because it adheres to this intuitive notion. Panqualityism, on the other hand, has some extra work to do because it needs to convince us to reject this notion that appears to have a lot of intuitive traction. Coleman has a double-headed argumentative strategy in favour of panqualityism. First, he calls into question the supposed counter-intuitiveness of the notion of unexperienced qualities, thus weakening the *prima facie* advantage that panpsychism seems to hold. Then, he presents a dilemma that panpsychists face due to maintaining the intuitive notion (which implies an awareness-feel). The result of this double-headed strategy, if convincing, would be the conversion of proponents of panpsychism to panqualityism. Given the rise in interest in panpsychism and the unique position panqualityism holds, it is worth exploring this further.

3.5.3.1 Independent phenomenal qualities as intuitive

Let us take a look at the first part of Coleman's strategy. I have said that the very notion of unexperienced qualities strikes most (not just panpsychists) as counterintuitive, but Coleman contends that on the common-sense way of thinking we can easily grasp the notion. He writes:

> We, in the everyday mode, think of objects as straightforwardly coloured. For example, we think of a red London bus as being straightforwardly red, much as if the redness were painted over the surface of the bus in a quite objective way (of course, what accounts for the redness of the 'paint' is something we don't consider, in this mode). As part of this conception, we take it, in an easy and uncomplicated way, that the bus is still red when we are not looking at it, and even when no-one is looking at it, as when it is waiting in its garage overnight … We have, on the commonsense way of thinking, no difficulty with the notion of qualities which exist with no-one there to experience them. I suggest we use this commonsense

> model to think now about unexperienced instances of phenomenal quality. We can, to take a next step, attempt to imagine a patch of phenomenal red, now as experienced by one of us, now as experienced by nobody, but still 'radiating' redness, much as we take the lonesome red London bus to do. Next, consider that this phenomenal redness permeates the spherical volume of a particle, a panpsychic ultimate. We have not yet been forced to think of this ultimate as itself a subject
>
> (Coleman, 2012, pp. 154–5).

I will not resist the claim that a London bus continues to radiate redness in the absence of experiencers, on a commonsense way of thinking. However, this is just an expression of the intuitive view that once a red London bus is out of sight it remains red. In the same way, as Coleman suggests, we can imagine a particle radiating redness internally without anybody experiencing it, but again, this is just the intuitive view that the particle remains red even when nobody is experiencing it as such. The problem, however, is that this commonsense view does not support the notion that a panqualityist requires, the notion that feels can exist unfelt. To support the panqualityist notion, a London bus example must focus on the phenomenal feel of the red-experience and not simply on the existence of redness. From a commonsense perspective, I accept that a red bus remains red when out of sight, but that does not entail the view that the *feeling* of the red-experience exists without a feeler perceiving the red bus. A more intuitive take would be that something about the bus (its redness) makes us, as feelers, feel a certain way (the red-experience) when we perceive it. I think that most people would answer 'no' if asked, 'Does a red London bus, when parked out of sight of anybody, radiate the *feeling* you have when you see its redness?' With this in mind, I do not think that the notion of unexperienced qualities is intuitive, despite Coleman's claims. As a result, I take the intuitive notion to be just that, an intuitive notion. Thus, I take it that on the face of it, the panpsychist, owing to their endorsement of the view that experiences require experiencers, has the intuitive advantage over the panqualityist.

While these considerations of intuitiveness are undoubtedly important for motivating us one way or another, the second head of Coleman's argumentative strategy is arguably more important, as it has the potential to override the pull of the common sense convictions just mentioned. For this reason, I will spend some time now focusing on it. The second strand of Coleman's argument is essentially a negative argument against panpsychism. The idea being that panpsychism's commitment to the intuitive notion leads to an impassable dilemma, the existence of which should drive panpsychists to reconsider their stance, and with panqualityism offering the best way forward for them.

Coleman's reasoning is something like the following: according to panpsychists, wherever there are phenomenal qualities, subjects must also be aware of those qualities (this is the intuitive notion). Moreover, their awareness of those qualities adds to their phenomenology; that is, it adds to the feel of the experience in the form of an awareness-feel (recall that panqualityism rejects this, which is why it purportedly faces the panqualityist zombie problem). However, Coleman's reasoning continues that it is peculiar that panpsychism maintains that there is an awareness-feel because it seems difficult to put one's finger on precisely what this feel is supposed to add to the experience of first-order qualities. If we cannot find the awareness-feel despite our searches, the reasonable conclusion is that it does not exist. We can break this bit down into two connected theses: a conclusive thesis that an awareness-feel does not exist, which we can call *the no awareness-feel thesis* (NF):

> **No awareness-feel thesis (NF)**: Awareness does not add anything to phenomenology.

And another thesis that says that as much as we search for the awareness-feel we cannot find it in our experience. An alternative way of saying this is that awareness is 'invisible' or 'transparent' in our searches.[19] Accordingly, we can call this *the awareness-feel transparency thesis* (AT):

> **Awareness-feel transparency thesis (AT)**: The purported awareness-feel is completely transparent in our experience.

We can see how these two theses are connected: AT underpins NF in the sense that it is because the awareness-feel does not appear to show up in our experience that Coleman suggests that there is no awareness-feel. Of course, the panpsychist will (and must) maintain that the awareness-feel does enter our phenomenology and will, therefore, reject AT. To do this, they must give an account of the awareness-feel and its contribution to experience. The problem, Coleman argues, is that to give an account they must claim one of two things about the relation between first-order qualities and the awareness-feel, but either is equally problematic. Let us explore the dilemma in more detail.

3.5.3.2 The awareness-feel dilemma for panpsychism

Let us call the dilemma Coleman presents *the awareness-feel dilemma* for panpsychists. In giving an account of the awareness-feel, Panpsychists, we are informed, must maintain either that:

1. The proposed awareness-feel is an isolated feel; 'a standalone qualitative ingredient in consciousness' (2017, p. 272) that is independent of first-order qualities, making no reference to them.

Or,

2. The proposed awareness-feel is interpenetrated, or suffused, with the first-order qualities of which we are aware.

[19] Mihálik (2022) refers to two similar theses when arguing against panqualityism, albeit on different grounds. I recommend his paper, 'Panqualityism, awareness, and the explanatory gap', to those readers wanting to consider alternative arguments against panqualityism.

Since we are supposed to have a dilemma here, either option should prove equally problematic for the panpsychist. These options remain somewhat opaque to me, so rather than attempting to go straight into giving a possible account of the awareness-feel, on behalf of the panpsychist, and then seeing how that account fares with respect to the dilemma, I think it is more important to get clearer on the precise details of the intended horns of the dilemma. I suspect that getting clearer about them will help rather than hinder the panpsychist, as we shall see.

Regarding (1), the first horn of the dilemma, it is not clear how to interpret the word 'standalone' or 'isolated' here. One interpretation might say something like the awareness-feel is isolated insofar as it is not hard-wired into the awareness of first-order qualities; it has character not owing to any particular token first-order quality. Another interpretation might say something like the awareness-feel is standalone in the sense that it is in-principle experienceable in the absence of any first-order qualities at all. With this in mind, I think we can draw at least these two interpretations of (1):

1.1 The awareness-feel exists independently of any particular token first-order quality.
1.2 The awareness-feel exists independently of any particular token first-order quality and is experienceable in the total absence of first-order qualities.

The question is: is the first horn of Coleman's awareness-feel dilemma intended to resemble option 1.1 or option 1.2? We will return to this question shortly, but the striking difference between the two options is that one (1.1) says that the awareness-feel is independent of any token first-order quality but leaves open the possibility that it is not experienceable in isolation from first-order qualities, while the other (1.2) adds the requirement that one can experience it in the total absence of first-order qualities.

Regarding (2), the option which says the awareness-feel is somehow suffused with the awareness of first-order qualities, it is not clear precisely how to interpret the terms 'suffused' or 'interpenetrated'. What sort of distinction between the awareness-feel and first-order qualities does the suffusion permit? One interpretation might say that the awareness-feel and first-order qualities are suffused just in case the awareness-feel is hardwired into the first-order qualities, with the awareness-feel not having a character independent of any particular token first-order quality. Another interpretation might say that the awareness-feel is suffused with first-order qualities just in case one is not distinguishable from the other in experience. Like before, I think this indicates (at least) two possible interpretations of (2):

2.1 The awareness-feel and first-order qualities are suffused insofar as the awareness-feel does not have an independent character in the total absence of first-order qualities.
2.2 The awareness-feel and first-order qualities are suffused insofar as the awareness-feel is not distinguishable from first-order qualities in experience.

Again, it is not clear whether option (2) is supposed to be like option 2.1 or 2.2. The striking difference, in this case, is that one (2.1) states that the awareness-feel does not have any character independent of at least some first-order quality, while the other (2.2) leaves open the possibility that it does have such an independent character but that we do not (or cannot) experience it as such.

Considering these more fine-grained interpretations of the dilemma's horns, it is intriguing to note that on one interpretation, the horns are compatible with one another; for example, (1.1) and (2.2) form a consistent set. The claim that the awareness-feel exists independently of any particular token first-order quality (1.1) does not preclude that the awareness-feel and first-order qualities are suffused insofar as the awareness-feel is not distinguishable from first-order qualities in experience (2.2). On this interpretation, at least, the dilemma is false because the awareness-feel proponent does not need to choose one horn or the other. For this reason, I suspect that this is not the set of horns that Coleman intends.

Let us now take a look at why Coleman thinks each horn of the dilemma is problematic for the awareness-feel proponent, in the hope that doing so might clarify which of the interpretations of each horn he has in mind. The first horn of the dilemma is unfavourable, we are told, because: 'If awareness has its own distinctive feel, which qualitatively speaking has nothing to do with, and makes no reference to, the other, first-order, qualities, then it is very hard to see how, in experiencing this quality, one could apprehend it as a feeling of awareness of these (first-order) qualities, i.e. as the very item it is supposed to be' (2017, p. 272). It is obvious that being able to apprehend the awareness-feel as the feeling of awareness of a given token first-order quality is central to the intended interpretation of (1). Such an apprehension seems to me straightforwardly incompatible with 1.1 because 1.1 leaves it open that the independence of the awareness-feel from first-order qualities might be unexperiencable as such, insofar as it is consistent with 1.1 that the awareness-feel is independent of any particular token first-order quality but that it cannot be experienced in isolation (for whatever reason). Since the above quotation clearly shows that the intended version of the first horn involves one's ability to apprehend the awareness-feel as independent, it would seem 1.2 is the intended interpretation.

For panpsychists who take the first horn of the dilemma, there is the obvious worry that there seem to be no candidates for the awareness-feel that fit the requirements of the horn (a qualitative feel that is distinct from first-order qualities and also experienceable as such). Putting that to one side, let us suppose the panpsychist proposes a candidate feel. The separation of first-order qualities from the awareness-feel that characterizes the experience of them seems problematic because if the awareness-feel is supposed to be the feel that characterizes the awareness of some first-order qualities, how can it be that that feel is experienceable completely apart from them (since the feel is supposed to be precisely the feel that characterizes the experience of those first-order qualities). Choosing this option is akin to claiming something like that it is possible to experience what it feels like to have a red-experience without any reference to a red-experience. This first horn, as I take Coleman to intend it, does seem to be tricky for the panpsychist, at least at first glance, but we will return to this shortly.

Turning to the second horn of the dilemma, which of the two interpretations is intended? This horn is unfavourable, we are told, because it entails a doubling-up of first-order qualities in experience that patently does not occur:

> But now the position appears to be this: I am aware of a set of first-order qualities, and aware, additionally, of an awareness-quale that phenomenally includes reference to (is 'stained by') these same first-order qualities. It seems to follow that I get every first-order quality twice in consciousness: once in its own right … and once more as 'staining' the feel of my awareness of all these first-order qualities.
> (2017, p. 272)

I am less confident about which interpretation of (2) Coleman intends, but I suspect that it is (2.2), as this is the weaker of the two interpretations, and I find no evidence that he intends specifically the stronger one.

The reason the second horn of the dilemma is supposed to trouble the panpsychist is that it implies that when I am aware of, for instance, a red-experience, there is in my consciousness the first-order redness quality and also the awareness-feel as it pertains to that same first-order redness quality, and this, Coleman says, means that we should have the redness-quality twice in our experience, but this simply does not tally with our experience because we do not have such a doubling-up of phenomenal qualities. I must admit that I find this reasoning a little puzzling. First, (assuming 2.2) it presupposes that because the awareness-feel is indistinguishable from first-order qualities in our experience, our experience must include a counterintuitive doubling-up of its first-order qualities. I am not convinced by this. Regardless, setting this scepticism to one side, if we accept for the sake of argument that this option does indeed entail a doubling-up of first-order qualities in experience, the assumption is that such an eventuality would be problematic. It is fair to say that for a doubling-up to be problematic, it must be discernible by the subject as such because it is the very fact that such a doubling-up would be noticeable in our experience that underpins this horn of the dilemma; that is, we should (if we grant Coleman's reasoning), but do not, notice a doubling-up of first-order phenomenal qualities in our conscious experience.

My problem with Coleman's reasoning here is that I have no idea what the difference between a single and a doubled-up red-experience would be. This qualitative doubling-up must be envisaged as something noticeable as such if it is to cause the panpsychist a problem. However, when I try to imagine the feel of a red experience compared to that same feel doubled up, I struggle to imagine any difference at all. At most, I can envisage the quality of redness printed as a little darker or fuller somehow, as a result of the double-printing (in the same way we might expect an image printed twice on the same piece of paper to perhaps appear a little fuller in colour). However, it is worth noting that in our binocular vision, almost all of the qualities in our visual fields are duplicated inputs to our visual system (one input for each monocular field), but we do not have in our overall binocular visual field a doubling-up of qualities in the imagined sense just noted. This can be illustrated by noticing that the colour qualities of our experience (in those with healthy sight) do not change when we close one eye. So, I do not think that the second horn of the dilemma is necessarily problematic for the panpsychist. For the panpsychist to be concerned, there would need to be further justification as to why we should expect a doubling-up of first-order qualities in our experience to be noticeable and, moreover, for us to be sure that a doubling-up is not something that we already routinely experience (just in a way indistinguishable to us).

I have so far offered some initial thoughts on the horns of the dilemma, and I have also indicated that there are at least two interpretations of each horn. Further, I have indicated that the interpretations Coleman intends for the horns of the dilemma are (1.2) and (2.2). Let us consider the dilemma so construed, that is, that the awareness-feel proponent must hold that either:

1.2 The awareness-feel exists independently of any particular token first-order quality and is experienceable in the total absence of first-order qualities.

Or,

2.2 The awareness-feel and first-order qualities are suffused insofar as the awareness-feel is not distinguishable from first-order qualities in experience.

This formulation of the dilemma is intriguing since both horns emphasize the distinguishability (or lack thereof) of the awareness-feel in experience. For example, the first horn (1.2) does not simply say that the awareness-feel exists independently of any particular token first-order quality. It also says that it must be experienceable in the total absence of first-order qualities. Similarly, the second horn (2.2) does not simply say that the awareness-feel is suffused with first-order qualities in the sense that it has no character independent of any token first-order quality. Instead, it says that the two are suffused insofar as they are not distinguishable in experience. Therefore, the first horn (1.2) rules out the possibility of the awareness-feel having an independent existence that cannot be experienced as such (of course, the question then is why should its being experienceable be so important), while the second horn (2.2) leaves open the possibility that the suffusion of the awareness-feel with first-order qualities is only a matter of experience.

Let us consider this more precise formulation of the dilemma in light of the core theses underwriting Coleman's approach. Earlier, I suggested that Coleman's commitment to the no awareness-feel thesis (NF) is underpinned by the awareness-feel transparency thesis (AT), which is the thesis that we are never aware of our awareness (i.e. that our awareness is transparent in our conscious experience). I believe that our new, more precise understanding of the dilemma's horns (being 1.2 and 2.2) reveals a further thesis underpinning AT (perhaps implicitly). This further, more foundational thesis has to do with the prominent role that the identifiability-in-experience of the awareness-feel (or lack thereof) plays in the horns of the dilemma. Let us call this new foundational thesis *the no identifiable awareness-feel thesis* (NI):

No identifiable awareness-feel thesis (NI): There is no awareness-feel clearly and distinctly identifiable as such in experience.

It seems to me that NI underpins AT in the sense that the supposed awareness-feel is said to be transparent in our experience because, in our experience, there is no such feel that is *clearly and distinctly identifiable* as the awareness-feel. If this is right, then Coleman's motivation is something like the following: NF is underpinned by AT, which is, in turn, underpinned by NI. This means that it is NI that really gets to the heart of Coleman's distrust of the awareness-feel. If this is right, then Coleman's principal concern is that we cannot experience the awareness-feel clearly and distinctly in our experience. The critical question then becomes: should the fact that we do not experience an awareness-feel clearly and distinctly as such in our experience be enough to conclude that there is no awareness-feel (i.e. does NI give us good reason to accept NF)? I think not. Consider the following two claims:

(a) *x* is not clearly and distinctly identifiable in *y*
(b) *x* is not in *y*

Claim (a) does not entail claim (b), as it is possible for some *x* to be in some *y* without being clearly and distinctly identifiable as such. If Coleman is equating (a) with (b), the implication for the first horn of the dilemma (1.2) is that unless the awareness-feel can be experienced in the total absence of any first-order qualities, then it does not exist independently of any token first-order quality(s). Thus, it makes the independent experiencability of an awareness-feel a requirement of its existence. The important question to ask is, therefore, can a plausible account be given such that the awareness-feel has an existence independent of first-order qualities without being experienceable as such? I believe we can give such an account. Even if providing such an account is only remotely possible, then 1.2 is redundant as the first horn because it collapses into 1.1. Recall that 1.1 says simply that the awareness-feel exists independently of any token first-order quality. It does not add the additional stipulation that for this to be so it must also be experienceable as such. Here is the thing, once we admit 1.1 as the dilemma's first horn, the panpsychist has an unobstructed path through. The panpsychist can claim that the awareness-feel is independent of any token first-order qualities but cannot be experienced in the total absence of first-order qualities (to put it a different way, the panpsychist can claim that the awareness-feel is independent of any given instance of any given phenomenal quality, but it is not experienced when there is a complete absence of any phenomenal qualities whatsoever). It may still do well to give an account, even though it cannot be clear and distinct, of the awareness-feel's contribution to conscious experience. We will turn to this point momentarily.

The implication – of equating (a) with (b) – for the second horn (2.2) is that the suffusion of the awareness-feel and first-order qualities only needs to be skin deep because 'suffusion' means only that the awareness-feel and first-order qualities are not clearly and distinctly distinguishable in experience. However, this leaves open the possibility that the awareness-feel and the first-order qualities are independent but that that independence is simply not apparent in experience. To call the second horn (2.2) into question, all we need is for it to be remotely plausible that we could experience the two as suffused even though they actually possess an independent existence.

I think this is plausible because I do not see a good reason to deny the possibility that the awareness-feel and first-order qualities might always (or just almost always) be experienced together. Importantly, nothing about that entails that they are not independent from each other.

If this is plausible, then option 2.1 becomes viable. Recall that 2.1 says that the awareness-feel and first-order qualities are suffused insofar as the awareness-feel does not have an independent character in the total absence of first-order quality. Importantly, according to 2.1, suffusion goes deeper than skin deep; whether or not the first-order qualities are suffused with the awareness-feel is not simply a matter of whether we can experience them independently. It leaves open the possibility that the two have an independent existence regardless of our ability to experience them in isolation.

This leaves us with a dilemma where each horn contains two sub-options, meaning there are a total of four pathways through it. To put it all in one place:

Horn 1: The awareness-feel and first-order qualities are independent

> Option 1.1 The awareness-feel exists independently of any particular token first-order quality.
>
> Option 1.2 The awareness-feel exists independently of any particular token first-order quality and is experienceable in the total absence of any token quality.

Horn 2: The awareness-feel and first-order qualities are suffused

> Option 2.1 The awareness-feel and first-order qualities are suffused insofar as the awareness-feel does not have an independent character in the total absence of first-order qualities
>
> Option 2.2 The awareness-feel and first-order qualities are suffused insofar as the awareness-feel is not distinguishable from first-order qualities in experience.

We now bring this critical exploration together and consider what it means for the panpsychist. The panpsychist only needs to be able to traverse one of the four pathways, of course. Still, in the next section, I will outline an account that is open to the panpsychist and sits equally well with 1.1 and 2.1. Before we move on to that task, I should say a little about what is required of any account of the awareness-feel to get the panpsychist through 1.1 or 2.1. First, to pass through 1.1, the purported awareness-feel must, in principle, exist independent of any particular token first-order quality; for example, the awareness-feel must exist independent of the qualitative pinkness of my cat's nose or the qualitative blackness of her tail. But, importantly, 1.1 does not preclude the possibility that there is no awareness-feel in the absence of first-order qualities *tout court*. This leaves open the possibility that the awareness-feel is such that whenever we experience first-order qualities, we also experience the awareness-feel, but that the awareness-feel has an independent existence apart from any given token first-order quality. Second, to pass through 2.1, the purported awareness-feel can be said to be suffused with first-order qualities in so far as it does not have an independent phenomenal character in the total absence of first-order qualities. This leaves the possibility that the awareness-feel exists independent of any given first-order quality while not having a character in the total absence of first-order qualities.

Putting the two together, we can see that 1.1 and 2.1 form a consistent set. The panpsychist can pass through either path if the purported awareness-feel is such that it has an existence independent of any token first-order property (e.g. the pinkness of my cat's nose) while having a character only in the presence of first-order qualities. What I have in mind is that the awareness-feel is not dependent on any particular token first-order quality but is only experienced in the presence of some or other first-order quality (or qualities). In other words, the awareness-feel shows up in our experience only in the presence of first-order qualities, but it is independent of any particular token first-order quality. In the next section, I will outline an account in this spirit on behalf of the panpsychist.

3.5.3.3 Navigating the awareness-feel dilemma

Although, following my previous reasoning, the dilemma does not, strictly speaking, stand because it does not demonstrate that the awareness-feel proponent is forced into a dead end (no matter which horn they take), the panpsychist – an awareness-feel proponent, of course – would do well to pick out the proposed awareness-feel in rough outline, even though it is not clearly and distinctly distinguishable (as it need not be, I have argued). Doing this will add to the intuitive appeal of the notion that phenomenology adds to awareness, and will thereby bolster the panpsychist position.

We can elucidate one plausible proposal for the awareness-feel by considering the juxtaposition between the goings-on on the set of a television show (e.g. actors reading their lines, moving in this way and then in that way) and that same goings-on as captured by a video camera recording the show. We might say that the goings-on on set are presented to, or disclosed to, the video camera. It seems to me that in recording the goings-on, the video camera adds a feel that is not present on the set itself. For example, it adds a particular (more or less) unique angle from which the goings-on on the set are viewed. Additionally, it adds a boundedness not present on the set itself insofar as it demarcates a portion of a more expansive view and a plausible feel that accompanies that boundedness. Perhaps it also adds a feel of there being more to the sides or behind than that presented from the camera's viewpoint – perhaps this is the feeling of limitation or exclusion rather than inclusion.

We can extract this line of thinking and apply it directly to our own conscious experience by replacing the purview of the video camera with our own subjective point of view and substituting the set of the television show with the world as it is presented to our subjective points-of-view. It seems to me plausible that a contribution to our phenomenology comes hand-in-hand with our being aware that what is presented to our visual field (for example) is bounded, discreet and limited due to our particular point of view. Again, it seems plausible that the anticipation of there being more to the scene, just outside of its purview, makes a phenomenological contribution.

To be clear, I propose that there is a phenomenology to the awareness of first-order qualities (i.e. an awareness-feel) owing to subjects of experience being inherently perspectival. Subjects being inherently perspectival is highly intuitive; it could not tally any better with our subjective experience. I propose that there is an additional feel to the bounded, discreet, persisting for-me-ness of awareness of qualities, that is not accounted for by the first-order awareness of qualities alone.

Coleman (or the panqualityist in Coleman's mould) may respond that this boundedness can be accounted for by taking the 'subject' to be identical to the central experiential screen, which integrates (i.e. represents) the inputs from suburban phenomenal screens. He might say that each 'macro-subject' is identical to a central experiential screen; their ever-changing, bounded phenomenology equal to the ever-changing, bounded (by being limited to a particular brain) representation of ever-changing suburban phenomenal screens by their central experiential screen. However, the point would remain: if subjects are central experiential screens, the point (following my suggestion) is that it *feels* like something to be a central experiential screen; that boundedness feels like something, just like it feels like something to be a unified and persisting point-of-view in the face of continual change regarding all other phenomenal content (i.e. first-order qualities). Remember that, given our re-statement of the dilemma, the awareness-feel proponent does not need to be able to clearly and distinctly distinguish the awareness-feel in experience for them to avoid the dilemma.

Suppose that the panpsychist considers the awareness-feel synonymous with the phenomenological contribution that being a conscious perspective makes to subjective experience. In that case, they can pass through either horn of the purported dilemma. I suspect that taking the second option is the better of the two. In this case, the panpsychist can maintain that the phenomenal feel of awareness is only apparent in the presence of first-order qualities, while still being clear that its phenomenological contribution is distinct (though not experienceable as such) from the first-order awareness of those qualities alone. If there is a phenomenology to perspectives, then it would not be surprising that the awareness-feel is only apparent in the presence of first-order awareness of qualities because what perspectives do is frame experience. Moreover, it seems intuitive that a framed experience is qualitatively different from an unframed one. Intuitively, we can think of perspectives as unique windows onto the world, which frame our conscious experience and, in framing our conscious experience, qualitatively add to it.

Let us briefly summarize the original motivations behind the dilemma and take stock of where we are. It is fair to say that affirming the awareness-feel is the dominant view (especially among those who endorse a fundamental approach to the problem of phenomenal consciousness). Coleman challenges this dominant view by stating that, although widely accepted, it is largely unsupported because proponents have yet to clearly identify the awareness-feel. Coleman reasons that, given that nobody seems to be able to pinpoint the awareness-feel, it is strange to maintain that there is such a thing. . The burden of proof, therefore, falls on the proponent to identify the awareness-feel. Moreover, he points out that it is strange to suggest that panqualityists are somehow in a conceptual deficit because they deny the existence of something the character of which nobody seems able to confirm. From here, Coleman presents his awareness-feel dilemma, which is supposed to show that any attempt to identify the awareness-feel will lead to a dead-end. The result, in Coleman's view, is that there is no awareness-feel and therefore, panqualityism does not face the panqualityist zombie problem (note that the barrier to suggesting that HOTs generate awareness of first-order qualities was the purported existence of an awareness-feel).

This chapter's detailed examination shows that the dilemma is not a severe concern for the awareness-feel proponent because they can find a way through. The horns of the dilemma do not represent dead ends for the proponent. I have suggested one possible account of the awareness-feel that is open to the proponent (although many others will no doubt also be open to them), the suggestion being that the awareness-feel is synonymous with the phenomenological contribution of a conscious perspective to experience. The result, if what I have said holds up to scrutiny, is twofold; first, we have shown that the panpsychist can plausibly pass through the awareness-feel dilemma untroubled, by, for example, following the suggestion just outlined. Second, given that the panpsychist can pass through the awareness-feel dilemma, the panqualityist faces the panqualityist zombie problem.

3.5.4 A quandary for panqualityism

Let us take a moment to speculate on a potential quandary for panqualityism that arises if perspectives contribute phenomenology to experience. Consider these likely commitments of the panqualityist:

1. Macro-perspectives exist.
2. Micro-perspectives do not exist.
3. Macro-perspectives are nothing more than the awareness of qualities.
4. HOTs suitably account for the awareness of qualities.

It is hard to maintain these commitments if one must admit that it feels like something to be a conscious perspective. Taking one commitment at a time, I will explain why the panqualityists should affirm it, before showing why it is hard for them to do so. The panqualityist will want to maintain (1) because its truth is immediately and pervasively apparent in our first-person experience. While (2) must be accepted because of the rejection of subjects at the micro-level. Subjects and perspectives can be considered synonymous for present purposes, so if subjects are absent from the micro-level, then perspectives are as well. They will hold (3) because macro-perspectives are supposed to be nothing over and above the awareness of qualities (since subjects are nothing over and above the awareness of qualities). This commitment implies that there is no awareness-feel. If this commitment is not upheld, they face the panqualityist zombie objection (because it would be difficult to reductively explain the added phenomenology in virtue of a HOT generating awareness). Instead, the panqualityist will likely maintain (4) that HOTs adequately generate the required awareness.

The problem is that if perspectives are associated with an awareness-feel, then (3) and (4) are false. If (3) and (4) are false, then to hold to panqualityism, the panqualityist needs another way to account for macro-perspectives in the absence of micro-perspectives. Remember that the conjunction of (1) and (2) is more or less what defines panqualityism (i.e. the view that there are macro but not micro-level subjects); to hold to panqualityism means to hold to (1) and (2). The problem is that if perspectives are associated with an awareness-feel, we have novel phenomenology entering the picture at the macro-level. Thus, we have the emergence of perspectives from the aperspectival. Moreover, it would appear that this would be a case of strong emergence because there can be no hint of perspectives at the micro-level without returning us to a distinctly panpsychist position (which the panqualityist will want to avoid).

In summary, if perspectives account for the awareness-feel, then panqualityism may face a version of the problem of strong emergence: the problem of accounting for (novel phenomenology-bearing) perspectives from an utterly aperspectival base. An alternative would be to reject panqualityism in favour of panpsychism.

3.5.5 The unhappy compromise objection to panqualityism

In response to what I have said, the panqualityist will likely be steadfast in rejecting an awareness-feel and will double down on their view that there is nothing in experience besides first-order phenomenal qualities that cannot be functionalized by HOTs. In this case, we will be left with a battle of intuitions, where arguably what counts is which account has enough intuitive force to convince. Let us finish our exploration of panqualityism by looking at the relevant battle of intuitions.

Consider HOT theorists who suggest that phenomenal consciousness can be given a purely functional explanation, on the one hand, and panpsychists who suggest that it is a fundamental feature of reality, evading functional explanation, on the other. Panqualityism is supposed to be a happy compromise between the two, evading the repercussions of locating phenomenal consciousness (in particular, its subjectival dimension) at the fundamental level while resisting the counterintuitive claim that it is nothing over and above a mere functional state. A possible objection to the panqualityist project says that this is an unhappy compromise because it is not clear who it is supposed to convince (or, indeed, who it has the power to convince). Panpsychists are unlikely to be convinced because it arguably amounts to giving up a central intuition underpinning their panpsychist thinking: that phenomenal consciousness necessarily involves phenomenal properties instantiated by a subject. Meanwhile, HOT theorists are likewise unlikely to be convinced because it arguably amounts to giving up their central intuition that consciousness, in its entirety, can be functionalized. HOT theorists will likely be unhappy to admit a component of phenomenal consciousness fundamental status. At the same time, panpsychists will likely be unhappy to revoke the fundamental status of a component of phenomenal consciousness.

Considering that this may be a battle of intuitions, where what counts is if one's intuitions are either already accepted or forceful enough to convince, Coleman's panqualityism is in a bind. There is little doubt that the panpsychist intuition – that phenomenal consciousness consists of subjects instantiating phenomenal properties – is more widely accepted than Coleman's intuition that phenomenal qualities (i.e. the felt qualities that characterize conscious experience) can exist without subjects. Moreover, given the unhappy compromise just outlined, I see little chance of panqualityism convincing either HOT theorists or panpsychists of the forcefulness of this intuition.

3.5.6 Panqualityism vs panpsychism, cosmopsychism and perennialism

How fruitful is panqualityism as an approach to the problem of phenomenal consciousness, compared to panpsychism, cosmopsychism and perennialism? As we said at the start of this section, panqualityism seems hopeful initially because it avoids the subject combination and derivation problems associated with panpsychism and cosmopsychism, respectively. Like perennialism, it correctly pinpoints the origin of those problems as their stipulation that phenomenality on the fundamental level of reality is subject-involving. And, again like perennialism, panqualityism evades these problems by doing away with subjects on the fundamental level. However, for panqualityism, this amounts to doing away with subjects of experience at the microphysical level rather than the cosmic level. Both panqualityism and perennialism are built on the rejection of the intuitive idea and touted conceptual truth that consciousness necessarily involves a subject instantiating phenomenal properties. Motivating the rejection of this apparent conceptual truth is thus key to panqualityism's success, in much the same way that motivating the plausibility of the non-dual ground is key for perennialism. I hope to have shown that the motivation on offer is weak because the proposed dilemma is not a choice between two dead ends. Moreover, it seems to me that panqualityists are in a quandary over what position to take on the existence of conscious perspectives, that is, if conscious perspectives are synonymous with an awareness-feel. Everything considered, panqualityism does not seem to be a more fruitful or plausible approach to the problem of phenomenal consciousness than panpsychism.

3.6 Conclusion

This chapter aimed to explore the viability of two interesting approaches to the problem of phenomenal consciousness that share a similar starting point. Both perennialism and panqualityism seek to overcome the subject problems of cosmopsychism and panpsychism, respectively, by rejecting the problematic stipulation that phenomenality at the fundamental level is subject-involving. Although this move appears to evade the target problems, I have shown that in both cases, doing so gives rise to additional problems. Furthermore, the additional problems are arguably equal to the very problem(s) (in kind and scale) that motivate the move to panpsychism (and, by transition, to cosmopsychism) in the first place. I, therefore, conclude that, as it stands, perennialism and panqualityism should not be considered successors to cosmopsychism and panpsychism. Focus should instead be retrained on the subject problems for panpsychism and cosmopsychism for the best chances of making progress. It is to this task that we now turn in the next chapter.

References

Albahari, M. (2019). 'Perennial idealism: A mystical solution to the mind-body problem'. *Philosophers Imprint*, 19(44), 1–37.

Albahari, M. (2020). 'Beyond cosmopsychism and the great I am: How the world might be grounded in universal Advaitic consciousness'. In W. Seager (Ed.), *The Routledge handbook of panpsychism* (pp. 385–406). New York: Routledge.

Alter, T., & Nagasawa, Y. (2012). 'What is Russellian monism?' *Journal of Consciousness Studies*, 19(9–10), 67–95.

Alter, T., & Nagasawa, Y. (Eds.) (2015). *Consciousness in the physical world*. New York: Oxford University Press.

Brüntrup, G. (2017). 'Emergent panpsychism'. In G. Brüntrup & L. Jaskolla (Eds.), *Panpsychism: Contemporary perspectives* (pp. 48–72). New York: Oxford University Press.

Chalmers, D. J. (2003). 'Consciousness and its place in nature'. In S. Stich & T. Warfield (Eds.), *The Blackwell guide to the philosophy of mind* (pp. 102–42). Oxford: Blackwell.

Chalmers, D. J. (2006). 'Strong and weak emergence'. In P. Clayton & P. Davies (Eds.), *The re-emergence of emergence: The emergentist hypothesis from science to religion* (pp. 244–54). New York: Oxford University Press.

Chalmers, D. J. (2010). 'Consciousness and its place in nature'. In *The character of consciousness* (pp. 103–42). New York: Oxford University Press.

Chalmers, D. J. (2017a). 'The combination problem for panpsychism'. In G. Brüntrup & L. Jaskolla (Eds.), *Panpsychism: Contemporary perspectives* (pp. 179–214). New York: Oxford University Press.

Chalmers, D. J. (2017b). 'Panpsychism and panprotopsychism'. In G. Brüntrup & L. Jaskolla (Eds.), *Panpsychism: Contemporary perspectives* (pp. 19–47). New York: Oxford University Press.

Chalmers, D. J. (2020). 'Idealism and the mind-body problem'. In W. Seager (Ed.), *The Routledge handbook of panpsychism* (pp. 387–406). New York: Routledge.

Coleman, S. (2012). 'Mental chemistry: Combination for panpsychists'. *Dialectica*, 66(1), 137–66.

Coleman, S. (2014). 'The real combination problem: Panpsychism, micro-subjects, and emergence'. *Erkenntnis*, 79(1), 19–44.

Coleman, S. (2017). 'Panpsychism and neutral monism'. In G. Brüntrup & L. Jaskolla (Eds.), *Panpsychism: Contemporary perspectives* (pp. 101–22). New York: Oxford University Press.

Eccles, J. C., & Popper, K. (1977). *The self and its brain: An argument for interactionism*. Abingdon: Routledge.

Fine, K. (2012). 'Guide to ground'. In F. Correia & B. Schnieder (Eds.), *Metaphysical grounding: Understanding the structure of reality* (pp. 37–80). Cambridge: Cambridge University Press.

Foster, J. (1991). *The immaterial self: A defence of the Cartesian dualist conception of the mind*. London: Routledge.

Goff, P. (2017). *Consciousness and fundamental reality*. New York: Oxford University Press.

Goff, P. (2020). 'Cosmopsychism, micropsychism and the grounding relation'. In W. Seager (Ed.), *The Routledge handbook of panpsychism* (pp. 369–84). Oxford: Routledge.

James, W. (1909). *A pluralistic universe*. Cambridge, MA: Harvard University Press.

Kastrup, B. (2018). 'The universe in consciousness'. *Journal of Consciousness Studies*, 25 (5–6), 125–55.

Lewis, D. (1986). *On the plurality of worlds*. Oxford: Blackwell.
Lockwood, M. (1989). *Mind, brain and the quantum: The compound 'I'*. Oxford: Blackwell.
Mathews, F. (2011). 'Panpsychism as paradigm'. In M. Blamauer (Ed.), *The mental as fundamental* (pp. 141–66). Frankfurt Heusenstamm: Ontos Verlag.
Mihálik, J. (2022). 'Panqualityism, awareness, and the explanatory gap'. *Erkenntnis*, 87(3), 1423–45.
Montero, B. (2010). 'A Russellian response to the structural argument against physicalism'. *Journal of Consciousness Studies*, 17(3–4), 70–83.
Mørch, H. H. (2014). *Panpsychism and causation: A new argument and a solution to the combination problem* (PhD thesis, University of Oslo).
Mørch, H. H. (2019). 'Is consciousness intrinsic? A problem for the integrated information theory'. *Journal of Consciousness Studies*, 26(1–2), 133–62.
Nagasawa, Y., & Wager, K. (2016). 'Panpsychism and priority cosmopsychism'. In G. Brüntrup & L. Jaskolla (Eds.), *Panpsychism: Contemporary perspectives* (pp. 113–29). New York: Oxford University Press.
Nagasawa, Y., & Wager, K. (2017). 'Panpsychism and priority cosmopsychism'. In G. Brüntrup & L. Jaskolla (Eds.), *Panpsychism: Contemporary perspectives* (pp. 113–29). New York: Oxford University Press.
Nagel, T. (1979). 'Panpsychism'. In T. Nagel, *Mortal questions* (pp. 181–95). New York: Cambridge University Press.
Rosen, G. (2010). 'Metaphysical dependence: Grounding and reduction'. In B. Hale & A. Hoffmann (Eds.), *Modality: Metaphysics, logic, and epistemology* (pp. 109–36). New York: Oxford University Press.
Rosenberg, G. (2004). *A place for consciousness*. New York: Oxford University Press.
Rosenthal, D. (1993). 'Thinking that one thinks'. In M. Davies & G. W. Humphreys (Eds.), *Readings in mind and language, vol. 2. Consciousness: Psychological and philosophical essays* (pp. 197–223). Oxford: Blackwell.
Rosenthal, D. (2005). *Consciousness and mind*. Oxford: Oxford University Press.
Russell, B. (1928). *The analysis of matter*. London: Kegan Paul.
Seager, W. (2010). 'Panpsychism, aggregation and combinatorial infusion'. *Mind and Matter*, 8(2), 167–84.
Seager, W. (2017). 'Panpsychist infusion'. In G. Brüntrup & L. Jaskolla (Eds.), *Panpsychism: Contemporary perspectives* (pp. 229–48). New York: Oxford University Press.
Shani, I. (2015). 'Cosmopsychism: A holistic approach to the metaphysics of experience'. *Philosophical Papers*, 44(3), 389–437.
Shani, I. (2022). 'Eden Benumbed: A Critique of panqualityism and the disclosure view of consciousness'. *Philosophia*, 50 (1),233–56.
Stoljar, D. (2001). 'Two conceptions of the physical'. *Philosophy and Phenomenological Research*, 62(2), 253–81.
Strawson, G. (2006). 'Realistic monism: Why physicalism entails panpsychism'. *Journal of Consciousness Studies*, 13(10–11), 3–31.
Strawson, G. (2008). *Real materialism and other essays*. New York: Oxford University Press.
Wager, K. (2011). *Dual-aspect priority monism and the combination problem for panpsychism* (PhD thesis, University of Birmingham).
Wager, K. (2020). *Panpsychism and cosmopsychism* (PhD thesis, University of Birmingham).

4

The subject problem for panpsychism and cosmopsychism

4.1 Introduction

As we have already seen, recent years have brought a groundswell of interest in novel approaches to the problem of phenomenal consciousness.[1] Let us recap. One such approach is panpsychism, which takes phenomenal consciousness as a fundamental and ubiquitous feature of the universe. Panpsychism, however, has an Achilles' heel in the form of the combination problem. A typical formulation of panpsychism, called constitutive panpsychism, takes it that the microphysical ultimates of the universe are themselves conscious and that human consciousness is constituted by consciousness at the microphysical level. Hence, the combination problem arises due to the need to explain how micro-level consciousness combines to constitute human-level consciousness. Cosmopsychism is an alternative view which avoids the combination problem by turning panpsychism on its head.[2] Like panpsychism, cosmopsychism says that human consciousness is dependent on a more fundamental form of consciousness, but while panpsychism claims this is found at the micro-level, cosmopsychism claims it is to be found at the level of the cosmos. Rather than maintaining that human consciousness is formed of combinations of micro-level consciousness, cosmopsychism claims they are derived from a larger, cosmic consciousness. This does, however, give rise to a parallel problem – the derivation problem. Arguably, the most promising version of cosmopsychism is constitutive cosmopsychism, which states that derivative macro-consciousness is constituted by fundamental consciousness, like constitutive panpsychism. However, in this case, the basic form of consciousness is the cosmic consciousness.

[1] At least in the sense that they are novel to the contemporary debates about phenomenal consciousness.

[2] Again, a simple formulation of cosmopsychism, called priority cosmopsychism, proposed by Nagasawa & I (2017) states that the cosmos as a whole instantiates fundamental consciousness. Arguably the most promising version of cosmopsychism is one that adds to this simple blueprint the claim that the cosmos, as a whole, is the one and only fundamental physical entity, as well as the one and only fundamental form of consciousness (Goff, 2017b, 2020; Nagasawa & Wager, 2017; Shani, 2015; Wager, 2011).

The combination problem for constitutive panpsychism can be understood as having three relatively distinct, although overlapping, aspects relating to the combination of phenomenal qualities, structure and subjects. It is generally accepted that the most challenging aspect is the subject combination problem. Likewise, the derivation problem can be understood as having the same three aspects, and similarly, the *subject* derivation problem is considered the most troubling.

Constitutive cosmopsychism is considered a promising alternative to constitutive panpsychism because it does not face the combination problem. It, therefore, stands to reason that if it is to be a viable alternative, it must deal with its subject derivation problem better than panpsychism can deal with its subject combination problem (or at least not be any worse off in this regard). In this chapter, I argue that the two problems are almost identical because they both hinge on inconsistencies in what I call synchronous perspectives scenarios. For both constitutive panpsychism and cosmopsychism, the most troubling inconsistency highlighted in the literature is the purported metaphysical impossibility of synchronous perspective scenarios. I situate these inconsistencies in *metaphysical impossibility arguments* against the respective views before offering alternative *epistemic implausibility arguments* that highlight an inconsistency between synchronous perspectives scenarios and our everyday first-person experience. I then propose a model for positing synchronous perspectives scenarios unproblematically. Notably, the model is available to both constitutive panpsychism *and* constitutive cosmopsychism. In addition, I consider some alternative responses. I conclude that if there is to be a clear advantage for either view over the other, then it is not to be found by comparing their subject problems. However, far from leaving these views where we found them, this chapter motivates both simultaneously by revealing that their subject problems are, in fact, one and the same, and by offering a unified way of addressing them.

Before proceeding to the main body of the chapter, it will be beneficial to cover some relevant preliminaries. Some of these points have already been covered, but it will be helpful to refresh our memories.

4.1.1 Combination and derivation problems

This chapter revolves around just one aspect of the combination and derivation problems, the subject aspect, so it will be helpful to distinguish the different combination problems and their derivation equivalents. It is now widely accepted that the combination problem for panpsychism is a catch-all term for a family of closely related (and possibly overlapping) problems. Following David Chalmers (2017), we can say that there are three core aspects or sub-problems: the quality combination problem, the structure combination problem and the subject combination problem.

The quality combination problem is the problem of explaining how micro-qualities can combine to form macro-qualities. The qualities being referred to are phenomenal qualities such as the quality of redness, which is the quality that characterizes what it feels like to see red, or the quality of pain, which is the quality that characterizes what it feels like to be in pain. The question in need of an answer is: how is it that small instances of qualities, or proto-qualities, combine into full-blown redness or even a complex of full-blown qualities? Chalmers notes that a particularly difficult aspect of this problem is *the palette problem*, which is the problem of accounting for the vast array of macro-qualities (that we are acquainted with in our experience) in terms of a presumably very small number of micro-qualities. There are a limited number of fundamental particles, so we should presumably expect an equally limited number of micro-qualities to match.

Another of the problems is *the structure combination problem*. The problem is that panpsychists must account for how micro-experiential structure (together with microphysical structure) can combine to form macro-experiential structure. Experience at the micro-level just does not seem to be capable of being structured in the same way that our macro-experience is; our macro-experience is rich, including complex visual and auditory structure, and it is not clear how this can be the result of micro-experience combining. A particularly challenging aspect of this problem is what Chalmers calls *the structural mismatch problem*. This is the problem of addressing the apparent mismatch between the macrophysical structure of our brains and the macro-phenomenal structure of our experience. While the claim that there is a close correspondence between physical and experiential structure at the micro level (because tiny distinct microphysical ultimates correspond with tiny distinct fragments of phenomenal structure) seems plausible, it appears rather less plausible that the macro-physical structure of our brains (an aggregate of microphysical ultimates and their corresponding distinct fragments of phenomenal structure) closely corresponds to the macro-phenomenal structure in our experience (which is smooth and continuous).

The subject combination problem is the problem of explaining how micro-subjects combine to constitute macro-subjects. The most challenging aspect here is *the subject summing problem*. This is the problem of accounting for the apparent lack of metaphysical dependence from micro-subjects to macro-subjects. It does not seem like any combination of the micro-subjects necessitates a further macro-subject.[3]

For each of the above combination problems for panpsychism, there are similar derivation problems for cosmopsychism. *The quality derivation problem* is the challenge of deriving macro-qualities from quality at the cosmic level. *The structure derivation problem* is the challenge of deriving macro-structure from cosmic-level structure. Finally, *the subject derivation problem* is the problem of how to derive macro-subjects from the cosmic subject. This chapter focuses on the subject derivation problem and, more specifically, an aspect that I call *the synchronous perspectives problem*. The problem emerges when perspectives are said to exist synchronously on different levels of reality, with perspectives on one level of reality subsuming those at lower levels. As we will see, positing perspective-subsuming perspectives in this way can motivate claims of metaphysical impossibility and epistemic implausibility.

[3] Additionally, there are problems that relate to, but that perhaps do not fit neatly into, the above, for example, the grain, unity and boundary problems. However, the focus of this chapter is the subject combination problem.

4.1.2 Subjects and perspectives

A crucial postulate underpinning much of the material covered in this chapter is that subjects of experience are inherently perspectival. That is to say, subjects are integrally the bearers of a unique conscious point of view. It is typically accepted as a conceptual truth that to be a subject of experience at all is to have a subjective perspective. The notion that subjects of experience are inherently perspective-bearing is endorsed by, for example, Chalmers (2017), Coleman (2012, 2014), Goff (2017a, 2017b, 2020), Shani (2015), Albahari (2020) and Matthews (2011). We can get a good feel for what is being referred to when we talk of perspectives by considering the following passage from Sam Coleman (2012):

> Consider a cluster of experiences, proprioceptive, emotional, cognitive-phenomenal and perceptual, that are together associated in a single phenomenal perspective. What it means to say that these experiences together constitute this one phenomenal perspective, and not any other, can be captured by thinking about an act of introspection performed from within that phenomenal perspective. Such an act of introspection will disclose just the aforementioned experiences and no others, it will not disclose the set of experiences that belongs to any other conscious mind. Intuitively, phenomenal perspectives – minds, subjects – include at a time a discrete set of phenomenally conscious elements, to which an introspective act on the part of one such phenomenal perspective has access. These spheres of experience, each one bound up by the reach of its particular potential introspective access, are by their fundamental nature closed off from one another. For if there is a question over whether a certain experiential element is part of your mind or part of mine, the question is to be settled by which of our minds has (or could have) introspective access to that element. Whichever way the matter falls, we will have two distinct phenomenal perspectives here and not one.
>
> (p. 145)

Meanwhile, Itay Shani (2015) describes phenomenal perspectives like this:

> Each perspective can be thought of as an opening to the world from a given point of origin and, as shown above, it is the form, or shape, of that opening – the dynamic configuration giving it structure – which defines how things are viewed from this particular point of origin. Thus, we can think of a perspective as an angle whose conscious point of origin is its vertex and whose form is limited by the rays emanating from that vertex.
>
> (p. 424)

Freya Mathews (2011) also highlights this unified, bounded and introspectively accessible aspect of subjects (though she does not explicitly contemplate perspectives):

> [A] subject, understood as a centre of subjectivity, is necessarily an indivisible unity: there are no scattered subjects, and the boundaries between subjects are

> not nominal. The individuation of subjects, or centres of subjectivity, is objectively determined: a thought objectively belongs to you or me; it is not up to a third person, qua knower, to decide where the boundaries of our respective subjectivities will be drawn.
>
> (p. 144)

A working definiton of a conscious perspective is that it is a spatially bounded and phenomenologically limited locus of experience, expressing a singular point of view on the world, being as such only accessible by introspection on the part of the perspective's holder. In this chapter, I proceed on the (largely) uncontroversial assumption that subjects of experience are inherently perspectival. It may turn out that there are compelling arguments against this, but none are currently apparent.

4.1.3 Levels of reality

Finally, before moving on, it is important to outline, again, some of the key terminology I will use. *Panpsychism* refers to constitutive panpsychism unless otherwise stated, and *Cosmopsychism* refers to constitutive cosmopsychism unless otherwise stated. Moreover, I take it that panpsychism affirms the existence of subjects at the micro-level and that cosmopsychism affirms the existence of a subject of experience at the cosmic level. Throughout the chapter (as I have been throughout the book so far, including in the previous sentence), I will frequently refer to entities at three 'levels' of reality: micro-level entities, macro-level entities and a cosmic-level entity. In addition, I also refer to entities at all levels below the cosmic level as sub-cosmic entities.

Micro-level: When I refer to the micro-level I am talking about the level of the microphysical, namely, the sub-atomic level. I mention not only microphysical entities but also micro-subjects, micro-perspectives and micro-qualities. Each of these relates to the same microphysical level of sub-atomic particles. For example, for panpsychists, the microphysical level is the ultimate level of reality, and each microphysical ultimate instantiates consciousness. Therefore, each one is also a micro-subject and instantiates micro-qualities. Whenever I refer to the 'micro' level, I refer to the 'smallest' level of reality: the microphysical and/or its respective micro-conscious aspects.

Macro-level: The macro-level is anything between the micro and the cosmic. For panpsychists, the microphysical level is fundamental, so we can talk of the microphysical *ultimates* from which all else is formed. In this case, anything composed of a combination of micro-level entities is a macro-level entity (until you reach the level of the cosmos as a whole).

Cosmic level: The cosmic-level entity is the cosmos as a whole. Sub-cosmic entities are any entity that sits below the level of the cosmos; this includes both micro- and macro-level entities. For cosmopsychists, the cosmos is the fundamental level of reality, so all micro- and macro-level entities are derived from the cosmic level.

4.2 The subject combination problem for panpsychism

In this section, I summarize some of the existing literature on the combination problem before, doing the same for the derivation problem in the subsequent section. I outline perhaps the first anticipation of the combination problem by William James (1895) in his *Principles of Psychology*, before covering three contemporary portrayals of the problem, offered by Philip Goff (2006), Sam Coleman (2012) and William Seager (2010). I then show one response to the problem offered by Goff (2017a).

4.2.1 James: Private minds remain private

One of the earliest anticipations of the subject combination problem is presented by William James in his 'Principles of Psychology' (1895). He writes:

> Where the elemental units are supposed to be feelings, the case is in no wise altered. Take a hundred of them, shuffle them and pack them as close together as you can (whatever that may mean); still each remains the same feeling it always was, shut in its own skin, windowless, ignorant of what the other feelings are and mean. There would be a hundred-and-first feeling there, if, when a group or series of such feelings were set up, a consciousness belonging to the group as such should emerge. And this 101st feeling would be a totally new fact; the 100 original feelings might, by a curious physical law, be a signal for its creation, when they came together; but they would have no substantial identity with it, nor it with them, and one could never deduce the one from the others, or (in any intelligible sense) say that they evolved it.
>
> Take a sentence of a dozen words, and take twelve men and tell to each one word. Then stand the men in a row or jam them in a bunch, and let each think of his word as intently as he will; nowhere will there be a consciousness of the whole sentence ... The private minds do not agglomerate into a higher compound mind.
>
> (1895, pp. 15–16)

The first passage illustrates James's contention that 'feelings', or minds, do not combine; he urges us to consider the fact that a group of minds grouped together always remain sealed off from one another, with no additional mind emerging as a result of any such grouping. The second paragraph illustrates the same sentiment by way of considering a grouping of people, each thinking of a different constituent word of a sentence, and the apparent lack of an emergent subject that has in its thoughts an entire sentence formed of the combination of each constituent word-thought. The takeaway message is that separate minds, in whatever manner they are arranged in relation to each other, always remain separate. Moreover, a compound mind cannot emerge from the combination of separate minds, since the compound mind would be irreducible to those minds from which it is said to have emerged.

4.2.2 Goff: Experiences do not aggregate

James's thinking has been turned into a convincing argument against constitutive panpsychism by Goff (2006); he says:

> Imagine that each of the ultimates in my brain feels slightly pained. It is unintelligible why the arrangement of these ultimates in my brain should give rise to some new subject of experience, over and above the billion slightly pained subjects of experience we already have. The emergence of novel macroexperiential properties from the coming together of microexperiential properties is as brute and miraculous as the emergence of experiential properties from non-experiential properties.
>
> (p. 54)

The basic idea is that for constitutive panpsychism to be true, the experiences of macro-subjects must be formed entirely of the experiences of micro-subjects, meaning a macro-subject's experience must include the experiences of micro-subjects. However, it is not clear that we can give an account of a combination that satisfies this, and without one, the emergence of macro-experience from micro-experience remains unintelligible.

To illustrate, Goff asks us to consider a composite macro-subject constituted by numerous micro-subjects. The experience of each of the constituent micro-subjects is that of being 'slightly pained', while the experience of the composite macro-subject is that of being 'severely pained'. The core argument is as follows:

1. For a macro-subject to be *intelligibly* constituted by a number of micro-subjects, the macro-subject's experience must include, as parts, the experience of the micro-subjects (or else it is unintelligible how the macro-subject's experience is constituted by a set of micro-subjects' experiences).
2. The micro-subjects' experience is all and only that of being slightly pained.
3. The macro-subject's experience is all and only that of being severely pained.
4. Therefore, the micro-subjects' experience is not present in the macro-subject's experience.
5. Therefore, the macro-subject cannot *intelligibly* be constituted by micro-subjects.
6. Therefore, constitutive panpsychism cannot account for macro-experience.

The argument above is essentially an argument against the intelligibility of macro-experience constituted by a combination of micro-experiences, on account of the experiences of micro-subjects being seemingly absent from the experience of the macro-subject. It does not go so far as to argue the metaphysical impossibility of subjects summing; it says only that the notion of macro-subjects constituted by micro-subjects remains unintelligible (but not impossible). Underpinning Goff's argument, it seems, is the assumption that the only viable way for x and y to constitute z is for z to be a mere aggregate of x and y. In other words, that aggregation is the only viable form of constitution.

The perspectival nature of subjects is crucial in understanding the motivation behind the first premise. If constitution means aggregation, then the idea that the numerous experiences of slight pain (instantiated by micro-subjects) can combine to constitute a singular instance of severe pain (instantiated by the macro-subject) becomes untenable when subjects are considered under their perspectival aspect. By taking the inherently perspectival nature of subjects into account, we can see more clearly why relying on 'summing', or mere aggregation, fails as an account of combination that allows Goff's scenario to obtain (i.e. a scenario where instances of slight pain accumulate into an instance of severe pain). What is missing on the combination-as-aggregation view is that the pained-ness of the subjects should not be understood as pained-ness *simpliciter*. Rather, pain is a phenomenal property instantiated by a subject. An aggregation of pain is conceivable if considered simply as a phenomenal quality, but this does not take into account the fact that, in Goff's scenario, the summing of instances of slight pained-ness is, at the same time, the summing of perspectives. It is subjects being the bearers of a perspective that gives them their marked boundedness, and it is this boundedness that gives rise to the core problem with Goff's scenario. It is not just that there are lots of little bits of pain that add up to a bigger pain, it is that there are lots of 'little' subjects experiencing mild pain that are supposed to add up to one 'big' subject experiencing severe pain. When we consider the perspectival aspect of subjects, we can see that, as Goff illustrates, their combination cannot be simply a case of aggregation, because a mere aggregation of perspectives is nothing more than a grouping of individually bounded perspectives.

Goff's claim is that it is not clear that there is any intelligible way in which micro-subjects can combine to constitute macro-subjects since the only intelligible form of constitution, he tells us, is aggregation. But again, this argument is not a strong argument against constitutive panpsychism because it concludes only that it is not easy to see how the constitution could occur. As we will see shortly, Coleman (2014) uses the inherently perspectival nature of subjects to highlight a metaphysical incoherence in the idea of combining subjects.[4] First, we look at Seager's (2010) claim, which aligns with Goff's, that combination is not aggregation.

4.2.3 Seager: Combination is not aggregation

Constitutive panpsychists might hold that macro-consciousness is formed of aggregations of micro-consciousness, where the aggregation functions like the aggregative property of mass. Consider the mass of a rock, for example, its total mass is straightforwardly an emergent property of the sum of the masses of all its massive parts. While I believe there are numerous problems with holding consciousness to be aggregative in this way, Seager (2010) draws attention to a prominent one, which is not dissimilar to Goff's objection. The problem with holding that consciousness is aggregative in the same way as mass, he says, is that it is not able to account for the apparent fact that complex parts, or sub-whole aggregations, will themselves be

4 We have, of course, already come into contact with this argument in the previous chapter.

conscious while at the same time contributing their consciousness to the overall state of the macro-consciousness.

He notes two problems that motivate this worry: *the intelligibility problem* and *the problem of the irrelevance of the totality*. The intelligibility problem is the general concern that the notion of conscious states aggregating appears unintelligible. Seager says:

> Consciousness cannot aggregate merely by the co-occurrence of some set of conscious states nominally taken to be 'parts' of a putative total and more complex conscious state. And while aggregation is not in general a function of mere co-occurrence (not even in the case of mass), it is not unfair to ask how precisely the aggregation of conscious states is supposed to occur.
>
> (2010, p. 177)

The problem of the irrelevance of the totality is the concern that, on the mass model, aggregative wholes do not offer an opportunity for the whole to be novel in any important sense. Yet, it seems like macro-subjects *are* novel in many respects. For example, macro-subjects, even if formed of aggregations of micro-subjects, must be novel singular subjects of experience. However, they are also said to be constituted by numerous micro-subjects, each of which maintain their own singular subjective experience. The subjective experience of the whole is not supposed to be a mere collection of micro-subjects' experiences; it is supposed to be a singular subjective experience of its own. It does not appear that subjects can aggregate in such a way as to allow the whole its own novel subjective experience. Seager explains the point like so:

> If we suppose that some massive body is an aggregate of massive parts, then if we know the positions and masses of the parts we know all there is to know about the mass of the totality. There is nothing novel, with respect to mass and its effects, possessed by the total system ... The mass of the totality and all of its effects are completely and fully determined, and exhausted by the masses of the parts and their joint effects. In general, with aggregative properties, the property of the whole is nothing but a reflection of the property as distributed through all the parts of the whole. The 'totality' is thus in a sense irrelevant.
>
> (2010, p. 177)

Neither Goff nor Seager explicitly argues that the idea of subjects combining is metaphysically impossible. Rather, they suggest that it appears unintelligible. For Seager, the unintelligibility of the aggregative model means that combination must be something other than aggregation. For Goff, if combination is not mere aggregation (and he agrees that it is not), then the constitution of macro-subjects of micro-subjects is doomed to unintelligibility.

4.2.4 Coleman: Perspectives cannot combine

While both Goff and Seager illustrate why combination for panpsychists cannot be mere aggregation, and conclude that it is hard to see how subjects *can* combine, Coleman thinks it is easy to see that they *cannot* combine. He holds that the combination of subjects is 'precluded by the metaphysical logic of points of view' (2014, p. 34). Coleman's claim, therefore, is much stronger than the others, as he argues that there is a metaphysical incoherence in the very notion of combining subjects. Coleman's target, like the others, is constitutive panpsychism, which, by definition, states that macro-subjects are constituted by the combination of micro-subjects of microphysical ultimates.

His argument is based on the idea that subjects are inherently perspectival. As stated previously, to possess a perspective is to possess a discrete, unified point of view. Each individual subject has a unique view of the world stage, isolated from the stage views of all other subjects: '[a] subject, then, can be thought of as a point of view annexed to a private qualitative field' (Coleman, 2014, p. 30). The incoherence in the notion of combining subjects resides in the incoherence of perspectives combining. Coleman purports to show that it is 'a demonstrably incoherent notion' (p. 29), thus ruling out constitutive panpsychism.

We have already seen Seager's concerns with aggregation as the mode of combination for panpsychism. Similarly, Coleman makes an important distinction between *mere aggregates* and *combinations* of entities. Mere aggregates of entities are assemblages that do not imply a necessary unity. A paradigm example is a heap of sand, where the proximity of grains does not imply a unified whole. In contrast, combinations are unions of entities that imply new wholes, which include, as constitutive parts, the combined entities. In combinations, the combined entities survive in the new whole, for they must do so for the whole to be constituted by them. A familiar example of a combination is ingredients combining into a cake. Combinations, in contrast to mere aggregates, have properties that are owing to their parts but which their parts do not themselves instantiate. For example, none of the cake's ingredients has the property of 'cake-ness', but their combination does. Cake-ness is not a problematically emergent property, however, since we can intelligibly trace its origin to a mixture of the ingredients' properties and interactions among them. Moreover, each initial ingredient survives the combination into the finished cake.

The aim, for Coleman, is to undermine constitutive panspychism by demonstrating that a metaphysical incoherence follows from a set of theses to which it is committed: (1) subjects are inherently perspectival, (2) combinations of micro-perspectives constitute macro-perspectives and (3) combination is understood in a non-aggregative way that unites the constituent perspectives such that a novel perspective intelligibly arises.

Coleman's contention is that it is impossible for perspectives to combine. He states that since constitutive panpsychists require that micro-perspectives survive the combination into a macro-perspective, it cannot be the case that, say, two micro-perspectives integrate into a single macro-perspective, as we would then have one perspective where we previously had two, and it is not possible for one macro-perspective to have two micro-perspectives as constituent parts if the two constituting perspectives no longer exist. Bear in mind that the constitutive relationship between micro-perspectives and macro-perspectives is synchronous; at any given moment, the macro-perspective is constituted by micro-perspectives.

Not only does this reasoning rule out the case of two micro-perspectives somehow integrating into a single macro-perspective, but it also rules out the case in which the macro-perspective inherits only one of the micro-perspectives of the two constituents, even if it inherited the phenomenal *contents* of both. This is because we would be left with one perspective purportedly constituted by two; hence, one would have disappeared and, thus, cannot partake in the constitution.

Coleman also says that we can rule out the possibility of both micro-perspectives surviving the combination into the new macro-perspective. Recall that what we want is a combination of perspectives, as opposed to a mere aggregation. So, it will not do that the macro-perspective is the aggregate of the two micro-perspectives side-by-side, so to speak, because such an aggregation would lack the required unity of a combination, and so would lack the generation of a new perspective subsuming the constituting perspectives.

Consider the possibility that the two micro-perspectives survive a combination into a macro-perspective that contains each of them as partial aspects of its new overall purview; this is the only option, given the above, that would genuinely see micro-perspectives constituting macro-perspectives. However, Coleman claims that this is not a possibility either. To understand why, he asks us to imagine two hypothetical micro-perspectives, Blue and Red (as you may recall from the previous chapter). Blue's perspective is exhausted by the experience of blue to the exclusion of all else. Red's is exhausted by the experience of red to the exclusion of all else. For a macro-subject to be constituted by the combination of Red and Blue, and for Red and Blue to survive as unitary perspectives, the composite macro-subject must contain, as partial aspects, both the experience of blue to the exclusion of all else *and* the experience of red to the exclusion of all else, at the same time. However, this represents an inconsistent set.

We can summarize Coleman's reasoning by isolating three possible post-combination scenarios and showing why each is problematic:

Scenario 1: Micro-perspectives exist, but a macro-perspective does not exist.
Scenario 2: A macro-perspective exists, but no micro-perspectives exist.
 2a: Both micro-perspectives cease to exist.
 2b: One of the micro-perspectives becomes the macro-perspective.
Scenario 3: Both micro-perspectives and a new macro-perspective exist.

Scenario 1 is problematic since the result is a mere aggregate. Scenario 2 will not do because the constitution relation fails to be the synchronous relation it needs to be; this is the case in both sub-scenarios 2a and 2b. Finally, Scenario 3 results in an inconsistent set of perspectives, so it is of no use. In a nutshell, Coleman's claim is that the instantiation of Scenario 3 is the only one that would involve a genuine constitutive combination. However, since it involves a metaphysically impossible conjunction of perspectives, we can say that it is impossible and that constitutive panpsychism is, therefore, false.

I am not convinced that Scenario 3 is metaphysically impossible, but we will return to this point in some detail later. Next, I briefly outline one proposed solution to the subject combination problem for panpsychism.

4.2.5 The phenomenal bonding solution

Goff (2017a) proposes a solution to the subject combination problem called the phenomenal bonding solution. The basic idea is that subject-combination from micro-level to macro-level subjects occurs in virtue of a specific kind of relation – the phenomenal bonding relation – that can hold between micro-subjects. When thinking in terms of aggregation, we are really only thinking in terms of spatio-temporal relations holding between micro-subjects, i.e. that a given group of micro-subjects are bunched closely together. As noted previously, this does not leave space for the required combination of subjects. However, the significance of the phenomenal bonding solution is that it tells us something is going on in addition to mere aggregation.

The idea is that bonding relations hold between micro-subjects and their mental states and, under at least some conditions, come to hold between those and other micro-subjects and/or their mental states, giving rise to macro-subjects. This raises some pressing questions: first, whether we can make sense of distinctly phenomenal relations, and second, how these relations play a vital role in allowing the micro-subjects to constitute a macro-subject.

Regarding the first question, Chalmers (2017) suggests the possibility of thinking of phenomenal bonding relations as the categorical bases of relational properties, just as Russellian monists hold that phenomenal properties underpin physical properties. Goff (2017a) says that it is not surprising that we do not have a grasp of the precise nature of the phenomenal bonding relation, because our physics deals with the relational nature of the world (by this, I mean how physical entities behave in response to one another) and not the categorical nature of those properties:

> [I]t is not surprising that we lack a transparent grasp of the phenomenal bonding relation – if such a thing there be – given the nature of our epistemic situation. Our most basic empirical science, physics, yields understanding only of the world's mathematico-causal structure, and the phenomenal bonding relation is not a mathematico-causal relation: conceiving of subjects standing in mathematico-causal relations does not remove their conceptual isolation, and hence does not remove their metaphysical isolation. Apart from its mathematico-causal structure, arguably the only feature of the world we transparently understand is consciousness. And consciousness is a monadic property. Our unfortunate epistemic situation does not afford us a transparent understanding of the (non-mathematico-causal) relations which conscious things bear to each other.
>
> (pp. 292–3)

If consciousness, as per Russellian monism, is the intrinsic or categorical nature of the physical world, and our current physics describes only its relational aspects, then phenomenal bonding relations would fall within what is hidden from our current science. In addition to this, he says the only access we have to this categorical nature is through introspection, so we cannot experience subjects as related because we only have introspective access to the subject that we are.

In response to the second question, regarding how phenomenal bonding relations help us to get from numerous micro-subjects to a new unitary macro-subject, Chalmers considers calling on the co-consciousness relation: 'A natural candidate here is the co-consciousness relation: a relation such that whenever it relates two phenomenal states, they are experienced jointly. When this relation holds among the states of distinct microsubjects, those states will be experienced jointly by a new subject' (2017, p. 200). However, he says that it is hard to find a microphysical relation with this kind of character, and given that the idea is that the phenomenal bonding relation will be the intrinsic nature of a microphysical relation, it seems we cannot find a home for the proposed phenomenal bonding relation(s). Addressing this worry, Goff writes:

> None of the relations that appear in perception or in physics are conceived of as phenomenal bonding relations. In the same way, the brain does not appear from the outside as a subject of experience, and the properties of physics or neuroscience are not conceived of in those sciences as phenomenal qualities. But just as the panpsychist might identify charge with a form of consciousness, so the proponent of phenomenal bonding might identify some empirically known relation as the phenomenal bonding relation.
>
> (2017a, p. 293)

Additionally, Chalmers highlights an outstanding problem with the proposal: the phenomenal bonding solution may go some way to explaining how combination is more than just an aggregation, but it still needs to give an account of the circumstances under which the bonding relation holds between micro-subjects such that it gives rise to a macro-subject, and in which cases it does not. Presumably, there will be both cases where micro-subject groupings do and do not constitute a new macro-subject. For example, we might think that micro-subjects associated with brains are cases where we see the phenomenal bonding relations at play, whereas in the cases of chairs and tables, we do not. As Chalmers says: 'To yield human consciousness, we presumably want phenomenal bonding to bond a limited multiplicity of microsubjects associated with the human organism, without bonding these to microsubjects elsewhere' (2017, p. 201).

Goff calls the above problem *the special phenomenal composition question*. He claims that the constitutive panpsychist has the following options: (1) maintain that all combinations of micro-subjects give rise to further macro-subjects (unrestricted phenomenal composition), (2) maintain that there is combination where there is an organism or (3) maintain that subjects never combine (nihilism).

Nihilism (3) is obviously a non-starter for the constitutive panpsychist, and Goff argues that (2) is vulnerable to issues when trying to give a semantic account of vagueness, so (1) is the natural candidate. This is quite counterintuitive, however, because it follows that there exists a macro-subject distinct from me, composed of a combination of the same token micro-subjects that constitute my macro-subjectivity, except that one micro-subject, corresponding to a single sub-atomic particle, is different. It does not seem like there are any (let alone many) near-identical macro-subjects constituted almost entirely by the same micro-subjects that constitute me. Additionally, it seems like we, as subjects of experience, have causal efficacy, but if that is the case why is the control of our whole body, for example, uniquely under the control of us as subjects rather than the almost identical subjects that are also supposed to exist? Furthermore, the phenomenal bonding solution still fails to account for the combination of perspectives. It is unclear whether the phenomenal bonding solution helps resolve Coleman's incoherence of combined *perspectives*.

What we have seen throughout this section is that the combination problem for panpsychism is very much a going concern. Since cosmopsychism is touted as a fruitful alternative to panpsychism, specifically in light of its ability to circumvent the combination problem, let us now explore how cosmopsychism deals with its equivalent subject problem.

4.3 The subject derivation problem for cosmopsychism

As we saw in the second chapter, the priority cosmopsychism blueprint proposes an alternative approach to the problem of phenomenal consciousness that turns panpsychism on its head. Instead of fundamental consciousness being exhibited at the micro-level, with macro-consciousness derivative of consciousness at the micro-level, the cosmopsychist blueprint proposes that fundamental consciousness is instantiated at the cosmic level, with macro-consciousness derivative of the cosmic consciousness. We have seen examples of how proponents and opponents of constitutive panpsychism address the subject aspect of the combination problem. Now, we will look closer at how proponents and opponents of constitutive cosmopsychism address the cosmopsychist equivalent to the subject combination problem: the subject derivation problem.

Recall that the broad derivation problem for cosmopsychism is the problem of explaining the derivation of macro-consciousness from the fundamental cosmic consciousness. The subject derivation problem is the aspect of the overall problem that pertains to the derivation of macro-level subjects from the cosmic subject. For constitutive cosmopsychism, the derivation involves constitution.[5]

This section takes a closer look at three cosmopsychist proposals. Each is broadly consistent with the priority cosmopsychism blueprint outlined in Chapter 2[6] and can be considered a development on it. Crucially, each addresses the subject derivation problem. I will briefly summarize each version of cosmopsychism, followed by a

[5] The derivation problem for cosmopsychism has been noted by others under various names; I have previously called it 'the decomposition problem' (Wager, 2011), as does Chalmers (2017); Mathews (2011) calls it 'the combination problem in reverse', while Albahari (2020), Goff (2017b) and Shani (2015) call it the 'decombination problem'. Here, I continue my earlier use (Nagasawa and Wager, 2017; Wager, 2020) in calling it 'the derivation problem' since it is the most general way to refer to the problem in question.

[6] Based on ideas from my earlier paper 'panpsychism and priority cosmopsychism' (2017) co-authored with Yujin Nagasawa.

cursory examination of how they approach the subject derivation problem. My aim is not to provide an in-depth analysis of the proposed or possible arguments against subject derivation at this point, but rather to outline existing work on the problem that will frame the subsequent discussion.

4.3.1 Goffian cosmopsychism

Goff (2017b, 2020) is a notable proponent of cosmopsychism. He proposes a version of cosmopsychism according to which the cosmos as a whole is the one and only fundamental entity and a subject of experience. We can see this as a view formed of the combination of panpsychism (in its simplest form) and priority monism. On this view, macro-subjects of experience are derived from the cosmic subject in virtue of being its partial aspects. Thus, the subject derivation problem is plain to see: how are macro-subjects of experience subsumed in the cosmic subject as its partial aspects? I call this aspect of the derivation problem *the problem of synchronous subjects*, but Goff refers to it as the problem of subject-subsuming subjects.

The problem of synchronous subjects – or the problem of subject-subsuming subjects – is tackled head-on. Goff says that while it is difficult to make sense of the idea of subjects which are themselves parts of further subjects, and indeed unimaginable to us, this does not mean that it is impossible. He highlights existing cases where things are unimaginable to us but where we nevertheless take them to be coherent: 'Certainly we cannot imagine such a thing by using our perceptual and/or introspective faculties. But nor can we imagine in this way a four-dimensional object, and we nonetheless take four-dimensional objects to be coherent' (2020, p. 151). The central message is that strangeness does not entail metaphysical impossibility. Furthermore, Goff suggests that our inability to positively conceive of synchronous subjects might be attributed to our lack of a complete understanding of subjects of experience. Thus, he appeals to a degree of epistemic ignorance to plug the gap between the kinds of synchronous subjects scenarios posited by cosmopsychism and our inability to conceive of them. Interestingly, Nagasawa and I (2017) have suggested appealing to epistemic ignorance to resolve similar gaps; only our suggestion was to appeal to ignorance about cosmic consciousness rather than consciousness in general (although this may amount to the same suggestion). As we will see in upcoming sections of the chapter, there *is* purportedly a metaphysical incoherence in the notion of synchronous subjects, which, if it stands up to scrutiny, undercuts Goff's response.

4.3.2 Cosmological panpsychism

Mathews (2011) offers a version of cosmopsychism – or, as she refers to it, a cosmological version of panpsychism – intended to rival materialism. For the purposes of this chapter, I will not focus on her arguments against materialism but will instead draw attention to her cosmopsychist proposal, her pre-emption of the derivation problem and her proposed solution.

On Mathews's proposal, 'the universe as a whole is the locus of mind' (2011, p. 141). For her, this means that the cosmos is the bearer of fundamental consciousness, which carries the added implication that the cosmos is a subject of experience. All matter in the universe, she says, is endowed with an exteriority, which is a physical dimension, and an interiority, which is a subjective dimension. Subjects are understood as necessarily indivisible, bounded centres of this subjectivity. In her own words:

> Subjective experience is, after all, the province of a subject. However, a subject, understood as a centre of subjectivity, is necessarily an indivisible unity: there are no scattered subjects, and the boundaries between subjects are not nominal. The individuation of subjects, or centres of subjectivity, is objectively determined: a thought objectively belongs to you or me; it is not up to a third person, qua knower, to decide where the boundaries of our respective subjectivities will be drawn.
>
> (2011, p. 144)

Mathews suggests that there is a need to reconcile the apparent fact of internally unified subjects with the observation that physical reality seems to exhibit, at best, only nominal unity. The best way to do this, she tells us, is to adopt a holistic, or cosmological, version of panpsychism. The core motivation for Mathews's cosmopsychism is that, taken at face value, there appears to be a jarring contrast between the unity of subjective experience and the disunity of the physical world. As such, it is not easy to see where consciousness fits into the physical world. Since we want to avoid offloading either the physical world or the unity of subjectivity, Mathews's project is to find a way to reconcile the two. She believes cosmopsychism is the answer: 'If physical reality as a whole, under both its material and non-material or field-like aspects, is seen as constituting a genuine, indivisible unity, then it could itself perhaps be regarded as a subject, or field of subjectivity, to which the entire differentiated physical manifold is subjectively present' (2011, p. 145).

The thinking is that if the cosmos as a whole is a unified subject, then we can say that the entire physical dimension is subjectively present to it at once, thereby reconciling the apparent disunity of the physical world with the unity of our subjective experience. However, this gives rise to the derivation problem. Or, as Mathews calls it, 'the individuation problem'. The picture she proposes is one in which the cosmos is a subject of experience to which the entire physical world is subjectively present; when we add the existence of sub-cosmic subjects, we appear in need of an answer to the question: how are unified sub-cosmic subjects differentiated from the overarching unity of the cosmic subject? Matthews explains the problem like so:

> [W]e face a *combination problem in reverse*: how are the entities, objects or beings we normally regard as distinct subjects to be individuated within such an all-encompassing holism? The problem is not, as it is for process philosophers, how are compound consciousnesses to be built up out of simple ones, but rather how can local, individual subjects come to differentiate themselves within the matrix of a global mind.
>
> (2011, p. 145)

Here, she makes the distinction between the combination problem for panpsychism, which is the problem of accounting for the combination of micro-subjects into macro-subjects, and the derivation problem for cosmopsychism, which is the problem of accounting for the derivation of sub-cosmic subjects from the cosmic subject. To answer the individuation problem, Mathews offers a more detailed sketch of her cosmological panpsychism. Her view posits a universe with an exterior physical aspect as well as an interior subjective aspect; its physical aspect forms an unbounded, indivisible and substantival plenum. About this plenum, she writes: '[T]he universe may be compared with a vast ocean coursed continually by currents and waves, some of which interfere to become vortices which hold their structure for long enough to give the appearance of independent or enduring existents' (2011, p. 146). The seemingly disunified objects of the physical world are, according to this view, enduring interference patterns in the vast indivisible 'ocean' that is the physical world. The way the plenum is structured strongly echoes the structure of priority monism (Schaffer, 2010), although Mathews does not reference it. The plenum is not structured in an aggregative manner but rather holistically, so we can perhaps infer that, just as with priority monism, the cosmos is not formed from a combination of parts; instead, the parts are derivative of the cosmos as a whole.

So far, we can see how Matthews proposes that objects derive from the universe as a whole (the plenum), but crucially, she must provide an account of the derivation of sub-cosmic subjects from the cosmic subject. Matthews refers to sub-cosmic subjects as *selves*. Selves, we are informed, are self-actualizing systems, 'defined, in systems-theoretic terms, as systems with a very special kind of goal, namely their own self-maintenance and self-perpetuation' (2011, p. 146). We can say, therefore, that all objects in the physical world are individuated within the whole as enduring interference patterns. In cases where such interference patterns constitute self-actualizing systems, they are also selves (sub-cosmic subjects). Selves are individuated within, yet embedded in, the indivisible whole. It may be worth pointing out that on Mathews's view, objects that are not selves are not considered truly things in their own right but rather just 'knotty bits of the matrix or plenum' (2011, p. 147).

This tells us how to differentiate between objects that are subjects of experience and those that are not when considering the universe from its external, physical aspect. But, considering the universe from its internal, subjectival aspect, there is also a crucial question of how macro-subjects are to be differentiated from the cosmic subject. The universe, considered from its subjectival aspect, is 'a field of subjectivity, a great, internally differentiated field of impulse, of intrinsic activity, of felt expansions, swellings, dwindlings, contractions, surges, urges and so forth' (2011, p. 147). This gives rise to a version of the synchronous subjects problem since we have an overarching cosmic subject that subsumes sub-cosmic subjects within it. It seems Mathews pre-empts the kind of perspectival issues highlighted by Coleman and Shani (more on Shani to follow): how can macro-perspectives be embedded within the cosmic perspective but also assert their relative independence? Or, to put it another way, how is it possible for macro-perspectives to avoid being absorbed into the cosmic perspective while remaining rooted in it? This is how Mathews presents the problem:

> If this is how the global field of subjectivity may be imagined from within, from the viewpoint of the One as Subject, the question of how finite selves embedded in

> this larger Subject may be imagined from within remains to be considered. How can relatively distinct subjectivities, the subjectivities belonging to the differentia we have identified externally as self-realizing systems in the geometrodynamic matrix, form within the field of a larger consciousness? How do such subjects manage not to be absorbed, experientially, into the larger field, and how does the larger Subject, of which they are a part yet from which they also differentiate themselves, experience them?
>
> (2011, p. 148)

Her solution is to call upon ideas from the psychoanalytic tradition. She proposes that just as the mental life of human beings is said to contain both conscious and unconscious aspects, so too does the mental life of the universe. She invokes Jung's (1960) notion of *autonomous complexes* to provide a model of how macro-subjects can be embedded in the cosmic subject. Autonomous complexes are parts of a person's psyche that have become annexed off from the rest and lead a life of their own, unaware of the fact that they are but parts of a greater psyche. Mathews suggests that this model illustrates how relatively distinct centres of subjectivity (macro-subjects) come to exist within the cosmic subject, without generating the problems associated with synchronous subjects. According to Jung, an autonomous complex-involving psyche is not aware of the existence of the autonomous complex despite its presence being felt. Moreover, the autonomous complex is not aware of its relation to the psyche which harbours it. Mathews explains this idea as follows: 'One as Subject may feel the effects of finite centres of subjectivity in the field of its own larger subjectivity, even though it may not be able actually to experience the way such finite selves feel to themselves' (2011, p. 149). The autonomous complex model offers a way for macro-subjects (and their perspectival natures) to exist within the cosmic subject (and its perspective) while remaining invisible to it, thereby avoiding concerns around their experiential absorption into the cosmic whole.

One notable problem with this view is that it does not seem to be able to satisfy the free lunch constraint on derivative entities. The constraint says that any non-fundamental entities should come at no additional ontological cost once the fundamental entities have been accounted for. We should be able to intelligibly explain all derivative entities in virtue of the fundamental entities; however, in the case of cosmological panpsychism, it is not obvious that derivative selves can be intelligibly explained in virtue of the cosmic subject. It may be that Mathews can elaborate on her view to demonstrate the intelligibility (and she makes it clear that her view is not fully worked out), but as it stands, it does appear to face a challenge in this respect.

4.3.3 Shanian cosmopsychism

Shani's view is in many respects like Mathews's cosmological panpsychism, with the key differences relating to how the proposal is presented and the finer details of its response to the subject derivation problem. Shani demonstrates a rich and systematic approach to presenting his view and addressing its challenges. According to his account of cosmopsychism, the cosmos as a whole is the one and only fundamental entity (he calls this the *absolute*). The absolute operates according to what he calls a *lateral duality principle*, having a dual nature with both a revealed and a concealed form. The revealed form equates to the world as revealed by physics, while its concealed form is a cosmic field of consciousness; he calls this an *endo-phenomenological expanse*. Macro-subjects (called *created subjects* in Shani's system) are derivative of the absolute's fundamental subjectivity, and thus the subject derivation problem arises. Shani provides what I take to be the most powerful argument against cosmopsychism, together with the most nuanced way of averting it. I will first present his argument against cosmopsychism and then very briefly summarize his response (I say 'very briefly' because I will return to it in more detail later in the chapter).

The stipulation that subjects of experience are inherently perspectival is central to Shani's argument against cosmopsychism. Recall how he describes perspectives:

> Each perspective can be thought of as an opening to the world from a given point of origin and, as shown above, it is the form, or shape, of that opening – the dynamic configuration giving it structure – which defines how things are viewed from this particular point of origin. Thus, we can think of a perspective as an angle whose conscious point of origin is its vertex and whose form is limited by the rays emanating from that vertex.
>
> (2015, p. 424)

With this understanding of perspectives in place, he claims a contradiction is plain to see, at least for panpsychism, which says combinations of micro-perspectives constitute macro-perspectives. Consider the view from a macro-perspective, *P*, with micro-perspective parts, *Q* and *R*. *P* transcends the boundaries of the views of either *Q* or *R* considered alone. That *P*'s perspective transcends *Q*'s, he suggests, presupposes the elimination of *Q*'s limitations, i.e. the elimination of the very perspective that is *Q*. The contradiction comes about because *Q* must exist in order to partially constitute *P*, but must also not exist in order that its existence does not preclude the possibility of an overarching perspective. This argument cuts against constitutive panpsychism and is just Coleman's (2014) argument against synchronous perspectives reframed.

Shani stretches the reach of the above reasoning even further. The problem is not just that micro-perspectives cannot by way of combination constitute macro-perspectives, but, moreover, that there can be no sense in which perspectives can stand in compositional relations with other perspectives *simpliciter*. This, if correct, would not only cut against constitutive panpsychism but also against any picture on which there are synchronous perspectives (perspectives that contain, as partial aspects, other perspectives). Continuing his comparison of perspectives to angles, he says:

> Now, if the perspective is to have parts each proper part must correspond to a division of the original angle brought about by the introduction of a ray on the interior of that angle (there is no other way to dissect an angle). Let us, then, think of P as our original perspective and of Q as a division within P … But now

> we are facing the problem just mentioned, for it follows from the simultaneous existence of P and Q that in viewing things from viewpoint P, which opens up the entire original angle, one also views things from viewpoint Q, which excludes the complement P-Q from sight. The result, as before, is a contradiction.
>
> (2015, pp. 424–5)

The result, according to Shani, is not just that the contradiction precludes the combination of subjects, but, moreover, '[i]f this analysis is sound, it precludes the existence of strict compositional relations between non-identical perspectives' (2015, p. 425). Thus, the problem stretches its reach to cosmopsychism just as much as panpsychism. This goes to say that wherever there are synchronous perspectives – perspectives within perspectives – we have entered the realm of metaphysical impossibility. According to cosmopsychism, macro-perspectives are partial aspects of a larger cosmic perspective, so the metaphysical impossibility of compositional relations among perspectives will rule out cosmopsychism as fast as it rules out panpsychism.

Let us unpack the difficulty for cosmopsychism a little. Cosmopsychism says the cosmos itself is a subject of experience, and given that inherent to being a subject of experience is having a perspective, a point of view, the cosmos must also have a perspective. Moreover, the cosmic perspective is the fundamental perspective from which all sub-cosmic perspectives are derived. Sub-cosmic perspectives are derived from the cosmic perspective as its partial aspects. The view from the cosmic perspective will be a view containing, as partial aspects, a multitude of sub-cosmic perspectives. It will be a variegated perspective fragmented by partitions corresponding to the boundaries of sub-cosmic perspectives. It is now clear to see why the apparent incoherence of synchronous perspectives will equally apply to cosmopsychism and panpsychism. For panpsychism, macro-perspectives are constituted by micro-perspectives, so the point of view of macro-perspectives will contain, as partial aspects, the views of various boundaried micro-perspectives. For cosmopsychism, the cosmic perspective grounds sub-cosmic (e.g. macro) perspectives as its partial aspects, so it will also contain the views of various boundaried macro-perspectives.

In both cases, the concern resides in the boundedness of the narrower perspectives existing as partial aspects of the broader perspective. Just as I was unconvinced by Coleman's argument against panpsychism, I am doubtful that what Shani's scenario demonstrates is metaphysical impossibility. Clearly, the scenario contains a logical incoherence of the form 'P&-P', but this may be an incoherence purely as a matter of logic (i.e. it may not entail metaphysical impossibility). What I mean is that, when formalized, a given state of affairs can be presented as contradiction-involving even if the apparent contradiction is merely the result of either a poor translation of the phenomena into logical terms or a poor understanding of the phenomena being translated. By way of an illustration, consider quantum superposition. An electron in superposition is in both a spin-up and spin-down state before it is measured. It is possible to present this formally as contradiction-involving, if understood through a common-sense lens according to which it is impossible for one thing to be in two states at the same time. In reality, superposition does not represent a contradiction.

Instead, any apparent contradiction is owing to the fact that our common-sense framework, including the view that one thing cannot be in two places at the same time, represents an incomplete understanding of quantum mechanics. Thus, we might say that superposition presents us with an incoherence purely as a matter of logic, because, of course, it is generally accepted that quantum superposition is not metaphysically impossible.

Whether or not the contradiction holds will be the subject of the second half of the chapter, and I will also look closer at Shani's response in the sections to come. Here, I will give only a basic outline of his response. Shani correctly highlights that the contradiction arises as constitutive cosmopsychism posits macro-perspectives as partial aspects of the cosmic perspective. He suggests that there is an alternative way to think about the grounding of sub-cosmic perspectives by the cosmic perspective that does not posit them as its partial aspects. The idea is that they are partially grounded and not fully grounded in the cosmic perspective. Full grounding dictates that the grounded be fully accounted for in terms of the ground, and partial grounding dictates only that the grounded be partially accounted for in terms of the ground. It appears accurate that fully grounding sub-cosmic perspectives in the cosmic perspective requires them to exist as its partial aspects, which is where the apparent contradiction arises; relying on partial grounding instead may be a fruitful approach. The partial grounding route involves the cosmic perspective being in some sense instrumental in the existence of sub-cosmic perspectives, while the derivative perspectives also exert their independence from it. Thus, Shani's suggestion that cosmopsychists endorse the partial grounding route does seem to avoid the problem of synchronous perspectives. I will cover Shani's approach in more detail in the later sections of the chapter.

Let us summarize what we have covered so far with respect to cosmopsychism. Goff's view supposes that sub-cosmic subjects are derived from the cosmic subject by being fully grounded in it as its partial aspects. Such a view entails problematic synchronous subjects scenarios (more on these to come), to which Goff responds that although it is strange to posit subjects as parts of other subjects, strangeness does not entail metaphysical impossibility. Mathews's cosmological panpsychism anticipates synchronous subjects scenarios and averts them by understanding sub-cosmic subjects according to a psychoanalytic autonomous complex model, which says that sub-cosmic subjects are to the cosmic subject what an autonomous complex is to the mind that harbours it. Shani homes in on the perspectival aspect of subjects and restates Coleman's argument against panpsychism as also an argument against cosmopsychism, whereby synchronous subjects scenarios (when subjects are considered as inherently perspectival) are shown to be metaphysically impossible. He proposes a solution based on the notion of partial grounding.

4.4 Synchronous perspectives scenarios and the subject-constitution principle

Bringing together the insights from this brief survey, we can see that the subject combination problem and subject derivation problem are essentially the same. The core of the problems is that they both entail scenarios in which subjects are parts of further subjects. For constitutive panpsychism, these arise because micro-subjects constitute macro-subjects, and for constitutive cosmopsychism, they arise because sub-cosmic subjects are constituted by the cosmic subject (as its partial aspects). I mentioned at the beginning of the chapter that I will mainly be considering subjects from their perspectival aspect because subjects are taken to be inherently perspectival, and it is the perspectival aspect that gives rise to the most pressing objections. With this in mind, I suggest that the core of both subject problems is the presence of troubling synchronous perspectives scenarios:

> **Synchronous perspectives scenarios**: Any scenario in which subjects on one level of reality constitute a subject on another level of reality.

The above definition relies on an understanding of what is meant by 'constitution'. For *x* to constitute *y*, *y* must be grounded in *x*. There is no universally accepted notion of grounding. Still, for our purposes, we need only a minimal understanding of it as a relation of dependence, but we could equally cash it out in terms of an 'in virtue of' relation. What I have to say is general and will work with most standard accounts of the grounding relation; if I equivocate on the notion I refer to, I do not do so to make a distinction. To say '*x* constitutes *y* if and only if *y* is grounded in *x*' still does not tell us what constitution means when we are talking about the constitution of subjects. Indeed, there are some particular conditions that we must take note of when considering the constitution of subjects by subjects. In order to say that a subject (or a group of subjects) is constituted by a further subject (or groups of subjects), the constituting subjects must survive in the constituted subject, or else there is no basis on which to say that new subject is constituted by them (or, in other words, there is no basis on which to say *y* is grounded in *x*). Furthermore, the constituted subject must be a genuinely novel subject and not just the mere aggregation of constituting subjects, nor can the constituted subject be just an arbitrary region of the constituting subject, or else the constituted subject would not really be a subject in its own right. Moreover, the constituted subject(s) cannot be strongly emergent from the constituting subjects because in cases of strong emergence it is not possible to deduce the emergent from the submergent. I propose that we put this together into the following principle:

> **The subject-constitution principle:** For a subject(s) to constitute a further subject(s) the constituting subject(s) must survive in the constituted subject(s) and the constituted subject(s) must be a genuine subject(s) not a mere aggregation, or arbitrary region, of the constituting subject(s). Moreover, the constituted subject(s) must not be strongly emergent from the constituting subject(s).

We can see the presence of synchronous perspectives scenarios in both Coleman's explication of metaphysical incoherence for constitutive panpsychism and Shani's for constitutive cosmopsychism. The problematic scenario for Coleman is the synchronous presence of micro-perspectives and macro-perspectives (macro-perspectives that are formed from the combination of micro-perspectives), while for Shani it is the synchronous presence of the cosmic subject and macro-subjects (macro-perspectives that are derived from the cosmic perspective as its partial aspects). We can also see the subject-constitution principle at work. The subject-constitution principle underpins the synchronous perspectives scenarios, because both constitutive panpsychism (by relying on subject combination) and constitutive cosmopsychism (by relying on subject derivation) are committed to it, and it guarantees the presence of subjects on multiple levels of reality, related to each other by constitution relations. In Coleman's example, the principle guarantees (or purportedly guarantees) that the two mutually exclusive constituting macro-perspectives must constitute a macro-perspective composed of conflicting micro-perspectives. In Shani's example, the principle guarantees (or purportedly guarantees) the simultaneous existence of the cosmic perspective and a macro-perspective as its partial aspect, which, considered together, reveal a contradiction (for the cosmic perspective must both affirm and deny the existence of whatever of its perspective sits outside of that of the macro-perspective constituent).

Coleman's and Shani's cases against constitutive panpsychism and constitutive cosmopsychism are arguably the most robust cases against the respective views. Both purport to show that the respective views entail a metaphysical impossibility based on their reliance on subjects combining (for panpsychism) or deriving (for cosmopsychism). Moreover, both focus on the perspectival aspect of subjects to demonstrate the impossibility. As I have shown, the problems are very similar and, at their core, centre around the implication of synchronous perspectives scenarios. It might be the case that one view or other has greater prospects of solving the problem due to its endorsement of a particular direction of dependence (recall that panpsychism is a bottom-up view, with derivative macro-subjects dependent on the fundamental micro-subjects, while cosmopsychism is a top-down view, with derivative macro-subjects dependent on the fundamental cosmic subject). However, I contend that the core of the problem is the same for both. This might be seen as disappointing for cosmopsychism because the view is often motivated by its ability to avoid the combination problem. Later, I will show that recognizing that the two problems are essentially the same allows us to address them simultaneously, with the intriguing result of jointly motivating panpsychism and cosmopsychism (at least when considering the combination and derivation problems under their subject aspects).

Now that I have argued that panpsychism and cosmopsychism (in their constitutive guises) both face the same problem, I want to situate the purported contradictions, highlighted by Coleman and Shani, within broader arguments from metaphysical impossibility against constitutive panpsychism and constitutive cosmopsychism. By 'broader arguments', I just mean arguments that include situating the contradictions in the context of the respective views' other commitments. I then propose alternative arguments from epistemic implausibility, which, instead of focusing on how synchronous perspectives scenarios are precluded by the metaphysics of perspectives, hinge on an inconsistency between what we should expect our experience to be like, given the postulates of the view, and what our experience is actually like.

4.5 Arguments from synchronous perspectives scenarios

We have seen that there are arguments that turn on the entailment from panpsychism and cosmopsychism to synchronous perspectives scenarios, with the presence of synchronous perspectives scenarios being underpinned by the subject-constitution principle. In this section of the chapter, I will attempt to formulate broad arguments from metaphysical impossibility against constitutive panpsychism and constitutive cosmopsychism. These are based on those offered by Coleman and Shani, but they situate the purported contradictions in the broader context of the views. As I have already stated, it is not immediately obvious to me that synchronous perspectives scenarios entail metaphysical impossibility (and since I might be missing something, I will take them seriously nonetheless). Instead, I suspect they are only epistemically implausible. By epistemically implausible, I mean that rather than metaphysical impossibility, such scenarios highlight an apparent mismatch between what we would expect our own macro-perspectives to be like (given the scenarios) and what they are actually like in reality. I will first formulate arguments from metaphysical impossibility before offering variations from epistemic implausibility.

4.5.1 Arguments from the metaphysical impossibility of synchronous subjects

Both Coleman and Shani purport to show a contradiction in synchronous perspectives scenarios. Coleman's target is constitutive panpsychism, and his conclusion is that this form of panpsychism is false because points of view do not combine. Shani builds on Coleman, by claiming that the metaphysics of points of view does not only rule out the *combination* of subjects but also rules out the *derivation* of subjects on which constitutive cosmopsychism depends. I will formulate broad arguments against both views, in line with Coleman's and Shani's objections.

4.5.1.1 A metaphysical impossibility argument against combining subjects

Let us first consider the case for an argument against constitutive panpsychism, which is in line with Coleman's project. As mentioned, the argument is based on the failure of points of view to combine. The argument against constitutive panpsychism from metaphysical impossibility can be presented as follows:

1. Constitutive panpsychism requires that physical ultimates are themselves subjects of experience.
2. Subjects of experience are inherently perspectival.
3. Therefore, constitutive panpsychism requires that physical ultimates are perspectival.
4. Macro-perspectives of humans are constituted by the combination of micro-perspectives of physical ultimates.
5. However, micro-perspectives must survive any combination into a macro-perspective.

6. A mere aggregate of perspectives does not count as a combination.
7. A combination equalling the strong emergence of a macro-perspective does not count as constitution.
8. Therefore, a successful account of combination must include the survival of any constituting perspectives (to satisfy 5), plus an additional novel perspective (to satisfy 6) formed of their combination, but not strongly emergent (to satisfy 7).
9. However, (8) results in synchronous perspectives scenarios.
10. If synchronous perspectives scenarios are metaphysically impossible, then perspectives do not combine.
11. Synchronous perspectives scenarios are metaphysically impossible.
12. Therefore, perspectives do not combine.
13. Therefore, constitutive panpsychism is false.

Remember that this argument is supposed to situate the purportedly contradictory synchronous perspectives scenarios in the context of a broader argument against panpsychism. It is not providing any motivation for the metaphysical impossibility, per se; rather, it is conditional on the truth of the contradiction.

With this in mind, we can examine the argument more closely. Many of the above premises are obviously true by the constitutive panpsychist's own lights. Premise (1) is generally uncontroversial, as it is the standard panpsychist claim that microphysical ultimates are subjects of experience. Premise (2) is also widely accepted, but most importantly, both constitutive panpsychism's proponents and opponents agree on the point. The conjunction of (1) and (2) straightforwardly entails (3), while (4) is true, by definition, for constitutive panpsychists. Premises (5), (6) and (7) state the minimal requirements of any proposed constitution, and so are also uncontroversial (to the constitutive panpsychist). They amount to what I have called the subject-constitution principle. Premise (8) is a restatement of (5)–(7). Premise (9) shows that, as a result of (8), any viable account of combination includes synchronous perspectives scenarios (here, we can see the subject-constitution principle underpinning the presence of synchronous perspective scenarios). Premise (10) is a simple conditional premise stating that if synchronous perspectives scenarios are metaphysically impossible, then perspectives do not combine; this is followed by (11), which affirms that synchronous perspectives scenarios are metaphysically impossible. The conclusion in (12) follows straightforwardly from (9)–(11), and (13), the conclusion that constitutive panpsychism is false, follows from (12).

The vital premise is (11), the premise that synchronous perspectives scenarios are metaphysically impossible. To restate, I am not, at this point, interested in providing a counterexample to premise (11). My interest lies in exploring where the contradiction, if it holds, sits in an argument against the view. I will, however, say a few words about my immediate reaction to it. As stated, Coleman highlights the contradiction by drawing attention to one possible scenario involving two micro-perspectives and their proposed combination into a new macro-perspective. The scenario posits two micro-perspectives, Red and Blue. Red's perspective – its point of view – is characterized by the experience of redness to the exclusion of all else. In contrast, Blue's point of view is characterized by the experience of blueness to the exclusion of all else. I think it is easy for us to conceive of such perspectives, but bear in mind that it is not simply supposed to be that Red's perspective is awash with the quality of redness, i.e. that the content of Red's perspective is redness and nothing else; instead, it is that there is a phenomenology to Red's experience being utterly exhausted by redness. In other words, there is a way it feels for one's point of view to be exhaustively red. And the same can be said of Blue's perspective.

Coleman's example proposes the combination of Red and Blue to constitute a 'bigger' perspective, Ub. We already know that Ub must have its own overarching perspective containing the perspectives of Red and Blue within its purview, since that is the only scenario in which the subject-constitution principle is maintained. Coleman argues that the contradiction arises because there is no possibility that the perspective of Ub can simultaneously include the contradictory perspectives of Blue and Red within its purview; it is impossible for Ub's perspective to be characterized by the experience of redness to the exclusion of all else *and* the experience of blue to the exclusion of all else, at the same time. But this is precisely what must obtain if constitutive panpsychism is to be upheld (so the argument goes). It is not immediately obvious to me that this is metaphysically impossible. It is certainly hard to imagine a single overarching perspective constituted by seemingly mutually exclusive parts, but that does not demonstrate that it is impossible.

My reluctance to join the calls of metaphysical impossibility is perhaps influenced by well-known accounts of a single consciousness instantiating seemingly mutually exclusive states of affairs. For example, it is very common for people to hold many contradictory beliefs and emotions, for instance, but their simultaneous instantiation by one consciousness is clearly not impossible. Moreover, there are examples of states of affairs that are inconceivable yet accepted as true; as I mentioned previously, take quantum superposition, for example. It is counterintuitive, granted, but that does not make it false.

4.5.1.2 A metaphysical impossibility argument against subject derivation

I now want to formulate a broad argument against constitutive cosmopsychism, which situates Shani's stated contradiction in the context of a complete argument against the view (as most typically understood). As with the previous argument, this one turns on synchronous perspectives scenarios being metaphysically impossible. We can formulate an overall argument against cosmopsychism as follows:

1. Constitutive cosmopsychism states that the cosmos is itself a subject of experience.
2. Moreover, the cosmic subject of experience is the fundamental subject.
3. Subjects of experience are inherently perspectival.
4. Therefore, cosmopsychism entails that the cosmos is perspectival.
5. Derivative sub-cosmic perspectives are constituted by (derived from) the cosmic perspective.

6. However, the only possible way for the cosmic perspective to constitute sub-cosmic perspectives is if they are its partial aspects.
7. Premise (6) implies that the cosmic point of view has within it the points of view of a multiplicity of sub-cosmic perspectives, synchronously (the implication of synchronous perspectives scenarios).
8. If synchronous perspectives scenarios are metaphysically impossible, then perspectives do not derive.
9. Synchronous perspective scenarios are metaphysically impossible.
10. Therefore, perspectives do not derive.
11. Therefore, constitutive cosmopsychism is false.

Premises (1)–(3) are uncontroversial to the constitutive cosmopsychist. It is possible to maintain some version of cosmopsychism and reject each of (1)–(3). Still, the typical constitutive cosmopsychist will want to maintain all of them (we will look at some alternatives that reject these premises later in the chapter). Premise (4) follows from (1)–(3). Premise (5) is also uncontroversial; it just states that the direction of dependence moves from the cosmic level to the sub-cosmic level(s). Premise (6) is an important premise based on the idea that cosmopsychism implies that the only way for sub-cosmic perspectives to be constituted by the cosmic perspective is for them to appear discretely and distinctly within the cosmic perspective. We will see later that this premise is controversial as there are ways to maintain constitutive cosmopsychism while rejecting premise (6) and/or premise (7). Premise (7) is simply a clarification of (6), stating that cosmopsychism implies synchronous perspectives scenarios. Premise (8) says that if such scenarios give rise to contradiction, then sub-cosmic perspectives do not derive from the cosmic perspective. Premise (9) is the key premise that affirms (8). Conclusions (10) and (11) follow straightforwardly.

Shani believes constitutive cosmopsychism can be rescued from the argument by denying premise (6), the claim that the only possible derivation of macro-perspectives from the cosmic perspective is for them to appear within the purview of the cosmic perspective as its partial aspects. Like Coleman, he argues that constitutive cosmopsychism appears to be ruled out due to its reliance on synchronous perspectives scenarios. However, Shani contends that these only arise if micro-perspectives are *fully* grounded in the cosmic perspective. Cosmopsychism he says, can be rescued by replacing the requirement for sub-cosmic subjects to be fully grounded in the cosmic subject with *partial* grounding instead. This is an astute solution and will be covered in more detail later in the chapter.

As with the previous argument, the most important premise is the one where the contradiction resides (9). Again, the contradiction is rooted in the entailment of synchronous perspectives scenarios. As I have already indicated, the most compelling objections to panpsychism and cosmopsychism are fundamentally equivalent for this reason. I will consider Shani's contradiction, which, as with Coleman's, I am not convinced demonstrates a metaphysical impossibility but rather an incoherence purely as a matter of logic. Recall that when I say 'incoherence purely as a matter of logic', what I mean is that there is indeed a contradiction of the formal form 'P&-P', but that this arises either as a result of a poor translation of phenomena into logic or as an incomplete understanding of the phenomena being translated. Nevertheless, let us return to Shani's declaration of metaphysical impossibility. Recall the following excerpt from earlier, as this is where the contradiction is demonstrated:

> That each subjective perspective is individuated in terms of a characteristic form is, in turn, instrumental in explaining why perspectives do not combine. To see why this is so, recall first how the combination problem arises in the context of perspectives. Suppose that a given perspective P is a compound made of other, more limited perspectives, say Q and R. As seen earlier, this seems to imply that viewing reality from viewpoint P consists, in part, in viewing reality from viewpoint Q. The trouble, however, is that the vista which P opens up transcends the limitations (or boundaries) of viewpoint Q, and therefore that it presupposes the elimination of such limitations. Thus, on the assumption that Q is a compositional component of P, it follows that Q must be both present and absent – a contradiction. In essence, this is the problem pointed out by Coleman but we are now in a position to say a little more about the nature of the problem.
>
> Each perspective can be thought of as an opening to the world from a given point of origin and, as shown above, it is the form, or shape, of that opening – the dynamic configuration giving it structure – which defines how things are viewed from this particular point of origin. Thus, we can think of a perspective as an angle whose conscious point of origin is its vertex and whose form is limited by the rays emanating from that vertex. Now, if the perspective is to have parts each proper part must correspond to a division of the original angle brought about by the introduction of a ray on the interior of that angle (there is no other way to dissect an angle). Let us, then, think of P as our original perspective and of Q as a division within P (see figure 1). But now we are facing the problem just mentioned, for it follows from the simultaneous existence of P and Q that in viewing things from viewpoint P, which opens up the entire original angle, one also views things from viewpoint Q, which excludes the complement P-Q from sight. The result, as before, is a contradiction. The moral, then, is that subjective perspectives are gestalts, namely, structural totalities which cannot be explained in terms of the combination of parts, because, when it comes to perspectives, the very existence of parts excludes the existence of the whole.
>
> (Shani, 2015, pp. 424–5)

For reference, let us also consider the 'figure 1' that Shani refers to (note: this is 'Figure 4' of our present inquiry).

In the first paragraph of the quotation, Shani restates the problem as presented by Coleman. Namely, that a scenario involving a macro-perspective, *P*, composed of micro-perspectives, *Q* and *R*, entails that *P* transcends the boundaries of *Q*'s perspective, thus eliminating the perspective that *Q* contributes to the constitution of *P* while simultaneously affirming the existence of *Q*'s perspective. This is Coleman's contradiction restated. In the second paragraph of the above quotation, Shani applies Coleman's thinking to cosmopsychism.

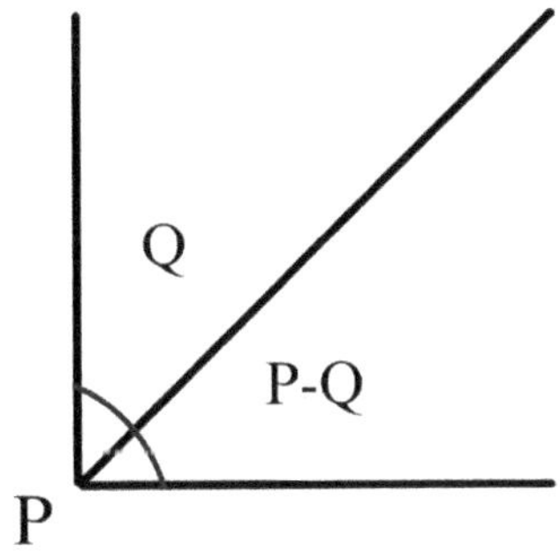

Figure 4 Shani's illustration of incoherent perspectives.

Shani starts by comparing perspectives to angles, with the point of origin of a perspective likened to the vertex on an angle (the point at which the two sides of an angle meet) and the boundedness, or limitations, of the perspective represented by the sides of the angle. This allows Shani to very simply illustrate his contradiction using Figure 4. The figure shows us angle *P*, which includes, as a part, sub-angle *Q*. In this illustration, *P* represents the fundamental cosmic perspective, and Q represents a derivative sub-cosmic perspective. Thus, it is illustrative of the kind of synchronous perspectives scenarios entailed by cosmopsychism. Shani then points out that this illustration shows us that the synchronous existence of perspectives *P* and *Q* entails that when the cosmic subject views things from its perspective, it also views from *Q*, but *Q* excludes the compliment *P-Q*. Therefore *P* must both include and exclude *P-Q*. Thus, we have a contradiction.

This contradiction is essentially the same as the one Coleman highlights against panpsychism. However, there is a subtle difference. The contradiction arises in Coleman's scenario due to the apparent impossibility of two mutually exclusive fundamental micro-perspectives constituting an additional derivative macro-perspective. In Shani's scenario, the contradiction arises as a result of the apparent impossibility of a sub-cosmic perspective deriving from the fundamental cosmic perspective, of which it is only a partial aspect. The similarity, however, allows us to object to the claim that the contradiction entails metaphysical impossibility on the same grounds as in Coleman's case. As with the previous argument, I am not focused on arguing against the metaphysical impossibility. Here, I am just situating the contradiction in the context of a broader argument against the view. However, on the face of it, it is not clear that there is a genuine metaphysical, rather than a purely logical, incoherence in the scenario. Just as we said in Coleman's case. It is undoubtedly difficult to conceive of a cosmic perspective that contains within its overarching purview a more limited perspective, which is characterized partly by its excluding the entire cosmic perspective minus its own parthood. However, we already know that some apparently inconceivable scenarios are metaphysically possible (e.g. quantum superposition/wave-particle duality, four-dimensional objects and contradictory beliefs and emotions).

Shani's contradiction, like Coleman's before it, is compelling. Shani's version, in particular, provides a powerfully clear demonstration of where the purported contradiction lies. However, as noted, I am not convinced that it highlights the *impossibility* of synchronous perspectives scenarios. As such, I do not think that we have grounds to reject constitutive cosmopsychism on this basis alone. At the very least, Shani frames a severe worry for cosmopsychism with striking clarity. My aim so far has been to show how the alleged contradictions fit into overall arguments against constitutive panpsychism and cosmopsychism. Although I have not yet presented any arguments against the presence of such contradictions, I have said in both cases that I have not yet been convinced of the impossibility of synchronous perspectives.

4.5.2 Epistemic implausibility arguments against synchronous subjects

While I remain unconvinced by the metaphysical impossibility arguments, I do think there are challenging arguments from epistemic implausibility. In this section, I make the case that the above arguments, although all purported to be metaphysical in nature, are underwritten by epistemic considerations, and that, given this, we can reimagine the arguments accordingly. When I say 'epistemically implausible', I mean that the arguments turn on introspection indicating that synchronous perspectives scenarios are *implausible*.

4.5.2.1 An epistemic implausibility argument against constitutive panpsychism

Consider the following argument against constitutive panpsychism:

1. Subjects of experience are inherently perspectival.
2. If constitutive panpsychism is true, macro-perspectives are constituted by a combination of numerous micro-perspectives.
3. Our macro-perspectives are not constituted by the combination of micro-perspectives.
4. Therefore, constitutive panpsychism is false.

The first premise relies on the constitutive panpsychist conceding that subjects of experience are inherently perspectival. I believe all accept this, so it is an uncontroversial premise (for our purposes, we can say the argument is conditional on accepting this premise). The second premise just describes the standard constitutive position that macro-subjects are constituted by a combination of micro-subjects; only this premise focuses specifically on the perspectival aspect of subjects. This premise is also uncontroversial. The third premise is the most important one. It states that, as the instantiators of macro-perspectives, our own human points of view should be formed of numerous 'smaller', bounded micro-perspectives, but they do not appear to be partitioned in any such way. My sense perceptions – visual and auditory, for example – are not variegated but unified. Given that the truth of constitutive panpsychism would entail our perspectives being formed from numerous discrete micro-perspectives, and the evident fact that our perspectives are not composed in such a way, constitutive panpsychism must be false.

This argument, unlike Coleman's and Shani's, does not purport to demonstrate metaphysical impossibility as it does not reveal synchronous perspectives scenarios to be impossible. Instead, it provides an argument that hinges on introspective observation of our own perspectives, highlighting an inconsistency between our actual experience and the way we should expect our experience to be if constitutive panpsychism were true. I suspect that our having a unified, *unvariegated* perspective may be at the heart of Coleman's argument, perhaps implicitly. However, we should be clear that this does not entail *metaphysical impossibility* but rather the weaker *epistemic implausibility*.

4.5.2.2 An epistemic implausibility argument against cosmopsychism

I believe my argument above is valid and makes a reasonable case against constitutive panpsychism, but we have yet to see if we can make a similar argument against cosmopsychism. Perhaps we could offer an argument like this:

1. Subjects of experience are inherently perspectival.
2. If constitutive cosmopsychism is true, we humans are sub-cosmic macro-perspectives constituted by the cosmic perspective in virtue of being its partial aspects.
3. Our macro-perspectives, in turn, constitute micro-perspectives in virtue of the micro-perspectives being partial aspects of our macro-perspectives.
4. If our macro-perspectives constitute micro-perspectives in virtue of the micro-perspectives being partial aspects of our macro-perspectives, then our perspectives should include numerous discrete micro-perspectives.
5. Our perspectives do not include numerous discrete micro-perspectives.
6. Therefore, constitutive cosmopsychism is false.

The above argument is more nuanced and controversial than the previous one, but I do not expect many constitutive cosmopsychists to reject any of its key premises, (1)–(3) in particular. I will say a little about why. The first premise is uncontroversial for reasons already stated. The second premise follows from the assumption that cosmopsychists typically seek to derive sub-cosmic perspectives from the cosmic perspective by claiming they are its partial aspects. Shani rejects this premise as part of his cosmopsychist solution to the subject derivation problem (more on this later). The third premise is important, and I will return to it at some length shortly. Essentially, it reflects a commitment to the ubiquity of consciousness (i.e. that both panpsychism and cosmopsychism agree that all matter is conscious but differ regarding which level of reality they claim is fundamental – the top or the bottom). The fourth premise follows directly from the third, and our own subjective experience confirms the fifth, as was the case with the identical premise in the previous argument.

Both the metaphysical impossibility and epistemic implausibility arguments centre on inconsistencies arising in synchronous perspectives scenarios, but while the former focuses on how the metaphysics of perspectives preclude such scenarios, the latter focuses on why the scenarios are at odds with our experience. I am not convinced that metaphysical impossibility arguments achieve their intended goal of demonstrating the impossibility of synchronous perspectives scenarios. However, I find the epistemic implausibility arguments more convincing, although they are more modest. In the next section, I propose a model of how to think about synchronous perspectives scenarios such that they do not give rise to these concerns.

4.6 The binocular model of synchronous perspectives

To address the inconsistencies, I suggest we need a model of how to conceive of synchronous perspectives scenarios that does not violate the subject-constitution principle while resolving the apparent contradictions they give rise to. This amounts to needing a model according to which our perspectives are not partitioned in accordance with the micro-perspectives they contain while still affirming that they contain further perspectives as parts. I believe there is a model fitting the criteria. I propose *the binocular model of synchronous perspectives*. The idea of the model is to base our thinking about perspectives on the workings of visual fields within binocular vision. To enable us to see how the model works when applied to perspectives, we first need to delve into the basics of binocular vision.

4.6.1 Binocular vision

Simply put, binocular vision is a visual field formed of the combination of two separate monocular visual fields. All animals with two eyes have binocular vision. In almost all cases, there is some degree of overlap between the two constituent fields (often, there is a significant overlap). The combined visual field allows for depth perception that the monocular fields, considered alone, do not allow for. The depth perception, known as 'stereopsis', arises due to what is known as 'binocular disparity', which is the difference in the images from the two eyes when appearing as a single combined visual field.

The question of how the two monocular fields come to constitute the binocular field is an interesting one. Physiologically, the process starts with inputs onto the retina of each eye. From there, messages are sent along the optic nerve to the thalamus and then through the optic radiation to the primary visual cortex. It is in the visual cortex that the monocular visual fields come together. In the thalamus, the views of the right eye and left eye are kept apart. By the time the messages reach the primary visual cortex, the right and left messages come together in the same layer of the neocortex (layer IV), but are partitioned from each other within that layer. They fully come together in layers I, II, III, V and VI of the neocortex in what are referred to as 'binocular cells'. Binocular cells 'record' from both right and left monocular cells at layer IV, producing the combined visual field.

What it means for monocular fields to 'combine' is not simply for them to be placed side by side or one on top of the other, but something much more nuanced (and mysterious). We can explore what goes on in the combination by looking at how various images are combined in disinct ways. Imagine two scenarios: in one, the images from each eye are similar, while in the other, they are very different.

In the scenario where the images are similar, they gain access to the visual system simultaneously and form a fused visual field. It is not known exactly what happens in this 'fusion', but what we do know is that the images are not simply aggregated (i.e. summed) and nor is the identity of each individual field lost. We know that the combination in question is not simply a case of the two monocular fields summing, because if it were, then the combined visual field would include the images of both individual fields. We can do an easy experiment to prove this is not the case: close one eye and notice that the brightness of the field from the other remains the same as the combined field. Furthermore, we know that the identities of each monocular field survive the combination, because if they did not, we would not be able to distinguish crossed from uncrossed disparity.

To understand the last sentence, we need to say a little about crossed and uncrossed disparity. A binocular disparity is simply the difference in an object's location in each monocular visual field. Whether a disparity is crossed or uncrossed has to do with its location relative to the horopter, which is the point in space that the eyes are fixating on plus an imaginary arc including all points at corresponding locations in the retinae. Crossed disparity occurs when an object is closer to the eyes than the horopter. It is so-called because the eyes must cross further to focus on it. In crossed disparity, the object appears further to the left from the right eye's view than the left eye's view. An uncrossed disparity is when the object is further away from the eyes than the horopter. It is so-called because the eyes must uncross to view it. In uncrossed disparity, the object appears further to the right from the right eye's view than the left eye's view. Now we understand this, we can say that the identities of each individual monocular field survive the combination, because we are able to differentiate objects with crossed and uncrossed disparities, and the ability to differentiate relies on the existence of the two independent visual fields.

What I have said so far is only about the first scenario, according to which the images from each monocular field are similar. To recap, in such cases, the two individual fields fuse, where the fusion is such that the individual images are not simply aggregated, and where their individual identities are also maintained.

Now let us consider the second scenario, according to which the images from each monocular field are very different (spatially or temporally). Scenarios like this give rise to 'binocular rivalry', where the two radically different images undergo alternating periods of dominance and suppression. In such a scenario, at any given moment, at any given point in the binocular visual field, only one image is being displayed. But what is displayed at any given moment, at any given point in the combined field, is constantly changing due to alternating periods of dominance and suppression among the individual visual fields. The most common illustration of binocular rivalry supposes two monocular visual fields, each displaying one of the images in Figure 5.

The two images in Figure 5 are very different. On the left side, we have only vertical lines, and on the right side, only horizontal lines. If the images were fused in the same manner as sets of similar images, we would expect the resultant binocular view to look something like Figure 6 (we would expect this intuitively, as well).

However, this is not what happens when the individual images are very different, as I have just noted. Instead, we see binocular rivalry resulting in something like what is depicted in Figure 7 (note: it is difficult to accurately depict binocular rivalry in a static

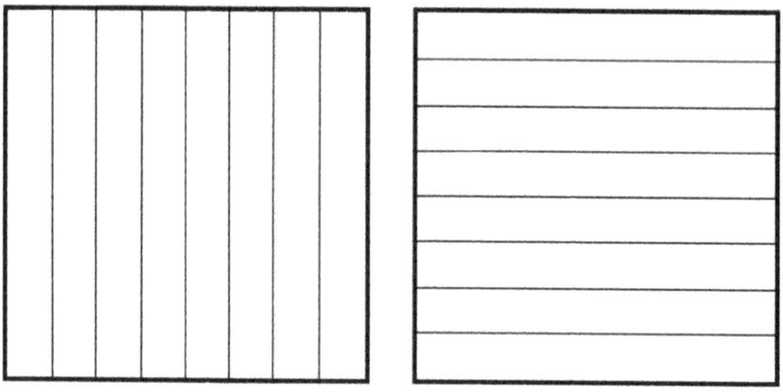

Figure 5 Component monocular fields.

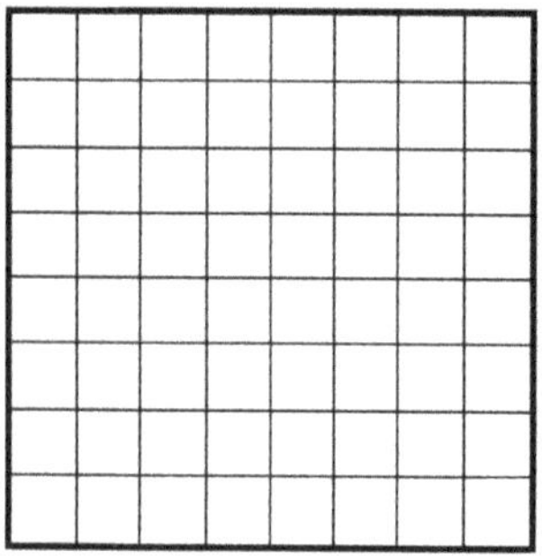

Figure 6 Anticipated binocular field.

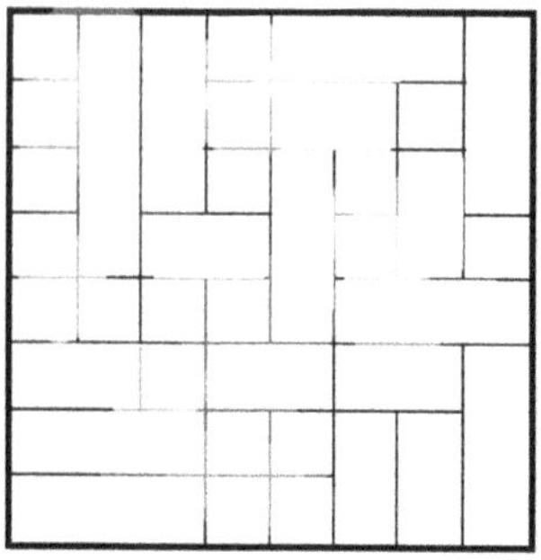

Figure 7 Binocular rivalry.

image since it would be dynamic, constantly changing in accordance with alternating periods of dominance and suppression between the horizontal and vertical lines).

At any one point in the binocular image, only one of the two monocular images is dominant, while the other is suppressed. We can see that when a disparity between the individual visual fields is too great, the combined binocular visual field is formed of a dynamic alternating 'mosaic' of the two monocular visual fields. In the example above, the combined binocular view would include (constantly changing) areas of horizontal line dominance and vertical line dominance. I should note that in cases of binocular rivalry, both images are processed initially, and even fused, albeit very briefly, but when the differences are too great, the images are separated out and processed sequentially.[7]

4.6.2 The binocular model for panpsychism and cosmopsychism

I propose that panpsychism and cosmopsychism can harness the basics of binocular vision to present a coherent model of synchronous perspectives scenarios. Recall that what they need is a model that allows for synchronous perspectives scenarios, in accordance with the subject-constitution principle, but which dissolves the apparent inconsistencies (between, for example, the expectation that our own perspectives be partitioned and the reality that they are not so partitioned).

4.6.2.1 The binocular model for panpsychism

I will present the model for panpsychism and then for cosmopsychism, although there is minimal difference between them. Imagine Coleman's synchronous perspectives scenario, involving two micro-perspectives, Red and Blue, combining to constitute a macro-perspective, Ub. What I propose is that we think of the micro-perspectives as equivalent to the two monocular fields of a binocular vision, where the combined binocular vision is equivalent to the macro-perspective. Coleman says his scenario is metaphysically impossible because it entails that the combined perspective must be formed of two mutually exclusive micro-perspectives. Remember that Red is a perspective characterized exhaustively by the experience of redness, and Blue is a perspective characterized exhaustively by the experience of blueness.

Reframing Coleman's scenario according to the binocular model, we can say that Red and Blue are equivalent to two individual monocular fields and that they combine to form Ub, the equivalent of a unified binocular visual field. Moreover, because Red and Blue represent mutually exclusive points of view, we can also say that their combining in a binocular visual field gives rise to a case of binocular rivalry. As we have just seen, in cases of rivalry, the combined image is not a fusion of the two individual images but rather a dynamic mosaic of alternating dominance and suppression across the two constituent images.

Recall what combination must amount to for the constitutive panpsychist: it must be more than mere aggregation but must allow the continued existence of the constituting entities (as per the subject-constitution principle). Accounts of combination that will not do include one on which the combined perspective is just the two micro-perspectives side-by-side (as this would amount to mere aggregation), one on which only one of the micro-perspectives survives, and one on which neither of the micro-perspectives survives (each of these amount to violations of the subject-constitution

[7] For more details on binocular vision and the processes I describe, see Howard and Rogers' (1996) book *Binocular Vision and Stereopsis* and Stidwill and Fletcher's (2010) *Normal Binocular Vision: Theory, Investigation and Practical Aspects.*

principle). The only viable option for the constitutive panpsychist appears to entail a synchronous perspectives scenario whereby the combined macro-perspective has as its partial aspects the two micro-perspectives. But this, according to Coleman, is metaphysically impossible because it amounts to the claim that a macro-perspective contains within its purview two mutually exclusive perspectives. It is impossible, for example, for Ub to share both Red's perspective of an experience exhausted by redness and Blue's perspective of an experience exhausted by blueness.

I have already said that I am not entirely convinced by the charge of metaphysical impossibility, but I will nonetheless address it. As I have said, I do think that there is an epistemic implausibility concern in the notion of synchronous perspectives scenarios. The implausibility arises as a result of the disparity between the expectation that our own perspectives will be perspectivally partitioned and the lack of such partitioning in our subjective experience.

So, how does the binocular model help the constitutive panpsychist? It helps by offering a model of combination according to which we would not expect perspectival partitioning in our experience even though our perspectives subsume further perspectives. Let us think again about Ub – constituted by a combination of Red and Blue – in light of the binocular model. As mentioned, we would expect their combination to result in binocular rivalry, leading to a dynamic mosaic of alternating dominance and suppression of Red's point of view (redness) and Blue's point of view (blueness). We would not expect to see an overall point-of-view split in two, formed half by Red's perspective and half by Blue's perspective. Rather, we would expect to see an overall point of view, which is a dynamic pulsating matrix of red regions and blue regions. Coleman's purported contradiction does not arise because Ub's point of view, at any given moment, does not include contradictory perspectives. Moreover, the epistemic implausibility does not arise because, given the model, we would not expect to see perspectival partitioning in our own subjective experience (the absence in our experience of which is what gives rise to the epistemic implausibility).

The question remains: does this model avoid violating the subject-constitution principle? This question concerns the need to ensure that the 'constitutive' part of constitutive panpsychism can be maintained. The constitution relation states that for *x* to constitute *y*, *y* must be grounded in (or obtain in virtue of) *x*. Chalmers (2017) notes that it can be understood intuitively as the claim that *x* somehow adds up to yield *y*. Remember that for constitutive panpsychism, the subject-constitution principle means that both the constituting perspectives (*x* in the above) must survive the combination, and in addition, we must have a new constituted perspective post-combination (*y* in the above), or else we cannot say that *x* grounds *y*. The answer to the question is that the subject-constitution principle can be maintained because, according to the binocular model of synchronous perspectives, the constituted macro-perspective is formed from a combination of the two micro-perspectives in such a way that their individual identities survive. In binocular vision, neither monocular field is ever extinguished in cases of binocular rivalry. This is evident from the dynamic mosaic of alternating dominance and suppression (which, recall, characterizes the overall binocular field), which presupposes the existence of both individual fields. Taking this as our model of subject-constitution, we can claim that the individual perspectives in the panpsychist combination likewise persist.

To summarize, according to the model I propose, constitutive panpsychism can avert both types of problems because it can offer an account of the combination of micro-perspectives into macro-perspectives, according to which the micro-perspectives' survival does not preclude the simultaneous existence of the macro-perspective constituted by them. Consider Coleman's metaphysical objection. In his argument, the two micro-perspective constituents (Red and Blue) are radically different, which he claims makes it impossible for them to jointly constitute a further perspective. However, as I have shown, on the binocular model, when two radically different perspectives constitute a macro-perspective, the macro-perspective exhibits rivalry (equivalent to binocular rivalry), which involves neither a contradictory perspective (*per impossible*) nor the elimination of the micro-perspective constituents.

Consider also the epistemic implausibility objection, which arises as a result of the discrepancy between what we would expect our own perspectives to be like, given the postulates of constitutive panpsychism, and what our perspectives are actually like when we introspect. The epistemic argument says that we should expect to see that our human perspectives are fragmented in accordance with the micro-perspectives which constitute them (i.e. micro-perspectives should appear as discrete and distinct parts of our perspectives), but since we do not see that in our experience, constitutive panpsychism must be false. The binocular model addresses this problem because, according to the model, it is not the case that we would expect the individual constituting perspectives to appear discretely and distinctly within the purview of the macro-perspective. What we would expect, in most cases, is perspectival fusion (in the vein of binocular fusion), while in rare cases, we would expect perspectival rivalry (in the vein of binocular rivalry). Given the model, some macro-perspectives will be constituted by fused micro-perspectives (those where the constituent perspectives are similar), and some will be constituted by rivalling perspectives (those where the constituent perspectives are very dissimilar). The binocular model of synchronous perspectives offers the panpsychist a response to the arguments from metaphysical impossibility and epistemic implausibility.

4.6.2.2 The binocular model for cosmopsychism

Let us now consider the binocular model for constitutive cosmopsychism. In this case, we will need to be a little more imaginative. In the panpsychist case, we benefit from the fact that binocular vision involves the combination of more limited visual fields into a composite field, which is like panpsychism insofar as it posits the combination of more limited perspectives into a composite one. The direction of dependence is the same: small entities combine to constitute larger entities, and the larger entities depend on the smaller entities. For cosmopsychism, the smaller entities derive from a larger entity and depend on the larger entity for their existence. So, we see a reversal in the direction of dependence. However, it does not mean we cannot apply the binocular model to address the subject derivation problem.

Recall that I said the subject combination and derivation problems are almost the same problem. Essentially, the metaphysical impossibility and epistemic implausibility problems centre around the entailment of synchronous perspective scenarios from both the panpsychist and cosmopsychist positions. To repeat, these are scenarios involving perspectives as parts of a further perspective(s). Panpsychism entails such scenarios because micro-perspectives are the fundamental parts of derivative macro-perspectives, while cosmopsychism similarly entails synchronous perspective scenarios because the fundamental cosmic perspective contains, as parts, derivative macro-perspectives. What the binocular model offers cosmopsychism is an unproblematic account of synchronous perspectives. It does not matter that there is no structural parity between cosmopsychism and binocular vision, in the sense that in binocular vision, the resultant combined visual field is formed of a combination of the more limited views, whereas in cosmopsychism, the overall perspective is prior to the more limited perspectives. What we are interested in, as far as cosmopsychism is concerned, is an account of synchronous perspectives that does not violate the subject-constitution principle.

Let us now run the model. Consider that the cosmic perspective is equivalent to the binocular visual field in the sense that it is an overall perspective containing further perspectives as parts. Now consider that two sub-cosmic perspectives, Red and Blue (we will stick to the same characters from Coleman's argument), are parts of the cosmic perspective, similar to how the individual monocular fields are parts of the binocular visual field. Now recall Shani's demonstration of metaphysical impossibility for constitutive cosmopsychism, which amounts to the claim that the cosmic perspective must both affirm and deny both Red and Blue. It must affirm Red because its perspective contains Red as a part, but it must also deny Red because its perspective (the cosmic perspective) contains Blue as a part, but Blue excludes Red, and vice versa. The purported contradiction does not arise on the binocular model because the cosmic perspective can be an unproblematic mixture of Red and Blue while still having Red and Blue as derivative parts. Consider that the cosmic perspective includes the two sub-cosmic perspectives, Red and Blue, as derivative parts. In line with the model, we can say that the cosmic perspective instantiates perspectival rivalry because its parts are radically different; its perspective is therefore characterized by a dynamic mosaic of alternating dominance and suppression of its derivative perspectives. This is the same scenario that occurs for panpsychism, except that in this case, the direction of dependence goes from top-down rather than from bottom-up. The metaphysical worry does not arise because Red and Blue are not present as discrete and distinct conscious perspectives within the cosmic perspective (due to suppression).

It is tempting to ask how the cosmopsychist can avoid violating the subject-constitution principle, perhaps also questioning how sub-cosmic perspectives could be derived from the cosmic perspective if they are not present as discrete and distinct conscious perspectives within it. The cosmopsychist can answer that the sub-cosmic perspectives are present in the cosmic perspective in the same sense that the micro-perspectives are present in the macro-perspective for panpsychism. We saw that the identities of the monocular fields are not lost in cases of binocular rivalry. Moreover, the fact that binocular rivalry is present proves the continued existence of the individual monocular fields. The same goes for the continued existence of micro-perspectives in the panpsychist case, and the existence of sub-cosmic perspectives in the cosmopsychist case. The subject-constitution principle is thus maintained.

Now, let us tackle the epistemic implausibility problem. It arises as a result of the discrepancy between what we would expect our own perspectives to be like, given the postulates of constitutive cosmopsychism, and what our perspectives are actually like in our subjective experience. The epistemic implausibility argument says that we would expect to see that our human perspectives are fragmented in accordance with the micro-perspectives which derive from them, but since we do not see that in our experience, constitutive cosmopsychism must be false. The epistemic worry for cosmopsychism hinges on its commitment to panpsychism; it says that micro-perspectives should appear as discrete and distinct conscious perspectives as parts of our perspectives, because, by transition, our macro-perspectives ground the micro-perspectives that they constitute. The binocular model addresses this problem because, according to the model, it is not the case that we would expect the individual derivative micro-perspectives to appear as discrete and distinct conscious perspectives within the purview of our macro-perspective. What we would expect, in most cases, is perspectival defusion (in the vein of binocular fusion, but in reverse to account for the reversed direction of dependence posited by cosmopsychism) and, in rare cases, perspectival rivalry (in the vein of binocular rivalry).

I should make a brief note on the 'defusion' I have just referred to. In the case of binocular vision, as I have mentioned already, when the images from the individual fields are similar, they undergo binocular fusion, whereby the two images are combined in such a way that the identities of the individual images are preserved but where they are not simply aggregated. In the panpsychist case, using the binocular model, we can say that the combination of micro-perspectives into a macro-perspective, when the micro-perspectives are similar to each other, is analogous to the case of binocular fusion. We can call this *perspectival fusion*. Additionally, in rare cases where the constituting perspectives are very dissimilar, the combination is analogous to binocular rivalry. We can call this *perspectival rivalry*. However, for cosmopsychism, the direction of dependence is reversed, meaning sub-cosmic perspectives are dependent on the cosmic perspective. So, it would not be appropriate for the cosmopsychist to say that in cases where sub-cosmic perspectives are similar, what we have is perspectival fusion, because that would imply a bottom-up direction of dependence among perspectives. Instead, they can say we have *perspectival defusion*, which is an exact reverse of fusion; perspectival defusion is a defusion of the cosmic perspective into sub-cosmic perspectives, such that the identity of the cosmic perspective is maintained.

One might complain that, at most, the model supports only the plausibility of synchronous perspectives scenarios, but does not indicate *how* the combination or derivation occurs. That is true. However, what is interesting is that the binocular model can draw from our understanding of binocular vision an endorsement of a kind of mysterianism about combination (and derivation), in the sense that even in the case of something as seemingly uncontroversial as the combination of two monocular fields into a binocular visual field, there remains a deep mystery regarding how the combination actually occurs. In the case of binocular vision, there is a well-understood *physiological* account of combination, by which I mean that combination occurs in certain instances and in particular cells in the brain. For example, we know that binocular fusion occurs in binocular cells in layers I, II, III, V and VI of the occipital lobe of the neocortex (which contains the primary visual cortex), but it is a mystery as to how the two fields are actually combined in the way we know they are combined (owing to our experiential acquaintance with them). It would be strange, therefore, to object to the model of combination and derivation that I present on account that it does not explain exactly how the combination and derivation occur. Given that something as simple as the combination in binocular vision is still deeply mysterious, we should perhaps not be surprised that the combination and derivation of perspectives (and, therefore, subjects) remain mysterious. It seems to me that providing a model of synchronous perspectives on which the reported problems do not arise should mark welcome progress, even if it is not a complete solution.

Perhaps a natural concern with the binocular model is that it only applies to the combination and derivation of the visual aspect of perspectives. Furthermore, one might be concerned that it is limited to such combinations and derivations as they occur in a single subject, because binocular vision is a phenomenon occurring in a single subject. This concern stems from overemphasizing the model's basis in binocular vision. The claim is not that perspectives are distinctly visual affairs. Nor is the claim that instances of binocular vision (and binocular vision alone) are actual wholescale instantiations of synchronous perspectives scenarios. The relevance of binocular vision to the model is less direct; it is that our understanding of the phenomenon underwrites the *plausibility* of synchronous perspectives scenarios. The idea is that the existence of binocular vision cuts against concerns that such scenarios are impossible or implausible.

It does this by claiming that the two are suitably similar, such that the accepted actuality of one underpins the plausibility of the other. The idea is that synchronous perspectives scenarios are structurally equivalent to binocular vision. In binocular vision, two narrower visual fields combine to form a wider visual field. In synchronous perspectives scenarios, two narrower perspectives combine to form a wider perspective.[8] In the case of combining perspectives, the problem is that the subject-constitution principle must be adhered to, but this seems impossible (or implausible) because it seems impossible (or implausible) that the combining subjects can survive in the combined subject – for the reasons we covered previously. The combining of visual monocular fields in binocular vision does not strike us as impossible or implausible because we know it to be actual, and we have a *relatively* good understanding of how the combination works. What is striking is that a case of binocular vision represents an instantiation structurally analogous to that deemed impossible or implausible in the case of synchronous perspectives scenarios: that is, narrower visual fields combine to constitute a wider visual field, and do so even if the constituting visual fields contradict one another.

Suppose we did not know about binocular vision and how it works. In that case, we might reasonably argue that it is impossible or implausible for the same reasons synchronous perspectives scenarios are said to be impossible or implausible. The idea,

[8] I am treating synchronous perspectives as involving combining perspectives to avoid confusing the main point. The idea is that synchronous perspectives scenarios are analogous to binocular vision scenarios, regardless of whether we take perspectives to combine or derive.

then, is that binocular vision provides actual instantiations of scenarios structurally analogous to synchronous perspectives scenarios, and in doing so, underwrites their possibility and plausibility. It does not matter that the model is based on a visual phenomenon occurring in a single subject. The model does, however, benefit from the fact that a visual aspect is a paradigmatic (though not necessary) aspect of conscious perspectives and, relatedly, that most arguments against synchronous perspectives scenarios are couched in terms of the visual sense.

4.7 Alternative responses to the metaphysical impossibility and epistemic implausibility arguments

While I believe the model I have provided is likely the best proposal for underwriting combination and derivation, some notable alternatives may be preferable to others. By alternatives, I mean different responses to the two kinds of arguments I have outlined. All of the alternative responses I state maintain the constitutive aspect of constitutive panpsychism and constitutive cosmopsychism. In most cases, there is a panpsychist and a cosmopsychist version of the response. I will cover three kinds of responses: those that reject the full grounding of derivative perspectives in favour of partial grounding, those that reject the panpsychism stipulation, and those that maintain the panpsychism stipulation but reject subjects at the microphysical level. To restate my aim, I am interested in how panpsychism and cosmopsychism can handle their respective subject problems, and if their ability, or inability, to handle them strengthens either view in contrast to the other.

4.7.1 The partial grounding response

The first kind of alternative response involves uncovering an assumption in the arguments that perspectives on one level must exist as discrete and distinct partial aspects of perspectives on another level (for cosmopsychism, this is the assumption that the derivative macro-perspectives must be discrete and distinct partial aspects of the fundamental cosmic perspective, while for panpsychism, this is the assumption that fundamental micro-perspectives must exist as discrete and distinct partial aspects of derivative macro-perspectives), since that is the only option available for grounding one perspective in another in accordance with the subject-constitution principle.

4.7.1.1 Shani's partial-grounding response for cosmopsychism

Shani (2015) provides arguably the most significant alternative response to the arguments above, on behalf of cosmopsychism. I will spend a considerable amount of time detailing his approach because it is, to my mind, the most developed version of cosmopsychism in the literature. We have heard a little about his position previously (in this chapter and those prior), but it will do us no harm to retread some of this ground as we explore deeper.

Shani's approach is to reject the premise that the only way to derive sub-cosmic perspectives from the cosmic perspective is by them being its partial aspects. He does not argue against the claim that this must be the case if sub-cosmic perspectives are to be *fully* grounded in the cosmic perspective. Rather, he argues that because of the metaphysical impossibility he illustrates, we should offer an account according to which the grounding relation is one of *partial* grounding instead. To say that sub-cosmic perspectives are partially grounded in the cosmic perspective is to say that, while a given sub-cosmic perspective is dependent on the cosmic perspective, it is not exhausted by that dependency. For Shani, sub-cosmic perspectives are, in some respect, anchored in the cosmic perspective, while being, in another respect, independent from it. In this way, both arguments we have considered against cosmopsychism are averted, because the derivative perspectives are not partial aspects of the cosmic perspective.

Let us explore this first option for the cosmopsychist further by examining how Shani's proposal works. Shani proposes a rich and nuanced view according to which the cosmos as a whole is the one and only fundamental entity. In addition, the cosmos is a conscious subject of experience. He refers to this conscious cosmos as *the absolute*. The absolute operates on a *lateral duality principle*, according to which it has both a revealed and concealed nature. The revealed nature equates to the world as revealed by our current physics, while its concealed nature is an intrinsic ocean of consciousness that he calls an *endo-phenomenological expanse*. The two dimensions are described as follows:

> [The] revealed side … appears as a spatially extended medium, evolving in time, and differentially structured into various phases and configurations. In short, it appears as what, in common parlance, we identify as physical nature. The concealed side, however, is presumed, on the present account, to be an intrinsically sentient medium, a vast ocean of consciousness. Needless to say, the phenomenal contents of this medium, the ebbs and flows of experience coursing it, are private and inscrutable.
>
> (Shani, 2015, p. 411)

It is important to note that Shani's picture is thoroughly monistic and not, as it appears at first glance, dualistic. There is no ontological distinction between the revealed and the concealed; they are merely dimensions of the same ontological ultimate – the absolute. The absolute, with its revealed and concealed dimensions, is an intensely dynamic medium from which derivative entities arise on both a microscopic and macroscopic level. While all microscopic entities are subjects of experience, this cannot be said for all macroscopic entities. Consider what Shani has to say about microscopic entities and why they are all subjects of experience:

> [The] simplest of relatives … are dynamically differentiated, and therefore demarcated, from their oceanic ambience … as a result of such demarcation, the sentient medium inside the 'vortex' becomes uniquely regimented. Moreover, this regimentation of the internal experiential milieu is reciprocally connected to the revealed structure … Hence, as the 'vortex' becomes differentiated from its

> surroundings its experiential dynamics separates too … creating a knot, or bulge of consciousness with an appearance of self-containment, which serves to separate the system's inner reality from the inner reality of the ocean surrounding it … The result is an individual self (however primitive) engulfed in its own experiences and concerns while being ignorant of the deeper layers which bind it to the ground of all things.
>
> (2015, p. 418)

While all microscopic entities are subjects of experience, we can say this for only a subset of macroscopic entities. Shani refers to all non-absolute entities as *relatives*, and those relatives that are not subjects, he calls *pure objects*. Pure objects are not subjects but, owing to the lateral duality principle, are 'abodes of consciousness'. The difference between pure objects and objects with macro-subjecthood comes down to whether or not the micro-subjects that constitute them are unified in the right kind of way.

To recap, a relative is any entity that is not the absolute itself (every sub-cosmic entity is a relative). Some, but not all, relatives are subjects. Subjecthood requires that a condition be met regarding the unity of consciousness. Pure objects are a subset of relatives that lack subjectivity, though they are not entirely independent of consciousness. All relatives – subjects and pure objects – are abodes of consciousness; all relatives are loci of experience, but some are not distinct subjects of experience. All relatives are abodes of consciousness in the sense that all microscopic entities are subjects of experience, but although all macroscopic entities are formed of microscopic entities, they do not all demonstrate the requisite unity to become macro-subjects. Shani explains the relevant unity in terms of a distinction between what he calls *esonectic binding* and *exonectic binding* – the difference in binding marking the difference between the cases where the fragments of consciousness associated with micro-relatives do and do not unite into new macro-subjects. Shani explains an esonectic system as follows:

> An esonectic system is a compound whole whose micro-constituents are interrelated in such a manner that the system is not only cohesive in respect of its outward revealed form but is also unified in respect of its concealed experiential domain … esonectic systems are internally interwoven: the endo-phenomenological reservoirs of their micro-components join together in a coherent fashion, giving rise to a unified experiential domain.
>
> (2015, p. 419)

Whereas he explains an exonectic system as follows:

> [A]n exonectic system is a compound whole whose micro-constituents are interrelated in such a manner that the system is woven together only on the outside: it has a cohesive exterior, but it lacks a macro-level inner dimension to match with its macro-level revealed form – the endophenomenological reservoirs of its micro-components remain secluded from each other and do not bind together.
>
> (2015, pp. 419–20)

Pure objects, he says, are exonectic systems, whereas macro-subjects are esonectic systems. Shani concedes that the distinction between esonectic and exonectic systems is speculative, and that we do not currently have a model explaining how and in virtue of what some systems achieve the required unity, while others do not. However, he does offer a place to start looking for answers. He refers to structural differences between minerals and brains, whereby the structural bonds holding minerals together are strong, with minimal communication between spatially separated parts. In contrast, the exact opposite is true of brains. He suggests this may give us a clue as to why we should expect consciousness to scale up in humans and other animals but not in rocks and chairs. If the micro-level is populated with tiny fragments of consciousness, which are then organized into rigid structures lacking in internal communication, as is the case in minerals, we would expect no unification of the disparate parts. Yet, we might expect such unification in brains as they lack rigid structures and allow communication between spatially separated parts.

Most importantly, this still does not tell us how macro-perspectives are grounded in the cosmic perspective. Moreover, we have yet to hear how Shani deploys the notion of partial grounding to avoid the problem of synchronous perspectives scenarios. In other words, using Shani's terminology, the question is: how does the absolute partially ground creature consciousness in such a way as to avoid synchronous perspectives scenarios? To summarize his answer, consider his outline of the partial grounding in question (where 'AP' denotes the absolute's perspective and 'RP' denotes a relative's perspective):

> To say that [AP] is a partial ground for [RP] implies that while [RP] depends on [AP] it also amounts to something more and is not exhausted by this particular dependency relationship. Such a state of affairs is expected if there is a certain aspect under which the perspectives of relative subjects are anchored in the perspective of the absolute, and another aspect under which they assert their independence.
>
> (2015, p. 423)

This raises two further questions: (1) How are we to understand the anchoring of relative perspectives in the absolute perspective? And, (2) In what sense do relative subjects assert their independence? To answer these two questions, Shani makes another distinction, this time between two types of characters that each relative perspective has: a *specific character* and a *generic character*. The first question, regarding anchoring, is addressed with reference to a perspective's generic character, while the second question is answered with reference to its specific character.

The *specific character* of a perspective is its unique outlook. A localized, unique, bounded centre of, as Shani says, 'perceiving, feeling, categorizing, synthesizing, anticipating, evaluating, selecting, preparing for action, and so on' (2015, p. 423). He says: 'Such a unique way of relating to things intentionally is manifested dynamically as a coordinated network of interrelated dispositions, or attitudes, which maintains its structural integrity over time' (2015, p. 423). This specific character of a subject's perspective lies behind our intuitive ideas about the existence of perspectives. But this character also gives rise to the derivation problem that Shani and others highlight.

It is the *generic character* that anchors the relative perspectives in the absolute perspective. The idea is that each relative perspective inherits its perspectival nature from the absolute perspective. Shani states that there are two general features of perspectives that are inherited from the absolute in virtue of the fact that the absolute itself exemplifies the features. The two features are *sentience* and *core-subjectivity*. First, we are told that each relative perspective clearly involves sentience since perspectives are experience-involving. The relatives are experiential, on Shani's model, owing to their being grounded in the sentient absolute. That interference patterns are sentient mediums at all is due to the fact that the absolute in which they are formed is a sentient medium. Second, the notion of core-subjectivity can be captured by considering that each perspective has a point of origin from which its purview of the world is cast. This is the implicit sense of self that Shani describes as 'that to whom things are given, or disclosed, from a perspective' (2015, p. 426). Shani's cosmopsychism claims that relative perspectives exemplify core-subjectivity in virtue of the absolute exemplifying core-subjectivity.

In summary, relative perspectives are grounded in the absolute perspective due to the fact they inherit sentience (in a general sense) and the generic sense of self, i.e. core-subjectivity, from the absolute. But they are also independent, owing to their unique, specific, character. Thus, sub-cosmic perspectives do not appear in the cosmic perspective, and therefore, the metaphysical impossibility and epistemic implausibility arguments are neatly undercut.

A potential problem with Shani's picture is that it may be more complicated than both constitutive panpsychism and other versions of constitutive cosmopsychism. It requires that the sentience of the absolute be imparted to the micro-subjective-relatives, which then combine into macro-subjective-relatives. On the other hand, the standard versions of constitutive cosmopsychism and constitutive panpsychism only require one step each to get from the fundamental subjective level to macro-subjects. In the case of panpsychism, it is one step from the micro- to the macro-level, and in the case of other accounts of cosmopsychism, it is one step from the cosmic to the macro-level. Related to the first, a second problem is that Shani's thinking seems to motivate an arguably more plausible alternative to cosmopsychism, which I call *Shanian panpsychism*. Shanian panpsychism arises because, if the partial grounding solution were to be pursued, it is not clear that the best way to do it is via a cosmopsychist rather than a panpsychist approach. The reason is that Shanian panpsychism may be simpler than Shanian cosmopsychism for precisely the reasons just mentioned.

4.7.1.2 Shanian panpsychism

Let us sketch a version of panpsychism inspired by Shani's model and consider if it might be a viable alternative response (to the two arguments) for the constitutive panpsychist.[9] We can say Shanian panpsychism is committed to the following tenets:

[9] To be clear, Shani does not make the claim that his insights can be used in the way I suggest, to form a version of constitutive panpsychism. He may well have good reasons for rejecting what I say here. I merely offer it as a possible version of panpsychism inspired by his rich insights.

1. Physical ultimates have revealed and concealed natures. Their revealed nature is their nature as revealed by current physics, and their concealed nature is their subjective consciousness.
2. Physical ultimates are micro-subjects that combine to form macro-subjects.
3. Combinations of physical ultimates form macro-subjects only under conditions where combinations result in esonectic systems. They do not form macro-subjects when their combinations result in exonectic systems.
4. Physical ultimates, as subjects of experience, are perspectival, and it is owing to such perspectivality that macro-subjects are perspectival.
5. Macro-perspectives are partially grounded in micro-perspectives of physical ultimates in the sense that they inherit generic sentience and core-subjectivity from micro-perspectives but maintain independence insofar as they exhibit a specific character not shared with any micro-perspective.

Essentially, I am proposing to take Shani's position minus the holism. Panpsychism is atomistic rather than holistic, so we can say that reality, on this panpsychist variant, involves a plurality of entities, each operating on a lateral duality principle whereby all fundamental entities (i.e. microphysical ultimates) have a revealed as well as a concealed nature. We can also borrow Shani's distinction between esonectic and exonectic systems to demarcate where combinations of ultimates are likely to give rise to novel created subjects. In esonectic systems, we expect the formation of created subjects, but not in exonectic ones. Moreover, this version of panpsychism avoids the problem of synchronous perspectives scenarios by appealing to partial grounding, explained in terms of a distinction between the generic and specific character of fundamental subjects (just as is the case for Shanian cosmopsychism). One could claim that derivative subjects inherit sentience and core-subjectivity from the concealed side of the microphysical ultimates but remain independent in the sense of having a specific character not shared with the fundamental subjects.

It is not immediately obvious that there are any additional problems for Shanian panpsychism over and above Shanian cosmopsychism. However, it is potentially easier to defend because it is arguably the simpler of the two. As mentioned, the cosmopsychist picture requires an absolute sentience being imparted to micro-sentience, which combines into macro-sentience. In contrast, the panpsychist picture requires only micro-sentience combining into (or imparting to) macro-sentience (the same holds true for core-subjectivity). The panpsychist version can do away with the absolute entirely. This version of panpsychism would not be undercut by the metaphysical impossibility or epistemic implausibility arguments against panpsychism because it does not posit synchronous perspectives scenarios.

The option of rejecting the full grounding of derivative subjects in fundamental subjectivity in favour of partial grounding is promising. However, it appears to be more promising for constitutive panpsychism than constitutive cosmopsychism, because the panpsychist variant is simpler, without any obvious additional costs. There is one additional worry for Shanian views that is worth noting. It regards the status of constituting subjects post-combination: does esonectic binding preserve the identities of the bound micro-subjects or not? It is not clear to me either way, but if it turns out that it does not, then both the panpsychist and cosmopsychist variants of the Shanian approach would contravene the subject-constitution principle.

4.7.2 The reject panpsychism response

The second response worthy of note only applies to cosmopsychism and only addresses the epistemic implausibility problem. It involves rejecting the stipulation of a modest version of panpsychism, which says that all microphysical entities are conscious. On the face of it, it might seem strange that constitutive cosmopsychists typically endorse a modest version of panpsychism, but they do. However, for constitutive cosmopsychism, it is precisely this stipulation that gives rise to the epistemic implausibility in the first place, because, without it, the cosmopsychist picture does not include macro-perspectives with micro-perspectives as derivative partial aspects.

What does cosmopsychism without panpsychism look like? Cosmopsychism without panpsychism involves the claim that there is a cosmic consciousness, which is the ultimate form of consciousness. The ultimate cosmic consciousness constitutes all sub-cosmic consciousness by virtue of the fact that sub-cosmic consciousnesses are its partial aspects. In this case, however, the only sub-cosmic consciousnesses are those on the macro-level. The micro-level of reality is not consciousness-involving. Essentially, the resulting view combines the following two theses: (1) the cosmos as a whole is conscious, but (2) not every part of the cosmos is conscious. It entails that there are parts of the cosmos that are entirely devoid of consciousness, except that they are part of a whole which is conscious.

I do not immediately see any incoherence in the idea. It is perfectly acceptable for specific parts of systems to lack properties that other parts – and indeed the system as a whole – instantiate. Consider the body of a human person and the associated mind of that same human person. Next, let us accept that the mind of that human person is associated with the brain part of the body and not the body as a whole (this is the intuitive idea, which is generally accepted, that the brain is the seat of consciousness in a human person). We intuitively say that the mind is the locus of experience for the body as a whole. So, intuitively, we have a physical body, part of which is a brain, and we have a mind that (whatever it is) is associated with the human body's brain, but acts as a locus of experience for the body as a whole. To put this even more intuitively, it is typical to suppose that my mind *is in my head*, but is the centre of experience for my whole body; this might be why even if we were unfortunate enough to lose a finger, we would still think our consciousness intact.

The potential cosmopsychist response I am proposing here takes the cosmos to be analogous to a human body. As a whole, the cosmos is conscious, in just the same way that a human body is conscious as a whole, and just as we intuitively take only a part (or some parts) to be conscious in the human body (the brain part(s)), the cosmopsychist takes only some parts of the cosmos to be conscious (this may well tally with the brain-parts of brained creatures). Moreover, just like we intuitively take it that the conscious parts(s) of our human body are the locus of experience for the whole body, the present cosmopsychist account says that the conscious parts of the cosmos are the locus of experience for the whole cosmos.

So far, so good. But this response may bring with it its own problems. For example, on this view, consciousness is a rare feature of the cosmos (insofar as the vast majority of its parts must lack consciousness), which leaves consciousness, arguably, unable to play the crucial role that many cosmopsychists will want it to play. Namely, that consciousness is the categorical ground of the nomic spatiotemporal cosmos revealed by physics. I do not have space to get into this in any significant detail here, but as we have seen previously (and will see again in the book's penultimate chapter), a promising version of constitutive cosmopsychism accepts a Russellian monist stipulation that the cosmos as revealed by physics gives only a structural-relational picture of the cosmos, and so does not tell us what grounds that structure. The Russellian monist stipulation says that consciousness, or phenomenality in some sense, is uniquely placed to fill this role. The problem, as far as the present cosmopsychist response is concerned, is that it is hard to maintain a Russellian view if consciousness is very rare, because it would be difficult to explain how the vast spatiotemporal structure of the cosmos is grounded in an extremely small number of conscious parts.

Additionally, those convinced by the metaphysical impossibility of synchronous perspectives will still object that, on this proposal, the problem has not been addressed. However, in response, the cosmopsychist could use the binocular model outlined earlier to formulate a reply, or alternatively (or perhaps conjunctively), they can stand their ground and claim that the metaphysical impossibility argument stops short of demonstrating the impossibility of synchronous perspectives scenarios.

4.7.3 The reject micro-level subjects response

The final response that I will note before concluding this chapter is the option of rejecting the stipulation that there are subjects of experience at the micro-level. There is a response of this kind available for both panpsychists and cosmopsychists. For panpsychists, a response of this kind can address both the metaphysical impossibility and epistemic implausibility arguments, while for cosmopsychists, it can address only the epistemic implausibility problem. To be clear, this is distinct from the previous response, which rejects consciousness at the micro-level. This option maintains that phenomenality, in some sense, is present at the micro-level without subjects being present.

4.7.3.1 Panpsychism without micro-subjects

For the panpsychist, rejecting micro-subjects allows both the arguments from metaphysical impossibility and from epistemic implausibility to be evaded. The impossibility problem is avoided because without micro-subjects, there are no micro-perspectives, and without micro-perspectives, the problematic synchronous perspectives scenarios do not materialize. Meanwhile, the implausibility problem is avoided, because, without micro-subjects, we would not expect our own macro-perspectives to be fragmented in accordance with their micro-perspective parts, and it is the expectation of such fragmentation that gives rise to the implausibility of synchronous perspectives scenarios.

I do not need to propose a hypothetical response here because a view already exists that follows this path: panqualityism. Readers of the previous chapter will already be well aware of this view. Panqualityism, defended most notably by Coleman (in, for example, his 2012, 2014, 2017), drops the stipulation that the microphysical ultimates are subjects of experience. It does this in favour of the view that they are instead phenomenally qualitied. Phenomenal qualities are the qualities that characterize phenomenal experience, such as colour qualities like redness and blueness. It is usually taken as a conceptual truth that phenomenal consciousness involves a subject of experience instantiating phenomenal properties. Panqualityism is arguably a counterintuitive view from the start because it rejects this apparent conceptual truth by stating that phenomenal qualities can exist untethered from subjects of experience (i.e. they can, and do, exist unexperienced).

Since we covered this view at length in the previous chapter, I will not go into detail here. However, it is worth restating the core of the view: according to panqualityism, subjects are nothing more than the awareness of phenomenal qualities, and while the qualities exist ubiquitously in microphysical ultimates, awareness of them occurs only in rare cases involving a system's higher-order thoughts about first-order qualities. On this view, micro-subjects do not exist, so there are no micro-perspectives in the picture to play the problematic role in synchronous perspectives scenarios.

4.7.3.2 Cosmopsychism without micro-subjects

For the cosmopsychist, rejecting micro-level subjects addresses the epistemic implausibility argument but not the metaphysical impossibility argument. The impossibility problem remains because synchronous perspectives scenarios are still implicated due to the existence of both cosmic-level and macro-level perspectives. The implausibility problem is avoided because there are no micro-subjects to lead to the expectation that we would see our own macro-perspectives fragmented in accordance with their micro-perspective parts.

Unlike the panpsychist case, I do not know of any examples of existing views fitting this picture. However, a possible response for the cosmopsychist is to say that although there are no micro-subjects, the micro-level is still consciousness-involving. What I propose here is not a cosmopsychist equivalent of panqualityism,[10] whereby the cosmos is phenomenally qualitied but not a subject of experience; rather, it is a little more nuanced. The possible response involves maintaining the following seemingly inconsistent set of tenets:

1. There are no unexperienced phenomenal qualities.
2. The microphysical level is phenomenally qualitied.
3. The microphysical level is free from subjects.

The tenets seem to form an inconsistent set because the truth of the conjunction of (1) and (2) apparently precludes the truth of (3). However, I think there is a possible

[10] Although I have highlighted such a view in the book's opening chapter, and it may yet have promise.

way for cosmopsychism to maintain the set consistently. First, consider the all-encompassing cosmic subject (with its cosmic perspective), which subsumes all sub-cosmic subjects (in this case, all sub-cosmic subjects are macro-subjects). The cosmic subject instantiates all of the phenomenal properties that are in existence, including those phenomenal properties associated with macro-subjects on the macro-level and those associated with all entities on the micro-level. On such a picture, although there are no subjects at the microphysical level, the micro-level is consciousness-involving insofar as it involves phenomenal properties instantiated by the cosmic subject. This view does not entail untethering phenomenal qualities from subjects, as with panqualityism, because ubiquitous phenomenal qualities at the microphysical level are all experienced, or instantiated, by the cosmic subject.

4.8 Conclusion

The combination problem for panpsychism, especially its subject aspect, has inflicted constitutive panpsychism over the course of its relatively recent resurgence. Constitutive cosmopsychism seems to offer the possibility of maintaining the core motivations behind panpsychism while avoiding the combination problem. However, it does give rise to its own equivalent in the form of the derivation problem. I have suggested that for cosmopsychism to be a genuine alternative to panpsychism, it must be better able to respond to the associated problems without incurring additional ones of its own. In this chapter, I compared the two views with regard to their respective subject problems, which are generally considered their greatest challenges. Far from either one coming out better than the other, I have suggested that they both face the same problem, which is that they both seem to entail synchronous perspectives scenarios. However, I have shown that, rather than this shared circumstance *undercutting* both views at once, it has meant I have been able to *defend* both views from their respective problems at once. Despite both views being left in a better place than they were found, I must conclude that if there is to be a way to choose which to prefer, panpsychism or cosmopsychism, it will not be on the basis of how they handle their subject problems alone. With this in mind, in the next chapter we consider two further aspects of the combination and derivation problems – the phenomenal *quality* and *structure* aspects – to see if we will find there a disparity in how the respective views manage, and therefore, if consideration of those problems is instructive for our comparison.

References

Albahari, M. (2020). 'Beyond cosmopsychism and the great I am: How the world might be grounded in universal Advaitic consciousness'. In W. Seager (Ed.), *The Routledge handbook of panpsychism* (pp. 385–406). New York: Routledge.

Chalmers, D. J. (2017). 'The combination problem for panpsychism'. In G. Brüntrup & L. Jaskolla (Eds.), *Panpsychism: Contemporary perspectives* (pp. 179–214). New York: Oxford University Press.

Coleman, S. (2012). 'Mental chemistry: Combination for panpsychists'. *Dialectica*, 66(1), 137–66.
Coleman, S. (2014). 'The real combination problem: Panpsychism, micro-subjects, and emergence'. *Erkenntnis*, 79(1), 19–44.
Coleman, S. (2017). 'Panpsychism and neutral monism: How to make up one's mind'. In G. Brüntrup & L. Jaskolla (Eds.), *Panpsychism: Contemporary perspectives* (pp. 249–82). New York: Oxford University Press.
Goff, P. (2006). 'Experiences don't sum'. In A. Freeman (Ed.), *Consciousness and its place in nature: Does physicalism entail panpsychism?* (pp. 53–61). Exeter: Imprint Academic.
Goff, P. (2017a). 'The phenomenal bonding solution to the combination problem'. In G. Brüntrup & L. Jaskolla (Eds.), *Panpsychism: Contemporary perspectives* (pp. 283–302). New York: Oxford University Press.
Goff, P. (2017b). *Consciousness and fundamental reality*. New York: Oxford University Press.
Goff, P. (2020). 'Cosmopsychism, micropsychism and the grounding relation'. In W. Seager (Ed.), *The Routledge handbook of panpsychism* (pp. 369–84). Oxford: Routledge.
Howard, I. P., & Rogers, B. J. (1996). *Binocular vision and stereopsis*. Oxford: Oxford University Press.
James, W. (1895). *The principles of psychology*. New York: Dover Publications.
Jung, C. G. (1960). *The structure and dynamics of the psyche* (2nd ed.). London: Routledge.
Mathews, F. (2011). 'Panpsychism as paradigm'. In M. Blamauer (Ed.), *The mental as fundamental* (pp. 141–66). Frankfurt Heusenstamm: Ontos Verlag.
Nagasawa, Y., & Wager, K. (2017). 'Panpsychism and priority cosmopsychism'. In G. Brüntrup & L. Jaskolla (Eds.), *Panpsychism: Contemporary perspectives* (pp. 113–29). New York: Oxford University Press.
Schaffer, J. (2010). 'Monism: The priority of the whole'. *Philosophical Review*, 119(1), 31–76.
Seager, W. (2010). 'Panpsychism, aggregation and combinatorial infusion'. *Mind and Matter*, 8(2), 167–84.
Shani, I. (2015). 'Cosmopsychism: A holistic approach to the metaphysics of experience'. *Philosophical Papers*, 44(3), 389–437.
Stidwill, D., & Fletcher, R. (2010). *Normal binocular vision: Theory, investigation and practical aspects*. Oxford: Wiley-Blackwell.
Wager, K. (2011). Dual-aspect priority monism and the combination problem for panpsychism (PhD thesis, University of Birmingham).
Wager, K. (2020). *Panpsychism and cosmopsychism* (PhD thesis, University of Birmingham).

5

Problems of phenomenal quality and structure

5.1 Introduction

Panpsychism, the approach to the problem of phenomenal consciousness that admits rudimentary consciousness to all microphysical ultimates,[1] faces the seemingly intractable combination problem: how is it that the consciousness of microphysical ultimates can combine to form instances of macro-consciousness (like human consciousness)? The problem is often separated into three sub-problems, pertaining, in turn, to the combination of subjects, qualities and structure. Cosmopsychism is an alternative to panpsychism that is receiving growing attention;[2] it says that the cosmos, as a whole, is a conscious entity. Like panpsychism, cosmopsychism holds that macro-consciousness is derivative of more fundamental consciousness that is not at the macro-level, but while panpsychism posits fundamental consciousness at the micro-level, cosmopsychism posits it at the cosmic level.

An important motivation for cosmopsychism over panpsychism is its avoidance of the combination problem, which, as just noted, arises because according to panpsychism, instances of micro-level consciousness combine to form macro-level consciousness. Cosmopsychism straightforwardly avoids the problem because it does not claim that macro-consciousness is formed from a combination of micro-consciousness but rather states that macro-level consciousness is derived from a larger cosmic-level consciousness. So far, so good. The trouble, however, is that taking the cosmopsychist approach does not allow one to escape the heart of the combination problem. Rather than offering an account of the combination of micro-level into macro-level consciousness, the cosmopsychist approach suggests a derivation of macro-level from cosmic-level consciousness. Thus, those pursuing the cosmopsychist approach are left with what we might call a *derivation problem*, in place of the combination problem. Moreover, just as the combination problem can be separated into three sub-problems, so too can the derivation problem. We can therefore envisage derivation problems relating to structure, qualities and subjects.

[1] At least according to the most typical construal.

[2] For example, see Wager (2011, 2020), Shani (2015), Nagasawa & Wager (2017), Goff (2017, 2020) and Mathews (2011). For a particularly interesting scientifically informed version, see Shani & Keppler (2018).

The heart of the problem is that, in the case of both panpsychism and cosmopsychism, macro-level consciousness is taken to be derivative of consciousness at some more fundamental level. For panpsychism, macro-consciousness is dependent on instances of micro-consciousness combining. In contrast, for cosmopsychism, macro-consciousness is dependent on some form of derivation from a larger cosmic-level consciousness. In both cases, the proponent must at least defend the plausibility of the derivation of macro-consciousness from fundamental consciousness. When I say they must at least defend the plausibility, I mean that they must at least show that the possibility of the derivation is not metaphysically precluded. Ideally, they would also demonstrate precisely how the derivation happens, but given our present relative ignorance of the nature of consciousness, we should do well to defend the mere plausibility of these interesting views.

In the last chapter, we explored the subject problems for panpsychism and cosmopsychism; in this chapter, I will focus on the structure and quality problems. In the last chapter, I argued that the subject combination problem and subject derivation problem are very closely related as both are implications of the views entailing problematic synchronous perspectives scenarios, and I suggested that the respective problems can be avoided by endorsing my binocular model of synchronous perspectives. Their respective subject problems are typically taken to be the most serious challenges for panpsychism and cosmopsychism, so the conclusion reached in the last chapter – that their problems are, in an important respect, identical, and can be avoided – has an interesting dual consequence. First, it progresses both panpsychism and cosmopsychism simultaneously, and second, it recasts the emphasis on the lesser engaged combination problems (i.e. if we are interested in which out of the two views is most promising, then we need to look beyond the subject combination and derivation problems). With this in mind, I turn our attention to the quality and structure aspects of the combination and derivation problems. In this chapter, I suggest that in these two aspects of the combination problem we see a striking asymmetry in how the problems affect panpsychism and cosmopsychism, with cosmopsychism enjoying a marked advantage in its ability to overcome the challenges. I will take the target problems one at a time. For each, I will first frame the challenge for panpsychism, before demonstrating that the challenge is not nearly as formidable for cosmopsychism. I conclude that, in respect of the quality and structure problems at least, cosmopsychism is to be preferred over panpsychism.

5.2 The quality combination problem

Let us begin with the quality problem(s). Phenomenal qualities are the felt qualities we are acquainted with in our subjective experience. They are the *qualities* that characterize phenomenal properties. Or, to put it more simply, they are the qualities that characterize what it is like for us to have an experience. Examples of phenomenal qualities include sensory qualities like colour experiences, tastes, smells, sounds, pains, etc. For example, when I am experiencing the colour red, it feels like something to have that experience, and that *feel* is a phenomenal quality.

The quality combination problem for panpsychism, broadly conceived, arises because panpsychists hold that the phenomenal qualities we are acquainted with in our everyday experience (i.e. macro-level experience) are the result of combinations of micro-qualities present at the fundamental microphysical level. The panpsychist maintains that microphysical ultimates are consciousness-involving in some primitive form, and one aspect of such primitive consciousness is similarly primitive phenomenal quality. Accordingly, the general problem is how to account for such a combination of micro-level into macro level phenomenal qualities.

Chalmers (2017) highlights one particularly challenging aspect of this general problem concerning the combination of qualities. He calls it *the palette problem*. Another difficult aspect is what I will call *the quality grain problem*,[3] but let us begin with the palette problem.

The palette problem arises because panpsychism holds that the fundamental phenomenal qualities are those associated with the microphysical ultimates of matter, and therefore, the qualities we are acquainted with in our macro-experience (our macro-qualities) are formed of a combination of such micro-qualities. The difficulty arises when we consider that our macro-experience is characterized by a vast number of qualities, ranging in degrees of similarity from extremely similar to extremely dissimilar. Think of all the different ways it is possible to feel. At any moment, our experience is composed of numerous colour, shape, smell, taste and sound qualities (among others). For example, at this moment, the qualities characterizing my experience include (but are certainly not limited to) the smell of the coffee I have sitting on my desk, the lingering taste of my last bite of blueberry muffin, the sounds of the traffic passing outside my window and the sound of my cat crying for attention, not to mention the intricate colour qualities of the painting of Cappadocia at sunrise that sits above my computer display. These examples of macro-level phenomenal qualities, according to panpsychists, are formed from a combination of 'smaller' micro-qualities associated with the microphysical ultimates of matter. However, there are only a few different types of microphysical ultimates. At most, it would seem, there are only as many micro-quality types as there are fundamental physical particle types – a handful – which means that the astonishingly vast array of macro-qualities that we experience must be formed from an incredibly small palette of micro-qualities. How can so few rudimentary micro-qualities account for the huge number and variability of macro-qualities in our experience? This is the palette problem.

5.2.1 The palette problem for panpsychism

To address the palette problem, proponents of panpsychism must address the discrepancy in the variety of qualities between micro- and macro-levels. To do this, they must claim that one would be mistaken either in thinking that there are only a *few* qualities at the micro-level, or that there are *many* qualities at the macro-level.

[3] The grain problem is more commonly related to the structure combination/derivation problems, as we will see later, but it also has a distinctive quality aspect to it. I will separate these out in this chapter but we could just as well see them as two aspects of the same problem.

Thus, approaches to the problem can be split into two broad categories: small-palette approaches and large-palette approaches.[4] Small-palette approaches can be distinguished by the insistence that the range of macro-qualities in our experience are formed from combinations of a small number of micro-qualities. Large-palette approaches can be distinguished by their claim that there are a large number of micro-qualities from which macro-qualities are formed. Both approaches maintain, in their own ways, that the palette problem arises out of a mistaken view on the prevalence of qualities at some level. For the small-palette approaches, the problem arises out of the mistaken view that the range of macro-qualities cannot be formed from a relatively small number of micro-qualities, while for the large-palette approaches, the mistaken view is that the micro-qualities are few in number.

Regarding the large-palette approach, no contemporary proponent of constitutive panpsychism has sought to solve the palette problem in this way. However, one related panpsychist, albeit not a constitutive panpsychist, account that does take such an approach is worth noting. Lewtas (2017) seemingly resolves the discrepancy between the variety of micro-level and macro-level qualities by positing a vast array of micro-qualities, with many (but not all) of the qualities we are acquainted with in our experience already present at the micro-level. In so doing, he seemingly overcomes the palette problem because there is no longer the need to get a diverse range of macro-qualities from a very restricted base of micro-qualities. It is natural to wonder how one might posit more micro-quality types than the number of microphysical ultimate types. It is worth briefly outlining the view to help us understand this.

Lewtas's position is committed to the view that there are just a few microphysical ultimates (basic physical objects, in his words), but that there are, nonetheless, vastly more micro-qualities (basic experience types, in his words) than there are microphysical ultimates. This makes his position highly unusual because it entails that more than one fundamental quality is instantiated by (at least some) microphysical ultimates. On his view, each token instance of each micro-quality characterizes at least some microphysical ultimates. Or, to put it differently, there are only a handful of types of microphysical ultimates. At least some of these types instantiate fundamental phenomenal qualities (or basic phenomenal properties, as he calls them, which are phenomenal properties not formed of other phenomenal properties). The microphysical ultimates that instantiate micro-level phenomenal qualities simultaneously instantiate more than one micro-quality. This is how the view posits a plethora of micro-qualities but a dearth of microphysical ultimates that instantiate them.

This is where the view gets somewhat perplexing; in cases of the simultaneous instantiation of numerous micro-qualities, the experience of each quality, for that token microphysical ultimate, is isolated from every other. On this view, one token microphysical ultimate might instantiate a hundred distinct micro-qualities, with each filling a phenomenal field of its own, and related to a distinct subject. The idea is that a microphysical ultimate has physical properties that are unproblematically separate from each other, such as mass and spin. Likewise, so the reasoning continues, it will

[4] I am following Chalmers (2017) in using this terminology.

have phenomenal properties, like blue experiences and red experiences, which are as separate from one another as the ultimate's physical properties of mass and spin. Importantly, instantiated by a single microphysical ultimate type is not a single subject experiencing blue and green experiences at the same time, but multiple micro-subjects, one for each phenomenal quality that the ultimate instantiates.

Our focus here is not on the subject aspect of Lewtas's view; instead, I draw attention to it only to give an example of a large-palette approach to the palette problem. As far as the palette problem is concerned, Lewtas's proposal avoids the problem by claiming that the reason we can have such a wide range of phenomenal qualities in our macro-experience is that there is an equally wide range (at least) of phenomenal qualities present at the micro-level. However, suppose we were to consider the viability of Lewtas's proposal in contrast to the typical constitutive panpsychist picture. In that case, this ability to address the palette problem will be weighed against the broader viability of its metaphysical picture. Then it seems problematic as it represents a commitment to a vastly more complex picture of fundamental reality, and comes with the consequent metaphysical expense that the panpsychist will likely deem poor value.

Let us now turn to the small-palette approach, which, again, maintains that the palette problem can be addressed by recognizing the mistaken view that macro-level qualities are more numerous than the small number of micro-qualities (or, at least more numerous than the possible combinations of the few micro-qualities. Any small-palette approach is going to rely on phenomenal blending, whereby two or more simple (fundamental) phenomenal qualities are blended in such a way (in particular ratios, for example) as to result in (derivative) composite quality blends.

Roelofs (2014) offers an attractive case for the small-palette approach.[5] They argue that the apparent radical heterogeneity (i.e. the huge variety) of macro-level qualities that appear in our macro-level experience *could* be formed of blends of just a few fundamental qualities. Their argument hinges on the thought that we do not know what the fundamental qualities are like in isolation, because we never experience them in isolation. While fundamental qualities are present in our experience of macro-qualities, they are present only as ingredients of blends, and are not individually discernible. So Roelofs's point is not that the fundamental qualities do not enter our experience; rather, their point is that we only ever experience them as indiscernible ingredients in a composite qualitative blend. However, the question remains: how is it that we get the great variety of phenomenal qualities that are present in our macro-experience from a very small number of fundamental micro-qualities? The proposal is that the apparent heterogeneity of macro-qualities is due to our inability to recognize the underlying similarity among seemingly very dissimilar qualities. Roelofs's suggestion is that it is because we cannot recognize the similarities between apparently distinct qualitative feels in our macro-experience, that we judge them to be dissimilar. In reality, according to this proposal, it is plausible that rather than experiencing a great

5 See Roelofs's book *Combining Minds: How to Think about Composite Subjectivity* (2019) for a broader discussion of their approach to both panpsychist and non-panpsychist mental composition. The book is particularly interesting as it extends (and responds to) concerns of mental composition beyond panpsychism to functionalist accounts and to theories of personal identity.

variety of dissimilar qualities, we are actually experiencing a great variety of similar qualities. Notice that the claim is not that we are mistaken about the variety of qualities that we purport to experience; it is just that our judgement that they are dissimilar is incorrect. Given that the palette problem resides in the apparent discrepancy between the presumably small number of micro-qualities and the presumably large number of macro-qualities that they must form, Roelofs's approach certainly addresses the heart of the problem by dissolving the discrepancy.

However, another question arises. Let us assume, for the sake of argument, the core theses of Roelofs's approach: (1) that there is no issue with phenomenal blending, (2) that there are only a handful of micro-qualities (which we only ever experience in composite blends), and (3) that the macro-qualities of our experience bear a far greater degree of similarity to one another than is apparent to us. We must still ask whether it is plausible that the great variety of qualitative feels can be derived from blends of such a small number of fundamental micro-qualities. Even if the great variety of macro-qualities we experience are much more closely related than we typically recognize, we are presumably still correct in judging that they differ to some extent. If this is correct, we still have a vast array of different macro-qualities formed from a very small number of micro-qualities. Therefore, we still require an account of how such qualitative variety can arise from a small number of micro-qualities.

I believe this approach has some merit, so will attempt to motivate the idea that an impressive variety of macro-qualities can indeed arise from a very limited micro-quality base. I will do this with the help of a thought experiment. Let us call this *the quality equalizer*. An audio equalizer is a piece of sound recording equipment that allows for the volume adjustment of particular sound frequency bands within an overall audio mix. They vary in how many frequency bands can be adjusted, but let us picture one with three bands. On a standard audio equalizer, each band contains a slider that can be slid up and down to adjust the volume of the particular frequency associated with that band, in the combined output audio. Given that the audio equalizer we are imagining has three bands, the combined audio output will always be a mixture of three frequencies. The prominence of each in the combined output will be a function of the position of the slider on the relevant band (the higher the slider, the greater the prominence of that frequency in the combined audio output).

The quality equalizer is a device similar to the audio equalizer we have been picturing. It also has three bands, with a slider on each that can be set to a range of positions along a vertical plane. However, on the quality equalizer, each band relates to one of the three fundamental quality types (I have chosen this number somewhat arbitrarily to represent the small number of microphysical ultimate types). With the audio equalizer, each band feeds into an overall audio output, the constitution of which is determined by the position of each band's slider. With the quality equalizer, each band feeds into a composite quality output, which is likewise determined by the position of each band's slider. While moving a slider up on a standard equalizer increases the volume of the band's associated frequency in the overall output (measured in db), moving a slider up on the quality equalizer increases the amount of the band's associated quality in the composite quality output (in the quality case let us call the unit of measurement *qi* for qualitative instances). For any quality band, the slider can be set anywhere from 0qi at the bottom of the band to whatever the maximum qi is at the top of the band; let us say the maximum is 9qi. The composite quality output of the equalizer is determined by the location of the set of sliders on their bands, and each unique set determines a unique output quality.

Now it is time for some rudimentary mathematics to determine how many unique composite quality outputs can be generated by the quality equalizer. We have three qualities that can enter the mix, and each contributes from 0–9qi, so we have three sliders, each with ten possible positions. Therefore, our quality equalizer can generate 1,000 unique composite qualities from combinations of just three fundamental qualities. I think this underwrites Roelofs's contention that large numbers of unique composite phenomenal qualities can result from blends of a very small number of fundamental qualities.

However, this proposal is still likely to be deemed implausible. Despite demonstrating the plausibility of many composite qualities resulting from blends of a few fundamental qualities, the plausibility of the claim that these can account for the *range* of macro-level qualities we experience is still likely to be contentious. As mentioned, Roelofs contends that there is a very high degree of similarity among all macro-level qualities, but that we cannot tell this because we do not experience the fundamental constituents in isolation. The question is whether the panpsychist adopting this proposal can make a compelling case that the apparently diverse range of distinct macro-qualities we are acquainted with in our experience are – although genuinely distinct qualities – in fact, all variations within a remarkably narrow range. This is not a knockdown argument against the proposal, of course. However, it will likely need further motivating to convince many that, for example, the qualitative *feel* of fear, smelling freshly grated orange zest and hearing ocean waves breaking over rocks, are all profoundly similar (as is every phenomenal quality we are acquainted with in our experience).

5.2.2 The quality grain problem for panpsychism

The quality grain problem is a problem which arises due to an apparent mismatch between the homogeneity, or, if you like, the smoothness, of our everyday experience of phenomenal quality, and the purported fact that, according to panpsychism, it is formed from an abundance of individual micro-fragments of quality associated with the microphysical ultimates. How do such disparate micro-fragments of qualities combine to form such a smooth-qualitied macro-experience?

I call the problem I am interested in here the *quality* grain problem because it is closely related to (or perhaps an integral aspect of) a broader problem often referred to as *the grain problem*. The grain problem is typically construed as a problem related to phenomenal structure. Later in the chapter, we will return to the grain problem in this 'structure' sense. For now, I will focus on a distinct (or at least distinguishable) quality aspect of the more general problem, as it deserves attention quite apart from the structure aspect. However, we will see later that the problems might not be totally distinct.

Returning to the quality grain problem, this is closely related to the notion of phenomenal blending that came up in the previous section. We saw how, more or less, all approaches to the palette problem require fundamental phenomenal qualities to be blended into macro-qualities. Obviously, in the previous section, we were interested in the discrepancy between the small number of micro-quality types and the large number of macro-qualities types, and whether or not it is feasible to combine the few types at the micro-level in enough different ways to account for the myriad macro-qualities we are acquainted with in our experience. We were not particularly concerned, there, with whether blending was possible; rather, we were concerned with whether a few qualities might be capable of blending into the variety of qualities in our macro-experience. The quality grain problem is specifically concerned with the viability of blending, as it unifies fragmented micro-qualities into seamless macro-qualities.

On the typical panpsychist view, the microphysical ultimates instantiate micro-phenomenal qualities, which somehow combine to form macro-qualities. Pre-combination, these micro-qualities are distinct quality fragments in their pure, unblended state. Upon combination (whatever that may be and however that may work), these distinct fragments, presumably billions and billions of them, form a macro-quality. However, the macro-qualities in our experience do not appear to be composed of billions of quality fragments. Consider the qualitative field of a subject of experience – perhaps consider yours right now – the qualities you are aware of now do not seem to be formed of billions of distinct fragments of phenomenal quality; rather, the qualities present to your phenomenal field appear smooth and continuous, with no evidence of the billions of jagged joints that we might expect if they were the composite qualities that the panpsychist tells us they are.

A response to the quality grain problem will accomplish the following two interrelated tasks: first, it will motivate the notion of phenomenal blending (i.e. it will give us reason to think phenomenal blending *per se* is possible). Second, it will leverage the notion of blending (now rendered plausible) to make sense of why our macro-qualities are not fragmented in accordance with their micro-quality ingredients. Roelofs (2014) achieves both by drawing attention to our own macro-qualities. They argue that we have good reason to suppose that blending is possible because we experience it in our everyday macro-experience. They provide familiar examples of colour and olfactory blends: it seems plausible, for instance, that when we experience the quality of pinkness, we are experiencing a mixture of red and white qualities. Alternatively, when we experience the scent of a perfume, we are experiencing a blend of the olfactory qualities of its constituents. Roelofs further motivates the concept of blending by highlighting research in neuropsychology, which has shown that pain experiences consist of two qualitative components (i.e. they are phenomenal blends): one that renders the pain unpleasant and another that enables us to locate the pain as distinct from other negative feelings.

By highlighting the apparent presence of blends in our everyday macro-experience, Roelofs accomplishes both tasks. In answer to the first, the panpsychist can claim that the concept of phenomenal blending is motivated by its apparent existence in our everyday macro-experience, which certainly seems reasonable. Furthermore, by identifying examples of blends familiar in our macro-experience, Roelofs paves the way for an answer to the second task as well: the apparent presence of blends in our macro-experience undermines the expectation that the notion of phenomenal blending is inconsistent with the qualities of our macro-experience (since they are already present there!). Recall that the quality grain problem arises due to a mismatch between the homogeneity (i.e. the smoothness and seamlessness) of our macro-level qualities and the micro-level fragments of quality from which they are formed (according to panpsychism). Roelofs's response is intriguing because rather than undermining the expectation that our macro-experience should be fragmented in accordance with phenomenal blending, it challenges the (implicit) assumption that our macro-experience is not already host to qualitative blends.

Continuing this line of response, the panpsychist can claim that, just as the familiar examples of macro-level quality blends are not problematic (insofar as their presence in macro-experience does not lead to a fragmentation of macro-level phenomenal quality in conflict with our experience), neither are micro-level blends (because, just as we do not see macro-level blends present as fragmentary in our experience, neither would we expect micro-level blends to present as fragmentary qualities at the macro-level). One worry is that this relies on extrapolating from a few macro-to-macro blends to billions of blends at the fundamental micro-level, and this extrapolation may be questionable given the basis on which the former are deemed plausible. Consider the exemplar macro-level quality blends; it is their very discernibility as blends that allows them to factor in the panpsychist's case for blending. But notice that the quality grain problem concerns the expectation that micro-level blends will be discernible in macro-experience, and notice also that it is their apparent indiscernibility that causes the tension for the panpsychist (i.e. why is our macro-quality not fragmented in accordance with the micro-quality blends which compose it, according to panpsychism). Therefore, the fact that micro-quality blends are indiscernible in macro-experience, while (at least some) macro-quality blends are discernible as such in macro-experience, would seem to count against the plausibility of micro-level blending, and therefore, arguably cuts against panpsychism.

The problem is that the case for the plausibility of phenomenal blending is made based on cases that are different in an important respect to those they seek to explain. The cases of blending we are aware of in macro-experience are those where ingredient qualities are discernible (either while blended or intellectually). However, the cases at the heart of the quality grain problem are those where the ingredients are not discernible in experience while blended, and do not seem to be intellectually discernible. Why should we take the intelligibility of the former to excuse the unintelligibility of the latter? For Roelofs (2014), this comes back to the panpsychist response mentioned in the previous section: we may be unable to discern ingredient qualities because we never experience them in isolation. A worry here is that if this approach is accurate, each of the astonishingly vast number of phenomenal macro-qualities we experience is formed from a unique combination of a tiny number of fundamental micro-qualities. Although we may not experience such qualities in total isolation, and therefore may not have a perfectly complete picture of them as pure qualities, it seems to me that, on this picture, we would still have an intimate experiential handle on them (after all, every qualitative feel puts us in contact, albeit imperfect, with those fundamental qualities). One might worry that this approach is in danger of making us implausibly ignorant of the very qualities that constitute our conscious experience.

What we have seen is that panpsychism faces one problem relating to the formation of massively varied macro-qualities from a limited base of micro-qualities, and another which relates to the formation of smooth composite macro-qualities from the fragmented individual micro-qualities present in micro-level experience (of the microphysical ultimates). So far, I have only summarized the quality combination problem(s) for panpsychism, outlining possible responses along the way. The outlines sketched above demonstrate that the quality combination problem may not be insurmountable for panpsychism, but that the proposed solutions may still need further justification.

5.3 The quality derivation problem

I now turn to parallels for cosmopsychism. Cosmopsychists hold that the fundamental bearer of phenomenal quality is the cosmos as a whole and that the macro-qualities we are familiar with in our experience derive from the cosmic-level quality. The general quality combination problem for panpsychism is the problem of how macro-qualities are formed of combinations of micro-qualities. There is a parallel general problem for cosmopsychism. *The quality derivation problem* for cosmopsychism is the problem of how to account for the macro-qualities that we are acquainted with in our macro-experience in virtue of the phenomenal quality associated with the cosmos as a whole. In other words, it is the problem of accounting for the derivation of macro-qualities from phenomenal quality at the cosmic level. We might also present parallel versions of the two more fine-grained problems that we explored in the previous section: the palette problem and the quality grain problem. But is cosmopsychism similarly challenged by these two problems? Let us now examine this question.

5.3.1 The palette problem for cosmopsychism

Recall the palette problem for panpsychism, the problem concerning how a rich array of macro-qualities can be constituted by a limited number of micro-qualities. If macro-qualities are formed of combinations of micro-qualities, and micro-qualities are the phenomenal qualities associated with microphysical ultimates of matter, then given that there is only a very limited variety of microphysical ultimates, we have to somehow form these rich macro-qualities from a restricted variety of micro-qualities. Considering this problem in light of cosmopsychism, we can formulate its equivalent palette problem. In this case, the issue is that the rich phenomenal qualities in macro-experience are derived from an even more limited base of qualities at the fundamental level. For panpsychism, the issue was that there are only as many micro-quality types as there are different types of microphysical ultimate (i.e. a handful). On the face of it, for cosmopsychism, the palette problem is even worse than for panpsychism because, in the cosmopsychist case, there is only one physical ultimate – the cosmos. Therefore, the rich phenomenal qualities of macro-experience must be derived from the phenomenal quality of just one entity (which is much fewer than the handful panpsychism has to work with!).

However, on closer inspection, the palette problem dissolves when considered from the perspective of cosmopsychism. The problem for panpsychism arises because the micro-qualities associated with microphysical ultimates are presumably primitive compared to the macro-level qualities they jointly constitute. Given that micro-qualities are said to be primitive, it seems a push to then form rich and diverse macro-qualities out of this small number of primitive micro-quality types (again, there is a limited number of types because there is only a small number of types of microphysical ultimates). In contrast, cosmopsychism does not suffer from the palette problem because it does not have to form rich macro-qualities from primitive micro-qualities, nor does it have to derive rich macro-qualities from a primitive cosmic-level quality. Instead, the cosmic quality is itself rich, arguably much richer than the qualities we are associated with in our macro-experience. The palette problem arises for panpsychism, essentially, because the base qualities are primitive and are said to combine into something richer and more diverse. Cosmopsychism does not face this problem because rich macro-qualities are derived from an even richer cosmic quality. On the cosmopsychist view, each of the great variety of macro-level qualities that we are acquainted with in our experience is a part of a larger and more complex cosmic-level phenomenal quality.

Earlier, I noted Roelof's (2014) approach to resolving the palette problem for panpsychism. On one interpretation, their approach involves tweaking both the poverty of the micro-qualities and the richness of the macro-qualities to reduce the discrepancy between them and render plausible the claim that macro-qualities are the result of the phenomenal blending of micro-qualities. On this approach, micro-qualities are taken to be much richer than the microscopic rudimentary fragments of qualities that the ordinary panpsychist takes them to be. The true phenomenal character of the fundamental micro-qualities outstretches our experience because we are never aware of them in isolation. At the same time, in a sense, the phenomenal character of macro-level qualities is not as rich as we might ordinarily assume; instead, what we take to be a vast array of disparate qualities is actually a tightly clustered set highly similar qualities. Thus, with a set of more expansive micro-qualities and a far less diverse range of macro-qualities to blend them into, the sharp edge of the palette problem is somewhat blunted. However, there is work to do to satisfactorily enrich micro-qualities and impoverish macro-qualities. The palette problem for cosmopsychism does not force the cosmopsychist to make or endorse such tweaks to micro- or macro-level qualities. The cosmopsychist can maintain that macro-qualities are as rich and varied as our experience would lead us to believe. Moreover, they can maintain that the microphysical ultimates instantiate only very rudimentary phenomenal qualities (if they so wish), but doing so does not complicate their response to the palette problem. Thus, with regard to the palette problem, cosmopsychism has the advantage.

5.3.2 The quality grain problem for cosmopsychism

Now let us turn to the quality grain problem. For panpsychism, this arises due to an apparent mismatch between the fragmented nature of phenomenal qualities at the micro-level and the smooth nature of qualities at the macro-level. There appears to be a mismatch between the derivative macro-quality and the fundamental micro-qualities.

Is there a similar apparent mismatch for cosmopsychism? For cosmopsychism, there would be an equivalent problem if there were a mismatch between the homogeneity of phenomenal quality at the derivative macro-level and the fundamental cosmic level. However, there need not be any such mismatch for cosmopsychism. Qualitatively speaking, our subjective experience is clearly a smooth and homogenous affair, but unlike in the case of panpsychism, macro-qualities, on the cosmopsychist view, are not taken to be complexes of 'smaller' fragments of quality. Rather, they may be derivative partial aspects of a larger cosmic quality, which itself may be equally (or even more) smooth and homogenous. In the case of cosmopsychism, we have smooth, homogenous macro-qualities derived from a smooth, homogenous, cosmic quality. Therefore, an equivalent of the grain problem does not arise.

We saw earlier that (almost all) panpsychists must rely on some degree of phenomenal blending, that is, they count on the plausibility (at least) of distinct qualities blending to form new composite qualities. We also saw that the extent of blending needed varies from view to view, but even the most elaborate views will need some degree of blending. I argued, echoing Roelofs (2014), that panpsychists can at least make a decent case for blending (of some sort) being plausible. However, I suggested that troubles remain for the panpsychist because the blending they require involves composite blends whose ingredients we cannot discern and which are unlike examples given to render the notion of blending intelligible. I claimed that panpsychism still has some work to do in addressing the quality grain problem. As a result, as it stands, cosmopsychism maintains the advantage over panpsychism with respect to the quality grain problem.

Therefore, we can see that cosmopsychism does not face the two most problematic aspects of the general quality derivation problem. It does not face the palette problem because the fundamental phenomenal quality is the cosmic quality, which is (in contrast to panpsychism's fundamental qualities) a much more complex palette than the derivative qualities. Furthermore, it does not face the quality grain problem because (in contrast to panpsychism's picture on which discrete quality-fragments at the micro-level combine to form homogenous macro-qualities) the fundamental quality need be no less homogenous than derivative qualities. One might still contend, however, that cosmopsychism must explain the derivation of macro-qualities from the cosmic quality, i.e. that it must still answer the broad quality problem. By way of an answer to this question, they can simply say that macro-qualities are derived from the cosmic quality in virtue of being partial aspects of it: macro-qualities are literally parts of the phenomenal quality instantiated by the cosmos.

5.4 The structure combination problem

The second aspect of the combination problem that I will address in this chapter is referred to as the structure combination problem. We can take this problem to target several issues related to structure. When contemplating structure problems, 'physical' structure is taken to be the quasi-mathematical structure described by current physics and 'phenomenal' structure is the structure manifest in our phenomenology (e.g.

consider the spatial structure of our visual field, some things are nearer or further away than others, and things take up space in a specific way in a specific place). To say that our phenomenology is structured is just to resonate with what Mendelovici says in the following excerpt:

> Our mental states do not form an undifferentiated mass, or a set of totally isolated distinct mental states, but are instead related and structured in various ways. For example, a visual experience of a red apple on a brown table does not only involve an experience of reddness, an experience of a somewhat spherical shape, an experience of brownness, and an experience of a table-like shape. It also involves these experiences related in a certain way: The redness and the spherical shape are experienced as pertaining to the same represented object, the brownness and the table-like shape are experienced as pertaining to a distinct represented object, and the two represented objects are experienced as spatially related to each other.
>
> (2017, p. 12)

In general, structure combination problems relate to difficulties in bridging an apparent difference between the phenomenal structure at the fundamental level of reality and the phenomenal structure at derivative levels of reality, as well as difficulties in bridging an apparent difference between the physical structure and the phenomenal structure within a given level. The first of these I call inter-level structure bridging problems (i.e. problems where a disparity in phenomenal structure occurs across levels of reality - for example, between the micro-level and the macro-level). The second category I call intra-level structure bridging problems (i.e. problems involving a structural disparity between the physical and phenomenal domains within a single level: micro, macro or any other). For panpsychism, the most pressing intra-level problem is the disparity between phenomenal structure and physical structure at the macro-level. This is the structural mismatch problem. Meanwhile, the most pressing inter-level problem for panpsychism concerns the disparity between micro-phenomenal and macro-phenomenal structure. This issue is closely related to the quality grain problem discussed earlier, but it focuses on phenomenal structure rather than phenomenal quality. I call this the structure grain problem. We will see shortly whether cosmopsychism faces equivalents of the inter- and intra-level problems just outlined, or whether it possesses additional theoretical resources that might allow it to sidestep or resolve them more effectively than panpsychism (spoiler alert: I suspect that it does). However, before turning to cosmopsychism's potential advantages, let us first examine the structure-related challenges that arise for panpsychism.

Chalmers describes the broad structure combination problem for panpsychism as follows:

> The structure combination problem is roughly: How does microexperiential structure (and microphysical structure) combine to yield macroexperiential structure? Our macroexperience has a rich structure, involving the complex spatial structure of visual and auditory fields, a division into many different modalities, and so on. How can the structure in microexperience and microstructure yield this rich structure?
>
> (2017, p. 183)

From Chalmers's summary, we can see that, broadly conceived, the structure combination problem clearly has both the intra and inter aspects just mentioned. It is an inter-level problem in a sense because it asks how micro-phenomenal structure can combine to form macro-phenomenal structure. It is also an intra-level problem in the sense that there is a purported parity between micro-phenomenal and microphysical structure at the fundamental level, yet we do not see a structural parity between macrophysical and macro-phenomenal structure at the derivative level.

5.4.1 The inter-level structure bridging problem for panpsychism: The structure grain problem

As mentioned, the structure grain problem is closely related to the quality grain problem. Perhaps they are even inseparable. However, it does seem that there is both a quality and a structure aspect to the general problem, and it is on this basis that I separate my treatment of the problem in this chapter. The aspect I am here calling the *structure grain problem* relates not to phenomenal *qualities,* per se, but to the discrepancy between the *structure* of phenomenal fields at the micro- and macro-levels. On a typical construal of panpsychism, micro-level phenomenal fields are taken to be simple and static. Take a token microphysical ultimate; its phenomenal field will presumably consist of an unchanging experience with a simple structure. However, this does not match the structure of our macro-level phenomenal fields.

To get a rough handle on what this is getting at, let us imagine the structure of our phenomenal field if it was characterized exhaustively by a red experience. I think we can understand that, in such a case, our experience would lack complex phenomenal structure: we would have just a simple, unchanging red experience. I take it that this is the sort of phenomenal structure that the panpsychist would claim is present at the micro-level. Now, in reality, our human phenomenal fields are much more richly structured than the one just described. At any moment, our phenomenal fields are structurally complex, with their contents arranged according to various spatial relations and including multi-modal elements (sights, sounds, smells, tastes, pains, emotions, etc.). The structure grain problem is the challenge of explaining the complex phenomenal structure of macro-level experience in virtue of the simple phenomenal structure presumably present in micro-level experience (given that macro-level structure is formed from combinations of micro-level structure).

I do not know if panpsychists are generally concerned with the apparent need to bridge micro- and macro-level phenomenal structure. Still, it does seem that this raises a legitimate concern. Perhaps the most likely response is that macro-level phenomenal structure (e.g. the spatial arrangement of qualities in our phenomenal fields) straightforwardly follows from the rearrangement of the micro-level structure that underpins it. But this only raises the question of what underpins such micro-level rearrangements. For panpsychists, micro-level experience is instantiated by microphysical ultimates, so macro-level experience formed from a combination of micro-level experience must pertain (in some way) to an arrangement of microphysical ultimates. Micro-level rearrangements, then, are rearrangements of microphysical ultimates. However, no arrangement of microphysical ultimates gives rise to macrophysical structure equivalent to the macro-phenomenal structure panpsychists maintain (following this line of thinking) results from the rearrangement of micro-phenomenal structure. This brings us nicely to our next problem.

5.4.2 The intra-level structural bridging problem for panpsychism: The structural mismatch problem

When it comes to the structure combination problem, I think it is fair to say that the aspect often called *the structural mismatch problem* is the most concerning for panpsychists. Chalmers outlines the problem like so: 'Macrophysical structure (in the brain, say) seems entirely different from the macrophenomenal structure we experience. Microexperiences presumably have structure closely corresponding to microphysical structure (this is especially clear on a Russellian view), and we might expect a combination of them to yield something akin to macrophysical structure. How do these combine to yield macrophenomenal structure instead?' (2017, p 183). Levine presents a perhaps clearer illustration of the structural mismatch problem:

> If macro-phenomenal properties are realized in micro-phenomenal properties, and micro-phenomenal properties are instantiated in micro-physical properties (indeed, on the Russellian version, they constitute the categorical bases of the micro-physical properties), then one would expect an isomorphism between the structure of the relevant macro-physical properties and the quality spaces of the relevant macro-phenomenal properties. But what reason is there to think such an isomorphism exists? It certainly doesn't seem that there is.
>
> (2017)

The structural mismatch problem stems from the proposed intricate connection between the micro-phenomenal and the macro-phenomenal, together with the proposed relationship between the micro-phenomenal and microphysical. According to panpsychism (at least the most popular versions we are interested in here), the microphysical is isomorphic with the micro-phenomenal, and the macro-phenomenal is formed from a combination of microphysical entities and their micro-phenomenal natures. The problem is that macro-phenomenal structure does not seem to be isomorphic to macrophysical structure in the way that we should presumably expect it to be given the isomorphism between phenomenal and physical structure at the fundamental level. This is to say that the brain's physical structure differs greatly from the structure of our conscious experience. For example, consider our conscious experience, typically a smooth, continuous, multimodal experience involving a complex of sights, sounds and smells (to name a few), which appear to us in a highly structured quality space. The physical structure of our brains does not seem at all isomorphic with the structural complexity of our conscious experience. We can see the aforementioned quality grain problem as a mismatch problem between the homogenous, continuous *quality* of the macro-experience and the heterogeneous, discontinuous *quality* of the micro-experience that constitutes it. The structural mismatch we have here is a similar problem; this time, the mismatch is between the homogenous and continuous phenomenal *structure* of macro-experience and the heterogeneous physical *structure* of the physical brain. Nagasawa and I formulate the combination problem in structural terms, stating:

> The combination problem arises from the apparent discrepancy between a highly complex, structured aggregate of atoms and brain cells, on the one hand; and a smooth, uniform phenomenal experience such as a visual experience, on the other. The problem can be formulated as an objection to panpsychism as follows: Ordinary phenomenal experiences present themselves as smooth, continuous, and unified. They do have distinct aspects, but they have an underlying homogeneity. According to panpsychism, however, all physical ultimates instantiate phenomenal or protophenomenal properties and our ordinary phenomenal experiences result from combinations of these properties. It is hard to see, however, how phenomenal or protophenomenal properties of microphysical entities could add up to the homogeneous character of phenomenal experiences that we have.
>
> (Nagasawa & Wager, 2017, p 120)

Responses to the structural mismatch problem are few and far between. Chalmers (2017) notes some possible means to work around or through the problem but ultimately remains unconvinced about the prospects of a solution. An effective response to the problem will counter the claim that macrophysical and macro-phenomenal structure are non-isomorphic. The obvious way to do this is to show that the non-isomorphism claim is false because we are mistaken about either macro-phenomenal structure or macrophysical structure, such that, when correctly understood, the isomorphism between them becomes apparent. One option Chalmers highlights, but quickly rejects, is Stoljar's (2001) suggestion that the structure of the visual field, as it appears to us, is not part of the structure of an experience but only the structure *represented* by the experience. Following this line of reasoning, the panpsychist might state that we have no reason to assume that the phenomenal structure of macro-experience, as it is in itself, is not isomorphic with macrophysical structure. However, Chalmers considers it plausible that the representational content of our macro-experience is also part of our macro-phenomenal structure, which would challenge the viability of this approach.

Chalmers suggests that a panpsychist's best response to the structural mismatch problem might be to say that the problem rests on an equivocation on what 'macrophysical structure' is supposed to be. On the one hand, we might construe macrophysical structure as macro-level structure characterized in terms of physics (i.e. space, time, mass, etc.). On the other hand, we might construe it as any structure constituted by microphysics (this might be chemical, biological, informational, etc.).That said, the panpsychist could hold that the structural mismatch problem arises from confusion over the notion of 'macrophysical structure'. The apparent non-isomorphism (which characterizes the problem) results from assuming a narrow construal of macrophysical structure, which takes it as structure characterized in terms of physics. In this case, it seems quite clear that the macro-phenomenal structure of the brain (or parts of it) is non-isomorphic with the macro-phenomenal structure we are acquainted with in our experience. However, by taking a broad construal of macrophysical structure (which takes macrophysical structure to be any constituted by microphysics), it is not immediately evident that there is a lack of isomorphism between that broad macrophysical structure of our brain and the phenomenal structure in our macro-level experience. For example, the macro-phenomenal structure of our visual fields may be isomorphic with the broad macrophysical structure of visual information in the brain. However, it seems complicated to make this work because it requires that micro-level phenomenal properties constitute both narrow and broad macro-phenomenal structure. However, it is not at all clear why micro-level phenomena should give rise to broad structure at all, and even if it does, it is not clear how broad macro-phenomenal structure relates to narrow macro-phenomenal structure.

My focus here, as elsewhere in the chapter, has not been to provide a complete account of responses to the combination problems for panpsychism; instead, my aim has been only to demonstrate that each problem remains a serious challenge and that, therefore, we may do well to consider the equivalent problem for cosmopsychism. With this aim in mind, let us now consider if there is a parallel structure-related problem for cosmopsychism. We can state the broad structure derivation problem for cosmopsychism as the problem of how to account for macro-phenomenal structure in terms of a derivation from cosmic-level phenomenal structure. Furthermore, we can restate the structural mismatch problem for cosmopsychism as the challenge of accounting for any mismatch between macrophysical and macro-phenomenal structure. On the surface, the problem might appear to present just as it does for panpsychism. However, I will demonstrate that, on closer inspection, the structural mismatch problem does not affect the views equally, and that cosmopsychism is less vulnerable to the problem.

5.5 The structure derivation problem

Cosmopsychism does not face the same broad structure problem as panpsychism because the problem for panpsychism arises specifically as a consequence of the claim that macro-consciousness is formed from a combination of the micro-consciousnesses of microphysical ultimates. For panpsychism, the broad problem is how such rudimentary physical and phenomenal structure combine to create the structure found in our macro-experience. The problem is that the supposed structural parity between the physical and the phenomenal purportedly existing at the fundamental micro-level appears to inexplicably disappear at the macro-level. Cosmopsychism denies the claim that macro-phenomenal structure is formed from a combination of the structure of microphysical ultimates and the structure of their phenomenal natures. Instead, it claims that the phenomenal structure we are acquainted with at the macro-level is derived from the phenomenal structure of the cosmos. There is no combination of micro-level entities into macro-level entities but instead a derivation of macro-entities from the cosmic entity. Despite this, we can suggest an equivalent problem for cosmopsychism. We can call this the structure derivation problem for cosmopsychism: the problem of how to derive macro-phenomenal structure from the phenomenal structure of the cosmos. This is cosmopsychism's inter-level structure problem.

When addressing this inter-level problem, it is clear that in needing to account only for derivation as opposed to combination (as is the predicament for panpsychism), cosmopsychism does not face anywhere near as severe a problem as panpsychism. Recall that the broad problem for panpsychism arises due to the discontinuity between the fragmented structure at the micro-level (i.e. a vast multitude of individual microphysical ultimates and their bounded phenomenal natures) and the continuous structure at the macro-level (e.g. in our macro-experience we are acquainted with a homogenous, continuous, unified quality space). Therefore, for panpsychism, there appears to be a striking discrepancy between the structure at reality's fundamental and derivative levels. Cosmopsychism does not face such an inconsistency because it does not take the microphysical level to be fundamental, but rather, it states that the cosmic level is fundamental. Importantly, the cosmic level need not exhibit the kind of fragmented fundamental phenomenal structure that causes the inter-level structure problem to arise in the first place. The cosmopsychist can maintain that cosmic phenomenal structure has precisely the smooth and continuous character present in macro-experience. Therefore, there is no structure derivation *problem* because the cosmopsychist can easily account for the derivation of macro-experiential structure from the phenomenal structure at the cosmic level.

The inter-level structure problem is very similar to the quality grain problem for both panpsychism and cosmopsychism. The quality grain problem for panpsychism is the problem of how to explain homogenous macro-qualities in virtue of a combination of heterogeneous micro-qualities. For panpsychism, the inter-level *structure grain problem* is the problem of explaining homogenous macro-phenomenal structure in virtue of a combination of fragmented instances of micro-phenomenal structure. The grain problem turns on the fact that there is a disparity between the qualities at the fundamental and derivative levels of reality, with fundamental qualities being heterogeneous, fragmented and discontinuous, and derivative qualities displaying a continuous homogeneity. Cosmopsychism does not face the grain problem, as there is no such disparity between qualities at the fundamental and derivative levels. This is because the cosmic level, not the micro-level, is fundamental, and there is no reason for the cosmopsychist to hold that cosmic-level quality is not just as continuous and homogenous as our macro-level qualitative experience. Cosmopsychists can similarly address the inter-level structure derivation problem (i.e. the structure grain problem). The problem arises for panpsychism because there is a vital difference between the phenomenal structure at the fundamental and derivative levels of reality, with the fundamental level of reality – the micro-level – exhibiting fragmented phenomenal structure, and the derivative level – the macro-level – exhibiting smooth, continuous, phenomenal structure. This problem does not materialize for cosmopsychism because, again, cosmopsychism takes the cosmic level to be fundamental rather than the micro-level, and there is no reason to suppose that there is a vital difference between the phenomenal structure at the cosmic level and macro-level. It is plausible that both levels exhibit smooth, continuous, phenomenal structure, so there is no need to get smoothness and continuity from a combination of instances of fragmented phenomenal structure (as is the case for panpsychism); smooth macro-phenomenal structure can easily be derived from smooth cosmic-level phenomenal structure via partial abstraction. For example, cosmopsychists can maintain that the smooth, continuous phenomenal structure of our macro-consciousnesses are partial aspects of the even larger, smooth and continuous phenomenal structure of the cosmic consciousness.

5.5.1 The structural mismatch problem for cosmopsychism

Even if there is no inter-level structure problem, there might still be an intra-level one. Let us now explore whether cosmopsychism faces an equivalent of the structural mismatch problem. On the face of it, it looks like the intra-level problem is essentially the challenge of accounting for the structural inconsistency between a macro-level physical entity – i.e. the brain – and its respective macro-experience. Thus, it appears *prima facie* to be a problem restricted to one level of reality: the macro-level (hence why I call it an intra-level problem). If this is right, the problem would appear to be equally problematic for both panpsychism and cosmopsychism. In both cases, the challenge at hand is how to explain the difference in structure between derivative physical entities and their associated phenomenality. Both views take the macro-level to be derivative, so it is not clear there is any reason why the problem would not trouble both in equal measure.

However, on closer inspection, there appears to be a relevant difference between how the mismatch problem affects the two views. To illustrate this, let us think first about panpsychism. It indeed faces the problem of how to explain a disharmony between macrophysical structure (like, say, brains) and macro-phenomenal structure (such as a human visual field). As we have already noted, when we talk about differences in *structure,* we are essentially talking about differences in smoothness and continuity. For example, brains (which are macrophysical entities) seem to be formed by a complex of jagged, discontinuous microphysical constituents. In contrast, our macro-experience seems to be homogenous, with different aspects being integrated and disintegrated in a smooth and continuous manner. The structural mismatch problem arises for panpsychism because it maintains that the brain is a complex of micro-constituents, each exhibiting fragments of phenomenal structure, which, when combined, form the smooth macro-phenomenal structure present in our macro-experience. Hence, there is a mismatch between the physical structure of the brain (a complex aggregation of individual microphysical ultimates) and the phenomenal structure of our macro-experience (which, in the case of panpsychism, is taken to be formed from a combination of the phenomenal structure of the microphysical ultimates). On the one hand, there is a smooth and continuous macro-experience; on the other hand, there is an aggregation of individual atoms, the combined phenomenal structure of which is said to make up the structure of macro-level experience.

The mismatch between macrophysical entities and macro-phenomenality is not, as it first appears, a problem confined to one level of reality. It stems from a commitment to bottom-up micropsychism. In accordance with such a bottom-up commitment, we imply that there is a structural disparity between brains and macro-experience because of the assumption that brains are formed of complexes of fundamental micro-constituents. The problem is not so much about the structural mismatch between the physical and phenomenal at the macro-level. Rather, at its root, the problem hinges on the assumption that reality, in its physical and phenomenal guises, is bottom-up, such that what is observed and experienced at the macro-level must be formed of a combination of what is observed and (presumed to be) experienced at the micro-level. According to this thinking, brains are complex wholes that are dependent for their existence on their microphysical parts.

Cosmopsychism maintains that reality functions in a top-down manner, so the motivation for the structural mismatch problem is absent. According to cosmopsychism, macrophysical entities like brains are not constituted by microphysical entities. Instead, microphysical entities are derived from and dependent on the macrophysical (and ultimately, all sub-cosmic entities are derived from and dependent on the cosmos as a whole, which is the only fundamental entity). As such, it rejects the view that brains are complex wholes that are dependent on their parts. Since this is from where the structural mismatch problem stems, it does not present for cosmopsychism.

In other words, because cosmopsychism is not a bottom-up view, it is not committed to the problematic assumption that there must be a structural mismatch. That assumption has its roots in the notion that the brain is a derivative whole formed from a combination of individual, discontinuous fundamental microphysical ultimates. Understandably, one apprehends a mismatch when the brain, as the bearer of macro-phenomenal structure, is itself taken to be such a fragmented aggregate. But for cosmopsychism, the brain need not be understood that way at all because cosmopsychism is a top-down view. The cosmopsychist can maintain that the brain is prior to its parts. Rather than constituting the brain, its microphysical parts depend on the brain for their existence. On this picture, there is no need to think that there is a problematic mismatch in structure between the physical brain and the phenomenal structure of the macro-experience with which it is associated. This is because the mismatch worry stems from the idea that the brain is formed of a combination of many individual microphysical constituents (and from there that it is the structure of their micro-phenomenal natures that must combine to give rise to the macro-phenomenal structure in our experience). Cosmopsychism rejects this picture and, as such, does not face the structural mismatch problem.

5.6 Conclusion

Let us take stock of where we are. In Chapter 1, I started our exploration of the landscape of fundamental consciousness by clearing the cosmopsychist pathway and distinguishing it from the much more well-trodden micropsychism pathway. From there, my track took us, in Chapter 2, to the priority cosmopsychism blueprint. There, I outlined a framework of a cosmopsychist approach to the problem of consciousness that prescribes a fundamental cosmic consciousness on which all sub-cosmic consciousness depends. This blueprint sets forth an alternative to panpsychism, which avoids two of its most persistent challenges: the infinite decomposition problem and the combination problem. However, we also saw that the blueprint is vulnerable to the derivation problem. Our next stop, Chapter 3, highlighted some developments on (or consistent with) the blueprint and some formulations of the combination and derivation problems, including claims that the notion of combined or derived *subjects* of experience entails a contradiction. The body of the chapter was then premised on this perceived wisdom that the subject aspect of the combination and derivation problems are likely defeating for panpsychism and cosmopsychism, respectively. On this basis, the chapter focused on an examination of two views – Albahari's (2020) perennialism and Coleman's (2012, 2014, 2017) panqualityism – that are closely related to panpsychism and cosmopsychism but which purportedly avoid the subject aspects of the problems by rejecting subjects at the fundamental level of reality. I concluded that neither view is a viable successor to panpsychism or cosmopsychism because each comes with distinct challenges that negates its promise.

From here, we circled back to the subject combination and derivation problems, an investigation of which was the focus of Chapter 4; if Chapter 3 demonstrated that getting rid of subjects gave rise to more problems than we started with, then it made sense to revisit the purportedly contradiction-involving notions of combining and deriving subjects, in the hope of finding a route through the problems. In Chapter 4, I argued that, at the core, the subject combination problem (for panpsychism) and the subject derivation (for cosmopsychism) are the same, because both arise due to the respective views affirming what I called 'synchronous perspectives scenarios', the possibility of which appears to be metaphysically precluded. I made the case that underpinning concerns about such scenarios might be their epistemic implausibility rather than their metaphysical impossibility. But at any rate, I offered a model for understanding synchronous perspectives scenarios in an unproblematic way (i.e. which undercuts the charge of both metaphysical impossibility and epistemic implausibility). The somewhat surprising conclusion of the chapter was that, on the one hand, there is no significant difference between the subject aspects of the combination and derivation problems, so neither panpsychism nor cosmopsychism is more promising in this regard. On the other hand, the fact that the problems are essentially the same means that my proposed 'binocular model of synchronous perspectives' helps panpsychism and cosmopsychism simultaneously resolve their subject problems (which, recall, are their most persistent challenges).

This brings us to the present chapter. Recall that a central focus in this book is an assessment of the promise of cosmopsychism compared to panpsychism (considering, in particular, the constitutive versions of those views). Given that Chapter 4 was somewhat of a leveller regarding the views' subject-related problems, in this chapter, we shifted our focus to the other two core aspects of the general combination problem: the problems relating to the combination and derivation of phenomenal qualities and structure. The aim was to see if the views' handling of these problems marked a distinct difference in their overall promise. I suggested that cosmopsychism is at a distinct advantage when it comes to these two problems. Thus, it is in the consideration of these two aspects of the combination and derivation problems that we find the most significant disparity in the respective views' prospects in the face of the overall problems.

So far, much of the focus of the book has been on the core problems of panpsychism and cosmopsychism. While I have argued that a general cosmopsychist approach navigates its challenges more easily than a general panpsychist one, I have yet to offer a more specific account of cosmopsychism that builds on the more general approach. This will be my primary task in the next chapter.

References

Albahari, M. (2020). 'Beyond cosmopsychism and the great I am: How the world might be grounded in universal Advaitic consciousness'. In W. Seager (Ed.), *The Routledge handbook of panpsychism* (pp. 385–406). New York: Routledge.
Chalmers, D. J. (2017). 'The combination problem for panpsychism'. In G. Brüntrup & L. Jaskolla (Eds.), *Panpsychism: Contemporary perspectives* (pp. 179–214). New York: Oxford University Press.
Coleman, S. (2012). 'Mental chemistry: Combination for panpsychists'. *Dialectica*, 66(1), 137–66.
Coleman, S. (2014). 'The real combination problem: Panpsychism, micro-subjects, and emergence'. *Erkenntnis*, 79(1), 19–44.
Coleman, S. (2017). 'Panpsychism and neutral monism'. In G. Brüntrup & L. Jaskolla (Eds.), *Panpsychism: Contemporary perspectives* (pp. 101–22). New York: Oxford University Press.
Goff, P. (2017). *Consciousness and fundamental reality*. New York: Oxford University Press.
Goff, P. (2020). 'Cosmopsychism, micropsychism and the grounding relation'. In W. Seager (Ed.), *The Routledge handbook of panpsychism* (pp. 369–84). New York: Routledge.
Levine, J. (2017). [Review of the book *Panpsychism: Contemporary perspectives*. Edited by G. Brüntrup & L. Jaskolla]. *Notre Dame Book Reviews*. https://ndpr.nd.edu/reviews/panpsychism-contemporary-perspectives/.
Lewtas, P. (2017). 'Building minds: Solving the combination problem'. *Inquiry: An Interdisciplinary Journal of Philosophy*, 60(7), 742–81.
Mathews, F. (2011). 'Panpsychism as paradigm'. In M. Blamauer (Ed.), *The mental as fundamental* (pp. 167–84). Frankfurt Heusenstamm: Ontos Verlag.
Mendelovici, A. (2020). 'Panpsychism's combination problem is a problem for everyone'. In W. Seager (Ed.), *The Routledge handbook of panpsychism* (pp. 303–16). London: Routledge.
Nagasawa, Y., & Wager, K. (2017). 'Panpsychism and priority cosmopsychism'. In G. Brüntrup & L. Jaskolla (Eds.), *Panpsychism: Contemporary perspectives* (pp. 113–29). New York: Oxford University Press.
Roelofs, L. (2014). 'Phenomenal blending and the palette problem'. *Thought: A Journal of Philosophy*, 3(1), 59–70.
Roelofs, L. (2019). *Combining minds: How to think about composite subjectivity*. New York: Oxford University Press.
Shani, I. (2015). 'Cosmopsychism: A holistic approach to the metaphysics of experience'. *Philosophical Papers*, 44(3), 389–437.
Shani, I., & Keppler, J. (2018). 'Beyond combination: How cosmic consciousness grounds ordinary experience'. *Journal of the American Philosophical Association*, 4(3), 390–410.
Stoljar, D. (2001). 'Two conceptions of the physical'. *Philosophy and Phenomenological Research*, 62(2), 253–81.
Wager, K. (2011). *Dual-aspect priority monism and the combination problem for panpsychism* (MA thesis, University of Birmingham).
Wager, K. (2020). *Panpsychism and cosmopsychism* (PhD thesis, University of Birmingham).

6

An account of cosmopsychism

6.1 Introduction

In this chapter, I provide an account of, and motivation for, a version of cosmopsychism that, for want of a better name, I call *CRP cosmopsychism* (shorthand for constitutive Russellian priority monistic cosmopsychism). I start by outlining its core commitments: simple panpsychism, the priority cosmopsychism blueprint, Russellian monism and priority monism. Next, I motivate each core commitment independently and then as a set. I then consider arguments for cosmopsychism, and against panpsychism, from internal relations. In the penultimate section of the chapter, I consider some possible objections to the view I propose. In the final section, I conclude.

At points, this chapter will cover material that has already been discussed earlier in the book. However, in most cases, it will expand on the previous treatment, and here, the purpose is to present in one place an accumulative case for cosmopsychism. While this chapter will motivate the core commitments of the cosmopsychist view that I propose, as well as respond to some possible objections, one noteworthy omission is that it will not repeat material on its most notable problem – the derivation problem – since various aspects of that problem have been a core focus of the book and were covered in considerable detail in Chapters 3 to 5. With that in mind, the reader should supplement this chapter with the cosmopsychist responses to the derivation problem that I have offered in Chapters 4 and 5.

6.2 Core commitments

The account of cosmopsychism I present in this chapter is based on three core commitments: simple panpsychism, priority monism and Russellian monism. In this section, I will outline each, before summarizing motivations for them in the next.

6.2.1 Simple panpsychism

A simple formulation of panpsychism states that phenomenal consciousness is a fundamental and ubiquitous feature of the cosmos. Fundamental in the sense that its existence is not dependent on (or grounded in) anything else, and ubiquitous in the sense that it is everywhere in the cosmos, not just existing where there is a brain. Arguably, the most popular version of panpsychism is constitutive panpsychism, which adds to the above formulation that the fundamental form of consciousness is found at the level of the microphysical ultimates – the sub-atomic level – and that macro-consciousness, such as human consciousness, is constituted by a combination of instances of micro-consciousness. The first core commitment of the cosmopsychism I propose is simple panpsychism, by which I mean the claim that phenomenal consciousness is a fundamental and ubiquitous feature of the cosmos. However, it is not committed to constitutive panpsychism. So, we have the first postulate of CRP cosmopsychism:

1. Consciousness is a fundamental and ubiquitous feature of the cosmos.

6.2.2 Priority cosmopsychism blueprint

The second core commitment of CRP cosmopsychism is, unsurprisingly, the priority cosmopsychism blueprint. The blueprint, outlined initially by Nagasawa and me (2017), and covered in Chapter 2 of this book, offers an alternative to popular versions of panpsychism and makes for a more promising approach to the problem of phenomenal consciousness:

> According to priority cosmopsychism, an alternative to panpsychism that we propose ...,phenomenality is prevalent because the whole cosmos instantiates phenomenal or protophenomenal properties. It says, moreover, that the consciousness of the cosmos is ontologically prior to the consciousness of ordinary individuals like us ... We offer instead [of panpsychism] a blueprint for a new alternative to panpsychism and explain how such a view avoids some of the most persistent problems for panpsychism while maintaining several of its strengths.
>
> (Nagasawa & Wager, 2017, p. 113)

The blueprint proposes turning panpsychism on its head. While panpsychism says that phenomenality is prevalent because microphysical ultimates instantiate phenomenal properties, the priority cosmopsychism blueprint states that it is prevalent because the cosmos, as a whole, instantiates phenomenality. On the cosmopsychist picture, macro-consciousness (e.g. human consciousness) is derived from the cosmic consciousness, rather than being formed from combinations of micro-consciousness, as panpsychism maintains. Thus, the blueprint exemplifies a structural parity with priority monism, the view that the concrete cosmos is prior to its sub-cosmic concrete parts. The blueprint is structurally parallel because the cosmic consciousness is prior to its sub-cosmic conscious parts (i.e. it applies the priority monistic structure to phenomenal reality rather than concrete reality). Following the blueprint allows one to maintain the strongest motivation for panpsychism, by avoiding the problem of strong emergence, while at the same time avoiding its most pressing problem, by sidestepping the combination problem. The commitment to the priority cosmopsychism blueprint gives us our next two postulates:

2. Phenomenality is prevalent because the cosmos as a whole instantiates phenomenality.
3. The consciousness of the cosmos is prior to sub-cosmic consciousnesses.

The commitment to the priority cosmopsychism blueprint provides a structural parity with priority monism, but CRP cosmopsychism goes a step further and is committed to priority monism, too.

6.2.3 Priority monism

Priority monism (Schaffer, 2010b) states that the cosmos is the one and only fundamental concrete object in existence. This contrasts with priority pluralism, which states that there are numerous fundamental concrete objects in existence. It is important to distinguish priority monism from existence monism (Horgan & Potrč, 2000, 2008),[1] which states that only one concrete object exists. In contrast, priority monism allows for a plurality of concrete objects to exist, providing they are derivative of the cosmos' existence. Existence monism, conversely, does not permit a plurality of concrete objects to exist, in any conventional sense.

CRP cosmopsychism is committed to priority monism, in addition to the prior commitments to simple panpsychism and the priority cosmopsychism blueprint. As a result, we get the following additional postulates of the view:

4. The cosmos as a whole is the one and only fundamental concrete object.
5. There is a plurality of sub-cosmic concrete objects, but these are derivative of the cosmos as a whole.

The priority cosmopsychism blueprint brings the view closer to priority monism by adopting a structural parity with it, but while priority cosmopsychism is only structurally parallel to priority monism, CRP cosmopsychism adopts priority monism itself. Structural parity alone equates only to the proposal that the phenomenal domain in cosmopsychism is structured analagously to how the physical domain is structured according to priority monism. While the latter quantifies over only concrete reality, the former does so over only phenomenal reality. Building on the blueprint by combining it with a commitment to priority monism leaves CRP cosmopsychism with a structural mirroring in the physical and phenomenal domains: each existing in a top-down manner, with the cosmos as a whole being the fundamental level in each domain. In the physical domain, the concrete cosmos is the one and only fundamental object, while in the phenomenal domain fundamental consciousness is instantiated by the cosmos as a whole. Each domain permits sub-cosmic entities (or parts), but they are merely derivative of the cosmos as a whole. It is still an open question as to how the two domains – the physical and the phenomenal – relate to one another.

1 Existence monism is referred to as 'blobjectivism' by Horgan & Potrč (2000, 2008).

6.2.4 Russellian monism

To make some headway on the question of how the two domains relate to one another, we turn to the final core commitment of CRP cosmopsychism: Russellian monism. A very simple formulation of Russellian monism says that physics describes reality only in terms of its structure, relations and dynamics, but it remains silent about the properties that ground such structure and relations (or the question about whether such properties exist at all). At least some of those properties (called 'inscrutables' by Montero (2010) or 'quiddities' by Chalmers (2017)) are phenomenal properties, according to Russellian monism. So overall, on this picture, the world that physics describes only in terms of structure and relations is imbued with a categorical nature that grounds it. That categorical nature, according to all versions of Russellian monism, is at least partially phenomenal (or proto-phenomenal).

There are many more precise versions of Russellian monism, and I do not want to suggest that CRP cosmopsychism endorses, or is compatible with, all of them. However, Alter and Nagasawa (2015) provide a general formulation of Russellian Monism that captures the three central claims shared by all versions of the view. These are:

> *Structuralism about physics*: the basic properties physics describes are structural/relational properties.
> *Realism about inscrutables*: there are inscrutables, the natures of which are not wholly structural/relational.
> *(Proto) phenomenal foundationalism*: at least some inscrutables are either phenomenal or protophenomenal properties.
>
> (2015, p. 425)

Arguably, the most promising versions of panpsychism adopt some form of Russellian monism. For example, Russellian constitutive panpsychism says that phenomenal consciousness is fundamental and ubiquitous; fundamental because it is not grounded in anything non-phenomenal, and ubiquitous because everything instantiates it. Constitutive panpsychism says that macro-(phenomenal)consciousness, such as human consciousness, is constituted by the combination of micro-consciousness (and micro-consciousness is instantiated by microphysical ultimates). It is obvious that Russellian monism is a natural complement here. Microphysical ultimates, as described by physics in terms of structure and relations, are physical, but they also have a categorical nature which grounds it, and that nature is phenomenal. We can say that matter has both an external (physical) and an internal (phenomenal) nature. When microphysical ultimates combine to form brains, for instance, their phenomenal natures also combine to form macro-consciousnesses. With this, we have a final postulate of CRP cosmopsychism:

6. The cosmos has an external and internal nature. Its external nature equates to the world as described by current physics, while its internal nature equates to phenomenal consciousnes, and the latter is the categorical ground of the former.

We now have the six core postulates of CRP cosmopsychism, as follows:

1. Consciousness is a fundamental and ubiquitous feature of the cosmos.
2. Phenomenality is prevalent because the cosmos as a whole instantiates phenomenality.
3. The consciousness of the cosmos is prior to sub-cosmic consciousnesses.
4. The cosmos as a whole is the one and only fundamental concrete object.
5. There is a plurality of sub-cosmic concrete objects, but these are derivative of the cosmos as a whole.
6. The cosmos has an external and internal nature. Its external nature equates to the world as described by current physics, while its internal nature equates to phenomenal consciousness, and the latter is the categorical ground of the former.

6.3 Motivations for core commitments

In this section, I will provide motivation for the core commitments of CRP cosmopsychism. These motivations will either come in the form of a positive argument, or more commonly, through the avoidance of a persistent problem. I will by no means be providing an in-depth analysis of the arguments or problems that comprise these motivations, and much of what I say in the section will be to some extent contentious, I offer them merely to motivate the commitments. I should also note that CRP cosmopsychism does not necessarily depend on the success of the motivations I offer.

6.3.1 Motivating simple panpsychism

By far and away the greatest motivation for simple panpsychism is the avoidance of the problem of strong emergence, so this is what I take to be the primary motivation for its inclusion here. However, there are many other historical motivations for the view. I will very briefly summarize three arguments that seem to stand the test of time, which motivate panpsychism, but that I do not take to be primary, before turning to the problem of strong emergence.

6.3.1.1 The epistemic argument for panpsychism

The *epistemic argument for panpsychism* is, as the name suggests, only an epistemic argument. Meaning it moves from our epistemic position to the truth of panpsychism. In my opinion, it should not be taken to prove panpsychism true, but instead, its function is to provide the initial trigger to drive the overall panpsychist approach forward. Similar arguments have undoubtedly been made throughout history by numerous thinkers, including Plato (see Skrbina, 2005). However, I take this argument from the following passage by Skrbina (2005):

> Mind is real. I know this because I experience it first hand, and I hold it as an indubitable feature of reality (against eliminativism). Body is real. Rationally, intuitively, and empirically I have reason to believe that my body is a physical, material thing, situated in a physical universe (against pure idealism). There is thus both a material and a mental aspect to my existence; at my deepest, most fundamental level of being, I am a 'thinking thing'. Some aspects of my physical being are clearly not widely spread in this world – aspects such as 'male', 'homo sapiens', or 'alive'. But my material nature seems to be universal. Similarly, some aspects of my mental being are unique to me, or to others of my kind. But this does not preclude the possibility that something like a mental nature is universal. For both rational and empirical reasons I am convinced that I am not ontologically unique. Since my mentality is fundamentally connected to, or related to, my material body, I have good reason to believe that mentality, in some form, is connected to all material beings. Therefore panpsychism must be true. QED.
>
> (p. 254)

For Skrbina, this passage constitutes the core argument for panpsychism. In teasing out premises and a conclusion from the passage, it seems the argument, as presented, is invalid because its epistemic premises are said to lead to a metaphysical conclusion, which they cannot do. The argument can be reformulated in this way, however:

1. My consciousness is real because I experience it as such.
2. My body is a real and a physical entity situated in a physical world because I experience it as such.
3. Therefore, there is both a physical and a conscious aspect to my being.
4. Moreover, my physical nature seems to be universal, (in the general sense that I am but a part of a world filled with other physical parts)
5. Given that my physical nature seems to be universal, and there is both a physical and a conscious aspect to my being, it is reasonable to suppose that my conscious nature is likewise universal.
6. If conscious nature is universal, then panpsychism is true
7. Therefore, I have reason to suppose that panpsychism is true.

The above argument is epistemic in the sense that it is founded on our everyday experience and extrapolates from there to panpsychism. The conclusion is not the truth of panpsychism, but that it is reasonable to believe panpsychism is true. I take this argument much like a proof of concept, whereby it justifies that we have good *prima facie* reason to take panpsychism seriously. There is, of course, plenty to question here, but it is not imperative to my discussion that I defend this argument more substantially.

6.3.1.2 The argument from continuity

The *argument from continuity* says that, unlike other approaches to the problem of consciousness, panpsychism does not need to impose an arbitrary distinction between those things that are conscious and those that are not. This implies that other views arbitrarily distinguish between conscious and non-conscious entities, although they will likely reject this charge. Arguments of this general structure have been made in numerous ways, with differing views about what the relevant continuity consists in. Like the previous argument, I do not think that this is a key motivation for panpsychism, but I do think it carries some weight, so I will briefly include it here.

One possible version of the argument from continuity says that all forms of life, including some which are intuitively non-conscious, have come about through the same overall process of evolution, making the distinction between conscious living things and non-conscious living things seem arbitrary. Most people accept that humans are conscious, and many will also affirm the consciousness of some other animals (great apes, elephants, dolphins, etc.). However, many will reject the consciousness of a fruit fly, and many more will deny that a sea squirt is conscious. Almost all will deny that non-living things are conscious. While extreme comparisons may stoke a sense of discontinuity, say, if we compare an elephant to a pebble, the more interesting comparisons are the harder-to-call cases. Why is a bottlenose dolphin conscious, but a sea squirt is not? One might reply that it is because bottlenose dolphins have brains and sea squirts do not. However, sea squirts do have very rudimentary brains, containing a little over 200 neurons (compared to just under 13 billion neurons making up the bottlenose dolphin's brain).

How about comparing the sea squirt with a sponge (*Tethya wilhelma)*? The sponge does not have a brain. But is it uncontroversial to suppose that the sea squirt, with its ~200 neurons, is conscious and the sponge is not? Even this case is controversial. Interestingly, sponges appear to be able to control their bodies in simple ways. For example, they have been shown to contract both rhythmically and arhythmically in response to their surroundings. One way they have been observed to contract arhythmically is as a form of self-defence, effectively toughening their outer layer to protect themselves from damage. Most interesting is that, although the exact mechanism for such action is unknown, neurotransmitter-like chemicals are hypothesized to be involved in its co-ordination: 'The existence of subcontractions, significantly weaker than regular contractions, again indicates that the sponge is able to control this behaviour by means of integrating various internal (physiological) and external (environmental) information. Preliminary results of our ongoing research indicate that several neuroactive substances are involved in the coordination of contraction in *T. wilhelma*' (Nickel, 2004, pp. 4522–3).

My point here is not to argue that sponges are conscious even though they have no brains, and therefore, that brains cannot be the exclusive harbours of consciousness, as that would involve a commitment to knowing a lot more about consciousness than I do (or anybody else does, for that matter). Rather, it is to show that the argument from continuity may still carry some weight because, even if one takes a black-and-white criterion such as 'consciousness exists where brains exist', there are still grey-area cases. The example just offered highlights that even in the absence of a brain it is thought that neuroactive substances are still involved in the moderation of the animals' behaviour.

This can also be taken as a top-up argument to the argument from strong emergence (to be covered shortly). Adding the top-up could motivate an extension of the argument from strong emergence, taking the conclusion from the truth of the disjunction 'panpsychism or panprotopsychism or micropsychism or Microprotopsychism' to the truth of the disjunction 'panpsychism or panprotopsychism'.

6.3.1.3 The naturalized mind argument

The next argument I want to discuss briefly is *the naturalized mind argument*. Skrbina (who coined the argument's name) says of it: 'Panpsychism "truly naturalizes mind," because it deeply integrates mind into the natural order of the world. Furthermore it does so in a way that no other theory does' (2005, p. 252). As with the continuity argument, this is more of a general type of argument than one specific one. The general argument goes something like this: we want consciousness to integrate neatly into the natural world, but according to dominant approaches to consciousness, conscious minds do not fit neatly into the natural world. Physicalism, for example, either has to do away with the reality of consciousness or else have it emerging inexplicably from physical processes (more on this to come). Alternatively, dualism has consciousness sitting entirely distinct from the natural world. In panpsychism, however, we find a place for consciousness to fit neatly into the natural world; it no longer needs to exist entirely separate from the physical, or to emerge inexplicably from it.

In actual fact, there are numerous views, that are to some extent related to panpsychism, that can also claim to neatly naturalize consciousness. Furthermore, there are some such views that can be combined with panpsychism. One example is Russellian monism, another core commitment of the form of cosmopsychism I propose in this chapter.

6.3.1.4 The last man standing argument

A further argument highlighted by Skrbina (2005) is the *last man standing argument*. He summarizes the argument as follows:

> In light of 'the "terminal" failure of the approaches built on the Cartesian intuition about matter', panpsychism stands as the most viable alternative. This is an important point, and one that has been neglected in the past. If intensive critical inquiry of dualism and materialism over the past, say, few hundred years has failed to produce a consensus theory of mind, then it stands to reason that a third alternative like panpsychism, in some positive formulation, should gain in viability.
>
> (p. 252)

The last man standing argument is evident from the above quotation: despite massive investment of resources, neither physicalism nor dualism have yet to come up with a generally accepted solution to the problem of consciousness. The idea is that the failure of physicalism and dualism underpins, in some measure, the viability of alternatives, chief among which is panpsychism. If afforded similar resources, the panpsychist approach may prove fruitful where physicalism and dualism have not. Again, I do not consider this a robust argument for panpsychism so much as adding to the initial motivation for the approach.

6.3.1.5 *The problem of strong emergence*

The arguments I have presented are best thought of as providing initial motivation for further exploration of panpsychism. They stop short of counting as strong reasons for supposing it may be true (at least as I have presented them). The avoidance of this next problem, however, forms the basis of the single most significant argument for panpsychism.

The problem of strong emergence is a problem for physicalism. Avoiding it is a key motivation for panpsychism. Simply stated, the problem for physicalism is this: if consciousness is real and dualism is false, then either consciousness is present at the fundamental level of reality, or it emerges from fundamental entities entirely devoid of consciousness. The physicalist must opt for the latter or else be a panpsychist, but the kind of emergence entailed is ontological (i.e. strong) emergence, which is purportedly impossible.

Let us first formulate an overall argument for panpsychism on the grounds that it avoids the problem of strong emergence, before bolstering its crucial premises. There are a few important postulates of this argument: (1) realism about physics, (2) realism about consciousness and (3) the rejection of substance dualism. With this in mind, we can formulate the following argument:

1. Consciousness is real *and* the world as described by current physics is real *and* substance dualism is false.
2. A complete physical description of the world, according to our current physics, does not integrate consciousness.
3. If consciousness is to be integrated into a physical description of the world, it must either already be a feature of fundamental physical entities or emerge from certain combinations of fundamental physical entities (and relations among them).
4. If consciousness emerges, then it *strongly* emerges.
5. Strong emergence is impossible.
6. Therefore, consciousness does not emerge.
7. Therefore, consciousness is a feature of fundamental physical matter.
8. Therefore, panpsychism (or panprotopsychism or micropsychism or microprotopsychism) is true.

Let us take a closer look. Premises (4) and (5) are the most significant for us. Premise (1), for our purposes, is a stipulation to help us on our way to the issue at hand; it is the conjunction of realism about physics, realism about consciousness and the rejection of substance dualism. This is an argument against physicalism and in favour of panpsychism (or panprotopsychism), so it is uncontroversial to postulate the rejection of substance dualism and the acceptance of realism about physics. Stipulating that consciousness is real, as far as premise (1) is concerned, amounts to the rejection of eliminativism and views maintaining that there is nothing to be explained regarding consciousness. Premise (2) builds on the consciousness-is-real stipulation in premise (1) and is driven by common arguments against physicalism like the knowledge argument (Jackson, 1982), the conceivability argument (Chalmers, 1996), and the explanatory gap argument (Levine, 1983). Premise (3) follows from (1)–(2).

Premise (4) states that if consciousness emerges, then it strongly emerges. Strong emergence is distinguished from weak emergence (Chalmers, 2006). Weak emergence is an epistemic form of emergence, meaning that although a novel property appears to arise, this is a mere appearance and is due to an epistemic limitation on our part. In weak cases, the emergence of the property is surprising given the base conditions from which it emerges. With weak emergence, even if the emergent property is surprising, it is in principle deducible from the base: that is, if we were epistemically unlimited, we would be able to deduce the property from the conditions from which it emerges (by conditions, I mean the entities at the base together with any relations among them).

In contrast, strong emergence is an ontological kind of emergence, where the emergent property emerges not just as a result of some epistemic limitation. In strong cases, the emergence of the novel property is not just surprising given the base conditions, but it is not deducible from the base, even in principle: even from a God-like omniscient perspective, the emergence of strongly emergent properties would not be deducible from the base. The reason premise (4) is supposed to hold is that if consciousness were to only weakly emerge, then panpsychism (or panprotopsychism) would be true, as it would entail the emergence of consciousness as an epistemic phenomenon rather than an ontological one. Consciousness, if it were to emerge, must do so ontologically if panpsychism (or panprotopsychism) is to be avoided.

Following (4), premise (5) is the second crucial premise: it states that strong emergence is impossible. Weak emergence is unproblematic as we know of many cases where it obtains, for example, the emergence of liquidity from base entities entirely lacking liquidity (Strawson, 2006) and the gas-solid-liquid transformation (Popper, 1978). Strong emergence is much trickier to get a handle on. There have not been any widely accepted cases of strong emergence, with proposed candidates tending to turn out, on further reflection, to be cases of weak emergence. More importantly, according to Galen Strawson, cases of strong emergence violate the following apparent principle: 'For any feature Y of anything that is currently considered to be emergent from X, there must be something about X and X alone in virtue of which Y emerges, and which is sufficient for Y' (2008, p. 65). Proposed instances of strong emergence violate the above principle because they are not, even in principle, deducible from the base. Consequently, there is no basis on which to say that the emergent property emerges from the proposed base rather than some other basal conditions. By definition, it is not possible to say that there is anything at all about the base and the base alone in virtue of which the emergent property emerges, because the emergent property is, in principle, non-deducible from the base.

From here, it is straightforward: premise (6) follows from (4)–(5), then premise (7) follows from (3)–(6), and the ultimate conclusion follows from (7). Overall, it is fair to say that avoiding the problem of strong emergence is by far the strongest motivation for panpsychism. Presented as the argument above, it prompts a move from physicalism to panpsychism (or, more reasonably, to either panpsychism, panprotopsychism, micropsychism or microprotopsychism).

6.3.2 Motivating Russellian monism

Let us now consider some motivations for Russellian monism. As I have already mentioned, Russellian monism is an umbrella term for various closely related views that share some common theses. Given my other core commitments, as far as forming my account of cosmopsychism is concerned, my focus is on panpsychist Russellian monism (the version which says the inscrutables, or quiddities, are phenomenal properties, rather than merely proto-phenomenal properties). I will briefly summarize four motivations for Russellian monism.

6.3.2.1 The grounding physics argument

The most significant motivation for Russellian monism is inspired by its namesake Bertrand Russell's views on physics. I call this *the grounding physics argument*. It moves from the premise that physics reveals only the structural nature of the world, and remains silent on what it is that instantiates such structure, to the suggestion that Russellian monism is the best candidate approach to offer an explanation as to what the instantiator is. The core of the argument is contained in the following passage by Russell (1959):

> It is not always realized how exceedingly abstract is the information that theoretical physics has to give. It lays down certain fundamental equations which enable it to deal with the logical structure of events, while leaving it completely unknown what is the intrinsic character of the events that have the structure. We only know the intrinsic character of events when they happen to us. Nothing whatever in theoretical physics enables us to say anything about the intrinsic character of events elsewhere. They may be just like the events that happen to us, or they may be totally different in strictly unimaginable ways. All that physics gives us is certain equations giving abstract properties of their changes. But as to what it is that changes, and what it changes from and to – as to this, physics is silent.
>
> (p. 13)

We can formulate an argument from the starting point that consciousness seems at odds with physical descriptions of the world (highlighted by arguments such as the conceivability argument (Chalmers, 1995, 1996, 1997, 2003) and the knowledge argument (Jackson, 1982, 1986)), and on the understanding that consciousness fitting neatly into the physical nature of the world is desirable:

1. Consciousness seems at odds with physical descriptions of the world.
2. Physics reveals only the structural nature of the world.
3. There is more to the world than structure alone.
4. Therefore, physics does not reveal the complete nature of the world.
5. Physics does not reveal quiddities.
6. Quiddities ground the structure of the natural world that physics reveals.
7. Quiddities are part of the natural world.
8. Some quiddities are phenomenal (or proto-phenomenal) properties.
9. All phenomenal properties are quiddities.
10. Phenomenal properties are part of the natural world.
11. Physics does not reveal phenomenal properties.
12. Therefore, physics does not reveal phenomenal properties, even though they are part of the natural world, because it does not reveal the quiddities that ground the structure it does reveal, and at least some quiddities are phenomenal properties.

Let us take a closer look at the premises. Premise (1) is the observation that consciousness is at odds with the physical description of the world. The knowledge and conceivability arguments underpin this observation. The takeaway is that physicalism, as we know it, struggles to find a place for consciousness in the physical world. Premise (2) describes what physics does: uncovering the nomic spatio-temporal structure of the world. Premise (3) is pivotal. It amounts to a rejection of the view that structure is all that exists (some take (2) as evidence that structure is all that exists (Ladyman & Ross, 2007)). From (1)–(3), we conclude (4). Premise (5) follows Chalmers (2017) in referring to what physics does not reveal and what the structure it does reveal actually *is* as 'quiddities'. Premise (6) states what quiddities are. Premise (7) states that quiddities are nothing supernatural; they are part of the natural world. Premise (8) is the proposition that phenomenal properties make good candidates for quiddities, so at least some quiddities are phenomenal properties. Premise (9) is the sensible stipulation that there are no phenomenal properties aside from those which are quiddities. It is a sensible stipulation because the alternative would be metaphysically costly in terms of simplicity. For example, having some quiddities as phenomenal properties and some, but not all, phenomenal properties as quiddities unnecessarily complicates the picture of reality. Premise (10) follows from (7), and premise (11) follows from (5). The ultimate conclusion (12) follows from (4), (9) and (11).

6.3.2.2 The conceivability problem

The conceivability problem arises due to the conceivability of phenomenal zombies, which are complete physical copies of us but which lack consciousness. Granting that conceivability equals possibility, the argument continues that such zombies are metaphysically possible. If they are metaphysically possible, then the physical description of the world clearly omits something: consciousness.

The conceivability problem, so presented, is a problem for physicalism (though modifications of it have also been deployed against other views), and avoiding it is a motivation for Russellian monism. While there are versions of physicalism that reject the conceivability of zombies (classified by Chalmers (2003) as 'type-A materialism'), as well as versions that accept the conceivability of zombies but reject that they are metaphysically possible ('type-B materialism'), and versions that claim they are conceivable for us now but they would not be conceivable under ideal conditions in which we are not epistemically limited ('type-C materialism'), each faces their own challenges in the face of the conceivability problem.[2]

An argument for Russellian monism from the conceivability of zombies goes something like this: physicalism is an attractive solution to the problem of phenomenal consciousness because it maintains that physics accurately describes the world. However, it must respond to the conceivability problem, but in each of its varieties, it faces challenges in doing so. Russellian monism is well-placed to respond to the conceivability problem *and* maintain that physics accurately describes the world. Russellian monism responds to the problem by saying that zombies are conceivable but not metaphysically possible. They are conceivable because when we conceive of zombies we are conceiving of merely structural replicas of ourselves. However, according to Russellian monism, structural copies would also entail copies of the categorical ground of that structure, and that categorical ground amounts to consciousness. Russellian monism, as discussed already, also finds a neat place for consciousness without disturbing the claim that physics accurately describes the world. Physics accurately describes the world according to its structure (but remains silent on the categorical base of such structure).

6.3.2.3 The happy compromise argument

Torin Alter and Yujin Nagasawa (2015) present two arguments for Russellian monism. I will include both here. The first is *the happy compromise argument*, which motivates Russellian monism on the grounds that it is uniquely positioned between physicalism, on the one hand, and dualism on the other, retaining the advantages of each while overcoming some of their respective challenges. Centrally, it preserves the ontological elegance of physicalism by holding that there is no fundamental difference of substance between the physical world and consciousness, while also attributing consciousness a unique status kindred in spirit to dualism. They write: 'Monist versions of Russellian monism share the ontological elegance of physicalism. And like traditional dualism, all versions of Russellian monism succeed in affirming the uniqueness of consciousness. Yet Russellian monism allows consciousness to be integrated into nature in a much more substantial way than does traditional dualism'. (Alter & Nagasawa, 2015, p. 443).

A notable caveat here is that physicalism and dualism each admit of multiple formulations, with some more responsive to their respective difficulties than others. Chalmers (2003) classifies physicalism (referred to as 'materialism') into three categories: type-A materialism, type-B materialism and type-C materialism. Type-A

2 See Chalmers (2003) for a detailed discussion.

materialism rejects that there is a hard problem of consciousness, contending that there is no explanatory gap between the physical and the phenomenal, or at most, a very minor epistemic gap that is easily closed. Type-B materialism holds that there is an epistemic gap between the physical and phenomenal but no ontological gap. Here, the hard problem is taken to be epistemic rather than ontological in nature. Finally, according to type-C materialism, the gap between the physical and phenomenal is considered deep, though ultimately still an epistemic gap. On this view, the hard problem, although epistemic, may not seem solvable in physical terms but is in-principle solvable. Perhaps both type-B and type-C materialism can claim to affirm a certain level of uniqueness to consciousness; both views can claim to respect deeply held intuitions that consciousness is unique, while giving an account as to why such intuitions turn out to designate something only epistemically, rather than ontologically, novel. However, both views have additional serious problems (see Chalmers (2003) for a detailed account).

While I do not think that the argument from a happy compromise is a strong or conclusive one, it does motivate Russellian monism somewhat, similar to how some of the arguments for panpsychism nudge us toward the view without providing conclusive arguments (we might even see this argument as related to the naturalized mind argument for panpsychism).

6.3.2.4 The 'two birds with one stone' argument

The second argument that Alter and Nagasawa (2015) offer is what I call *the two birds with one stone argument*. This argument is powered by a perceived ability of Russellian monism to solve two seemingly unrelated problems simultaneously. On the one hand, some in the philosophy of science believe that there must be properties grounding the nomic spatiotemporal structure that physics describes that are not themselves structural (although others contend that there is nothing but structure). In the philosophy of mind, many want to find a neat way of integrating consciousness into nature, with traditional views rendering it incongruent in one way or another. Alter and Nagasawa connect these two seemingly unrelated problems by pairing what they describe as a 'help-wanted' problem in the philosophy of science with a 'job-wanted' problem in the philosophy of mind (pp. 444–5).

Philosophy of science is looking for outside help to ground the nomic spatiotemporal structure that physics describes so completely, while the philosophy of mind is looking for a job for consciousness, as it seems at odds to find a place for it in the physical world, such that firmly held intuitions about its causal importance are satisfied. Russellian monism, the argument states, can solve both problems at once. It solves the problem in the philosophy of science by offering consciousness the role of grounding the structure described by physics, while simultaneously solving the problem in the philosophy of mind by giving it a role in the causal scheme of the natural world.

I take this argument to be most effective when considered a top-up argument, that can be added to the grounding physics argument and the happy-compromise argument.

6.3.3 Motivating priority monism

The final core commitment of CRP cosmopsychism is priority monism. Schaffer (2010b) offers a variety of motivations for priority monism, but I will focus on two of them here. The first is avoiding the problem of infinite decomposition, and the second is the argument from quantum emergence. In addition to the two I provide here, I will return to another argument for priority monism in a later section of the chapter, when we consider internal relations and their relevance to cosmopsychism.

6.3.3.1 The problem of infinite decomposition

Priority monism can be motivated by *the argument from the possibility of infinite decomposition* (also called the argument from the possibility of *gunk*). Infinitely decomposable matter (sometimes called 'gunk') is matter every part of which has further proper parts. The argument from the possibility of infinite decomposition is an argument for priority monism by way of some modal considerations, and runs as follows:

1. Either the ultimate cosmos or its ultimate parts must be basic at all possible worlds.
2. There are possible worlds which are infinitely decomposable.
3. Therefore, the cosmos must be basic at all possible worlds.

The argument moves from the premise that what is basic must be basic at all possible worlds, through the premise that there are in fact worlds whose parts are infinitely decomposable, to the conclusion that the cosmos must be basic at all possible worlds. The truth of premise (1) is argued for on the basis that the direction of priority must be a necessary truth, or else there could be two worlds which were indiscernible in every sense, except that in one the cosmos is basic, while in the other its parts are basic. This is not likely to receive broad support. Schaffer argues convincingly for the truth of premise (2). All that is needed to satisfy the truth of the premise is to demonstrate that an infinitely decomposable world is possible. Schaffer provides three accounts on which it is possible. Each corresponds to a different level of threat to the view that an infinitely decomposable world is impossible, depending on the strength of the notion of possibility being deployed. However, all that the argument requires is one sense in which it holds. If there are possible worlds in which infinite decomposition obtains, then the conclusion (3) follows from the conjunction of (1) and (2).

At the least threatening level, it is *logically possible* that there is matter every part of which has further parts. This possibility amounts to the fact that there is no logical contradiction in the idea. Next, and more threatening, is that it is *metaphysically possible*: we can conceive of a world in which this is the case. If conceivability is considered a guide to metaphysical possibility, then a world in which there is matter every part of which has further parts, is metaphysically possible. Most damaging of all, however, is that it is *actually possible*. By that, I mean that it is possible that the actual world itself contains matter every part of which has further parts.

Reasons for thinking that the actual world is infinitely decomposable, as I see it, are threefold. First, from an intuitive point of view it seems plausible that the matter we are acquainted with in the actual world could be such that it is infinitely decomposable. Second is the lesson from the history of science: we have at many times believed we have discovered the ultimate constituents of matter only to find, along with advances in technology in our scientific endeavours, that we were wrong and that there was, in fact, a lower level to physical reality than previously thought. Take the atom, for example. It was considered the smallest building block for a long time, until J.J. Thompson discovered in 1897 that electrons were components of all atoms. We now know not only that atoms are made up of electrons, protons and neutrons, but that these are, in turn, made up of much smaller sub-atomic particles. I follow Schaffer (2010b) in highlighting Brian Greene's (1999) summation of the lesson from the history of science, when he says: 'History has surely taught us that every time our understanding of the universe deepens, we find yet smaller microconstituents constituting a finer level of matter'. (p. 141). Third, infinite decomposition is postulated in serious scientific theories about the actual world. For example, Dehmelt (1989) posits an infinite regression of sub-electron structure. Additionally, Montero (2006) highlights that physicists Weinberg (1992) and Bohm (1957) have both taken seriously the possibility of infinite decomposition.

6.3.3.1.1 *Infinite decomposition and consciousness*

In addition to the argument for priority monism from infinite decomposition, another related argument is relevant to the motivation of CRP cosmopsychism. Nagasawa (2012) argues that infinite decomposition cuts against *all* major approaches to the mind-body problem – physicalism, dualism, idealism, and neutral monism – because they are all versions of 'fundamentalism'. Fundamentalism, as Nagasawa (2012, p. 358) conceptualizes it, is the conjunction of the following three theses:

> The hierarchy thesis: the universe is stratified into levels.
> The fundamentality thesis: there is a bottom level, which is fundamental.
> The primacy thesis: entities on the fundamental level are primarily real and the rest are at best derivative, if they are real at all.

To avoid confusion, a note on the fundamentality thesis is in order. Central to the cosmopsychism I propose in this book is the notion that the fundamental level is the top level of reality rather than the bottom, but in order to track Nagasawa's argument, in this section of the chapter, when I refer to the 'fundamental level' I refer to the (proposed) bottom level of reality unless otherwise specified.

Returning to Nagasawa's argument, the thought is that all of the major approaches to the mind-body problem imply fundamentalism, and given that infinite decomposition is inconsistent with fundamentalism, if the world is infinitely decomposable, then fundamentalism is false, and therefore, so are all of the major approaches to the mind-body problem. Nagasawa presents his argument as follows (2012, p. 360, cited below with minor formatting adjustments):

1. If physicalism, dualism, idealism, or neutral monism is true, then fundamentalism is true.
2. If fundamentalism is true, then there is a bottom, fundamental level of reality.
3. There is no bottom, fundamental level of reality.
4. Therefore, fundamentalism is false (from 2 and 3).
5. Therefore, physicalism, dualism, idealism, and neutral monism are all false (from 1 and 4).

It is important to note that the conclusion is based on specific construals of the broad approaches cited. I think that premise (1) is, broadly speaking, clearly false, because there are possible formulations of each of the approaches that do not entail fundamentalism. Premise (3), as we have seen previously, is not a given but is certainly a possibility. Therefore, the argument is more limited in scope than claimed. What Nagasawa's argument does well is show that versions of physicalism, dualism, idealism and neutral monism that *do* affirm fundamentalism are vulnerable to the possibility of infinite decomposition. Let us present a modified version of the argument to reflect this critical point:

1. If fundamentalism is false, then fundamentalist versions of physicalism, dualism, idealism, neutral monism and panpsychism are false.
2. If infinitely decomposable matter is possible, then fundamentalism is false.
3. Infinitely decomposable matter is possible.
4. Therefore, fundamentalism is false.
5. Therefore, fundamentalist versions of physicalism, dualism, idealism, neutral monism and panpsychism are false.

Notice the difference between the third premise in each argument. My reformulation states that infinitely decomposable matter is *possible* but does not imply that it is actual, as in the original argument. This is because all we need to reach our conclusion is for infinite decomposition to hold in some possible world. We can then follow Schaffer in maintaining that what is fundamental must be fundamental in all possible worlds (or else we have two identical worlds except that one is fundamentalist and the other not): if it is possible in some world, then it is actual in this world.

One might still wonder why this argument is relevant to the motivation of cosmopsychism. The reason is that it purports to rule out all of the most common approaches to the mind-body problem, but as I have shown with my modified version, what it really does is rule out *fundamentalist* versions of those approaches. The version of cosmopsychism I propose, however, is a non-fundamentalist approach to the problem of consciousness, and as such, it evades the problem of infinite decomposition. It does this owing to its commitment to priority monism. In this respect, cosmopsychism enjoys a significant advantage: it avoids an obstacle that potentially rules out most competing views, including, most importantly, constitutive panpsychism (recall that a primary aim of this book has been to compare the viability of constitutive forms of cosmopsychism and panpsychism).

Nagasawa was initially sceptical of the prospects for a priority monist response to his argument. However, he later points out, with me (Nagasawa & Wager, 2017), in our priority cosmopsychism blueprint proposal, that adopting at least the structure of priority monism affords approaches to the problem of consciousness a way of avoiding the problem of infinite decomposition.

6.3.3.2 The argument from quantum emergence

Let us now consider another argument in favour of priority monism, offered by Schaffer (2010b): *the argument from quantum emergence*. It runs as follows:

1. The cosmos, as a whole, possesses emergent properties (due to quantum entanglement).
2. If the cosmos, as a whole, possesses emergent properties, then the cosmos, as a whole, is prior to its parts.
3. Therefore, the cosmos, as a whole, is prior to its parts.

The thinking here is that if the priority monist can show that the cosmos as a whole has emergent properties (note: the emergent properties in question are *weakly* emergent properties, not the problematic *strong* kind), then they could claim that the cosmos as a whole is prior to its parts. The notion of emergence that Schaffer has in mind is the failure of mereological supervenience. Supervenience is an asymmetrical dependency relation holding between a set of basal properties and a supervenient property (or properties). It is asymmetrical in the sense that the supervenient property is dependent on the basal properties, but the basal properties are not likewise dependent on the emergent property. If we call the basal properties A-properties and the supervening properties B-properties, the notion is that there can be no change in the B-properties without some change in the A-properties (but not vice versa). With this in mind, we can say that mereological supervenience obtains when the whole supervenes on the parts, i.e., where the parts form the supervenience base for the supervening whole. Since we are interested in emergence as the failure of mereological supervenience, we are looking for cases where the whole fails to supervene on the parts. Or, more precisely, where the *cosmos* fails to supervene on its parts.

The support for the first premise, that the cosmos is entangled and thus possesses emergent properties, comes from the claim that emergent properties of the aforementioned sort are found in entangled quantum systems, together with the claim that the cosmos is one such quantum system. As Schaffer says, '[a]n entangled system is one whose state vector is not factorizable into tensor products of the state vectors of its components' (Schaffer, 2010b, p. 51). This goes to say that the information contained in the components of an entangled system does not account for all the information contained in the system as a whole. The critical question is whether or not the cosmos is one such quantum system. Following Gribbin (1984) and Zeh (2003), Schaffer argues that there is reason to believe that the cosmos does indeed form one such entangled system since everything so closely interacted in the Big Bang.

The second premise – a conditional premise stating that if the cosmos is indeed an entangled whole, it will entail that it is prior to its parts – details a simple move from the fact that if the cosmos contains emergent properties (e.g. the correlation coefficients of the wave functions of its parts) due to quantum entanglement, then it is more than the sum of its parts, and therefore, its parts cannot be prior.

6.3.4 The combined motivation for cosmopsychism

So far, I have laid out some motivations for the core commitments considered in isolation, only occasionally alluding to their interplay. However, the conjunction of the commitments makes for a unique set of advantages for CRP cosmopsychism. Some motivating factors for individual commitments are forceful in their own right, but perhaps the most striking observation is that they form a consistent set: we might even go so far as to say a *symbiotic* set. Let us briefly explore how bearing this set positions cosmopsychism in comparison to panpsychism and physicalism. In this book, my principal interest is in the prospects of CRP cosmopsychism as an alternative to constitutive panpsychism. However, I am also incontrovertibly interested in a broader comparison between cosmopsychism and physicalism.

Consider first the comparison with panpsychism. Both views benefit from avoiding the problem of strong emergence by positing consciousness at the fundamental level of reality (although the fundamental level is different for each view, of course). Both can also benefit from the additional commitment to Russellian monism (this would make the resulting views *constitutive Russellian* panpsychism and cosmopsychism) and its motivating factors of the grounding physics argument, avoiding the conceivability problem and offering a place for consciousness to fit neatly into the natural world. It starts to get more interesting when we consider CRP cosmopsychism's additional commitment to priority monism because the advantages that come from this move cannot be carried over to panpsychism. CRP cosmopsychism benefits from the argument from quantum emergence and avoids the problem of infinite decomposition. In contrast, panpsychism is in tension with quantum emergence, and as a version of what Nagasawa calls 'fundamentalism', it is vulnerable to the possibility of infinite decomposition.

Now consider the comparison with a typical version of physicalism. Physicalism is vulnerable to the problem of strong emergence, leaves consciousness jarring with the physical world (granted that the operative version of physicalism is non-eliminativist), and is vulnerable to the possibility of infinite decomposition.

6.4 Internal relations and cosmopsychism

Continuing the theme of a symbiosis between the various core commitments of CRP cosmopsychism, I now want to explore in greater detail an additional motivation for cosmopsychism in contradistinction to panpsychism. This motivation relates to internal relations and several senses in which a consideration of them reveals support for cosmopsychism while ruling out panpsychism. What I have to say hinges on an argument for priority monism from internal relations, made by Schaffer (2010a). The argument is split into two steps: the first argues *against* priority pluralism, and the second argues *for* priority monism. This two-step argument can be seen as an addition to the section earlier in the chapter that focused on motivating priority monism as a core commitment of CRP cosmopsychism. I mentioned in that section that I would return to add extra weight to the motivation detailed there; well, here it is. In the second half of this section, inspired by Schaffer's argument covered in the first half, I formulate several arguments from internal relations that support cosmopsychism.

6.4.1 Internal relations, priority monism and priority pluralism

Schaffer aims to provide an argument for priority monism from the interrelatedness of all things. Taking the starting point that the free recombination of entities is central to the truth of priority pluralism, he offers a new minimal conception of an internal relation such that its existence would preclude the existence of free combination among its relata. The minimal conception of an internal relation is the internal$_{\text{constraining}}$ relation. The idea is that a minimal conception of an internal relation is a modally constraining relation such that it precludes the modal free recombination of its relata (the internal$_{\text{constraining}}$ relation is taken to be a minimal conception that maintains the common core of other conceptions of internal relations, namely that they preclude the possibility of free recombination). Modal freedom is required by priority pluralism because, if, as it maintains, there are numerous independent basic entities, they must be distinct entities and so capable of free recombination. Schaffer's definition of modal freedom says that, in order for it to obtain, it requires that there are no necessary connections between two entities. Take any two entities *x* and *y*. Modal freedom is true if: 'for any way, that x can be, and for any way that y can be, there is a metaphysically possible world w in which x and y are each these respective ways' (2010a, p. 352). He illustrates the idea in the following passage: 'Modally free entities are like multiple knobs on a stereo. There are no necessary connections between the setting of the one knob and the other. Any way the one knob can be set, and any way the other knob can be set, is a way both knobs can be set. All combinations are possible.' (2010a, p. 350). Now that we have a handle on the minimal conception of internal relations that Schaffer employs, and a grasp of modal free recombination, we can proceed to his argument.

6.4.1.1 The argument against priority pluralism from internal relations

The first step of Schaffer's argument goes like this: given that the free recombination of entities is central to priority pluralism, the existence of an internal$_{\text{constraining}}$ relation would entail its falsity (because, again, an internal$_{\text{constraining}}$ relation would preclude free recombination). Moreover, he proposes numerous reasonable candidates for such a relation. Regarding the first step of the overall argument (from internal relations to priority monism), Schaffer presents the following sub-argument from internal relations to the falsity of priority pluralism:

1. All things are related by relation R
2. R is an $internal_x$ relation
3. Thus, all things are $internally_x$ related

The idea is that if all things are internally related, then there are no independent things, and thus, no two things are freely recombinable; therefore, priority pluralism is false. Schaffer's argument depends on elucidating a suitable relation to take the place of *R* in the argument. Moreover, the $internal_x$ relation must equal an $internal_{constraining}$ relation. Crucially, we must have good reasons for thinking that any proposed candidate is pervasive (because the proposal is that *all* things are related by this relation). Schaffer suggests three candidate relations: causal connectedness, spatiotemporal relatedness and being worldmates. Let us briefly summarize each, starting with causal connectedness. About *causal connectedness* Schaffer says:

> One plausible candidate for a pervasive internal relation is causal connectedness, given the understanding of causation found in causal essentialism, and assuming some level of determinism. By causal connectedness, I mean the relation that obtains between any two things when there is a causal path (ignoring the direction of causation, and potentially running through intermediaries) from an event in which the one thing features to an event in which the other thing features. For instance, if two fragments are produced from one explosion, then one can find a causal path as follows: trace back from an event in which the one fragment features to the event of the explosion, and then trace forward from the explosion to an event in which the second fragment features.
>
> (2010a, p. 362)

Schaffer claims that we have good reason to think that causal relatedness is pervasive because in Big Bang cosmology, everything traces back to a single primordial explosion, so for any two things whatsoever, we can causally trace back from the first one to the big bang, and then back out from the big bang to the second one.

Furthermore, Schaffer notes that causal connectedness is a good candidate for the $internal_{constraining}$ relation, given causal essentialism, i.e. that entities bear causal powers and liabilities essentially (Shoemaker, 1980; Mumford, 1998; Ellis, 2001; Heil, 2003). Such a claim, we are told, can be understood as arising from two essence claims: (1) things fall under certain natural kinds essentially, and (2) natural kinds are endowed with certain causal powers and liabilities essentially (Schaffer, 2010a, p. 363). Given causal essentialism, causal connectedness entails modal constraints because it generates necessary connections between entities. Consider the following example offered by Schaffer:

> Recall that it is a necessary condition on modal freedom, that for any way that the one entity can be, and any way that the other entity can be, there is a world that realizes this combination (barring co-location, and leaving the remainder of the world as is). Now let *a* and *b* be two electrons – never mind how distant in space-time these might be. Draw up the list of ways that *a* can be. Perhaps a cannot vary

> its intrinsic nature, but it should be able to vary its location, and at any rate there will be the one way that *a* can fail to be. (Electrons are not necessarily existing beings!) Likewise draw up the parallel list of ways that *b* can be. Now consider combination pairs involving any variation to the location or existence of *b*, such as < *a* is as it actually is, *b* is elsewhere >, or < *a* is as it actually is, *b* does not exist >. What results – leaving the remainder of the world as it actually is – is a causally incoherent scenario. For *b* is enmeshed in chains of cause and effect. Relocating *b* leaves a rip in the causal network, and deleting *b* entirely leaves a hole in the causal network. Either would require there to be different causal powers and liabilities in the world (given determinism). And this is incompatible with the continued existence of either *a* or *b*, as both bear their causal powers and liabilities essentially.
>
> (2010a, pp. 363–4)

If we consider causal connectedness the internal relation we are looking for, then it seems to follow from the argument that there cannot be multiple distinct basic entities, and thus priority pluralism cannot be true. Thus, the argument would be effective.

The second candidate Schaffer proposes is *spatiotemporal relatedness* (i.e. belonging to a common spatiotemporal system, where spacetime is understood as that found in structuralist supersubstantivalism). As he states, it is obvious that this relation should be taken as pervasive since spacetime is the quintessential example of pervasiveness (i.e. if we understand pervasiveness in terms of spatiotemporal pervasiveness, then the best example is spacetime itself – nothing is more spatiotemporally pervasive than spacetime). Regarding its suitability as an internal$_{\text{constraining}}$ relation, Schaffer says: 'Given structuralist supersubstantivalism, the spatiotemporal distance relations between any two things will be essential to them, since the things *are* regions, and the distance relations are essential to the regions' (2010b, p. 365). Therefore, whether an entity *is* or fails to *be* will necessarily impact on the spatiotemporal distance relations between it and every other entity. And therefore, entities fail to be freely recombinable. This is illustrated by Schaffer, again with reference to two entities, *a* and *b*. We are asked to consider again combination pairs that involve one entity remaining as it actually is and the other as failing to exist (such as <*a* is as it actually is, *b* does not exist>). We are left with a spatiotemporally incoherent scenario because *b*'s failing to exist is incompatible with *a*'s continued existence, as *a* is what it is in virtue of its place in spacetime, and bears its totality of spatiotemporal relations essentially. Pulling *b* out of the spatiotemporal structure leaves a hole in the spacetime manifold and precludes the continued existence of *a* because *a* cannot bear spatiotemporal relations essentially that necessarily involve *b*'s existing.

The third candidate that Schaffer proposes is the relation of *being worldmates*. This suggestion is conditional on a commitment to counterpart theory. The case for the pervasiveness of the relation is straightforward: given counterpart theory, it is clear that the relation of being a worldmate at world *W* is pervasive in *W*. Moreover, it also appears to be a good candidate for an internal$_{\text{constraining}}$ relation. Schaffer's thinking is driven by David Lewis's stipulation in counterpart theory that 'nothing is in two worlds' (1968, p. 144, cited in Schaffer, 2010a, p. 367): all entities are world-bound. While entities *a* and *b* have counterparts in other possible worlds, *a* and *b* themselves are world-bound to the actual world. Consider Schaffer's elaboration:

> So consider any two given actual concrete objects *a* and *b*. Given the worldboundness thesis of counterpart theory, there is only one world at which a is found (namely, actuality), and likewise only one world at which *b* is found. So for the ways associated with a one only finds W_a = {*a* is as it actually is, *a* does not exist}, and likewise for the ways associated with *b* one only finds W_b = {*b* is as it actually is, *b* does not exist}. So now consider the following two combination pairs in $W_a \times W_b$: < *a* is as it actually is, *b* does not exist > and < *a* does not exist, *b* is as it actually is >. These combination pairs have no realizing worlds, for they describe modally incoherent scenarios. For if either of these entities is as it actually is, we can only be looking at the actual world, since this is the only world where either of these entities is at all. But if we are looking at the actual world then the other entity exists after all. In other words, deleting either entity from the world must take us to a different world where the other entity is not to be found. The world to which a given entity is bound turns out be a necessary accompaniment to that entity.
>
> (2010a, pp. 367–8)

Entities *a* and *b* can only exist in the actual world because, on counterpart theory, entities are world-bound. Therefore, any combination pair that involves *a* or *b* as it actually is can only be referring to the actual world, as that is the only world in which they exist. However, in the actual world, both entities exist, so some combination pairs do not have realizing worlds (e.g. <*a* is as it actually is, *b* does not exist>). Therefore, we see, again, a failure of free recombination.

To be clear, Schaffer does not argue for the truth of any particular candidate. He merely justifies their candidature. In doing so, he motivates his minimal concept of an internal relation, the internal$_{\text{constraining}}$ relation, and the work such a relation can do in revitalizing an argument against priority pluralism. We can summarize the argument against priority pluralism by supplementing Schaffer's argument with a chosen internal$_{\text{constraining}}$ relation and then adding the extra premise and conclusion as follows:

1. All things are related by relation R
2. R is an internal$_x$ relation
3. Thus, all things are internally$_x$ related
4. If all things are internally$_x$ related, then priority pluralism is false.
5. Therefore, priority pluralism is false.

6.4.1.2 The argument for priority monism from the internal relatedness of all things

The second step of Schaffer's argument moves from the falsity of priority pluralism, on the grounds of the failure of modal free recombination (due to the existence of a suitable internal$_{\text{constraining}}$ relation), to the truth of priority monism, by way of establishing an entailment from the existence of an internal$_{\text{constraining}}$ relation to the truth of priority monism.

The argument from the internal relatedness of all things to priority monism is straightforward and fairly untronversial. It simply says that once priority pluralism is taken off the table (due to the previous argument, for example), the only remaining options are priority monism or priority nihilism. The nihilist position can be rejected based on what Schaffer calls 'the tiling constraint' (2018). This constraint leaves priority pluralism and priority monism as mutually exclusive and jointly exhaustive, thereby ruling out priority nihilism. The tiling constraint says that the basic entities tile the cosmos without gaps or overlap: '*No gaps* expresses the requirement that the sum of all the basic entities is the cosmos as a whole. No portion of the cosmos is left uncovered. *No overlaps* expresses the requirement that the basic entities be mereologically disjoint, having no common parts' (Schaffer, 2018). Priority nihilism is ruled out because the no gaps requirement demands that the sum of all the basic entities is the cosmos as a whole, but the cosmos as a whole cannot be the sum of the basic entities if there are no basic entities. Since priority nihilism is the view that there are no basic entities, it is excluded. Thus, we can display the argument from internal relations to priority monism as follows:

1. Either priority pluralism or priority monism or priority nihilism is true.
2. If all things are internally$_{\text{constrained}}$ related, then priority pluralism is false.
3. All things are internally$_{\text{constrained}}$ related.
4. Therefore, priority pluralism is false.
5. Therefore, either priority monism or priority nihilism is true.
6. The no-gaps requirement of the tiling constraint requires that the sum of all the basic entities is the cosmos as a whole.
7. If there are no basic entities, then the no-gaps requirement of the tiling restraint cannot be met.
8. Therefore, priority nihilism does not satisfy the tiling constraint.
9. Therefore, priority nihilism is false.
10. Therefore, priority monism is true.

The previous section covered premises (1)–(4). Premise (5) tells us that two of the three contenders remain. Premise (6) is just the statement of the no-gaps requirement, while (7) is an uncontroversial extrapolation from (6). The ultimate conclusion (10) follows straightforwardly from the conjunction of (5), (8) and (9).

It is clear that the key premises (setting aside those dealt with in the previous section) are (6) and (7). However, both of these are uncontroversial if we accept, as Schaffer says, that: 'The central question under discussion is the *question of fundamental mereology*, which is the question of what are the basic actual concrete objects. This is the question of what is the ground of the mereological hierarchy of whole and part' (2010b, p. 38). Most crucially, this question presupposes that there are such things as fundamental entities and this clearly rules out priority nihilism.

6.4.2 Internal relations, panpsychism and cosmopsychism

Until now, we have seen Schaffer's proposed arguments *against* priority pluralism and *for* priority monism. Next, I suggest that we can extend Schaffer's reasoning such that it informs our comparison between panpsychism and cosmopsychism. More specifically, I suggest that doing so motivates cosmopsychism over panpsychism. First, I will formulate an argument against panpsychism from internal relations before providing an argument for cosmopsychism from internal relations. The first argument relates to the first step of Schaffer's argument, while the second relates to its second step.

6.4.2.1 The argument against panpsychism from internal relations

First, let us remind ourselves of the relevant details about panpsychism and internal relations (specifically internal$_{\text{constraining}}$ relations). Panpsychism holds that all microphysical ultimates instantiate fundamental phenomenality (this argument will also cut against versions of micropsychism that maintain that *some* microphysical ultimates instantiate fundamental phenomenality). Schaffer's minimal conception of an internal relation, as an internal$_{\text{constraining}}$ relation, is a relation such that its pervasive existence precludes modal free recombination of basic entities, where modal free recombination ensures that any entity can actually be any way it can possibly be, in any world; that is, that there is no world in which any basic entity is constrained by the existence of any other basic entity. Schaffer, as we have already seen, offers three candidates for such a relation. With these details fresh in our minds, we can consider the argument against panpsychism from internal relations that I propose:

1. Panpsychism entails priority pluralism.
2. Priority pluralism is true if and only if there are multiple basic entities that are open for free recombination.
3. There are not multiple basic entities that are open for free recombination (because of the existence of relevant internal relations that preclude recombination).
4. Therefore, priority pluralism is false.
5. Therefore, panpsychism is false.

Let us take a closer look at one premise at a time. Premise (1) claims an entailment from panpsychism to priority pluralism. This is a result of panpsychism's commitment to microphysical ultimates and thus to a multitude of basic entities. Recall that priority pluralism says there are multiple basic entities, so panpsychism's commitment to fundamental phenomenality being instantiated by microphysical ultimates represents a commitment to priority pluralism, with each microphysical ultimate considered a basic entity.

Premise (2) is supported by the first step in Schaffer's argument. Its consequent being a conjunction of the definition of priority pluralism (namely, that it stipulates a plurality of basic entities) and an essential feature of basic entities (namely, that there are no necessary relations between them and that they are open to free recombination). Thus, the important part is the stipulation that basic entities must be open to free recombination. As Schaffer states, this is the case because it would be strange if necessary relations held between basic entities because such a scenario would preclude their being basic entities (remember that the very notion of basicness is such that basic entities do not depend on any other entities for their existence).

Premise (3) is the rejection of the proposition that there exist multiple basic entities open to free recombination. The basis of the rejection is Schaffer's argument against priority pluralism, namely that the existence of pervasive internal$_{\text{constraining}}$ relations precludes the possibility of the existence of a plurality of basic entities. The conclusion (4) follows from (1)–(3), and then the ultimate conclusion (5) follows from (1)–(4).

The argument is undoubtedly valid, and the biggest question of soundness will be whether an appropriate internal$_{\text{constraining}}$ relation can be offered. As we saw a moment ago, Schaffer offers three potential candidates for the relation, each involving the commitment to some metaphysical doctrine or other (e.g. the candidate of causal connectedness involves the commitment to causal essentialism). Ultimately, this argument will likely stand or fall on whether a candidate for the internal$_{\text{constraining}}$ relation can be offered that the panpsychist is compelled to accept. I will not make a strong case here for which candidate is best suited, as there are numerous, and which relation is most appropriate may vary depending on which version of panpsychism, or panpsychist, is being opposed. Diverse views will likely have embedded within them different metaphysical commitments. However, it does seem likely to me that the typical panpsychist will endorse causal essentialism. Thus, the internal$_{\text{constraining}}$ relation of causal connectedness appears generally well placed to play the role of the relation needed.

Clearly, the effect that this argument has, on working out which to favour out of panpsychism and cosmopsychism, is that it motivates cosmopsychism. If the argument is sound, then it rules out panpsychism, so cosmopsychism wins as the last approach standing. However, even if the argument is contested on the grounds that no appropriate relation has yet been elucidated, for example, one might reasonably argue that it still counts against panpsychism that it is vulnerable to the possible existence of such a relation. However, I think our consideration of the relevance of internal relations (and Schaffer's argument, in particular) to our comparison of these fundamental approaches to consciousness can lend yet more favour to cosmopsychism; the argument against panpsychism is a negative argument for cosmopsychism, but there may also be a positive argument for cosmopsychism in the vicinity.

6.4.2.2 *The argument for cosmopsychism from internal relations*

What sorts of arguments for cosmopsychism can be made from internal relations? There are two kinds of arguments available. The first sort are still negative arguments in the form of 'last man standing' arguments. Let us call these *last approach standing arguments*. I think there are two last approach standing arguments in favour of cosmopsychism. The first is a simple argument, essentially the same as the one we just covered above, moving from the truth of priority monism (due to failure of recombination) to the falsity of panpsychism. The second last approach standing argument is more audacious, claiming to uniquely affirm cosmopsychism on the (controversial) basis that cosmopsychism is the only approach to the problem of consciousness that affirms priority monism. The second kind of argument (and the third argument we will look at) is a positive argument for cosmopsychism, given the assumption of fundamental consciousness.

6.4.2.2.1 The last approach standing argument for cosmopsychism over panpsychism

The last approach standing argument for cosmopsychism over panpsychism is an argument for cosmopsychism, insofar as we are concerned with which out of panpsychism or cosmopsychism to affirm. It concludes with the falsity of panpsychism. Therefore, given the binary choice between panpsychism and cosmopsychism, cosmopsychism prevails. As just noted, it is almost identical to the last argument I offered, except that this one makes explicit that cosmopsychism is not equally affected. This is potentially important because the previous argument against panpsychism motivates cosmopsychism due to panpsychism's failure, but it leaves open the possibility that cosmopsychism is equally affected. The simple argument, which excludes such a possibility, runs as follows:

1. Failure of modal free recombination entails priority monism.
2. Modal free recombination fails.
3. Therefore, priority monism is true.
4. Panpsychism denies priority monism.
5. Therefore, panpsychism is false.
6. Cosmopsychism affirms priority monism.
7. Therefore, cosmopsychism is not likewise false based on a denial of priority monism.

Premises (1) and (2) reflect Schaffer's argument. Premise (3) follows from (1)–(2). Premise (4) follows from panpsychism's commitment to priority pluralism and the incompatibility of priority pluralism with priority monism. The conclusion in (5) follows from (1)–(4). As I said, this is essentially the same argument as the one against panpsychism that I covered earlier. However, premise (6) and the ultimate conclusion in (7) make explicit that cosmopsychism is not vulnerable to the same argument.

6.4.2.2.2 The last approach standing argument for cosmopsychism simpliciter

The following argument purports to motivate cosmopsychism exclusively, on the basis that modal free recombination entails priority monism and cosmopsychism is the only approach to the problem of phenomenal consciousness that affirms priority monism. Consider the argument:

1. The failure of modal free recombination entails the truth of priority monism
2. Modal free recombination fails.
3. Therefore, priority monism is true.
4. Cosmopsychism is the only approach to the problem of consciousness that affirms priority monism.
5. Therefore, cosmopsychism is the only true approach to the problem of consciousness.

As it stands, the argument is weak because of the weakness of premise (4). Although it is true (as far as I am aware, at present) that cosmopsychism is the only approach to the problem of phenomenal consciousness that affirms priority monism, it does not rule out the possibility of others. For example, consider Chalmers's type-A materialism. Type-A materialism's approach to the problem of consciousness says that the hard problem of consciousness does not exist, maintaining either that consciousness does not exist at all (eliminativism: Paul Churchland, 1981; Patricia Churchland, 1986; Dennett, 1991) or that it is entirely explained in functional or behavioural terms (functionalism: Harman, 1990, or logical behaviouralism, respectively). It is perfectly possible that one could be both a type-A materialist and a priority monist. One's approach to consciousness might be eliminativist, but there is nothing about eliminativism that precludes one from also being a priority monist. More than ruling out possible approaches to the problem of consciousness, the argument can be seen as an instruction on how to be successful as an approach to the problem of consciousness (i.e. to affirm priority monism). I should say, though, that it may well be that some approaches – some versions of dualism, for example – are ruled out by the truth of priority monism (or the arguments that affirm priority monism). However, I do not have space to explore such possibilities here.

6.4.2.2.3 The last approach standing argument for cosmopsychism given fundamental phenomenality

The first last approach standing argument I presented is a strong one but is limited to motivating cosmopsychism over only panpsychism, while the second argument presented is relatively weak because it attempts to motivate cosmopsychism over all other approaches to the problem of consciousness. It would be progress to offer an argument that is less limited than the first, but stronger than the second. I think we can do just that. We can argue from internal relations to cosmopsychism, on the assumption of fundamental consciousness. Meaning that we can argue the truth of cosmopsychism over all other fundamental approaches to the problem of consciousness. The argument runs like this:

1. Either cosmopsychism is true or micropsychism is true (assuming fundamental consciousness).
2. If micropsychism is false, then panpsychism is false.
3. Micropsychism entails priority pluralism.
4. Cosmopsychism entails priority monism.
5. If priority pluralism is false, then micropsychism is false.
6. If micropsychism is false, then cosmopsychism is true.
7. Priority pluralism is false.
8. Therefore, micropsychism is false.
9. (Therefore, panpsychism is false.)
10. Therefore, cosmopsychism is true.

The argument is valid, but as always, its soundness will depend on the truth of its premises. We will take a look at each premise. Premise (1) states that the disjunction of cosmopsychism and micropsychism is exhaustive given fundamental consciousness. This argument aims to show that cosmopsychism is true to the exclusion of all other fundamental approaches to the problem of consciousness. An approach can be said to invoke fundamental consciousness if it posits consciousness as a fundamental feature of reality (and where fundamental reality is deemed consonant with the material universe—recall the definition of 'fundamental consciousness' in Chapter 1). The reason that the disjunction of cosmopsychism and micropsychism is exhaustive, given fundamental consciousness, is that it is entailed by another exhaustive disjunction: either fundamental consciousness is present at the micro-level or it is present at the cosmic level. It is possible to hold the view that macro-level consciousness (like human consciousness) is fundamental. For example, some versions of emergentist panpsychism claim that micro- and macro-level consciousness co-exist with both levels being fundamental (Rosenberg, 2004; Brüntrup, 2017), while other versions claim that fundamental micro-level consciousness gives rise to macro-level consciousness, but the micro-level consciousness is annihilated in the process, leaving macro-consciousness fundamental (Seager, 2010, 2017). Indeed, others (Mørch, 2014, 2019) maintain that macro-consciousness is formed by a fusion of fundamental micro-consciousness, but that micro-consciousness is not annihilated in the fusion; post-fusion, it is macro-consciousness that is fundamental. All these views have in common that they approach the problem diachronically, whereby fundamental macro-consciousness comes about through the process of emergence from fundamental micro-consciousness. Taken synchronically, these views seem to discredit the disjunction in premise (1), but taken diachronically, considering the process of the emergence of (emergently)fundamental macro-consciousness, we can still claim that the fundamental consciousness is that of the micro-level, because, diachronically, that is what macro-consciousness (whether or not it is fundamental) ultimately depends on (or owes its existence to).

Premise (2) is the conditional premise that if micropsychism is false, then panpsychism is false. For the purposes of this argument, micropsychism is understood as the view that *at least some* microphysical ultimates are conscious. Compare this to panpsychism (in its most typical bottom-up form, obviously[3]), which says that *all* micro-physical ultimates are conscious. It is clear that if it is false that *at least some* micro-physical ultimates are conscious, then the falsity of panpsychism will be entailed, because if it is not true that at least some are conscious, then it is certainly not true that all are.

Premise (3) is the premise that micropsychism implies priority pluralism. The defence of this premise is straightforward because micropsychism posits multiple fundamental microphysical ultimates, which are the plurality of basic entities that are posited by priority pluralism (see also the defence of premise (1) from my argument against panpsychism from internal relations, as the same reasoning applies).

Premise (4) is true, as cosmopsychism explicitly includes a commitment to priority monism (remember that here I am talking about CRP cosmopsychism). Premise (5) follows from (3). Premise (6) follows from premise (1), while premise (7) is supported

[3] I have argued at the start of this chapter that cosmopsychism can be considered a version of panpsychism insofar as panpsychism is the view that all fundamental entities are consciousness-involving, panpsychism, as used here, refers to the most typical understanding of panpsychism as a bottom-up view.

by the argument against priority pluralism from internal relations. From there, (8) follows from (7), and the ultimate conclusion (10) follows from (8). Premise (9) is just in the argument above to remind us that panpsychism – our main comparator with cosmopsychism – is also false if micropsychism is false.

6.4.3 Conclusions from internal relations and cosmopsychism

We have seen how Schaffer argues against priority pluralism and for priority monism. This alone can be seen as an addition to the earlier section of the chapter motivating priority monism. If priority monism is a core commitment of cosmopsychism and we wish to motivate our core commitments, then an argument showing that it must be true is an important motivation. Inspired by Schaffer's argument, I provided an argument against panpsychism. Recall that the debate that I am focused on (and which cosmopsychists generally are focused on) is the debate about which out of panpsychism and cosmopsychism to prefer. This argument suggests that we should prefer cosmopsychism as the other option in the binary debate is false (due to its commitment to priority pluralism, and the falsity of priority pluralism). This same motivation was then expressed in another argument, a kind of last approach standing argument for cosmopsychism. This is a strong argument but limited in scope. It differs from the first argument against panpsychism by making explicit that cosmopsychism is not equally as vulnerable as panpsychism (but other than that it is essentially the same argument). I then offered an alternative argument that is weak but greater in its scope. It states that, given the failure of modal recombination, cosmopsychism is the only true approach to the problem of consciousness because it is the only one that affirms priority monism. The final argument offers a balance between strength and scope, and in my mind is the most useful. It pitches cosmopsychism against all other fundamental approaches to the problem of consciousness, and concludes that, due to the failure of modal recombination (given an internal$_{\text{constraining}}$ relation), cosmopsychism is true. I think these arguments, either taken individually or collectively, offer a strong motivation for cosmopsychism, certainly as an alternative to panpsychism, but perhaps beyond that, too.

6.5 Possible objections

In one final attempt to fortify the account of cosmopsychism I offer in this chapter, let us now consider some possible objections and potential responses. Some of the objections that follow are objections made against panpsychism, which can plausibly be transferred to cosmopsychism, while others are more exclusively against cosmopsychism.

6.5.1 The objection from implausibility

The objection from general implausibility states that cosmopsychism is too implausible to be true. I can see two closely related objections that might contribute to this more general implausibility stance. The first is what Philip Goff (2022) calls *the incredulous stare objection*[4] to panpsychism; the other is what I will call *the three-wrongs-do-not-make-a-right objection.*

6.5.1.1 *The incredulous stare objection*

The incredulous stare is an objection often directed at panpsychism, amounting to the charge of sheer *prima facie* ridiculousness. Godehard Brüntrup and Ludwig Jaskolla note that it is perhaps the most common objection against panpsychism: 'The most common response to panpsychism is an incredulous stare. This is perhaps caused by the idea that panpsychism entails the belief that mountains and rocks, molecules and elementary particles enjoy an anthropomorphically conceived conscious life' (2017, p. 2). There are echoes of the incredulous stare in Thomas Nagel's statement that panpsychism has the 'faintly sickening odour of something put together in the metaphysical laboratory' (1986, p. 49). The cosmopsychist, perhaps even more so than the panpsychist, faces the incredulous stare. But what is an apt response to the charge of sheer counterintuitiveness? I follow Goff (2022) in responding that history is replete with examples of once highly counterintuitive proposals becoming generally accepted, so counterintuitiveness alone should not be cause to reject a view out of hand. After all, we see this in the natural sciences, the social sciences, and even further afield. Goff offers some scientific examples: 'Consider the thesis that we have a common ancestor with apes, or that time flows slower when travelling at high speeds, or that a particle can exist in a superposition between distinct locations; all of these theses are highly counter-intuitive, but this gives us little or no reason to think them false'. (Goff, 2022). It is the same general attitude that Arthur Schopenhauer alludes to in the preface of the first edition of his *The World as Will and Idea* (1818) when he writes: 'the weightiest knowledge of the truth, to which only a brief triumph is allotted between the two long periods in which it is condemned as paradoxical or disparaged as trivial' (1818, p. xvii). My response to the incredulous stare, then, is to insist that counterintuitiveness alone does not render a proposition false and there is a proven track record of propositions that, though initially counterintuitive, have come to be widely accepted as true.

6.5.1.2 *The three-wrongs-do-not-make-a-right objection?*

Another possible objection based on implausibility, though this time the objection is against CRP cosmopsychism specifically, is what I am calling *the three-wrongs-do-not-make-a-right objection*. This is the objection that says that CRP cosmopsychism is especially implausible because it is formed of a combination of three individually implausible theses. Simple panpsychism, Russellian monism and priority monism are all implausible in their own right, and surely implausibility compounds, so they must be even more implausible taken as a set.

[4] Borrowing the phrase from Lewis (2003), who used it to describe reactions to his modal realism.

My response is to highlight some of the content already covered in prior sections of this chapter. First, considered separately, although counterintuitive, there are good reasons for the core commitments of cosmopsychism. For example, avoiding the problem of strong emergence is a powerful motivation for simple panpsychism. It is especially powerful if we consider the choice the problem of strong emergence leaves in its wake: if the problem of emergence is convincing (and I think it should at least be taken seriously), and assuming that we have already rejected dualism (for the sake of argument) due to well-known problems, then the choice for those wanting to take a stance on the problem of consciousness looks like being between type-A materialism, which says either that consciousness does not exist or that it can be described entirely in functional or behaviourist terms, on the one hand, and simple panpsychism on the other. Although I do not have the space to go into detail, a case can be made that the problem of strong emergence undermines the middle-ground between those two options, and given those two options, simple panpsychism, for many, will not sound like such a ridiculous choice.

Next, take Russellian monism. On the face of it, it too may seem implausible, for it posits features of reality not revealed by our current physics (i.e. its 'inscrutables' or 'quiddities'), and for many it may seem spooky to posit something that by definition is not revealed by our best physics. However, as we saw earlier in the chapter, there are good reasons to accept Russellian monism. To take one example, there are reasons to think that the world as revealed by physics must be grounded in something that it does not itself reveal, and there are advantages to holding that consciousness plays the grounding role. Moreover, it slots consciousness, a hitherto awkward-to-place feature of the world, neatly into nature.

Likewise, there are good reasons to support priority monism. I will not go into details again here, but consider Schaffer's arguments from quantum emergence, internal relations and the argument from infinite decomposition. Together, these make a strong accumulative case for the *prima facie* counterintuitive view.

Moreover, contrary to the objection, considering the advantages of its core commitments as a set actually increases CRP cosmopsychism's overall promise. As we have seen throughout this chapter, the combination of the views allows for an approach to the problem of consciousness that seems uniquely placed to overcome a range of challenges.

6.5.2 The objection from the vulnerability to a conceivability argument

One might object that cosmopsychism is vulnerable to a version of a conceivability argument that says that it is conceivable that there is an exact phenomenal copy of the cosmic consciousness in the absence of an exact copy of the physical world. According to cosmopsychism, the cosmic consciousness is supposed to be the consciousness of the physical cosmos. Therefore, a possible separation (given that conceivability equals possibility) of the cosmic consciousness from the physical cosmos would be concerning.

However, recall that the cosmopsychism I propose in this chapter is committed to Russellian monism. As a result, it can respond to this worry in the same way that

Russellian monists can respond to the standard conceivability problem. The response to the problem goes something like this: zombies are conceivable but not possible. They are conceivable because when we conceive of exact physical copies of us (remember that a zombie is an exact physical replica of us but lacking consciousness), we are really only conceiving of exact *structural* physical copies. According to Russellian monism, physics accurately describes the world according to its spatiotemporal structure, but such structure is grounded by quiddities, at least some of which are phenomenal properties. While we can conceive of exact physical copies, structurally considered, we cannot (or could not) conceive of exact physical copies when also taking into account the relevant quiddities. Thus, Russellian monism can respond to the conceivability objection, and cosmopsychism, owing to its commitment to Russellian monism, can adopt the Russellian monism response to the particular conceivability objection we are considering here.

6.5.3 The objection from the causal inefficacy of cosmic consciousness

Cosmopsychism's commitment to Russellian monism means that it is vulnerable to one of the latter's most pressing objections. In recent years, there has been fierce debate over the viability of Russellian monism's contention that consciousness has causal efficacy in virtue of phenomenal properties being the categorical grounds of the relational structure revealed by physics. Let us consider the strongest line of objection,[5] which says that the Russellian monist's account of the causal efficacy of consciousness is untenable because there is an argument to show that any given type of quiddity is unable to make a distinctive contribution to physical causation. The argument has the following form: take any given type of quiddity and the physical disposition it grounds. It is conceivable that a different type of quiddity grounds that physical disposition. Therefore, the relationship between a type of quiddity and the physical disposition it grounds is metaphysically contingent. The problem is that if a different type of quiddity could have grounded a physical disposition to the one that actually grounds it, then the quiddity that actually grounds it cannot be contributing anything causally distinctive (because some other type of quiddity could have just as well done that job). There are at least two promising lines of response, and both are represented in the literature. Let us very briefly summarize each.

One line of response is for the Russellian monist to accept that the relation between a quiddity and the physical disposition it grounds is metaphysically contingent but to reject the claim that this is problematic. This line of response has been offered by Torin Alter and Sam Coleman (2021), who argue that the objection presupposes that causal relations must be metaphysically necessary, but that causal relations are not

5 Howell (2015) has presented what is arguably the paradigmatic argument of this kind, so I recommend that interested readers read his paper. Alter and Coleman (2021) have presented a generic argument which covers all arguments of this kind, including Howell's. Their paper is perhaps the best account of these kinds of arguments and the responses open to the Russellian monist. In the interest of space, I will keep things rather generic and simple in what I have to say.

typically so construed. We do not typically hold that the relation between one physical event that causes another must be metaphysically necessary, so why think it should be metaphysically necessary in the causal relations holding between quiddities and physical dispositions? Here is how they put it:

> Physical efficacy does not in general require metaphysically necessary connections among relata. For example, that physical event A causes physical event B does not entail that A metaphysically necessitates B. Perhaps A causes B in virtue of metaphysically contingent causal laws. A parallel point holds for the role of categorical grounding in physical causation. Suppose property C grounds physical disposition D. Plausibly, C is thereby physically efficacious if D is: if D has some physical effect E then, by grounding D, C helps D cause E.26 It does not follow that C grounds D in all possible worlds in which C is instantiated. Nor does it follow that C grounds D in all possible worlds in which D has the physical effects it actually has – or even that, in every such world, D is grounded at all. In the actual world, C might contribute to D's causing E in virtue of metaphysically contingent grounding laws. In sum, categorical properties contribute to the physical efficacy of the dispositions they actually ground even if there are metaphysically possible worlds in which those categorical properties do not make those same (or any such) contributions. There is no reason why there should be an exception to that general rule where the dispositions are those described by fundamental physics and the categorical properties that ground them are (proto)phenomenal quiddities.
>
> (Alter & Coleman, 2021, p. 413)

A second line of response is for the Russellian monist to reject the claim that the relation between a type of quiddity and the disposition it grounds is metaphysically contingent. Instead, the Russellian monist can hold that the relation is one of metaphysical necessity.[6] Robert Howell (2015) – a key proponent of the objection to Russellian monism we are considering here – argues that this line of response is untenable for the Russellian monist because it conflicts with a core motivation for the view: that traditional physicalist responses to the conceivability argument are deemed unsatisfactory. Howell contends that following this line of response requires the Russellian monist to adopt a position analogous to one of two traditional physicalist responses to the conceivability argument and, therefore, undercuts the very motivation to be a Russellian monist in the first place. Specifically, he suggests that Russellian monism is especially motivated by a rejection of both type-A and type-B physicalism's responses to the conceivability argument, which are based on the conceivability of the physical obtaining in the absence of the phenomenal. The type-A response is to reject that it is ideally conceivable (the term 'ideally' indicates that while the type-A physicalist might agree that it seems conceivable, nonetheless, they claim that, from an epistemically ideal vantage point, it is inconceivable). Meanwhile, the type-B response accepts that

6 For versions of Russellian monism which endorse metaphysically necessary relations between quiddities and the physical dispositions they ground, see Mørch (2014) and Coleman (2015).

it is conceivable but that the physical necessitates the phenomenal nonetheless. Howell contends that if Russellian monists claim that quiddities necessitate the physical dispositions they ground, then their response to the conceivability argument should be different: they should endorse either type-A or type-B physicalism because their responses are equivalent to the physicalist ones, so the further step to Russellian monism seems unmotivated.

Alter and Coleman (2021) explore this line of reply and respond to Howell's contention that it is untenable. Their response is to suggest that Howell would be right that the 'necessitarian' Russellian monist should endorse type-A or type-B physicalism *if* there were no additional motivating factors behind maintaining Russellian monism. However, they argue that there *is* additional motivation for maintaining Russellian monism, even on the necessitarian view. To illustrate this, they compare type-A physicalism with a version of Russellian monism they call 'type-A Russellian monism' (a version of Russellian monism on which the type-A response to the conceivability argument is adopted; a response which says that it is not ideally conceivable that the physical obtains in the absence of the phenomenal). Alter and Coleman's point is that type-A Russellian monists, unlike type-A physicalists, can claim that the conceivability of the separation of the phenomenal and the physical is merely apparent owing to a relatively plausible account of epistemic ignorance. This plausible variety of epistemic ignorance is what they call 'quiddistic ignorance', i.e. epistemic ignorance in so far as we do not understand the precise nature of quiddities. If this veil of quiddistic ignorance were lifted, so the reasoning goes, then the separation of physical and phenomenal (or, in other words, the separation of quiddities and the physical dispositions for which they are the categorical grounds) would no longer be conceivable. That is, the separation is inconceivable from the ideal vantage point wherein the epistemic distance has been overcome.

Alter and Coleman argue that type-A physicalists cannot anchor their claim that the conceivability is merely apparent in an equally plausible account of epistemic ignorance. Type-A physicalists, they claim, are instead committed to relatively implausible claims: some are committed to the functionalist claim (broadly accepted as implausible) that all phenomenal terms can be fully analysed in functional terms, while all type-A physicalists are committed to the (arguably implausible) claim that 'all macrophenomenal truths are a priori entailed by the complete structural truth'. (2021, p. 419). It is important to note that many Russellian monists are panpsychists (or panprotopsychists) who will be motivated to adopt panpsychism because of the problem of strong emergence. These Russellian monists will likely consider type-A Russellian monism far more plausible than type-A physicalism since the former can still avoid the problem of strong emergence. The point is that there are good reasons why, upon adopting a necessitarian view, the Russellian monist will continue to hold Russellian monism rather than collapsing into type-A or type-B physicalism, even though their adopting a necessitarian position brings them into closer alignment with those types of physicalism, in the respects Howell highlights.

These two lines of response to the objection are tenable for the Russellian monist. Therefore, I do not have the sense that Russellian monism has an insurmountable challenge in accounting for the causal efficacy of phenomenality.

This objection can be applied to CRP cosmopsychism owing to its commitment to Russellian monism. The objection, in this case, would be based on the thinking that it is conceivable that the categorical ground (i.e. the phenomenality) of the cosmos could have been different to what it actually is, and therefore, the relation between the cosmic consciousness and the physical cosmos is metaphysically contingent. Given this, the objection continues, it is hard to see how cosmic consciousness makes any distinctive contribution to physical causal relations. In response, the cosmopsychist can satisfactorily follow either of the two lines of reply that we have just explored.

The first response is open to the cosmopsychist because it seems that positing a merely contingent relation between the cosmic consciousness and the physical cosmos (of which it is the categorical ground) is irrelevant to the actual causal efficacy of cosmic consciousness. That the physical cosmos has a distinct categorical base in another possible world seems not to dent the prospects of the cosmic consciousness being causally efficacious in the actual world. The cosmic consciousness is not precluded from making a distinctive causal contribution to the physical world on the basis that the same contribution might be achieved by a distinct consciousness in some other possible world. I say this for broadly the same reasons covered by Alter and Coleman.

There may be independent reasons for the cosmopsychist to maintain that the relationship between the cosmic consciousness and the physical cosmos is one of metaphysical necessity. In this case, the cosmopsychist can follow the second line of response and make a case for necessitarian Russellian monism. The cosmopsychist who follows the second line of reply will arguably have more resources than the standard necessitarian Russellian monist, when making their claim that cosmopsychism remains motivated despite the necessitarian claim (recall Howell's argument that making such a claim renders Russellian monism untenable). They can, of course, like the standard necessitarian Russellian monist, base this motivation on quiddistic ignorance (i.e. they can claim that the merely apparent conceivability of the separation of the cosmic consciousness and the physical cosmos is grounded in our impoverished understanding of the nature of cosmic consciousness; if we were to lift this veil of quiddistic ignorance then the separation would be inconceivable). However, the cosmopsychist can also call on the additional motivation for Russellian monism arising from its contribution to cosmopsychism's overall promise (i.e. if the compound case for cosmopsychism is compelling, and Russellian monism contributes to the strength of that overall case, then that can be seen as an additional motivation for Russellian monism).

6.5.4 The no signs objection

The no signs objection to panpsychism objects to the view on the basis that there are no signs that things like rocks and chairs are conscious. Cosmopsychism can also be charged with the same objection on the basis that there are no signs that the cosmos is conscious. The panpsychist and cosmopsychist can respond by referring to the problem of other minds, which is, to put it simply, the problem of determining if other humans have minds like our own. They can even refer to the problem of animal minds, which is the problem of determining if other animals have minds like our own. The very existence of these problems highlights that we find it difficult to confirm whether things similar, although not identical, to ourselves, like other humans and animals, are conscious. Given this, the panpsychist can claim that we should not be surprised that it is hard to confirm that rocks, chairs or the cosmos are conscious. Furthermore, because we do not know the exact nature of human consciousness, we cannot reasonably expect to know the exact nature of either micro-consciousness or the cosmic consciousness.

The no signs objection implies that only direct signs would be satisfactory, but perhaps we should also consider indirect signs of a more pervasive existence of consciousness. For example, we can look to science to see whether there are cases in which the existence of some entity is proposed, on the basis that there appears to be a need for an entity with property *x* in order to fit the role *y*, and that entity gives us a complete explanation of some state of affairs. Indeed, we can find examples. To take just one, the existence of the Higgs boson was first proposed in 1964 to explain why particles have mass (via the Higgs mechanism), but it was not until 2012 that its existence was confirmed. My point is not that the existence of the cosmic consciousness will eventually be confirmed because the Higgs boson was eventually confirmed. Rather, the point is simply that it is not unusual to propose the existence of something owing to indirect evidence, i.e. because the proposed entity's existence would complete (or contribute to) our understanding of some other known but mysterious states of affairs.

6.5.5 The objection from the estrangement from current science

There are numerous possible objections rooted in the worry that cosmopsychism is estranged from current science. I will briefly cover two such possible objections here: the objection from the violation of causal closure and the objection from the preclusion of evolution.

6.5.5.1 The violation of causal closure objection

Next, let us consider *the violation of causal closure objection*, which says that cosmopsychism must be false because the cosmic consciousness would violate the widely held principle of the causal closure of the physical (given that the cosmopsychist will want to avoid the cosmic consciousness being merely epiphenomenal). Broadly speaking, the principle of the causal closure of the physical says that all the causal powers of the universe are accounted for in terms of the causal powers of the fundamental physical entities. Jaegwon Kim (1993) states this principle in relatively strong terms, as the proposition that all physical events are the result of only physical causes, whereas Montero (2003) states it in relatively weaker terms, as the proposition that all physical events have a physical cause. The core idea is that nothing causally novel breaks in and disrupts the causal structure of the universe. This idea is not entirely uncontroversial, but the basic idea, of viewing with extreme caution any proposed external interruptions to the causal web of the universe, is widespread.

Given that cosmopsychists are likely to claim that the cosmic consciousness is causally efficacious (to avoid cosmic epiphenomenalism), they face the following problem: How can the cosmopsychist account for the causal efficacy of the cosmic consciousness while adhering to the principle of the causal closure of the physical? The cosmopsychist has a straightforward response to the objection: it can uphold the cosmic consciousness's causal significance while also adhering to causal closure by virtue of its commitment to Russellian monism. Recall that according to Russellian monism, (at least some of) the properties that ground the structure revealed by physics are phenomenal properties. On such a view, phenomenality is afforded causal significance by way of being the categorical ground of all causal powers observed in physics. The idea is that this does not violate causal closure because its causal relevance is such that it does not interrupt the causal web revealed by physics – its causal efficacy is already accounted for in the physical causal picture (again, because it is the categorical ground of the structure revealed in that picture). Cosmopsychism, as it is committed to Russellian monism, inherits this same response to the objection from the violation of causal closure.

6.5.5.2 The objection from the preclusion of evolution

Another possible objection that stems from a worry about cosmopsychism's estrangement from current science is *the objection from the preclusion of evolution*. The idea is that there is an incompatibility between cosmopsychism and the evolution of life. The objection could go something like the following: the process of the evolution of life, from which we have materialized, is a process moving from simpler lifeforms to more complex ones over unimaginably long periods. Furthermore, we can infer the same direction of travel regarding consciousness, with more complex instances of consciousness materializing out of a long process taking consciousness from simple to more complex forms. Here is the problem: How could such a process occur if cosmopsychism is true? Does cosmopsychism not imply that the cosmic consciousness is the most complex form of consciousness, and given that it is undoubtedly the oldest form of consciousness, does it not preclude the evolutionary development of life (and consciousness)?

One aspect of this objection stems from the worry that the cosmic consciousness, as it is prior to sub-cosmic consciousnesses, is more complex than sub-cosmic consciousnesses, which seems contrary to evolution. Another aspect of the objection boils down to the worry that the top-down structure of the cosmopsychist worldview does not allow for seemingly bottom-up processes, like the evolution of life, to unfold.

The cosmopsychist can respond to the first worry by highlighting that the cosmic consciousness's being prior to sub-cosmic consciousnesses does not entail that it must be more complex than they are. For example, consider a painting on a huge canvas. Its entirety is perfectly smooth white, except for a tiny space in one corner containing the most intricately detailed and colourful brushwork. It is not strange to say that this painting is overall less complex than the tiny region in its corner. Likewise, the cosmos, overall, does not necessarily need to be more complex than its parts. But even if it *is* more complex, it is not clear that that precludes the evolution of bottom-up processes.

This brings us to the second worry, that cosmopsychism, as a top-down view, does not allow for seemingly bottom-up processes (like the evolution of complex life from simple life). Before responding, let us first distinguish between two general approaches: synchronic and diachronic. A synchronic approach tries to understand the world at a moment in time, while a diachronic approach tries to understand the world as it comes about in time. My approach in this chapter is generally a synchronic one, and this worry has to do with diachrony, but I will attempt to offer an answer, nonetheless.

With that in mind, in response to this objection, the cosmopsychist can note that the objection is rooted in its commitment to priority monism, and look to ways in which priority monists might reply to the same objection. On the face of it, there is no reason why priority monism precludes the possibility of seemingly bottom-up processes. The truth of priority monism does not entail a static whole grounding a plurality of static derivative parts. The derivative parts are not precluded from being dynamic in all manner of ways, and priority monism neither denies the existence of the entities at the microphysical level that physics studies, nor the kinds of interactions among them that physics observes. Priority monism simply says that the cosmos as a whole is prior to its parts. That is, it makes a claim about part-whole relations, but this does not entail that it rejects the unfolding of dynamical processes over time among its derivative parts. Cosmopsychism can reply to the present objection in kind.

6.6 Conclusion

To complement the cosmopsychist responses to the derivation problem in the prior two chapters, in this chapter, I have presented a more specific account of cosmopsychism created according to the priority cosmopsychism blueprint. We have explored its core commitments (simple panpsychism, Russellian monism and priority monism) and their motivations, both in isolation and as a set. We then explored the relevance of considerations regarding internal relations to comparisons between cosmopsychism and panpsychism (and potentially even more broadly). Finally, we considered some objections to the account of cosmopsychism on offer. I hope this chapter has demonstrated the viability of a more filled-out account of cosmopsychism and spotlighted its advantages over panpsychism. There is yet plenty of work to be done to articulate cosmopsychism and substantiate the material covered here. However, I hope this provides a helpful springboard for further progress.

References

Alter, T., & Coleman, S. (2021). 'Russellian monism and mental causation'. *Noûs*, 55(2), 409–25. https://doi.org/10.1111/nous.12318.

Alter, T., & Nagasawa, Y. (2015). 'What is Russellian monism?' In T. Alter & Y. Nagasawa (Eds.), *Consciousness in the physical world: Perspectives on Russellian monism* (pp. 422–522). Oxford: Oxford University Press.

Bohm, D. (1957). *Causality and chance in modern physics*. London: Routledge and Kegan Paul.

Brüntrup, G., & Jaskolla, L. (2017). 'Introduction'. In G. Brüntrup & L. Jaskolla (Eds.), *Panpsychism: Contemporary perspectives* (pp. 1–16). New York: Oxford University Press.

Chalmers, D. J. (1995). 'Facing up to the problem of consciousness'. *Journal of Consciousness Studies*, 2(3), 200–19.
Chalmers, D. J. (1996). *The conscious mind: In search of a fundamental theory*. New York: Oxford University Press.
Chalmers, D. J. (1997). 'Moving forward on the problem of consciousness'. *Journal of Consciousness Studies*, 4(1), 3–46.
Chalmers, D. J. (2003). 'Consciousness and its place in nature'. In S. P. Stich & T. A. Warfield (Eds.), *Blackwell guide to the philosophy of mind* (pp. 102–42). Oxford: Blackwell.
Chalmers, D. J. (2006). 'Strong and weak emergence'. In P. Clayton & P. Davies (Eds.), *The re-emergence of emergence: The emergentist hypothesis from science to religion* (pp. 244–54). New York: Oxford University Press.
Chalmers, D. J. (2017). 'Panpsychism and panprotopsychism'. In G. Brüntrup & L. Jaskolla (Eds.), *Panpsychism: Contemporary perspectives* (pp. 19–47). New York: Oxford University Press.
Churchland, P. M. (1981). 'Eliminative materialism and the propositional attitudes'. *Journal of Philosophy*, 78(2), 67–90.
Churchland, P. S. (1986). *Neurophilosophy: Toward a unified science of the mind-brain*. Cambridge, MA: MIT Press.
Coleman, S. (2015). 'Neuro-cosmology'. In P. Coates & S. Coleman (Eds.), *Phenomenal qualities: Sense, perception and consciousness* (pp. 66–102). Oxford: Oxford University Press.
Dehmelt, H. (1989). 'Triton, … Electron, … Cosmon …. An infinite regression?' *Proceedings of the National Academy of Sciences*, 86(22), 8618–19.
Dennett, D. C. (1991). *Consciousness explained*. New York: Penguin Books.
Ellis, B. (2001). *Scientific essentialism*. Cambridge: Cambridge University Press.
Goff, P. (2022). 'Panpsychism'. In E. N. Zalta (Ed.), *The Stanford encyclopedia of philosophy* (Summer 2022 ed.). https://plato.stanford.edu/archives/sum2022/entries/panpsychism/.
Greene, B. (1999). *The elegant universe: Superstrings, hidden dimensions, and the quest for the ultimate theory*. London: Vintage.
Gribbin, J. (1984). *In search of Schrödinger's cat: Quantum physics and reality*. New York: Bantam Books.
Harman, G. (1990). 'The intrinsic quality of experience'. *Philosophical Perspectives*, 4, 31–52.
Heil, J. (2003). *From an ontological point of view*. Oxford: Oxford University Press.
Horgan, T., & Potrč, M. (2000). 'Blobjectivism and indirect correspondence'. *Facta Philosophica*, 2(2), 249–70.
Horgan, T., & Potrč, M. (2008). *Austere realism: Contextual semantics meets minimal ontology*. Cambridge, MA: MIT Press.
Howell, R. (2015). 'The Russellian Monist's problems with mental causation'. *The Philosophical Quarterly*, 65(258), 22–39. https://doi.org/10.1093/pq/pqu058.
Jackson, F. (1982). 'Epiphenomenal qualia'. *Philosophical Quarterly*, 32(127), 127–36.
Jackson, F. (1986). 'What Mary didn't know'. *Journal of Philosophy*, 83(5), 291–5.
Kim, J. (1993). *Supervenience and mind: Selected essays*. Cambridge: Cambridge University Press.
Ladyman, J., & Ross, D. (2007). *Every thing must go: Metaphysics naturalized*. Oxford: Oxford University Press.
Levine, J. (1983). 'Materialism and qualia: The explanatory gap'. *Pacific Philosophical Quarterly*, 64(October), 354–61.
Lewis, D. (1968). 'Counterpart theory and quantified modal logic'. *Journal of Philosophy*, 65(5), 113–26.

Lewis, D. (2003). *On the plurality of worlds*. Oxford: Blackwell.

Montero, B. (2003). 'Varieties of causal closure'. In S. Walter & H.-D. Heckmann (Eds.), *Physicalism and mental causation: The metaphysics of mind and action* (pp. 173–87). Exeter: Imprint Academic.

Montero, B. (2006). 'Physicalism in an infinitely decomposable world'. *Erkenntnis*, 64(2), 177–91.

Montero, B. (2010). 'A Russellian response to the structural argument against physicalism'. *Journal of Consciousness Studies*, 17(3–4), 70–83.

Mørch, H. H. (2014). *Panpsychism and causation: A new argument and a solution to the combination problem* (PhD thesis, University of Oslo).

Mørch, H. H. (2019). 'Is the integrated information theory of consciousness compatible with Russellian panpsychism?' *Erkenntnis*, 84(5), 1065–85.

Mumford, S. (1998). *Dispositions*. Oxford: Oxford University Press.

Nagasawa, Y. (2012). 'Infinite decomposability and the mind-body problem'. *American Philosophical Quarterly*, 49(4), 357–67.

Nagasawa, Y., & Wager, K. (2016). 'Panpsychism and priority cosmopsychism'. In G. Brüntrup & L. Jaskolla (Eds.), *Panpsychism: Contemporary perspectives* (pp. 113–29). New York: Oxford University Press.

Nagasawa, Y., & Wager, K. (2017). 'Panpsychism and priority cosmopsychism'. In G. Brüntrup & L. Jaskolla (Eds.), *Panpsychism: Contemporary perspectives* (pp. 113–29). New York: Oxford University Press.

Nagel, T. (1986). *The view from nowhere*. Oxford: Oxford University Press.

Nickel, M. (2004). 'Kinetics and rhythm of body contractions in the sponge *Tethya wilhelma* (Porifera: Demospongiae)'. *Journal of Experimental Biology*, 207(26), 4515–24.

Popper, K. (1978). 'Natural selection and the emergence of mind'. *Dialectica*, 32(3–4), 339–55.

Rosenberg, G. H. (2004). *A place for consciousness: Probing the deep structure of the natural world*. New York: Oxford University Press.

Russell, B. (1959). *My philosophical development*. Abingdon: Unwin Hyman.

Schaffer, J. (2010a). 'The internal relatedness of all things'. *Mind*, 119(474), 341–76.

Schaffer, J. (2010b). 'Monism: The priority of the whole'. *Philosophical Review*, 119(1), 31–76.

Schaffer, J. (2018). 'Monism'. In E. N. Zalta (Ed.), *The Stanford encyclopedia of philosophy* (Winter 2018 ed.). https://plato.stanford.edu/archives/win2018/entries/monism/.

Schopenhauer, A. (1818). *The world as will and representation* (7th ed.). London: Kegan Paul, Trench, Trubner.

Seager, W. (2010). 'Panpsychism, aggregation and combinatorial infusion'. *Mind and Matter*, 8(2), 167–84.

Seager, W. (2017). 'Panpsychist infusion'. In G. Brüntrup & L. Jaskolla (Eds.), *Panpsychism: Contemporary perspectives*(pp. 229–48). New York: Oxford University Press.

Shoemaker, S. (1980). 'Causality and properties'. In P. van Inwagen (Ed.), *Time and cause* (pp. 109–35). Dordrecht: Reidel.

Skrbina, D. (2005). *Panpsychism in the West*. Cambridge, MA: MIT Press.

Strawson, G. (2006). 'Realistic monism: Why physicalism entails panpsychism'. *Journal of Consciousness Studies*, 13(10–11), 3–31.

Strawson, G. (2008). *Real materialism: And other essays*. New York: Oxford University Press.

Weinberg, S. (1992). *Dreams of a final theory*. New York: Pantheon Books.

Zeh, H. D. (2003). 'There is no 'first' organisation'. *Physics Letters A*, 309, 329–34.

7

Non-constitutive alternatives and the broader significance of cosmopsychism

7.1 Introduction

We have reached the final leg of our exploration of cosmopsychism and its local context. Let us conclude by recapping where we have been throughout this journey before taking the opportunity to reflect on further alternatives and cosmopsychism's broader significance. Specifically, we will survey a handful of influential versions of non-constitutive panpsychism and cosmopsychism which contrast with the constitutive proposals that have taken centre place in the preceding pages. I mentioned such views in Chapter 1 but did not elaborate on them. This was not only because they were not my main focus, but also due to the richness and nuance of the specific examples. At that early point in the volume, readers may have lacked the conceptual resources, developed throughout the book, which might have greatly assisted in understanding these alternatives. Therefore, it is fitting to include reflections on these alternatives here, at the end of our study, where we can deploy some of the resources gathered over its course. Finally, we will close with some brief reflections on the potential significance of cosmopsychism (or broadly cosmopsychist thinking) beyond its relevance to the problem of phenomenal consciousness. As an illustrative case study, I discuss how a cosmopsychism-based pantheist view might contribute to discussions in the philosophy of religion. Let us begin with a brief recap of where we have been.

We began by uncovering a landscape of fundamental approaches to the problem of consciousness, an intriguing middle space between dualism and physicalism. The claim here was that recent explorations have been limited to the micropsychism pathway (along which we find panpsychism), and that the cosmopsychism pathway, although potentially teeming with promise, has remained un(der)explored. In Chapter 2, we honed the focus on the priority cosmopsychism blueprint, a framework of an approach to the problem of consciousness which marks an advantageous alternative to panpsychism (as typically construed), because it allows those views devised according to it to evade panpsychism's most pressing challenges – the problem of infinite decomposition and the combination problem – while remaining consistent with its core motivation. However, the problem with the priority cosmopsychism blueprint is that those views built upon it must answer the derivation problem.

At the start of Chapter 3, we explored some developments on the blueprint. We then highlighted some objections based on the subject-related aspect of the derivation problem, which seemed to render cosmopsychism a dead-end. Taking these objections seriously, we spent the majority of the chapter studying two alternatives to panpsychism and cosmopsychism – perennialism and panqualityism – which purportedly avoid the subject combination and derivation problems by dropping the claim that the fundamental level of reality is subject-involving. With these two alternatives found lacking, in Chapter 4, we recast our attention back to the subject problems for panpsychism and cosmopsychism in the hope of making progress. I suggested that the problems for the two views are, at their core, identical, because they are both based on the untenability of what I call synchronous perspectives scenarios. In the face of this charge, I proposed a binocular model of synchronous perspectives to underwrite the plausibility of such scenarios. Doing this had the intriguing result of simultaneously motivating both panpsychism and cosmopsychism. Consequently, I suggested that a deciding factor when comparing the two views may not be their potential to respond to their respective subject problems (because, in response, both can adopt the binocular model).

In Chapter 5, we explored the quality and structure aspects of the combination and derivation problems. Here, I argued, we see a distinct difference in how cosmopsychism and panpsychism can manage their respective problems. I suggested that the challenges they pose are far less acute for cosmopsychism. Finally, in Chapter 6, we considered a more complete account of cosmopsychism, consistent with the responses to the derivation problem(s) covered in Chapters 4 and 5. I presented and motivated its core commitments and considered some possible objections.

With that overview in place, let us now turn our attention to non-constitutive versions of cosmopsychism and panpsychism. The driving force of these views is that they purportedly avoid the combination problem, the issue with which we have been centrally concerned. They do so because, on their proposals, macro-level consciousness is not constituted by consciousness at a lower or higher level; it is neither formed from a combination of micro-level consciousness nor derived from the cosmic-level consciousness in virtue of being a partial aspect. If this claim survives scrutiny and the views do not suffer serious problems elsewhere that constitutive approaches do not, then they would appear to hold significant promise. Let us begin by considering a version of cosmopsychism along these lines, before turning to survey a few versions of panpsychism.

7.2 Non-constitutive cosmopsychism: SED cosmopsychism

Itay Shani and Joachim Keppler (2018)[1] present a novel version of cosmopsychism anchored in stochastic electrodynamics (SED). SED, being a physical theory, says

[1] The same core ideas are also presented in Keppler and Shani (2020), but for the sake of terminological simplicity I will limit my consideration to Shani and Keppler (2018).

nothing about consciousness, but Shani and Keppler augment its physical account of reality with phenomenality to provide an intriguing place for consciousness.

Standardly, SED is an extension of classical electrodynamics – which describes how electrical and magnetic fields interact with charged particles – supplementing it with a *stochastic* (i.e. random) background electromagnetic field. This background field is typically described as a zero-point field (ZPF) exhibiting random fluctuations. Broadly, the idea is that quantum-like effects (e.g. Casimir effect and stability of atomic orbits) can be reproduced on a classical account by reference to the ZPF's interactions with charged particles. On this view, the ZPF is posited as a real (i.e. an actual) field that pervades the universe and exerts real forces on charged particles (this contrasts with quantum electrodynamics, where vacuum fluctuations are typically taken to be mathematical constructs).

Intriguingly, Shani and Keppler base their cosmopsychist proposal on a rather non-standard interpretation of SED (and oddly, this does not appear to be made explicit). Broadly, this non-standard interpretation drops the standard idea that quantum-like effects can be explained in classical terms and instead proposes that quantum mechanics *emerges* from the interaction of matter with the ZPF (with the ZPF being the fundamental submergent base of an emergent quantum mechanics, rather than being a consequence of quantum mechanics). Furthermore, the ZPF is characterized in ways that contrast strikingly with its characterization in standard SED. On the standard view, the ZPF is a passive field that stays perpetually unstructured despite charged particles' interactions with it. On this non-standard view, in contrast, the ZPF is an active structuring field, which structures matter, and moreover, is structured by its interactions with matter.

This mutual structuring of the ZPF and physical systems (their electrically charged components, to be more precise) occurs in cases where the energy exchange between the oscillating components of a physical system (i.e. the movement of electrons resulting from their interaction with the ZPF) and the ZPF field modes involved in the interaction reaches equilibrium (i.e. the energy absorbed from the ZPF and re-emitted to the ZPF is equal). In these cases, the interaction with the ZPF constrains the system's dynamics, leading to quantum behaviour. Conversely, physical systems not only interact with the ZPF but also exert influence on its internal structure and dynamics. Their interaction generates local organization in the ZPF such that the set of relevant field modes becomes highly correlated, meaning they start to exhibit a system-specific degree of order and coordination (rather than the prior independent random fluctuations). In such dynamically stable systems as just described, the relevant field modes become phase-locked, meaning that the charged components of the system interact with the ZPF in a way that creates coherence among them. Thus, the system enters a coherent state through its interaction with the ZPF, where coherence equates to long-term dynamic stability and system-wide integration. All this goes to say that physical systems (i.e. coherent structures) emerge through the selective filtering of the full spectrum of frequencies constituting the ZPF.

After outlining their preferred account of SED, Shani and Keppler move to situate consciousness into its physical picture. Let us explore, in outline, how this works. They propose that the ZPF has both an external and internal character. Externally, it is a 'vibrant pool of activity', and internally, it is a 'formless sea of consciousness' (or, an unstructured conscious expanse) (Shani and Keppler, 2018, p. 399). Crucially, immanent in this unstructured conscious expanse is a dazzling array of phenomenal qualities.

Given the ZPF's dual nature, Shani and Keppler propose – mirroring the emergence of physical systems – that *conscious* systems (what we have been calling micro- and macro-level consciousnesses) extract their states of consciousness from the array of phenomenal qualities immanent in the internal character of the ZPF (what 'immanent' means here is crucial and we will return to it shortly). That is to say that any given pattern of phase-locked field modes (i.e. any given unique ZPF information state) determines a quantum system's physical and phenomenal properties. Recall that any coherent structure is a quantum system. The range of phenomenal properties available to a quantum system is determined by the set of 'attractors' (i.e. phase-locked field modes), and the extent of the system's consciousness equates to the degree of phase-locking in the system. What this means is that systems with a more restricted set of attractors, and an overall lesser degree of phase-locking, will be associated with a more rudimentary form of consciousness, while systems with a more diverse range of attractors, and a greater degree of phase-locking, will be associated with more complex forms of consciousness (for our purposes we can consider atoms and molecules examples of the former and complex cell assemblies in animal brains examples of the latter).

Let us now contemplate how the various combination/derivation problems arise for SED cosmopsychism. Confusingly, Shani and Keppler present the quality and structure combination/derivation problems (which we explored in Chapter 5) as anchored in the subject problem and the problematic synchronous subjects scenarios therein (which we explored in Chapter 4), because *subjects* on one level extract their qualities and structure from *subjects* on another level. As a result, they maintain that these problems do not concern SED cosmopsychism at all, because, on this view, synchronous subjects scenarios do not manifest (we will return to this shortly). However, this presentation of the quality and structure problem is peculiar. First, the problem of synchronous *subjects* does not entail a problem of synchronous qualities or structure; *subjects* are difficult to account for when nested, not necessarily their phenomenal qualities or structure. Second, the quality and structure problems exist quite apart from the subject problem. As we will see, the claim that SED cosmopsychism completely sidesteps these problems in virtue of avoiding synchronous subjects scenarios is misplaced.

Most generally, we can state the problems as follows: how is the phenomenal quality and structure of non-fundamental forms of consciousness derived from the fundamental form of consciousness? Recall that the fundamental form of consciousness is the interiority of the ZPF – an unstructured expanse of pure consciousness. Consequently, the challenge to SED cosmopsychism is: how does the phenomenal quality and structure of non-fundamental forms of consciousness derive from the conscious interiority of the ZPF (i.e. the cosmic consciousness)? We can see that these problems are distinct from the subject problem.

To respond to the quality problem, we must ask what the cosmic consciousness is like in terms of phenomenal qualities (we will return to the question of structure shortly). The key claim is that the cosmic consciousness, in its pure unstructured state, does not explicitly or '*in actu*' contain phenomenal qualities (remember, we are here referring to the qualities that characterize subjective experience), but they exist within it implicitly or '*in potentia*'. It is the selective filtering of the cosmic consciousness by a conscious system that gives a system its phenomenal character. Thus, selective filtering somehow realizes *in actu* phenomenal qualities from their mere *in potentia* existence. Another key claim here is that phenomenal qualities exist implicitly or *in potentia*. So SED cosmopsychism's quality problem regards how the explicit or *in actu* qualities of conscious systems are derived from their implicit or *in potentia* existence in the cosmic consciousness. To answer this question, it is crucial to make sense of the notion of qualities' implicit or *in potentia* existence in the cosmic consciousness, central to which, in turn, is getting a grasp on what the filtrata are when conscious systems selectively filter cosmic consciousness to extract their phenomenal characters.

Let us consider two intuitive ways that they might cash out this implicit or *in potentia* existence. One option is that they have in mind a cosmic consciousness that is analogous to white light's relation to the wavelengths of visible light, noting that white light is the result of combining all wavelengths of visible light together; pure consciousness might involve all phenomenal qualities combined together, and from there quantum systems selectively filter phenomenal qualities resulting in the phenomenal properties of the quantum system. However, this model is not available to Shani and Keppler. First, each wavelength of light is present, actually and explicitly, in white light, not merely *in potentia* or implicitly. We can see that all wavelengths are present by shining white light through a prism, which, through dispersion, reveals the separate wavelengths. Consider another option, perhaps they mean something analogous to the way in which encoded in DNA is the potential for a biological organism of immensely rich structure even though the DNA itself is not as richly structured. However, DNA is a *structured* series of molecules, and according to Shani and Keppler the cosmic consciousness, in its pure state, is unstructured. Again, this option is not viable.

The only option is that phenomenal qualities *strongly emerge* from the cosmic consciousness, as there seems to be nothing about the cosmic consciousness in virtue of which they intelligibly emerge. In the absence of an intelligible relation holding between the two, it appears phenomenal qualities are ontologically novel. This undermines a core motivation for panpsychism and cosmopsychism over physicalism, and begs the question: why not just posit phenomenal qualities as strongly emergent from the *physical* picture that SED presents (or elsewhere).

So, why do Shani and Keppler not posit phenomenal qualities as existing *in actu* in the cosmic consciousness, as parsimony and simplicity would dictate? The reason is likely that doing so would require the unstructured ZPF to be more structured than it should be, given their formulation of SED. Perhaps doing so would also undermine their account of a cosmic subject, which in turn would undermine their response to the subject derivation problem: if the cosmic consciousness is teeming with phenomenal qualities, it would be theoretically prudent to posit those qualities as characterizing the experience of the cosmic subject, but this would imply that the cosmic subject is perspectival, which would undermine their response to the subject problem, because their response is based on dropping the claim that the cosmic subject is perspectival (we have got ahead of ourselves, but we will return to this shortly).

Now, let us turn to the structure problem(s). As we explored in Chapter 5, there are two key kinds of structure problems, which I referred to as *intra-level* and *inter-level* structure problems. The former relates to explaining any disparity between the phenomenal and physical structure on any given level. The latter refers to the challenge of explaining any discrepancy between the phenomenal structure at one level and that of another. Despite Shani and Keppler's claim to the contrary, SED cosmopsychism faces a particularly taxing version of an intra-level problem. It has an intra-level structure problem as it must explain the structural disparity between the ZPF's active external nature and the undifferentiated nature of its interiority (i.e. the problem of explaining the discrepancy between the phenomenal and physical structure of the ZPF). It also faces an inter-level structure problem because we know from our own introspection that macro-level experience has a dynamic, smooth, continuous structure, but it seems like this structure is at odds with the discontinuous or fragmented structure of a distinct set of phase-locked field modes that underpins, according to this view, our conscious experience (i.e. animal brains, as quantum systems, extract their (smooth, continuous) phenomenal picture from a (distinct, discontinuous) set of phase-locked field modes).

Regarding its intra-level problem, recall how the contrasting external and internal natures of the ZPF were described, 'the ZPF can therefore, from the external perspective, be regarded as a vibrant pool of activity, and from the internal perspective be looked upon as a *formless sea of consciousness* or unstructured ocean of awareness' (Shani and Keppler, 2018, p. 399). Also, recall that the ZPF's random fluctuations are fundamental to the SED's account of physical reality. Hence, externally, it is 'a vibrant pool of activity'. These random fluctuations (this vibrant pool of activity) clearly exemplify structure, albeit fleeting, but how can this structured medium's interior remain unstructured? One possible response is to deny that structural correspondence between interiority and exteriority is required. We might use the analogy of an ocean that, while it exhibits disturbances (i.e. structure) on its surface, these are not mirrored in the body of water beneath. In this analogy, the ocean's surface is the ZPF's exterior, while the body of water beneath is its interior. The problem is that in the case of the ocean, the body of water beneath its surface is structured in accordance with the structure of its surface. However, the depth of the water will determine the degree of mirroring (the deeper in the water, the weaker the structural mirroring).

Of course, Shani and Keppler need the interiority to be completely unstructured in the presence of random fluctuations in the exteriority. This makes it difficult to maintain the desired interior-exterior coupling, which raises the pressing challenge: in what sense is the cosmic consciousness the interiority of the ZPF rather than some distinct entity? It seems like the intra-level structure problem might actually be especially damaging to SED cosmopsychism, because it seems to force the conclusion that the cosmic consciousness is actually a distinct entity from the ZPF. If this line of reasoning is infective, the view looks like a version of substance dualism (or a metaphysically uneconomical form of idealism) and would inherit its suite of problems.

Regarding its inter-level problem, SED cosmopsychism may fare better. It may avoid a disparity between cosmic-level phenomenal structure and the phenomenal structure of conscious systems by appealing to the nature of phase-locked field modes in general. On Shani and Keppler's proposal, conscious experience is underpinned by a set of distinct phase-locked field modes, which, despite being phase-locked, remain distinct entities (e.g. in terms of spatial structure, frequency, polarization) and are thus, to an extent, discontinuous. So, it would appear that the view still needs to explain the smooth and continuous macro-phenomenal structure of conscious systems in virtue of the phenomenal structure associated with a set of distinct phase-locked field modes. However, in general, phase-locked field modes often have the appearance of smoothness and continuity despite the individual modes remaining discrete. This is because the complex interactions of phase-locked modes can result in a continuous wavefront. Therefore, it seems that the present view could maintain that in this continuity in the wavefront, we find structural parity with the smooth and continuous phenomenal structure we find in macro-consciousness. In fact, I think other panpsychists and cosmopsychists can appeal to an *analogy* with phase-locked field modes to respond to their own intra-level problems (especially at the macro-level where there is an apparent disparity between the physical structure of the brain and the macro-level phenomenal structure to which it is associated).

Let us now turn to the subject problem. At its most general, the subject derivation problem is the problem of accounting for derivative subjects in virtue of the fundamental form of subjectivity. As we saw in Chapters 3 and 4, for constitutive approaches, the problem resides in synchronous subjects scenarios (particularly owing to the entailment of synchronous *perspectives* scenarios). SED cosmopsychism evades the subject derivation problem, as formulated against constitutive views, by dropping the claim that the fundamental form of consciousness is perspectival. You may recall Chapter 3, where we explored perennialism and panqualityism. Those views make an equivalent move by denying subjects at the fundamental level. In doing this, Shani and Keppler can claim that synchronous perspectives scenarios never obtain, and therefore, that the subject derivation problem never arises. Although it is true that their view does not face the subject problem as it pertains to constitutive views (owing to their entailment of purportedly intractable synchronous perspectives scenarios), it does still face a subject derivation problem. Namely, how does SED cosmopsychism account for the derivation of the subjectival aspect of conscious systems in virtue of the subjectival aspect of the cosmic consciousness?

Before assessing whether this poses a serious problem, we need to know in what sense the cosmic consciousness is a 'subject', if not owing to its being a conscious perspective. As covered earlier in the book, it is generally accepted as a conceptual truth that being a subject of experience is having a conscious perspective. Simply put, the typical view is that having a conscious perspective is to be a locus of experience. Dropping this conceptual truth is costly and will need significant motivation (recall the discussion in Chapter 3 of panqualityism and perennialism's rejections of this apparent truth). Regardless, for there to be such a thing as a subject minus a perspective, we need to know what remains in the absence of a perspective. Interestingly, Coleman, our chief panqualityist interlocutor from Chapter 3, rejected the conceptual truth precisely because subjects are *nothing but perspectives*, and perspectives can be explained functionally without remainder.

Here, Shani and Keppler invoke the concept of a 'pure subject'. They suggest that various 'constraining factors serve to delimit and shape one's experiential flow' (2018, p. 403) and indicate that this constraining constitutes a perspective. Thus, it is this constraining of one's experiential flow that the cosmic consciousness, as a pure subject, lacks. But what exactly is left of a subject once a perspective has been subtracted? The claim is that a subject minus a perspective is *ipseity*, which, common in the phenomenology literature, is a sense of self or 'me-ness'. However, I am not sure how to make sense of the notion of ipseity without invoking a perspective; that is, a sense of self or 'me-ness' sounds very much like a perspective. A conscious perspective equates to a locus of experience or, in other words, a minimal sense of experiential givenness. More plausibly, to my mind, ipseity is a perspective in the absence of additional phenomenal content (i.e. an empty perspective, but a perspective nonetheless). If it turns out that ipseity cannot be made sense of in the absence of perspective, and thus the cosmic consciousness is admitted perspectivality, then SED cosmopsychism will face the same subject problem as constitutive views. Again, this turns on the problematic implication of synchronous perspectives scenarios. Consequently, this is not a live option.

So far, regarding subjects, we have seen that Shani and Keppler face a challenge because they jettison the apparent conceptual truth that the very mark of a subject is its being a conscious perspective. Additionally, they face a challenge owing to the difficulty of making sense of a 'pure subject' without invoking a perspective. Perhaps more dramatically, it is not entirely clear why the cosmic consciousness should be imbued with pure subjectivity at all. If it does not equate to perspectivality, and we cannot say what it is without invoking a perspective, then it does not seem to play an explanatory role. Concerning the latter problem, the simplest solution is to maintain that the cosmic consciousness is a subject of experience, but this is not a viable option, because, for one, it would raise the constitutive subject derivation problem it seeks to avoid.

Bracketing those concerns for a moment, let us consider an outstanding subject problem: how do perspectival ordinary subjects derive from the fundamental non-perspectival pure subject? Essentially, the SED cosmopsychism proposal responds as follows: conscious perspectives are formed through the dynamic structuring of the cosmic consciousness occurring in conscious systems. This dynamic structuring partitions the pure subjectivity of the cosmic consciousness such that the me-ness (i.e. the ipseity) of the cosmic consciousness becomes the me-ness of the local conscious system. From there, the structuring of the conscious system gives rise to a perspective. Perspectives are constituted entirely by how the conscious system is constrained by their 'inner reality and the world around them'. As Shani and Keppler put it, 'Regular subjects experience their inner reality and the world around them in a *conditioned* manner constrained by the unique particularities of their creaturely being: their body physique; the qualities of their senses; their present situatedness; past experience and accumulated memory; drives, desires, and conscious purposes; established knowledge structures; attitudes and judgments; unconscious complexes and tendencies; language;

social and cultural conditioning' (2018, p. 403). The problem is that it seems like a minimal perspective is a precondition of the modes of structuring mentioned here, rather than their result. For example, for a subject to be conditioned by their sense experiences, memories, desires, language, etc., they must first have a perspective. I think the aforementioned forms of structuring represent higher-level ways in which perspectives can become *more* structured, rather than the mechanism through which perspectives are generated from the non-perspectival.

In summary, contrary to the claim of evading the derivation and combination problems entirely, SED cosmopsychism faces a daunting patchwork of problems pertaining to the overall issue of accounting for the derivation of macro-consciousnesses from the cosmic consciousness. First, regarding the quality problem, it faces the challenge of making sense of the notion of phenomenal qualities existing *in potentia* (or implicitly) in the cosmic consciousness in such a way that avoids the implication of either their being strongly emergent from the cosmic consciousness or existing *in actu* (or explicitly) in the cosmic consciousness after all. Second, regarding structure, its principal challenge is to make sense of how the exteriority and interiority can be uncoupled in the way claimed, while maintaining enough coupling for it to make sense to say that the cosmic consciousness is the interiority of the ZPF rather than a distinct entity in its own right. Third, regarding subjects, as we have just seen, it must motivate the rejection of an apparent conceptual truth (that the mark of a subject is its being a conscious perspective), then make sense of the notion of a subject existing absent of a perspective (and part of the challenge here will be accounting for the fact that the ways in which ordinary subjects are said to be conditioned, and therefore perspectival, presuppose the existence of a perspective). Thus, SED cosmopsychism is far from evading the derivation problem.

Aside from its quality, structure and subject derivation problems, SED cosmopsychism also faces the additional (although related) problem of needing to underwrite the plausibility of the proposed cosmic consciousness: an expanse of pure, unstructured consciousness which is non-perspectival and in which phenomenal qualities exist only *in potentia* (or implicitly).

Let us first consider how we might positively motivate such a medium. One source of support for the plausibility of the cosmic consciousness is the explanatory power of the overall theory of which it is a part. However, this is severely constrained by the outstanding derivation problems. Shani and Keppler suggest that an added source of support for the cosmic consciousness can be garnered from first-person reports of religious and spiritual practitioners who claim to experience pure consciousness directly through meditation or other practices. For now, I will bracket any concerns about the reliability or plausibility of such reports, and their limitations as sources of evidence, etc., and instead take them at face value. The problem is that to suggest such experiences (if such there be any) motivate the SED cosmopsychist view of cosmic consciousness is clearly self-defeating: on Shani and Keppler's account, such practitioners (or their brains, or parts thereof) are phase-locked macroscopic quantum systems whose conscious states are determined by the *selective filtering* of the ZPF. Thus, they cannot possibly be experiencing the ZPF in its pure, unstructured state. Either such practitioners experience pure consciousness, in which case SED cosmopsychism is thereby undermined, or they are not experiencing pure consciousness, in which case their experiences do nothing to motivate the notion of pure consciousness.

Now let us consider a challenge to the cosmic consciousness that is not targeted directly at its plausibility, per se, but its ability to help address the problem of consciousness (SED cosmopsychism's *raison d'etre*). The challenge is whether we can make sense of the cosmic consciousness as a form of *consciousness*. The worry is that it is at risk of being unrecognizable as a form of consciousness, at least in any way that can help with the problem of consciousness. The problem of consciousness arises because of human conscious experience, particularly its qualitative and subjective (i.e. perspectival) aspects. But in these respects, the cosmic consciousness seems to be nothing like human consciousness. For example, the cosmic consciousness lacks phenomenal qualities *in actu* (since they exist merely *in potentia* within it). Thus, it has no phenomenal character. Moreover, it lacks a conscious perspective, meaning it is not a locus of experience, i.e. it lacks any sense of givenness. Therefore, it is natural to wonder in what sense this medium is a form of 'consciousness'. The risk is that the two are so radically dissimilar that considerations of parsimony start to lean in favour of forms of physicalism that rely on strong emergence, because, after all, SED cosmopsychism seems to rely on the strong emergence of consciousness from the unrecognizably conscious, but brings with it all the other aforementioned problems in addition.

Shani and Keppler do an admirable job presenting a novel and rich account of non-constitutive cosmopsychism embedded within a specific scientific theory of the physical world. Nonetheless, on balance, it is an unattractive proposition compared to its constitutive relatives. As I mentioned at the outset of this section, standard SED is a somewhat fringe position in physics, and the present proposal is based on a non-standard version of SED, which is an even more fringe position. Therefore, SED cosmopsychism represents an attempt to supplement a relatively fringe view of physical reality with a conscious dimension to address the problem of consciousness. This feels like an overstretch, partly because SED of the preferred non-standard form does not benefit from adopting a conscious dimension, the conscious dimension is only needed to address the problem of consciousness. However, as I have indicated, the cosmic consciousness with which the proposal supplements SED, despite Shani and Keppler's claim, raises severe versions of all the derivation problems, and additional problems unique to the proposal. Let us turn now to consider some non-constitutive forms of *panpsychism*.

7.3 Emergent panpsychism

The most promising non-constitutive accounts of panpsychism are forms of *emergent* panpsychism. While constitutive panpsychism says that macro-level consciousness is constituted by a *combination* of micro-level consciousness, non-constitutive panpsychism rejects that the relevance of micro- to macro-consciousnesses is that the former combine into the latter, rather, they typically hold that the former are instrumental in *causing* the latter. Emergent panpsychists typically maintain that consciousness at the macro-level *emerges* from the micro-level, and here, the micro-consciousness is instrumental in the emergence of the macro-consciousness. Moreover, it would seem (although, as we will see, this is questioned) that these emergent views will require *strong* emergence if they are to avoid collapsing into constitutive views.

As stated in Chapter 1, since a core motivation for panpsychism is that its account of reality does not involve the strong emergence of consciousness, it may seem rather surprising to find panpsychists adopting positions that depend on that very notion. However, the crucial distinction here is that, unlike the physicalist, who must endorse the strong emergence of the conscious from the non-conscious, the emergent panpsychist only needs to endorse the strong emergence of macro- from micro-level consciousness (possibly together with microphysics). Brüntrup (2017) refers to the radical form of emergence confronting the physicalist as 'superstrong emergence' instead of 'strong emergence', because, for the physicalist, strong emergence involves not only the emergence of a novel, irreducible consciousness with novel causal powers, and the submergent entities appear to be of an inexplicably different kind from the emergent entity: recall Strawson's (2006) suggestion that consciousness emerging from the entirely non-conscious is akin to something spatially extended emerging from something without spatial extension.

We will explore a few examples of emergent views momentarily, but before that, let us note the key motivation and problem for this general approach. The primary motivation for emergent panpsychism is that its rejection of the constitutive position means it avoids the formidable combination problem that has plagued constitutive panpsychism. However, the emergentist approach also faces significant obstacles. For example, the supposedly lighter-weight form of strong emergence endorsed by emergent panpsychists is still quite heavy, because they maintain that emergent macro-consciousnesses are irreducible novel entities with novel causal powers, which is akin to the emergence of new fundamental entities. It is important to note that emergent panpsychist accounts typically argue that the emergence of macro- from micro-level consciousness is, in some sense, intelligible, thus emphasizing the distinction from the type of strong emergence required by the physicalist, and deemed so unfavourable by constitutive panpsychists.

Such accounts also face a more specific problem relating to the tension between the causal efficacy of emergent consciousnesses and the desirability of upholding the principle of the causal closure of the physical. As we have seen previously, the desire to maintain that macro-consciousness is, in some sense, causally efficacious is near-ubiquitous; after all, we are ourselves examples of macro-consciousnesses, and it feels like we contribute to the causal unfolding of the world, in part, by dint of that fact. Furthermore, for reasons we have touched on in the preceding chapters, it is widely considered crucial that a view does not violate the causal closure of the physical. The tension exists because it is challenging to offer a non-reductive account of consciousness which both allows for mental causation and preserves causal closure. For example, in Chapter 1, we discussed how this tension is a significant challenge to substance dualism. In Chapter 6, we discussed how, arguably, constitutive panpsychists could maintain both notions by reference to macro-consciousness being constituted by causally efficacious micro-level consciousnesses. However, emergent panpsychists are in a position more akin to substance dualism because macro-level consciousness is not similarly constituted by micro-level instances. Of course, either of these notions could be rejected, but that route will likely be deemed highly undesirable.

Let us briefly examine three promising and influential versions of emergent panpsychism and assess their viability as alternatives to their constitutive siblings.

7.3.1 Seager's emergent panpsychism: Combinatorial infusion

Seager (2010, 2012, 2017) proposes a form of emergent panpsychism in which macro-level consciousness emerges from micro-level consciousness through a non-constitutive mode of combination he calls 'combinatorial infusion'. Combinatorial infusion involves the emergence of a novel simple (i.e. partless) entity as the result of existing entities infusing or absorbing into the emergent entity, with the latter inheriting the character of the former. Importantly, on this proposal, the submergent entities do not survive the infusion. Seager suggests that combinatorial infusion is such that an intelligible relation holds between the emergent entity and the inherited character(s) of the submergent entities; therefore, strong emergence, at least in its most worrying form, is avoided. He offers black holes and quantum entanglement as potential examples of combinatorial infusion in the physical domain. I question whether these are examples of the type of infusion that Seager describes, but this need not concern us presently.

Translated into the key of mental combination, combinatorial infusion involves the emergence of a novel macro-consciousness (instantiated by macrophysical entities) as the result of micro-level consciousnesses (instantiated by microphysical entities) infusing or absorbing into a new macro-consciousness, with the latter inheriting the character of the former. Again, on this proposal, the submergent micro-consciousnesses do not survive the infusion. Still, mental infusions involve an intelligible relation holding between the emergent consciousness and the inherited phenomenal characters of the submergent consciousnesses, and therefore, strong emergence is avoided.

A crucial feature of Seager's view is that combinatorial infusion is a *diachronic* process, and this plays a key role in the aforementioned intelligibility of infusions (which, Seager contends, keeps his infusion view from implicating strong emergence, where there would be no intelligible link whatsoever from the emergent to the submergent); infusions, considered *synchronically*, exhibit no intelligible link between the infusing micro-consciousnesses and the infused macro-consciousness, and therefore, *appear* to be instances of strong emergence. However, when correctly understood as a *diachronic* process, combinatorial infusion maintains an intelligible relation between submergent entities pre-infusion and the infused emergent entity post-infusion. Regarding the question of precisely when and why combinatorial infusion takes place, Seager says we are in the dark. He says, 'Panpsychist combinatorial infusion would thus postulate a set of fundamental properties of consciousness that are assigned to the fundamental physical entities which constitute our world. It holds that, under certain conditions of which we remain quite ignorant, mental fusion will occur, generating a new state of consciousness that is a function of the precursor states' (2017, p. 239). However, he does suggest invoking new (contingent) fundamental combinatorial infusion laws that govern when micro-consciousness infuses into macro-consciousness (Seager, 2017). While Seager's proposal goes some way to averting typical concerns expressed in the previous section regarding emergent panpsychism's reliance on strong emergence, it still faces several significant problems. Space limits me to highlighting the implications of just one tension in the proposal.

Let me first note a friction between two features of Seager's proposal that may not be obvious, before elucidating the consequent problems. First, the view holds that the fundamental forms of consciousness are 'assigned' to the fundamental physical entities (i.e. the microphysical ultimates) and that the infusion annihilates the infusing micro-consciousnesses. Second, it says that combinatorial infusions of micro-into-macro consciousnesses operate in (or are only apparent to) the phenomenal domain, by which I mean that in the case of the infusion of a set of micro-consciousnesses into a single new simple (i.e. partless) macro-consciousness, the infusion will not be mirrored in the physical domain, i.e. the microphysical ultimates to which the infusing micro-consciousnesses are 'assigned' will not themselves undergo infusion into a new macrophysical simple. This is key because if the proposal suggested that infusions are mirrored in the physical domain, then it would appear demonstrably false in virtue of the fact that our brains are not partless simples; they are collections of microphysical ultimates.

I propose that the conjunction of these two features – which says that microphysical entities have their individual consciousnesses annihilated while maintaining their physical individuality – raises the following interrelated problems: the fundamental uncoupling problem, the problem of consciousness-eradication, the problem of a partial phenomenal emptiness in microphysics and the causal efficacy dilemma. Let us briefly summarize.

The fundamental uncoupling problem arises because an implication of the proposal is that microphysical entities have their individual consciousnesses annihilated while maintaining their physical individuality, which leads to a radical but unexplained uncoupling of fundamental consciousness from fundamental physical reality. How can we make sense of this uncoupling in a way that is not so metaphysically costly – in terms of theoretical redundancy and inelegance, for example – that it undermines the proposal?

The problem of consciousness-eradication arises because microphysical entities whose phenomenal natures have been annihilated by infusion presumably remain phenomenally empty henceforth. The implication here is that every time an infusion occurs, the total number of individual consciousnesses in existence is irredeemably reduced. Over time, this would eradicate consciousness from the universe. This awkwardly positions the view as more of a transient micropsychism on the road to eliminativism, than a thoroughgoing panpsychism, thus somewhat contradicting its purpose.

The problem of partial phenomenal emptiness in microphysics arises because the view implies that some microphysical ultimates are phenomenally empty (by dint of being involved in consciousness-eradicating infusions) and some are not, which leads to a worrying asymmetry in fundamental physics. If microphysical ultimates are divided into conscious and non-conscious entities, this should manifest in an empirically detectable difference in their behaviour, but no such difference is revealed by physics. In the absence of a detectable difference, we would need a formidable theoretical justification for the asymmetry, but none is provided.

This informs the final problem, in the form of *the causal efficacy dilemma*: is the causal efficacy of a non-conscious microphysical ultimate altered by virtue of its lack of consciousness? If so, we would expect the differences between causally efficacious and causally inert microphysical ultimates to be empirically detectable, but they are not. If not, then consciousness seems causally inert, which raises the threat of epiphenomenalism.

One response would be to claim that microphysical ultimates do not permanently lose their consciousness in the infusion process but only temporarily loan their individual phenomenality to the infused macro-consciousness. The problem is that this response describes a constitutive view and, as such, is vulnerable to the combination problem. Thus, combinatorial fusion, as it stands, either collapses into constitutive panpsychism and faces the combination problem as a consequence, or remains emergence-based and faces the theoretical challenges above. As it stands, it seems less plausible than either constitutive panpsychism or substance dualism. Next, let us consider Mørch's emergent panpsychism and see how it fares in comparison.

7.3.2 Mørch's emergent panpsychism: A modified integrated information theory

Mørch (2019) presents a variation of the infusion view (which Mørch refers to as 'fusion' views, so in this section, we will follow suit) that represents a modified version of the integrated information theory of consciousness (IIT). Before we delve into Mørch's proposal, it will be helpful to summarize IIT. Developed by Giulio Tononi (2004, 2008), IIT aims to explain consciousness in terms of a system's capacity to integrate information. It begins with an analysis of conscious experience, breaking it down into its essential properties. From this foundation, it seeks an explanation of consciousness. These essential properties confer IIT's five axioms: intrinsic existence, composition, information, integration and exclusion. IIT derives five postulates from these axioms that collectively specify the physical conditions a system must satisfy to be conscious. This means that the physical correlates of consciousness will be physical systems that adhere to the postulates.

The central claim is that consciousness comes in degrees, with systems exhibiting higher degrees of consciousness corresponding to those achieving greater *integrated information*. The theory quantifies the amount of integrated information in terms of Φ. A system with high Φ is one whose causal interactions are both highly differentiated and highly unified. According to IIT, conscious systems are those with maximum Φ, namely, any system such that its Φ is greater than any of its parts *and* greater than any system of which it is a part. Importantly, according to IIT, the consciousness of a system is not reducible to the consciousness of its parts (i.e. a system's consciousness is not merely a sum of the consciousness of its parts); rather, it is a function of the causal interactions among its parts. Essentially, the theory states that when conscious systems themselves become parts of a greater conscious system (because the system to which they are a part achieves maximum Φ), then the consciousnesses of the parts fuse into the new greater consciousness of the overall system.

It is natural to associate IIT with panpsychism because it posits that any system that integrates information, even to a minimal degree, will possess some degree of consciousness. This implies that conscious systems could exist far beyond the bounds of biological systems and, therefore, far more widely than ordinarily supposed. A panpsychist interpretation of IIT takes this to the extreme and claims that *all* things integrate information to some degree and, therefore, are conscious. However, one challenge for panpsychist interpretations – which I will call *the problem of partless systems* – is that it seems unlikely that sub-atomic particles will count as conscious systems if they lack parts, because, arguably, parts are required to count as a system at all: it is not clear how a partless entity could integrate information. One option would be to reject that parts are required for something to count as a system. For example, perhaps a proponent could argue that electrons can be considered systems on the basis that they are, properly considered, quantum field excitations rather than partless point-like entities, and that these field excitations evolve according to a wavefunction, which, considered as a whole, exemplifies causal structure. But this is a challenge, to say the least. Meanwhile, non-panpsychist versions of IIT arguably leave the core of the hard problem of consciousness untouched; why is it that systems with Φ are conscious at all (see Chalmers, 2017)? Let us leave these challenges to one side for a moment.

We are now in a position to return to Mørch's emergent panpsychism. Mørch notes that IIT is a kind of fusion view (like Seager's combinatorial infusion) because when a system reaches maximum Φ, it becomes conscious, and as such, its parts lose their consciousness. This is owing to its exclusion postulate, which says that consciousness does not overlap among systems. That is, if a brain is a conscious system, then its neurons are not individually conscious, just the brain as a whole. This postulate blocks the implausible implication that my brain includes many distinct consciousnesses, many of which are nearly identical to my consciousness. For example, imagine my consciousness with just one more or less neuron included. Let us continue: we previously noted how the apparent lack of a physical correlate for conscious fusions undermines fusion views. Mørch points out that IIT offers precisely what fusion views seem to be missing; according to IIT, the physical correlates of fusions are physical systems with maximum Φ.

However, Mørch also highlights a problem for IIT: the coarse-graining problem. This problem relates to the fact that for a given physical system, there will likely be various spatiotemporal 'grains' (i.e. levels of differentiation) at which one could assess the system's Φ, together with the fact that, according to IIT, assessments made at coarser grains result in higher Φ. Mørch offers two examples where coarser-grained assessments have higher Φ. To give a spatial example, the assessment of a brain's (or a part thereof) Φ at the coarser grain of neurons will result in higher Φ than if the assessment had been made at the finer grain of sub-atomic particles. The same can be said for temporal grains. An essential aspect of determining how much information a system integrates is the extent to which a state of that system at one time-point is determined by the state of the system at the time-point immediately prior. Accordingly, in addition to various possible spatial grains, numerous possible temporal grains are available and depend on what is classed as 'immediately prior'. Mørch compares the difference between classing it as a nanoseconds-long interval versus a milliseconds-long one. Assessments based on a milliseconds-long 'immediately prior' moment will have a higher Φ. The reason that coarse-graining is a problem is that, as a consequence, any finer grains are structurally irrelevant to the system's consciousness, and therefore, there is a decoupling of micro- and macro-level structure.

Non-panpsychist versions of IIT can sidestep this problem by affirming the multiple realizability of macro-consciousness, that is to say, that different underlying physical bases can realize an identical macro-consciousness. It can make this claim because being conscious is a matter of a system's integrating information rather than what physical components make up the system. However, this option is not available to the panpsychist because uncoupling the consciousness of a system from its parts undermines (Russellian) panpsychism's core claim that the intrinsic nature (i.e. phenomenal properties) of microphysical ultimates determines their dispositional properties and, consequently, the dispositional properties of a system as a whole. However, there is a potent motivation for the panpsychist over the non-panpsychist interpretation. Namely, in its standard form, IIT is vulnerable to a version of the conceivability argument (Chalmers, 1996): we can conceive of systems exemplifying integrated information – that is, systems with a non-zero Φ – in the absence of consciousness. Given that conceivability equals possibility, it is possible that systems with non-zero Φ lack consciousness. If it is possible that systems with non-zero Φ lack consciousness, then they do not necessitate consciousness. If there is no necessary connection, then IIT does not explain consciousness. Even if one rejects the conceivability argument, there at least seems to be a compelling explanatory gap, just as there is for other forms of physicalism. Chalmers (2017) has suggested that fundamental laws might be posited that explain why systems that integrate information become conscious. However, this would seem to entail strong emergence, and thus, the view would be left with the familiar theoretical burden that initially motivates panpsychism. Therefore, it is worth exploring the viability of panpsychist interpretations.

Mørch suggests a way of modifying coarse-graining in IIT so that panpsychist interpretations can also address the coarse-graining problem. She begins by drawing our attention to a curious asymmetry between the structure and quality combination problems, and the tension therein between macro-consciousness and its microphysical correlate. The structure combination problem (or one aspect thereof) arises because there is not enough macro-level phenomenal structure to match the microphysical structure of our brains; our macro-level experience is structured, of course, but apparently not in accordance with the structure of the billions of microphysical ultimates that constitute our brains. On the other hand, the quality combination problem (or the aspect called the palette problem) arises because there are too many phenomenal qualities in macro-consciousness to match the few phenomenal qualities that are instantiated by the few types of microphysical ultimates. So, macro-level consciousness seems to have *too little structure* and *too many phenomenal qualities* to match its microphysical correlate. Mørch proposes that this asymmetry hints at a solution to the coarse-graining problem for IIT. The suggestion is that the missing structure appears in macro-consciousness as phenomenal *qualities*, not phenomenal *structure*. Mørch suggests that a macro-level phenomenal quality might reflect microphysical structure 'in virtue of the many complex ways it differs from other possible macro-phenomenal qualities' (2019, p. 1081).

Mørch suggests that IIT might be modified to state that macro-level phenomenal *structure* is multiply realizable, whereas macro-level phenomenal *quality* is not. This means that different microphysical bases could yield structurally identical consciousnesses (i.e. consciousnesses with identical causal relations and degrees of integration) but with different qualitative characters. According to this proposal, macro-level quality is how microphysical structure manifests in macro-consciousness. This allows IIT panpsychism to uphold – like other iterations of IIT – that two conscious systems can exhibit identical macro-level dispositions while simultaneously possessing different microphysical dispositions; microphysical dispositions arise from the micro-phenomenal qualities of the specific ultimates involved in each system, and the macro-level dispositions result from the macro-phenomenal structure emerging as a consequence of the system's being a maxima of Φ. Thus, the proposal preserves panpsychism and, consequently, avoids the apparent explanatory gap (and vulnerability to a conceivability argument) that confronts non-panpsychist versions of IIT.

However, the problem of partless systems (and any resulting theoretical complications) remains challenging, as well as the obvious broad issue of why microphysical structure should show up as macro-phenomenal quality (crucially, micro-phenomenal structure cannot be an intermediary in any viable response as that would lead us back to the coarse-graining problem). A further hurdle is to explain how and why the missing *fragmentary* structure of the microphysical correlate of consciousness shows up in macro-consciousness as *smooth* phenomenal qualities. Phenomenal qualities in macro-experience are varied but smooth and continuous, whereas microphysical structure is fragmented and discontinuous. On this view, we should expect our qualitative macro-phenomenal fields to be highly discontinuous, but they are not.

Additionally, it is not clear how a numerically vast but extremely range-limited (i.e. at the micro-level, there are vast numbers of a limited range of structure-instances) array of phenomenal structure at the micro-level should give rise to the wide range of phenomenal qualities we are acquainted with in our macro-conscious experience (bear in mind that micro-phenomenal structure will be isomorphic with microphysical structure, and microphysical structure is very minimal at the fundamental level). If this correctly identifies a disparity between macro-phenomenal qualities and microphysical structure, then the implication is that macro-phenomenal quality lacks a sufficient physical correlate. Regardless, we can see this as a form of palette problem: how does the limited range of microphysical structure give rise to the wide range of qualities in macro-experience? Note that this palette problem is extra complicated because the limited palette also needs to account for the structure-to-quality transformation outlined in the previous paragraph.

For the sake of argument, let us grant that sense can be made of drawing macro-level phenomenal quality from micro-level phenomenal structure. There is another problem in the vicinity, which relates to the aforementioned problem of partless systems, and arises because of the apparent missing physical correlate of the ultimate ground of phenomenal quality: if macro-phenomenal quality is just the way that micro-phenomenal structure shows up at the macro-level, we might take this to imply that micro-level phenomenal quality is just the way that phenomenal structure at some even lower sub-micro-level shows up at the micro-level. However, there does not seem to be a candidate lower level that can be considered physically structured in any way that would entail phenomenal structure (assuming physical-phenomenal structural isomorphism). Moreover, even if there was a candidate lower level, it would just transfer the problem down another level, *ad infinitum*.

Furthermore, it is unclear if this proposal can satisfactorily make sense of *subjects* of experience. Before proceeding, it is crucial to highlight an implication of Mørch's view. By grounding macro-phenomenal quality in micro-phenomenal structure and positing macro-phenomenal structure as owing to a system's causal relations, it purportedly avoids the combination problem, because any overlap between micro-phenomenality and macro-phenomenality is avoided (macro-phenomenal quality is grounded in micro-phenomenal structure, and not micro-phenomenal quality, so there is no overlap (i.e. sharing) of micro- and macro-level quality or structure).

As we saw in Chapter 4, I do not think the subject combination problem is as serious a challenge to constitutive panpsychism as it first appears. However, if Mørch's view were to face the subject combination problem, it would undermine the primary emergentist motivation: avoiding the combination problems of constitutive views. So, where do subjects fit into the view? In Mørch's proposal, subjects are not persistent containers of experience. They are not some entity that has experiences, but instead, experientiality is a fundamental existent, and individual experiences are specific forms it takes. 'Subjects' are just a matter of experientiality taking a specific form as an experience. Importantly, subjects so conceived do not persist through time. What we think of as a subject persisting through time is merely a series of causally related individual experiences. This means that when a system reaches maximum Φ and becomes a new consciousness, no subjects are thereby eradicated, nor do any subjects need to be combined. Instead, experiences unproblematically fuse. Fusions involve phenomenal continuity from the fusing of experiences into the new consciousness, but the forms of those experiences are lost.

There is a problem here regarding identifying the physical correlate of fundamental experientiality. Let us assume the most likely answer: microphysical ultimates. If experientiality, rather than any given experiences, is fundamental, then we would expect to find experientiality in its pure form at the fundamental level. That is, we would expect to find experientiality that has not been structured into specific experiences. If it is already structured at the fundamental level, then it is not clear why we should consider experientiality rather than structured experiences fundamental. But if structured experiences are fundamental, then it looks like we have subjects of experience (of the container form Mørch wants to avoid) there, too. If we have subjects at the fundamental level, then the subject combination problem arises, as it arises for constitutive panpsychism. For Mørch's fusion view, this would amount to the problem of explaining how micro-subjects can fuse into a new unified macro-experiential field rather than a new macro-level field formed of an aggregation of micro-experiential fields.

This ties in with the problem regarding the need to account for microphysical ultimates as partless systems: the theory needs microphysical ultimates to have parts in order to be systems with maximum Φ, but they also need a lack of structure to exhibit pure experientiality (to avoid container-like subjects existing at the fundamental level, and thus giving rise to the subject combination problem), so there is a tension here. A possible response might be to shift the fundamental level 'lower' and call on quantum fields (and excitations thereof), but as we saw with Shani and Keppler's (2018) proposal, such moves tend to come with distinct complications.

7.3.3 Rosenberg's emergent panpsychism: Natural liberalism

Let us consider one final proposal. In *A Place for Consciousness*, Gregg Rosenberg (2004) argues for a version of emergent panpsychism as an integral and inseparable part of a broader metaphysical account of reality called 'Liberal Naturalism'. A warning: this account is rich, innovative and challenging in equal measure, and getting to grips with its core ideas can be daunting. Rosenberg's overall project is driven by the contention that physics fails on two counts: first, to make adequate sense of consciousness, and second, to make adequate sense of causation. Liberal Naturalism remedies this by providing a revisionary account of causation, which places consciousness at its heart. At its core, it comprises three interconnected theories that we must understand to appreciate the view: the theory of causal significance, the carrier theory of causation and the theory of natural individuals. Critical within this package of theories are four types of properties: effective, receptive, phenomenal and experiential. And what is called a 'receptive connection'. Let us see what these are and how they fit together in the overall account of reality.

The *theory of causal significance* is essentially a rejection of typical accounts of causation which maintain that it is to be understood in terms of regularities such as laws of nature, e.g. David Hume (1739), or counterfactuals, e.g. Lewis (1973a, 1973b). Instead, it rests on an account of 'causal significance' according to which causation involves a matching of two aspects of causal significance: an effective aspect, which pertains to an entity's dispositions to effect other entities, and a receptive aspect, which relates to its capacity to be effected by the effective properties of other entities (i.e. the capacity to receive another's effective properties). That is to say, on this picture of causation, for one thing to cause another, the former must possess the requisite 'effective properties', and the latter must have the complementary 'receptive properties'. When the two are matched, we have causation.

The *carrier theory of causation* supplements the theory of causal significance and its effective and receptive properties with the claim that these properties need to be 'carried'. The idea is that effective and receptive properties are extrinsic, or merely structural, and thus must be carried by intrinsic properties (we can see here that Rosenberg's view is a form of Russellian monism). The carrier theory of causation holds that consciousness is uniquely placed to play the required carrier role. According to the view, effective properties are carried by 'phenomenal properties', and receptive properties by 'experiential properties'. Phenomenal properties are relatively easy to define: they refer to the felt qualities that characterize our macro-level experience (e.g. varied qualities of colour, sound, taste, smell and touch). In contrast, it is not easy for me to grasp precisely what experiential properties are supposed to be, but we can say they are supposed to be some sort of proto-subjective properties. We will return to this issue shortly.

The *theory of natural individuals* helps tie up some loose ends. It tells us which things are conscious and details their emergence. As such, this theory allows us to see how the view evades the combination problem. On Rosenberg's view, 'natural individuals' are entities that engage in causal relations. He presents a layered view of nature according to which natural individuals exist on various levels simultaneously. This will prove central to his view. To understand the layering of nature, it will help to drop the layering we have used throughout the book in terms of micro-, macro- and cosmic levels and instead follow Rosenberg and refer to sequentially numbered layers starting from Level 0 as the fundamental level. Let us contrast natural individuals (henceforth 'NIs') on Level 0 and non-zero levels. Non-zero level NIs are conscious entities, with those on any particular level emerging from NIs at lower levels. Meanwhile, NIs on Level 0 are not conscious. To explain why, we need to understand how the levels are related, and how the different types of properties (effective, receptive, phenomenal and experiential) and the notion of a 'receptive connection' fit in.

Beginning at the bottom level, Level 0 NIs, we are told, are mere *possibilia* – they are indeterminate abstract effective and receptive properties. In the abstract space of Level 0, effective and receptive properties exist – *per impossibile* at higher levels – in a pure state independent of each other. Recall that phenomenal properties carry effective properties, and experiential properties carry receptive properties. Thus, all four property types are present at Level 0. Level 1 consists of NIs that emerge when receptive and effective properties at Level 0 bind together and give rise to emergent Level 1 receptive properties, which bind with Level 0 effective properties in a receptive connection. These receptive connections are our emergent Level 1 NIs. The same process occurs for all other non-zero levels. For example, Level 2 NIs emerge when receptive and effective properties at Levels 0 and 1 give rise to Level 2 receptive properties that then bind with effective properties at Levels 0 and 1 in receptive connections, thus giving rise to Level 2 NIs, and so on.

Receptive connections are of central importance for understanding the emergence of consciousness; I noted before that Level 0 NIs are not conscious, but all those on Level 1 or above *are* conscious. The instantiation of receptive connections at non-zero levels equates to the emergence of subjects of experience (i.e. consciousnesses). The view purportedly avoids the combination problem because macro-level consciousness is not formed from a combination of micro-level consciousnesses. Instead, macro-consciousness *emerges* from the interactions of effective and receptive properties at lower levels. Moreover, the emergence at play here is supposed to be strong (albeit not of the 'superstrong' kind that standard emergentists rely on). Recall that strong emergence involves the emergence of novel entities that are not reducible, even in principle, to the submergent base, and which exemplify novel causal powers; macro-level (i.e. Level 1+) consciousness fits this bill.

Let us first explain the sense in which they are novel and irreducible and then explain their novel causal powers. Subjects of experience (i.e. macro-consciousnesses) formed by receptive connections are novel entities. The subjects do not exist before the receptive connection. Moreover, subjects are irreducible because they are not composed of an aggregate of subjects of experience at lower levels. In fact, lower-level subjects are not incorporated into the new subject of experience at all. The question of how Level 1+ consciousnesses exhibit novel causal powers is slightly tricky to convey. At the risk of oversimplifying, NIs on non-zero levels (especially levels 2+) have novel causal powers because the lower-level effective properties, which are bound in the receptive connections which give rise to the NIs, are causally constrained by their being bound in the receptive connection. This is important because it avoids the view facing the problem of mental causation. The idea is that macro-consciousness is able to be causally efficacious (and thus satisfy our intuitions about the causal efficacy of our macro-consciousnesses) unproblematically by way of constraining the potential of the bound lower-level effective properties.

I mentioned earlier that I find it difficult to grasp what experiential properties are supposed to be. I think the vague presentation of these properties raises significant concerns for Rosenberg's view. It will help outline my concern with experiential properties to recap an apparent conceptual truth that we have visited several times throughout the present volume: that phenomenal consciousness equates to a subject of experience bearing phenomenal properties, which means that the subject of the experience necessarily instantiates the phenomenal properties that characterize the quality of the experience. This is the intuitive notion that there is no experience without a subject of experience. Although the idea is that this analysis sets out conceptual components of phenomenal consciousness that are, in fact, not metaphysically separable, the two components therein seem to provide a comprehensive formulation of phenomenal consciousness.

We are now better positioned to see why Rosenberg's experiential properties are mysterious. As noted earlier, they do not pertain to *subjects* of experience because subjects of experience, on this view, are strongly emergent through receptive connections at levels 1+. We also know they are not phenomenal properties because phenomenal properties carry effective properties. Thus, if the intuitive notion that a subjective experience (i.e. phenomenal consciousness) is comprehensively conceptualized by reference to a subject and the phenomenal properties that characterize their experience, then there seems to be nothing left for experiential properties to be.

Here is my concern: I suspect the reason that *experiential* properties are posited is to make the overall theory work, but I worry that this may be ad hoc. Rosenberg's overall theory requires two distinct kinds of intrinsic properties: one carries the effective properties and the other the receptive properties. With phenomenal consciousness deemed the only candidate carrier (given that it is the only thing that, so to speak, sits outside a structural picture of the world), it must be split in some way into two distinct kinds of properties. It makes sense to split it into phenomenal properties and subjectivity. (As mentioned, these are typically considered only conceptually, and not metaphysically, separable, but Rosenberg can potentially sidestep related worries by positing the separation of effective and receptive properties only at Level 0, where they exist as mere *possibilia*). The problem is that Rosenberg cannot stop at separating phenomenal properties and subjectivity because subjectivity is the very thing that is supposed to emerge from receptive connections (thus giving us *subjects* of experience), and receptive properties need distinct properties to carry them. If experiential properties were already subjective, then we would face the same combination problem as constitutive panpsychism. Therefore, the theory must try to further distinguish between subjectivity and some form of proto-subjectivity. But herein lies the problem. I cannot see how to make sense of 'experientiality' without some minimal sense of givenness, that is, some minimal sense that experience is had by a subject (recall the equivalent problem with Shani and Keppler's cosmopsychist proposal). Note that Rosenberg cannot rely on phenomenal qualities to make sense of non-subjective experientiality because phenomenal properties are already put to work carrying effective properties. This raises the question: what makes these properties experiential as opposed to non-experiential? It seems that 'experiential' properties are merely mysterious intrinsic properties about whose nature we are ignorant and, indeed, whose 'experiential' nature plays no explanatory role in the emergence of consciousness.

The recourse to referring to these properties as 'experiential' rather than non-experiential may simply be to hold together the overall theory; as it stands, receptive properties must be carried by some property related to consciousness (because of the prior commitment in the carrier theory of causation, to consciousness being the only candidate for sorts of intrinsic properties capable of carrying physical structure), that is neither phenomenal qualities nor subjectivity. Thus, properties that are non-subjective and not phenomenal qualities, yet still mysteriously experiential, are posited to fulfil the required role. This feels a little too much like bending reality to account for the theory rather than bending the theory to account for reality. Nothing about experiential properties makes them uniquely suited to giving rise to subjectivity.

Because the link between experiential properties and subjectivity is so mysterious, their supposed experiential nature plays no explanatory role in accounting for consciousness (i.e. subjective experience at levels 1+). The explanatory work resides in being an intrinsic property that carries receptive properties. But this does not explain the emergence of subjectivity at all. Any other intrinsic carrier would do the job just as well. Rosenberg's view is thus left with a dilemma: either backtrack and accept that experiential properties are subjective but face the combination problem (as it arises for constitutive panpsychism) as a consequence, or maintain that experiential properties are non-subjective, in which case the view looks even less favourable than standard emergentism (because we see a resurgence of strong emergence that is unintelligible, but with the unfavourable addition of massive theoretical redundancy; standard emergentism has greater simplicity and elegance, and, arguably, no less explanatory power).

Assessing Rosenberg's solution to the problem of consciousness is challenging due to its deep connection to a revisionary account of causation. It is an all-or-nothing proposition. Consequently, it has not garnered significant support. However, even if we broadly accept Rosenberg's account of causation, there remains, as I indicated above, the issue of defining experiential properties in such a way that makes sense of the 'experiential' ascription without incorporating subjectivity.

In the preceding two sections, we have explored some prominent non-constitutive examples of cosmopsychism and panpsychism. These views take up positions on the landscape of fundamental consciousness that I presented in Chapter 1, but stand in contrast to the constitutive views which have been our main focus and are generally considered more promising. Each of these non-constitutive proposals should be commended for the sustained engagements with the problem of consciousness that they represent, their philosophical ingenuity, and their daringness to attempt more precise accounts of how macro-consciousness arises from consciousness at the fundamental level. However, as I have indicated, I suspect these views tend to be more theoretically burdensome than constitutive proposals. This does not necessarily undermine their promise, if it is outweighed by a capacity to avoid the persistent problems that arise for constitutive views, the principal among which is the combination or derivation problem. However, if my suggestions above stand up to scrutiny, then each of the non-constitutive accounts we have considered appears to either face the combination or derivation problem or else rely on a version of strong emergence that makes physicalist accounts relying on strong emergence seem relatively favourable. Of course, the brief summaries and critiques that I have provided here may inadvertently cloud enlightening nuances that tip the balance back in favour of these emergent forms of panpsychism and cosmopsychism, so I invite interested readers to engage directly with the primary materials to gain a more full-bodied understanding of these sophisticated views.

7.4 A broader significance of cosmopsychism

Before drawing to a close, let us allow a few words of consideration to the potential broader relevance of cosmopsychism. It is natural to suppose that the potential significance of cosmopsychism extends only to its prospects for solving the problem of phenomenal consciousness and, therefore, has no relevance to other areas of philosophy or other academic disciplines. Certainly, one might suppose that it has no practical relevance to actual human lives. I believe cosmopsychism's potential contribution to human endeavours far outstrips its relevance to the problem of phenomenal consciousness. It seems to me that cosmopsychism (or broader views incorporating cosmopsychism) has much to offer other areas of philosophy and academic scholarship, and perhaps more unexpectedly, to the practical structuring of human lives.

Much of my thinking in this regard is based on the fact that cosmopsychism, in various ways, renders intimate the relationship between the parts of the cosmos and the cosmos as a whole - both in terms of their physicality, since all are parts of the physical cosmos on which they physically depend, and in terms of their phenomenality, since all are parts of the cosmic consciousness on which their consciousnesses depend. From a cosmopsychist perspective, on the one hand, human beings (in terms of both their physical and phenomenal natures) turn out to be less significant in comparison to the non-human world than is often assumed. On the other hand, despite this great levelling of disparities in the significance among parts, on cosmopsychist thinking, we might see all parts (i.e. all things) as inheriting a distinct kind of significance that is not grounded in how sub-cosmic parts compare to other sub-cosmic parts, but instead in their relation to the cosmos as a whole; all sub-cosmic things, regardless of their form, are parts of the cosmos, on which, considered as a whole, their existence depends. This broad cosmopsychist perspective challenges a common worldview that puts human beings at the forefront when determining the relative significance of things in the world as they pertain to the ultimate nature of things. This radical reassessment will likely impact a range of disciplines within and beyond philosophy and, indeed, the conduct of ordinary human lives.

To take one example, cosmopsychism's portending of a radical reassessment of the place of human beings in relation to the wider world will likely be relevant to discussions in environmental philosophy. For example, cosmopsychist thinking is likely to be of consequence for the broad debate between anthropocentrism and ecocentrism, as well as related conversations about the value of nature (e.g. whether or not the non-human world has 'intrinsic' value and how that might be conceived). It may also be relevant to those subsequent debates about what nature's value, so conceived, means for how we human beings should behave (e.g. what moral obligations we might have to the non-human world). A cosmopsychist perspective may also have implications for how we should respond to the environmental challenges of our day. Perhaps chief among them are the two arguably interrelated challenges of overconsumption and climate change; cosmopsychism's foregrounding of the interrelatedness of things (including minds), for example, may be instructive here. Moreover, it may also have implications for how we think about the value of non-human animals, and how human beings might be obligated to act accordingly.

Additionally, cosmopsychism may have relevance to cosmology, and certainly to the philosophy of cosmology, at least so far as they are concerned with what Ellis (2017) calls 'cosmologia'; the study of the physical universe plus its philosophical implications for human meaning and purpose: 'Cosmologia necessarily considers major themes in philosophy and metaphysics, perhaps relating them to issues of meaning and purpose in our lives, and is of great public interest and concern' (p. 4). Cosmologists, of course, are principally concerned with the nature of the physical cosmos. Still, they may be interested in cosmopsychism insofar as its account of the cosmos and its relation to consciousness represents a compelling account of reality, and insofar as the cosmopsychist picture of the cosmos has such philosophical implications for human meaning and purpose.

While I believe cosmopsychism may have far-reaching significance in areas just mentioned and others, we do not have space to meaningfully explore these broad axes of relevance here. However, it would be beneficial to examine more closely at least one area in which cosmopsychism (or, in this case, a broader cosmopsychism-based view) might fruitfully engage to illustrate a case in point. Let us use the philosophy of religion as our case study.

7.4.1 Philosophy of religion: A case study in the broader significance of cosmopsychism

In the last decade or so, there has been an increasing interest in alternative concepts of God, with a growing emphasis on pantheist and panentheist concepts of God (Buckareff & Nagasawa, 2016, 2019; Buckareff, 2022). There has also been some interest in the potential relevance of views in the philosophy of mind to these discussions in the philosophy of religion (Nagasawa & Wager, 2017; Brüntrup et al., 2020; Nagasawa,

2020). Cosmopsychism might contribute to the discussion on alternative concepts of God by, for example, underpinning pantheistic accounts of divinity. Levine (1994) and Oppy (1997) argue that central to pantheistic views (which, bracketing some caveats, state that the universe is God) is their providing an account of unity, and a related account of divinity, such that the universe as a whole can plausibly be said to be divine.[2] Cosmopsychism might be apt to underpin a pantheistic worldview because, for example, it exemplifies a robust account of unity (i.e. in terms of fundamental reality: all reality, physical and phenomenal, depends on the cosmos as a whole), and arguably, there are various ways that the cosmos so conceived might plausibly be taken as divine.

Cosmopsychism's relevance to the philosophy of religion may be broader still. There is a recent movement in the philosophy of religion, sometimes referred to as 'the humane turn', which seeks to expand the scope of the field beyond its typical focus on the internal consistency of a particular God concept (almost exclusively the God of traditional theism: an all-powerful, all-knowing, all-loving, agentive God who created and sustains the universe) and the problem of evil in relation to God so conceived. Philosophers of religion following this 'humane turn' take seriously the lived dimension of religious and spiritual lives.[3] They consider the practices, feelings and other practical aspects of religious and spiritual lives, and the relationship between these and the relevant metaphysical commitments. A broader consideration of cosmopsychism might contribute to this movement by, for example, coupling its underpinning of a pantheistic conception of God with a consideration of its practical implications for the lives of pantheists.

Indeed, I have explored this possibility myself (Wager, 2024), drawing on the life and works of pantheist poet Robinson Jeffers (1887–1962), who is something of an inspirational figure within contemporary pantheist movements in the 'West'. A summary of this work may illustrate a way in which a cosmopsychist account of reality might underwrite a mode of 'spiritual well-being', and thereby make a valuable contribution to this recent turn in the philosophy of religion, as well as the broader project of deepening our understanding of the lived reality of religious and spiritual worldviews (including non-religious spiritual worldviews). In the aforementioned work, I present a general conceptualization of the spiritual life, the successful living of which constitutes spiritual well-being, and then present a pantheist account, drawn from Jeffers's life and works, that is consistent with the general conceptualization. A key idea in this approach is to emphasize the practical implications of a worldview rather than a critical assessment of its metaphysical commitments. Thus, the viability of this (or any other) pantheistic account of spiritual well-being will be an indicator of its practical significance for pantheists.

To outline the general conception of spiritual well-being and the consonant pantheist account drawn from Jeffers, I refer to the following excerpt from the conclusion of

[2] I am talking here about what I call 'realist' versions of pantheism. For an explanation of my distinction between realist and non-realist versions of pantheism, please see my paper 'Falling in Love Outward: Pantheism and Spiritual Well-Being' (2024).

[3] See Wager and Wynn (2024a, 2024b) for a recent collection of papers in this vein.

my paper 'Falling in Love Outward: Pantheism and Spiritual Well-being' (for a more complete understanding of the views I present here, please see the full paper)[4]:

> Let us recap the conception of spiritual well-being that I presented earlier. According to this conception, spiritual well-being consists of a spiritual life that is going well for a person. The spiritual life, as I conceived of it here, comprises three components: a conception of ultimate reality; a conception of the human condition, which is formed of two sub-elements: a view on the position human beings actually find themselves in and a vision of the ideal position of human beings in accordance with the ultimate nature of things, and; a guide to the practical structuring of a human life such as to bring about a transformation from its actual to its ideal position. Based on this understanding of spiritual well-being, my task was to present a pantheistic account of the spiritual life, which would, in turn, underpin an account of spiritual well-being … I extracted an account from the life and works of Robinson Jeffers. As we have seen, it was possible to draw out each of the components of the spiritual life: the universe as a whole is the fundamental concrete entity and instantiates the fundamental forms of beauty and phenomenality (forming the first component); human beings actually find themselves in a position of introversion, but their ideal position is exemplifying Inhumanism. The two features of which are: exemplifying a general inhumanist attitude and recognising, through the experience of falling in love outward, the relation one bears to the universe (forming the second component), and; spiritual engagements are the method of a person's transformation from their actual to their ideal position.
>
> (Wager, 2024, pp. 67–8)

From the above, we see that Robinson Jeffers expresses a broadly cosmopsychist worldview, according to which the cosmos itself is a conscious entity, and all things are derivative conscious parts of it. However, Jeffers also attributes beauty to the cosmos as a whole, a measure of which all its parts inherit (and this feature plays a central role in the account of spiritual well-being I present, as we will see). This forms the core metaphysical picture proposed by Jeffers, fulfilling the account of the spiritual life's first component.

Regarding the second component, Jeffers maintains that diverse forms of human suffering result from 'introversion', an excessive self-focus of human beings on

[4] For guidance on the primary sources for Jeffers's views, I recommend referring to my paper 'Falling in Love Outward: Pantheism and Spiritual Well-Being' (2024). However, see Jeffers (2011, pp. 604–5) and (2000, pp. 411–12) for succinct summaries of his 'religious attitudes'. For an explanation, in prose, of his inhumanism, see both the published and unpublished versions of the preface to *The Double-Axe and Other Poems* (for the published version, see Jeffers (1948, p. vii) and see Jeffers (2000, p. 418) for the unpublished version). For a depiction of inhumanism in verse, see the poem 'The Double-Axe' in Jeffers (1948), and for a depiction of falling in love outward, in verse, see the poem 'The Tower Beyond Tragedy' in Jeffers (1925, pp. 81–2). Finally, for a depiction of Jeffers view that it is only considered in isolation that parts of the cosmos appear evil, see the poem 'The Answer' in Jeffers (1937, p. 107).

human affairs to the exclusion of recognizing their proper relation to the cosmos as a whole (namely, their being a proper part of it). For Jeffers, fostering an attitude of 'inhumanism', which is a course correction of this over-emphasis on human affairs, together with a recognition by human beings of their status as parts of the conscious cosmos, offers a kind of salvation from suffering.

Finally, concerning the third component, we can derive from Jeffers a practical guide for fostering such recognition through what I call 'spiritual engagements'. This is where the notion that the cosmos as a whole embodies the fundamental form of beauty – and consequently, that all sub-cosmic entities participate in that beauty – becomes relevant. According to Jeffers, it is through experiences of beauty (which he calls 'mystical experiences') that human beings come to recognize their parthood with the cosmos and, more importantly, fall in love with the cosmos as a result of such experiences. Thus, 'spiritual engagements', I suggest, are engagements with the world that have the propensity to result in aesthetic experiences wherein a person comes to identify themselves with the cosmos, i.e. mystical experiences.

Since the above is a rather incomplete summary, I recommend those interested read the full paper. Here, we have space only for an imperfect sketch, and Jeffers's views are nuanced and apt to be misunderstood. However, this sketch serves our modest purpose of highlighting how cosmopsychist views might fruitfully engage discussions beyond the philosophy of mind, in this case, by contributing to both the alternative concepts of God literature and the growing discussion around taking seriously the practical dimensions of spiritual life.

Let us now explore how this view, a Jeffers-inspired cosmopsychism-based version of pantheism, might be brought into deeper engagement with the philosophy of religion by considering one of the discipline's core foci: the problem of evil. Moreover, let us consider, in particular, Yujin Nagasawa's (2024) recent ingenious argument that aims to transform the problem itself. Let us begin with a summary of the argument before providing some objections and considering how a Jeffers-inspired pantheist might respond (note that I will use 'Jeffers-inspired pantheism' to refer to the kind of cosmopsychism-based view we just outlined, and for our purposes, we can take it that this view will count as a version of 'non-theism' in Nagasawa's proposal).

The problem of evil is usually considered a problem for traditional theists. However, Nagasawa's intriguing argument carries the striking conclusion that not only does the problem of evil apply to both theists and non-theists, but is, furthermore, *more severe* for non-theists. In short, Nagasawa first reduces the problem of evil to what he calls 'the problem of systemic evil for modest optimists', which applies equally to theists and non-theists, and then argues that theists are significantly better resourced than non-theists to respond to this problem.

Let us first consider the reduction of the problem of evil. Nagasawa points out that the problem of evil essentially comprises a tension between on the one hand the unexpectedness of evil and, on the other hand, the existence of evil. Next, Nagasawa argues that the unexpectedness of evil is grounded in 'modest optimism', which is the conviction that 'Overall and fundamentally, the environment in which we exist is not bad'. (2024, p. 142). It is important to note that the phrase 'environment in which we exist' is required to limit the optimism-defeating effects of considering an overly broad state of affairs. For example, people are less likely to be optimistic about the state of the totality of existence, which is largely unknown to them, than about their local environment, with which they are quite familiar. Thus, 'the environment in which we exist' restricts what modest optimism quantifies over to 'a relatively local environment to which we belong' (p. 142). The basic idea is that modest optimism is upheld when the ratio of good to evil in the local environment (or our judgements about such a ratio) does not favour evil. With this conception of modest optimism in place, Nagasawa makes the case, underpinned by empirical findings, that most theists *and* non-theists are likely to be modest optimists (i.e. they are both likely to affirm that their local environment is not overall bad). Therefore, the problem of evil, now renamed 'the problem of systemic evil for modest optimists',[5] is just as much a problem for non-theists as theists.

Having brought theism and non-theism to parity concerning the problem of evil, Nagasawa makes the surprising claim that theism is much better placed to respond because it can call upon vast supernatural resources to smooth over the tension between modest optimism and the existence of evil. Crucially, these resources are not available to the non-theist. Roughly, the idea is that the theist can posit sources of value in a transcendent spiritual domain, which can offset any apparent imbalance of evil over good in our environment. The resources called upon here are those familiar to existing theodicies (e.g. the free will defence (Plantinga, 1974; Augustine, 2008) and the soul-making theodicy (Hick, 1966)). Moreover, Nagasawa claims that the theist can also call upon whatever non-supernatural resources might be available to the non-theist. Thus, we arrive at the striking conclusion that it is non-theism for which the existence of evil poses the most significant challenge.

Although this argumentative strategy is ingenious, it seems to me to have some serious flaws. Let us briefly explore these potential flaws before considering how our Jeffers-inspired pantheism might be brought into engagement with the discussion.

The first issue is that, even by Nagasawa's lights, the theist response does not address the problem of systemic evil for modest optimists (and, by transition, does not address the problem of evil *simpliciter*). Recall that the problem reportedly resides in the tension between modest optimism and the reality of evil. The issue is that the theist response does nothing to dissolve the tension because it does not maintain modest optimism. Recall that modest optimism quantifies over only 'a relatively local environment', but note that the supernatural resources that the proposed theist response calls upon are external to a relatively local environment. Therefore, supernatural resources do nothing to change the modest optimist's calculation of good over evil because modest optimism quantifies over only a local environment. That is, supernatural resources do not help the theist dissolve the tension between *modest* optimism and the reality of evil. Such resources help dissolve a tension between

[5] By 'systemic evil', Nagasawa is referring to the evil inherent in and resulting from the biological process of evolution. This is chosen as it captures a maximal amount of evil of different types under a single concept. It will not be important for our discussion to focus on this conception of 'systemic evil', we can stick to more typical ways of construing evil as it will simplify the discussion and not lose anything too significant. I will however still use the term when I mention the names of problems.

what we can call *transcendent optimism* and the existence of evil, but that is not the problem of evil, on Nagasawa's view. This new problem, which we can call *the problem of systemic evil for transcendent optimists,* does not apply to non-theists (as they likely do not ground their optimism in a transcendent domain), it seems to boil down to the problem of evil as ordinarily conceived. Thus, the 'local environment' restrictions are vital to maintaining modest optimism, and modest optimism is essential to extending the reach of the argument to non-theists (the restrictions were placed on the conception of modest optimism precisely because doing so brought almost everyone, including theists and non-theists, into its orbit). Therefore, if the theist cannot dissolve the tension between *modest* optimism and the reality of evil, they are not touching the problem (as conceived in Nagasawa's proposal). Therefore, they are no better placed than the non-theist.

A second issue is that reducing the problem of evil to the problem of systemic evil for modest optimists obfuscates a critical asymmetry in the seriousness of the challenge posed by evil for theists and non-theists: for theists, the challenge is existential to their *theism*, but the non-theist does not find their *non-theism* challenged. This difference in what is at stake, i.e. the very existence of the worldview, is what makes the problem of evil so concerning for the theist.

With some persistence, we *can* get this asymmetry to show up in the problem of systemic evil for modest optimists. To do this, we need to recognize that the unresolved tension is an existential threat not just to the modest optimism of the person concerned, but also to whatever underpins that modest optimism. To illustrate, consider my optimism about my having hair at age thirty-seven. Reality is in tension with this optimism because I am thirty-seven and unequivocally bald. What is at stake if I cannot dissolve this tension is not just my optimism about my having hair at thirty-seven but also whatever the reason is that I anticipate having hair (e.g. my belief that I inherited the relevant genetic code governing my hair from my father, who has maintained a full head of hair); the tension is an existential threat to both my optimism and its reasons. Turning back to theists and non-theists, let us highlight the asymmetry: What underpins modest optimism in the case of theists is their *theism*. For theists, traditional theism is at stake in the problem of evil (i.e. it calls into question the existence of the God which characterizes their theism). In the case of non-theists, their modest optimism is not underpinned by their non-theism (i.e. it is not because they reject traditional theism that they affirm that overall, fundamentally, their local environment is not bad). Thus, the problem of systemic evil for modest optimists poses an existential threat to theism, but not to non-theism, and therefore is a far more significant challenge to theists than non-theists.

So far, I have claimed that, on Nagasawa's proposal, the theist cannot draw on supernatural resources to answer the problem of systemic evil for modest optimists. As such, they have no resources over and above the non-theist. Moreover, I have claimed that theists are in a far worse position because the tension comprising the problem is an existential threat to theism but not non-theism. I also noted that the problem could be tweaked to allow access to supernatural resources, but doing so would extend the context beyond modest optimism to transcendent optimism, and thereby render the problem inapplicable to non-theists (because while non-theists are likely modest optimists, they are not likely to be transcendent optimists). It seems that the problem of evil is best presented, as is typical, as a problem for theists based on a tension between a particular concept of God and the existence of evil. Conceptualizing the problem this way is, contrary to Nagasawa's claim, better for the theist because it allows access to supernatural resources.

However, Nagasawa raises a legitimate question for the non-theist, even if not accompanied by an existential threat: How do non-theists account for their modest optimism given a world replete with evil? One obvious response is that modest optimism is not in tension with evil per se but the balance between good and evil. The non-theist can maintain that the balance of evil in the local environment does not seem tipped to favour evil over good. This is an unproblematic response for the non-theist because all that modest optimism requires is that the local environment is not *overall* bad, i.e. the existence of evil per se does not challenge non-theism. Contrary to Nagasawa's contention, it is not clear that the theist can make the same claim, and the reason further highlights why the problem of evil is not equivalent to the problem of systemic evil for modest optimists. Plausibly, for the theist, *any* amount of evil in their local environment is *prima facie* in tension with their theism. It seems irrelevant whether the overall balance falls in favour of good. Given theism, the very existence of evil demands a response. However, remember that the usual theodicies, which would otherwise be called upon to respond, cannot be wheeled out in response to this formulation of the problem of evil. Thus, the non-theist might have *more* resources available than the theist.

Let us now return to cosmopsychism and consider how it might contribute to this discussion. More specifically, let us return to the Jeffers-inspired pantheism outlined earlier (which, again, exemplifies a form of cosmopsychism), and explore how it might respond to the problem of systemic evil for modest optimists. First, let us sketch Jeffers's view of evil (or, more accurately, my interpretation of it). It is important to note that we can find two views on evil in Jeffers: one from the human perspective and another from a divine cosmic perspective. From the human perspective, many forms of suffering result from human 'introversion', an over-emphasis on human affairs. The idea is that an exaggerated inwardness of human beings (and humanity as a whole) in their conduct results in evil behaviour and consequences (i.e. moral evil). Crucially, Jeffers sees the cosmos as a whole as an internally dynamic entity whose dynamism exemplifies a kind of 'violence', that is, it is not a calm, tranquil entity but a ferocious creative medium, and this creativity is responsible for evil – natural and moral – as well as everything else (note: the cosmos is not conceived as agentive, so this creativity does not equate to the intentional action of an agent). Critically, from a divine cosmic perspective, the cosmos as a whole is neither good nor bad. Such moral ascriptions apply only to its parts considered in isolation from the whole (an isolation which is impossible in actuality). We can thus provide the following general picture of evil: From a human perspective, evil is real and results from human activity. However, evil (and goodness) does not exist from the divine cosmic perspective. The cosmos, when properly considered holistically, is neither good nor evil. However, when, from the human perspective, its parts are (*per impossibile* in actuality) considered in isolation, they can be evil. This idea is tricky to grasp, but it need not concern us here as we are not presently concerned with critically assessing the metaphysics of the worldviews.

Given this, how might a Jeffers-inspired pantheist respond to the problem of systemic evil for modest optimists? Interestingly, my previous objection, which blocks the theist's access to supernatural resources, also blocks our Jeffers-inspired pantheist (and would block other cosmopsychist views, too) from appealing to the nature of the cosmos as a whole to address the problem. Appeal cannot be made to the cosmos as a whole because it is a non-local environment. However, they may still be able to maintain modest optimism by reference to Jeffers's notions of 'introversion' (as the source of local moral evil) and its antidote in the form of 'inhumanism'. Of course, one option is to take the aforementioned stance and claim that the balance of good and evil in the local environment is not tipped in favour of evil. However, for the sake of argument, let us assume that the balance tips in favour of evil, and thus, modest optimism is in tension with reality. The Jeffers-inspired pantheist we are considering may still be able to provide a response by reference to introversion and inhumanism. Introversion provides an explanation of moral evil in the local environment, while inhumanism provides a way to reduce the local level of moral evil over time (recall that this is supposed to be a shifting of emphasis from the human to the non-human, thereby reducing the negative consequences of an over-emphasis on human affairs). So, even in a local context where evil outweighs good, we might think modest optimism can be maintained by reference to the fact that the current balance of evil over good can shift in a positive direction over time. Of course, for this to work, modest optimism would need tweaking so that it quantifies over a period of time that extends somewhat into the future, but the period could be relatively short, and such an amendment would not affect the prevalence of modest optimism (which is what guarantees the argument has maximal applicability to theists and non-theists). Bear in mind that a similar response will not be effective for the theist because, again, *any* amount of evil poses an existential threat to their theism.

You will notice that the response I just proposed involved human beings' optimism being proactively maintained by their response to evil. The idea that a reply might involve a sense in which evil can be *responded to* brings us to a critical point, where I must admit that the preceding discussion has had a dual function. We saw how cosmopsychism (by way of our Jeffers-inspired pantheist) might engage with, and deepen, existing discussions in the philosophy of religion. But it also serves the somewhat different purpose of illustrating a limitation with the standard discussions on the problem of evil in the analytic philosophy of religion, namely that the focus is typically on *explaining* evil in such a way that preserves the traditional theistic concept of God. However, some philosophers criticize this standard philosophical engagement with evil on the basis that it says nothing about how to *respond* to evil. For the average person, evil poses a direct problem because it demands a response. While a peruse of the standard philosophical literature might give the impression that the only contribution philosophers of religion can make on the topic is providing abstract God-preserving explanations of evil, philosophers sympathetic to the recent 'humane turn' in the philosophy of religion have sought to focus on ways in which religious and spiritual traditions might provide resources for *responding* to evil (Cottingham, 2005, 2014; Moser, 2008; Clack, 2018). Cosmopsychism, in this case via our Jeffers-inspired pantheism, can make a meaningful contribution to the discussion here, too.

Recall the general account of spiritual well-being that I presented earlier, and its purpose to contribute to the humane turn literature by presenting a general conception of spiritual well-being, the adoption of which allows spiritual worldviews to demonstrate their practical relevance. Here, the focus was not on assessing the metaphysical accounts of a worldview but on exploring how metaphysical accounts underpin (and/or are underpinned by) practical modes of spiritual life. Notably, the relevance of this conceptualization extends beyond religious and spiritual *traditions* to include non-religious forms of spirituality, too. Our Jeffers-inspired pantheist is a case in point.

Given this way of conceptualizing spiritual well-being, my claim that Jeffers-inspired pantheism can provide a practical response to evil is perhaps unsurprising. The response is something like this: Evil (moral evil, at least) is the result of human introversion, and this can be remedied by developing an inhumanist attitude (i.e. a proactive shifting of emphasis from the human to the non-human). Moreover, on this view, the ultimate aim of the spiritual life is for a person to 'fall in love outward', that is, to come to recognize their inseparable identity with the cosmos as a whole and, as a result, to fall in love with the cosmos. The vehicle of falling in love outward, according to Jeffers, is a form of aesthetic experience – wherein one experiences their identification with the cosmos – which he calls 'mystical experiences', and it is mystical experience that causes one to fall in love outward. Thus, we can extract a form of spiritual practice from Jeffers's view, which involves 'engagements with the world that foster aesthetic experiences, and in particular, those experiences of beauty which have a particular propensity to result in a person identifying with the universe as a whole, and indeed falling in love with that universe' (Wager, 2024, p. 64). This is relevant to the problem of evil because, according to Jeffers, as a result of falling in love outward, one attains something closer to the cosmic perspective we noted earlier. That is, there is an understanding that evil (moral evil) exists from a human perspective and can be remedied through inhumanism, but also a recognition that against the vast backdrop of the cosmos as a whole (with which one now identifies), earth-bound moral and natural evils are *relatively* insignificant: the cosmos which they love and with which they recognize they are continuous is beyond the goods and evils of the human perspective. Thus, this is an analogue of the supernatural resources available to the theist: in this case, the spiritual domain is broadly naturalistic, yet it arguably provides resources that, in a sense, balance out any imbalance of evil over good.

The aim of this section was to use the philosophy of religion as a case study of how cosmopsychism, or cosmopsychist-based views, might effectively engage with and enhance existing discussions, thereby demonstrating a potential example of cosmopsychism's broader relevance. On this occasion, I focused on Jeffers-inspired pantheism, which is rooted in cosmopsychism, however, there are undoubtedly other ways that cosmopsychist views could contribute to the discussions covered here (and indeed, others might call more substantially on the conscious aspect of the cosmos in course of their engagement). I do not intend to suggest that the Jeffers-inspired view explored here is ultimately defensible, rather, I present it to illustrate how one particular cosmopsychism-based view might critically and fruitfully engage with existing debates. As I mentioned previously, my focus in this section has not been to interrogate the metaphysical foundations of the account. Furthermore, the broader ideas I introduced at the beginning of the section are merely speculative reflections. It is crucial to note that I am not claiming that adopting a cosmopsychist approach to the problem of consciousness commits one to any of the ideas discussed in this section. These are potential avenues for exploration that interested parties may wish to take up. Indeed, for my own part, I defer to future occasions a detailed examination of cosmopsychism's broader relevance.

7.5 Conclusion

As I mentioned at the outset of the book, I hope that by spotlighting the landscape of fundamental consciousness and conducting the explorations contained within its chapters, this book will serve a dual purpose: first, to make a modest contribution to contemporary debates on the problem of phenomenal consciousness (principally, though not exclusively, by providing a defence of cosmopsychism), and second, to catalyse further explorations of the landscape and perhaps its broader relevance. I believe that fundamental approaches to the problem of consciousness, in general, but especially those following the cosmopsychism pathway, are teeming with untapped potential. Many positions remain unexplored. Future expeditions into the landscape will no doubt map and evaluate these positions. Some will inevitably turn out to be dead ends. Nevertheless, any genuine explorers searching for a solution to the problem of phenomenal consciousness would do well to take these vast, hitherto unexplored regions of the map seriously.

References

Augustine (2008). *Confessions*. Translated by H. Chadwick. Oxford: Oxford University Press.

Brüntrup, G. (2017). 'Emergent panpsychism'. In G. Brüntrup & L. Jaskolla (Eds.), *Panpsychism: Contemporary perspectives* (pp. 48–71). New York: Oxford University Press.

Brüntrup, G., Göcke, B. P., & Jaskolla, L. (Eds.) (2020). *Panentheism and panpsychism: Philosophy of religion meets philosophy of mind*. Paderborn: Mentis.

Buckareff, A. A. (2022). *Pantheism*. Cambridge: Cambridge University Press.

Buckareff, A. A., & Nagasawa, Y. (Eds.) (2016). *Alternative concepts of God: Essays on the metaphysics of the divine*. New York: Oxford University Press.

Buckareff, A., & Nagasawa, Y. (2019). 'Guest editorial preface: Special issue on pantheism and panentheism'. *International Journal for Philosophy of Religion*, 85(1), 1–3.

Chalmers, D. J. (1996). *The conscious mind: In search of a fundamental theory*. New York: Oxford University Press.

Chalmers, D. J. (2017). 'The combination problem for panpsychism'. In G. Brüntrup & L. Jaskolla (Eds.), *Panpsychism: Contemporary perspectives* (pp. 179–214). New York: Oxford University Press. https://doi.org/10.1093/oso/9780199359943.003.0009.

Clack, B. (2018). 'Evil, feminism, and a philosophy of transformation'. In N. N. Trakakis (Ed.), *The problem of evil: Eight views in dialogue* (pp. 123–50). Oxford: Oxford University Press.

Cottingham, J. (2005). *The spiritual dimension: Religion, philosophy and human value*. Cambridge: Cambridge University Press.

Cottingham, J. (2014). *Philosophy of religion: Towards a more humane approach*. Cambridge: Cambridge University Press.

Ellis, G. F. R. (2017). 'The domain of cosmology and the testing of cosmological theories'. In K. Chamcham, J. Silk, J. D. Barrow, & S. Saunders (Eds.), *The philosophy of cosmology* (pp. 3–39). Cambridge: Cambridge University Press.

Hick, J. (1966). *Evil and the god of love*. New York: Harper & Row.

Hume, D. (1739). *A treatise of human nature*. Edited by E. C. Mossner. Mineola, NY: Oxford University Press.

Jeffers, R. (1925). *Roan Stallion, Tamar and other poems*. New York: Boni and Liveright.

Jeffers, R. (1937). *Such counsels you gave to me and other poems*. New York: Random House.

Jeffers, R. (1948). *The double-axe and other poems*. New York: Random House.

Jeffers, R. (2000). *The collected works of Robinson Jeffers volume 4: Poetry 1903–1920 prose, and unpublished writings*. Edited by T. Hunt. Stanford, CA: Stanford University Press.

Jeffers, R. (2011). *The collected letters of Robinson Jeffers, with selected letters of Una Jeffers: Volume two, 1931–1939*. Edited by J. Karman. Standford, CA: Stanford University Press.

Keppler, J., & Shani, I. (2020). 'Cosmopsychism and consciousness research: A fresh view on the causal mechanisms underlying phenomenal states'. *Frontiers in Psychology*, 11, Article 371, 1–7. https://doi.org/10.3389/fpsyg.2020.00371.

Levine, M. P. (1994). *Pantheism: A non-theistic concept of deity*. Abingdon: Routledge.

Lewis, D. (1973a). 'Causation'. *Journal of Philosophy*, 70(17), 556–67.

Lewis, D. (1973b). *Counterfactuals*. Malden, MA: Blackwell.

Mørch, H. H. (2014). *Panpsychism and causation: A new argument and a solution to the combination problem*(Doctoral dissertation, University of Oslo).

Mørch, H. H. (2019). 'Is the integrated information theory of consciousness compatible with Russellian panpsychism?' *Erkenntnis*, 84(5), 1065–85.

Moser, P. (2008). *The elusive God: Reorienting religious epistemology*. New York: Cambridge University Press.

Nagasawa, Y. (2020). 'Panpsychism versus pantheism, polytheism, and cosmopsychism'. In W. Seager (Ed.), *Routledge companion to panpsychism* (pp. 259–68). New York: Routledge.

Nagasawa, Y. (2024). *The problem of evil for atheists*. Oxford: Oxford University Press.

Nagasawa, Y., & Wager, K. (2017). 'Panpsychism and priority cosmopsychism'. In G. Brüntrup & L. Jaskolla (Eds.), *Panpsychism: Contemporary perspectives* (pp. 113–29). New York: Oxford University Press.

Oppy, G. (1997). 'Pantheism, quantification and mereology'. *The Monist*, 80(2), 320–36.

Plantinga, A. (1974). *The nature of necessity*. Oxford: Oxford University Press.

Rosenberg, G. H. (2004). *A place for consciousness: Probing the deep structure of the natural world*. New York: Oxford University Press.

Seager, W. (2010). 'Panpsychism, aggregation and combinatorial infusion'. *Mind and Matter*, 8(2), 167–84.

Seager, W. (2012). 'Emergentist panpsychism'. *Journal of Consciousness Studies*, 19(9–10), 9–10.

Seager, W. (2017). 'Panpsychist infusion'. In G. Brüntrup & L. Jaskolla (Eds.), *Panpsychism: Contemporary perspectives* (pp. 229–48). New York: Oxford University Press.

Shani, I., & Keppler, J. (2018). 'Beyond combination: How cosmic consciousness grounds ordinary experience'. *Journal of the American Philosophical Association*, 4(3), 390–410.

Strawson, G. (2006). 'Realistic monism – Why physicalism entails panpsychism'. *Journal of Consciousness Studies*, 13(10–11), 3–31.

Tononi, G. (2004). 'An information integration theory of consciousness'. *BMC Neuroscience*, 3(5), Article 42. https://doi.org/10.1186/1471-2202-5-42.

Tononi, G. (2008). 'Consciousness as integrated information: A provisional manifesto'. *The Biological Bulletin*, 215(3), 216–42. https://doi.org/10.2307/25470707.

Wager, K. (2024). 'Falling in love outward: Pantheism and spiritual well-being'. *AGATHEOS – European Journal for Philosophy of Religion*, 1(3), 35–70. https://doi.org/10.69574/aejpr.v1i3.29806

Wager, K., & Wynn, M. (2024a). 'Editorial: God concepts and spiritual well-being'. *AGATHEOS – European Journal for Philosophy of Religion*, 1(3), 1–2. https://doi.org/10.69574/aejpr.v1i3.29815.

Wager, K., & Wynn, M. (Eds.) (2024b). 'God concepts and spiritual well-being [Special issue]'. *AGATHEOS – European Journal for Philosophy of Religion*, 1(3).

Index

www.ingramcontent.com/pod-product-compliance
Ingram Content Group UK Ltd.
Pitfield, Milton Keynes, MK11 3LW, UK
UKHW021832051225
465743UK00004B/25

9 781350 508613